A TANNER'S WORTH OF TUNE
Rediscovering the Post-War British Musical

A Tanner's Worth of Tune is the first book to be written on the post-war British musical, and the first major assessment of the British musical for a quarter of a century, reviving interest in a vast archive of musicals that have been dismissed to the footnotes of theatrical history. This timely reappraisal of the genre and its social background, before the 'international' British musicals began appearing in the 1970s, argues for a radical understanding of the shows and their writers, and a rethinking of our attitude towards them.

The musical plays of Ivor Novello and Noel Coward – both pre- and post-war – are discussed in detail, as are the two composers who came to dominate the 1950s, Sandy Wilson and Julian Slade, and the little school of *plein air* musicals that threaded through that decade. The book brings together 'adopted' British musicals, discusses the rise and fall of the British 'verismo' and the biomusical, whether of Dr Crippen or the Rector of Stiffkey, finally charting the collapse of the British musical's nationalism in the 1960s as witnessed by John Osborne and Lionel Bart. The book draws on Adrian Wright's lifelong passion for British theatre music, its writers, composers, performers and craftsmen. Provocative, idiosyncratic and unfailingly entertaining, *A Tanner's Worth of Tune* makes a compelling plea for a rediscovery of an era of pleasures which have too long been forgotten.

ADRIAN WRIGHT is the author of *Foreign Country: The Life of L.P. Hartley* [1996], *John Lehmann: A Pagan Adventure* [1998], *The Innumerable Dance: The Life and Work of William Alwyn* [2008] and the novel *Maroon* [2010]. He lives in Norfolk, where he also runs Must Close Saturday Records, a company dedicated to British musical theatre.

A TANNER'S WORTH OF TUNE
Rediscovering the Post-War British Musical

Adrian Wright

THE BOYDELL PRESS

First published 2010
The Boydell Press, Woodbridge

ISBN 978 1 84383 542 4

The Boydell Press is an imprint of Boydell & Brewer Ltd
PO Box 9, Woodbridge, Suffolk IP12 3DF, UK
and of Boydell & Brewer Inc.
668 Mount Hope Ave, Rochester, NY 14604, USA
website: www.boydellandbrewer.com

A CIP catalogue record for this book is available
from the British Library

The publisher has no responsibility for the continued existence
or accuracy of URLs for external or third-party internet websites
referred to in this book, and does not guarantee that any content
on such websites is, or will remain, accurate or appropriate.

This publication is printed on acid-free paper

Designed and typeset in Brittanic Bold
and Adobe Warnock Pro by
David Roberts, Pershore

Printed in Great Britain by
CPI Antony Rowe, Chippenham and Eastbourne

'Nonsense, yes, perhaps –
but oh, what precious nonsense!'

W. S. Gilbert, *Patience* (1881)

Contents

List of Illustrations   viii

Acknowledgements   x

1   **Before and After**   1
    Identifying the British Musical

2   **Delusions of Grandeur**   14
    Ivor Novello

3   **Mastering Operetta**   45
    Noel Coward

4   **Pastiche and Esoteric**   70
    Sandy Wilson

5   **Resounding Tinkles**   95
    The *plein air* Musicals of Julian Slade and Dorothy Reynolds,
    Geoffrey Wright and Donald Swann

6   **Away from Home**   123
    Adopted British Musicals

7   **Community Singing**   139
    Realism and the British Verismo Musical

8   **Specifically British**   169
    David Heneker, Monty Norman, Julian More and Wolf Mankowitz

9   **To Whom it May Concern**   195
    The British Biomusical

10 ***Fin de Partie***   222
    John Osborne, Lionel Bart and After

Appendix 1   Original Productions of British Musicals   249

Appendix 2   Adaptations from Other Works, 1946–78   278

Notes   283

Select Bibliography   289

Index of Musical Works   293

General Index   298

Illustrations

1 *Six of One*: sheet music cover   2

2 *Tough at the Top*: sheet music cover   7

3 Vivian Ellis LP cover image   9

4 'Ivor Novello Talks to You': *Theatre World* advertisement   19

5 Jacket of Hester W Chapman's novel *King's Rhapsody*   24

6 Vanessa Lee, Harry Acres, Ivor Novello, Phyllis Dare, Olive Gilbert and Denis Martin at the recording session for *King's Rhapsody*   37

7 *Gay's the Word*: advertisements in theatre programme   40

8 Frankie Howerd and Judith Bruce in the original London production of *Mister Venus*   43

9 Stanley Parker's impressions of Coward's *Operette* in *Theatre World*   50

10 The stars of *Ace of Clubs* in the original theatre programme   55

11 *Sail Away*: sheet music cover   63

12 *The Boy Friend*: fortieth birthday Players' Theatre programme cover   74

13 Sandy Wilson   79

14 *Valmouth*: sheet music cover   81

15 Patricia Michael and Philip Gilbert in the original London production of *Divorce Me, Darling!*   87

16 Dorothy Reynolds, Denis Carey and Julian Slade at a dress rehearsal for *Salad Days*   96

17 Bob Harris and Joe Greig in the original London production of *Salad Days*   99

18 Marion Grimaldi and Newton Blick in the original London production of *Follow That Girl*   104

19 *Wildest Dreams*: LP cover   108

20 Anna Dawson around the time of *Wildest Dreams*   110

21 *Wild Thyme*: sheet music cover   120

22 *Golden City*: sheet music cover   124

23 *The Crystal Heart*: sheet music cover   127

24 *The Love Doctor*: sheet music cover   130

25 *Troubador*: flyer handbill   136

26 Judith Bruce in the original Australian production of *Irma la Douce*   149

27 Elisabeth Welch and Jack MacGowran in the original London production of *The Crooked Mile*   152

28 *House of Cards*: sheet music cover   156

29 *The Lily White Boys*: cover of book of lyrics   160

30 *Johnny the Priest*: theatre programme   164

31 Playbill for the premiere of *Half a Sixpence*   170

32 Three stage designs for the original London production of *Half a Sixpence*   172–3

33 *Belle*: sheet music cover   180

34 Contemporary *Punch* cartoon of Davy Kaye and George Benson in *Belle*   185

35 *Joey Joey*: sheet music cover   199

36 Stuart Damon and Judith Bruce in the original London production of *Man of Magic*   203

37 *The Prostitutes Padre*: theatre programme cover   209

38 Margaret Burton in the original London production of *Annie*   219

39 Roy Dotrice and Judith Bruce in the original London production of *Tom Brown's Schooldays*   234

40 *Scapa!*: theatre programme cover   237

41 Judith Bruce in the original London production of *Maggie May*   242

42 Judith Bruce, with her daughter Nancy, in the star dressing room during the original London production of *Maggie May*   246

Acknowledgements

My first thanks must go to the late Vivian Ellis. Too many years ago, when I first thought of writing a book about the British musical, I wrote to ask if he would agree to speak to me about his work. His answer was typically polite and brief. *No.* In a few words, he explained his reason: 'Because I am so weary of being talked to by people who really know nothing about my career I have decided not to give any more interviews. However, I can see that you mean business and know your stuff. I have passed your name to my agent, who has agreed to take on your book.' This was an act of great kindness, although Ellis had already distanced himself from it. His agent (who then became *my* agent) Eric Glass assured me that there would be no difficulty in finding a publisher for so worthy a tome. It was, anyway, little more than a synopsis, but as the months went by in unnerving silence, this promising beginning had no happy ending. Nearly forty years later, the book that even then (and for years before) was rolling about in my head has at last appeared, because my publisher asked 'Do you have any ideas for other books?' I had thought I might persuade him to let me write a life of the redoubtable Dame Ethel Smyth, but his eyes only lit up when I introduced the book you now hold in your hands.

All books of non-fiction must feed on facts dug out by those that have gone before, and I acknowledge Kurt Gänzl's two-volume history of British musicals, although my views on British musicals are very different from his. Although I have nowhere quoted from Gänzl's text, this has been a dependable source of reference for production details. Other crucial original sources include theatre programmes, reviews, and much-treasured complete runs of theatre magazines. Among the many other books consulted, details of which may be found in the Bibliography, I would particularly recommend the following for further reading: for a sharply critical slant Gervase Hughes' *Composers of Operetta*; for Noel Coward, Graham Payn's illuminating *My Life with Noel Coward* and Cole Lesley's memoir; for Ivor Novello, Sandy Wilson's excellent *Ivor*, the no-nonsense biography by James Harding, and the sometimes effusive but always informative biography by W. Macqueen-Pope. Unfortunately, the British musical has attracted a number of writers whose knowledge, discrimination and recall of facts leaves the informed reader short-changed, but these the reader must discover for himself. Good or bad, all have been digested in the years over which this book has bubbled away unwritten.

I have to thank the many composers, writers, directors, performers, producers and musicians who have, over the years, contributed to my knowledge of British musicals, and have only space here to name a few. Leon Berger, archivist for the

Donald Swann estate, introduced me to the glories of *Wild Thyme* and made it possible for me to record songs from its score.

Artists contributing memories and ideas to this book throughout its long gestation include Gyles Brandreth, Dora Bryan, Margaret Burton, Peter Byrne, Anna Dawson, Stephen Hancock, Doreen Hermitage, Pip Hinton, Cheryl Kennedy, Jean Kent, Vivienne Martin, Patricia Michael, the late Ralph Reader, Patsy Rowlands, Anna Sharkey, Ronnie Stevens, Terri Stevens, Jean Marion Taylor, Norman Warwick and David Wheldon-Williams. A long friendship with Gordon Duttson, Ivor Novello's last secretary, gave me insights into Novello's life and work that would otherwise have been denied. Gordon was also generous in arranging meetings with composers and performers he had known during his career. Performers, however, are not always the fount of knowledge one might wish. I was delighted to be asked to lunch by the pianist Courtney Kenny, and was hoping to learn everything I didn't already know about *Wildest Dreams*, for the long tour of which he accompanied Julian Slade on another piano. Alas, Mr Kenny could remember absolutely nothing about it. Performers, too, are not always accurate in their recollections, and I have preferred, where possible, to put my faith in the solidity of the written word, in those cases where the writer may be considered trustworthy.

David Huckvale introduced me to James Bernard and Paul Dehn's *Battersea Calypso*, and I thank him for not only making it possible for me to hear the score but for the colourful story surrounding it. Gordon Langford gave me interesting information about several London productions for which he provided orchestrations, including *The Crooked Mile* and *House of Cards*. I am grateful to the writer and actor Ron Pember for information about *Jack the Ripper*.

I have to thank the late Lionel Bart for agreeing to be interviewed, the late Ronald Cass, and the late Peter Greenwell who spoke to me of his work and entrusted me with private recordings of his scores. The late Hugh Hastings told me of his experiences with *Scapa!* (a score which had been lost). With his assistance and the piano transcriptions of William Rayner we restored the score. Geoffrey Wright was generous in his memories of the many musical productions in which he was involved, including *The Burning Boat*, and I value our collaboration on the never completed *Bella*.

My friendship with Julian Slade was a continuing thread through a lifelong obsession with the British musical, and he was unstinting in his generous assistance. I am also indebted to Monty Norman, the late David Heneker, Peter Ingold, Philip Lane, the late Peter Myers, Diana Payne-Myers, Leslie Orton, the late Ned Sherrin, the late Christopher Whelen, the late Reginald Woolley and Peter Worsley. The late Robb Stewart not only enthusiastically played me songs from his unperformed *The Girl on the Ostrich*, but recollected the history of his *Chrysanthemum* and his long association with Noel Coward.

The encouragement of John Knowles, Roger Mellor and Michael Thornton was appreciated, as was the support of Michael King and Terence Dunning.

Invaluable information has been provided by the Victoria and Albert Theatre Collection, and the ever-welcoming and helpful staff of its Reading Room. Peter Hunter unearthed material that I imagined I would never find. Ronnie Troughton was helpful beyond the call of duty with photographs, as was Judith Bruce. I have used several photographs from her albums to show the sort of career a musical performer, working both in American *and* British musicals, had during the period covered in this book. *A Tanner's Worth of Tune* (the title, by the way, is stolen from a song title in a 1960 British musical, *Johnny the Priest*) bears traces of a long friendship and many discussions with Stewart Nicholls, who has done so much to reinvigorate interest in the British musical. Paul Guinery listened to my sometimes unformed ideas and tactfully made comments and suggestions. He also read the book in manuscript, and went on tactfully making comments and suggestions, some of which I hope he will find reflected in the final text.

Michael Middeke at the Boydell Press commissioned the book and has been a firm supporter during its genesis. I thank him and the team at Boydell, including Michael Richards and Mike Webb, for the attention they have paid to the *Tanner*'s production. Every effort has been made to trace the holders of copyright for any material included in the book. Apologies are made for any omissions, which the publisher will be pleased to correct in any subsequent editions.

Lastly, I have my late aunt, Beryl Wright, to thank for setting me on the road. Everyone needs an aunt who points the way. She started me off by taking me to see a touring version of the original production of *Salad Days* and thereafter was a quiet champion of the sort of British musical that has fascinated me for a lifetime.

Adrian Wright
Norfolk, 2009

1 Before and After
Identifying the British Musical

Any search for identity must begin with a birth. W. S. Gilbert's epitome of official pomposity in *The Mikado*, Pooh-Bah, could trace his ancestors 'back to a protoplasmal primordial atomic globule'. Does the British musical go back as far? Cavemen, after all, must have whistled. The beginnings of British musical theatre may well go back to Greek theatre. (Was not the Chorus an essential component of its drama?) In its links with opera, the works of Charles Dibdin and Thomas Linley, of John Gay, the British musical may have found its apotheosis in the nineteenth century when Gilbert's first collaboration with Sullivan, *Thespis*, was produced at Christmas 1871. In Britain, the operas of Gilbert and Sullivan were the first most recognisable manifestations of what was to become its nationalistic contribution to the genre. But *were* they operas? In 1981, when the D'Oyly Carte Opera Company presented its final London season, posters described the G & S operas as 'The World's Greatest Musicals', and if they *were* musicals they were certainly the longest-running in the world, D'Oyly Carte having toured them for over a hundred years.[1]

When it comes to the British musical, nomenclature is and always has been under discussion. If we allow that Gilbert and Sullivan *did* write opera, it makes sense that Richard D'Oyly Carte should have set up an *Opera* Company to perform them. Before meeting Sullivan, it had anyway seemed that Gilbert was writing something that might *become* opera, or at least *ballad* opera. (His *Bab Ballads*,[2] which now seem almost to be songs without music.) Arthur Seymour Sullivan, that most respected of establishment composers, was beguiled into his collaboration with Gilbert much to the disapproval of many critics who only longed for another weighty oratorio from his pen, a *Te Deum* to mark the end of the Boer War, or a choral extravaganza for the Leeds Festival choristers to get their teeth into.

To satisfy Sullivan's craving to write something of substance, the 'lighter' operas represented by such works as *Iolanthe* and *The Gondoliers* were interrupted by the more 'serious' *The Yeomen of the Guard*. Perhaps, after all, *this* work was truly opera? Gilbert obviously considered it more so than their other works, and felt himself the inferior partner in its making. This, dammit, was as serious as Gilbert was prepared to be, and he saw no reason why Sullivan should not be satisfied with having been given the chance to write a serio-comic opera for the masses. Within the D'Oyly Carte Opera Company some distinction was always made between the more popular works in the repertoire and those that contained music which demanded rather more singing. A soprano with sound

technique and accurate top notes was usually singled out for Elsie in *The Yeomen of the Guard* and the title-role in *Princess Ida* with its taxing (for G & S) 'Invocation', an obvious reaching-up to 'real' opera.

A further distinction was made in 1891 when Richard D'Oyly Carte built the Royal English Opera House (now the Palace Theatre) expressly to 'establish English Grand Opera', in effect Sullivan's *Ivanhoe*: 'I am doing a serious opera now,' the composer informed Dion Boucicault.[3] D'Oyly Carte's new theatre was to be devoted to this 'Grand Opera', and he had no intention of allowing any of the works Sullivan had written with Gilbert (presumably not 'serious' and certainly not 'grand') to be staged there. D'Oyly Carte's announcement of his plans for the house contained a phrase that resonates through the history of twentieth-century British musical theatre, when he described *Ivanhoe* as being 'a subject of national interest', a problem with which managements, writers and composers have on and off battled ever since. Sullivan's new opera was considered so vital to the musical health of the nation that it was dedicated to Queen Victoria, who showed her appreciation by not turning out to see it. She would not be the last person to ignore the relevance of the British opera or British musical play to the health of the nation. She may have made the right decision, for *Ivanhoe* proved a deadly bore, and Sullivan the opera composer became Sullivan the operetta composer again.

Nevertheless, the difficulty of adequately describing what the British opera or musical might be persisted. It was Boucicault who suggested that he and Sullivan collaborate on a new subject, 'comic-idyllic but *not* burlesque' and *Thespis* had been regarded by many as burlesque, an acceptably skittish concept to the Victorian. Would such a work have turned out a musical, a musical comedy, a musical play, a musical entertainment, an opera, a light opera, an operetta or an operette? You may add your own descriptions as you will. Noel Coward would spend much of his musical career writing a form of operetta, one of the least successful indeed calling itself *Operette*, and who was to say that it was not, even if some of it seemed more like a musical or, spasmodically, a revue. In its day, *Thespis* was described by the press as an 'English *opéra-bouffe*' and, as we have already seen, as 'burlesque', another Sullivan work (written with B. C. Stephenson), *The Zoo*, as a 'musical folly', and *Trial by Jury* is described on the title-page of its vocal score as a 'dramatic cantata'! Faced with these bewildering signposts, how did the Victorians make up their minds as to what they wanted to see?

The Trades Description Act has never been brought to bear against the British musical, yet we probably all feel we understand what sort of territory its various manifestations indicate. Light opera? Something aspiring to the important, but frolicsome? The British equivalent of Franz Lehár or Edward German or Jacques Offenbach? Something with scantily clad girls in it, lined up like prancing Viennese horses? Good tunes and a happy ending? Even though they didn't find the scantily clad girls, the British would probably demote Gilbert and Sullivan operas to this category of 'light opera', the neither chalk nor cheese hinterland of musical theatre. The terminal D'Oyly Carte Company stooped to pulling in the crowds by offering up G & S as musicals. During its last months the management understood that the Arts Council had resolved to transform it into the National *Light Opera* Company of Great Britain, when alongside the works of Gilbert and Sullivan it would present, in its opening season, German's *Merrie England* and Messager's *Véronique*. From Opera Company to Light Opera Company through musicals? – an interesting journey!

British musicals and the television booth

Half a century ago, the revue writer Peter Myers and the composer Ronald Cass had a series on BBC television, the title of which I cannot remember. A popular singer of the time (Carole Carr? Jill Day?) hovered in the background. The studio audience was asked to come up with titles for an unwritten song. Imagine yourself in that audience, and come up with titles of your own. The suggestions would settle on one title, and armed only with this, some manuscript paper and a pencil or two, Myers and Cass slipped into a soundproof booth. I seem to remember that we, sitting at home, were not allowed inside the booth, perhaps for fear that we might discern the magical process at work within, and I cannot for the life of me remember what happened on screen while the writers were incarcerated. I cannot recall if Ms Carr or Ms Day immediately went into the booth with them, but sooner or later (they only had a half hour programme) she was in there. A few minutes short of the end credits, the three emerged with a song made to order, and delivered it there and then. I suspect not one of those television booth numbers was ever heard of again.

One wonders if George and Ira Gershwin ever agreed to such a charade, or Rodgers and Hammerstein, or Loewe and Lerner?[4] Locking *them* away for twenty minutes might have produced something to write home about, but Myers and Cass were not of their class. Their contribution to British revue was considerable, but when it came to songs, their work was not in the first division, and on the few occasions they tried their hand at writing musicals they were not conspicuously successful. Never mind. They were British and seen to be having a go. Still, their remarkable feat begs the question, why did they not have a long list of musicals to their name? At the rate of one song every thirty minutes, working a seven hour day with coffee and tea breaks and an hour for lunch, they should comfortably have polished off fourteen songs before knocking off. At this rate, they should have been writing five musicals a week. This is not as ambitious as it sounds. We have no idea how long it took Shakespeare to write *Hamlet*. Did he polish it off during a week's holiday up the road from Stratford-upon-Avon at Royal Leamington Spa? ('It rained all week so I stayed in and wrote *Hamlet*.') We know for a fact that Noel Coward could write a play within two or three days, pieces whose popularity has endured for much longer. Masterpieces have begun life on the backs of envelopes, on the backs of cigarette packets, in the corner of napkins, and in gentler days on starched shirt cuffs. If Myers and Cass had set their minds to it, they would have been falling over themselves with musicals.[5] They were obviously shirkers.

The programme with the booth was homespun, and things have changed. The relationship between television and the British musical has developed in a way that Myers and Cass would not have dreamed of. In the 1960s television was not averse to giving it space,[6] as indeed did BBC radio, mostly via Saturday night variety programmes which would sometimes harbour lengthy extracts from new productions. Even earlier than this, television was leading the way, which could be wayward. When shows of superior quality were available, the BBC elected to broadcast a complete live performance of *Carissima*, an ungainly semi-musical, semi-operetta by Eric Maschwitz and the composer Hans May. They did it live *twice*, once in 1950 and once in 1959 with Ginger Rogers.[7] The fact that Maschwitz was an executive with the BBC may have had nothing to do with it, but he may have marvelled at its selection, for nobody is going to stand up for *Carissima* as a masterpiece. The eighty-two separate scenes had to be shared between two studios, an organisational nightmare (called 'Multi-studio working') that someone must have thought worth while.

British musicals infiltrated the annual Royal Variety Performance in 1938 with a finale begun by Lupino Lane and company singing 'The Lambeth Walk' with its catchy cry of 'Oi!' from the Victoria Palace success *Me and My Girl*. It was 1951 before the British musical was represented again, this time by Cicely Courtneidge and her *Gay's the Word* company, and in 1955 there was a scene from Julian Slade and Dorothy Reynolds' *Salad Days* (but no *The Boy Friend*). It took eight years to bring the British musical once more before the Queen, with scenes from *Half a Sixpence* and *Pickwick* in 1963, and then nothing more throughout the period covered by this book. Only now and then would a complete performance of a British musical make it onto the small screen; those chosen include Ivor Novello's *The Dancing Years* and *Salad Days*, but the transition from stage to small screen was usually disappointing.

There was a time when ITV's *Sunday Night at the London Palladium* devoted a segment of the hour-long programme to a current London show. These were often Broadway imports. It was now that I first vowed allegiance to the wide-mouthed Libi Staiger of Frank Loesser's *The Most Happy Fella* singing 'Happy to Make Your Acquaintance'. In 1962 it was the turn of the British *Scapa!* Note the exclamation mark, a trend encouraged by *Oklahoma!* and, after *Oliver!*, much used in the forlorn hope of bringing public excitement to fever pitch. Alas, as with so many other shows featured in this book, few now remember Hugh Hastings' musical, set on Scapa Flow, adapted from his own much more successful straight play *Seagulls over Sorrento*. One wonders how those extracts ever found their way onto television in the first place. Was there some Supreme Televisual Being to whom appeals might be made when British musical productions were in dire straits? One suspects it was often a case of managements helping managements, but being nautical it is not surprising that television all but scuppered *Scapa!*

There was no more luck for *Chrysanthemum*, vaguely promoted as a British ragtime musical which was supposed to make a musical comedy couple out of husband and wife Hubert Gregg and Pat Kirkwood. With the production already in difficulties, the company did extracts on television, which Gregg insisted had only a negative effect on the box-office. A more cunning scheme was worked in the 1950s by the impresario and librettist Jack Waller, who had made his name in the 1920s with the British production of *No, No, Nanette*, and gone on to write vastly entertaining musicals of the 1930s with the composer Joseph Tunbridge. Waller was putting on a new British musical, *Wild Grows the Heather*, based on J. M. Barrie's play *The Little Minister.*[8] This time his collaboration with Tunbridge was the easiest it had been, for Tunbridge was already dead; the music came out of his trunk. According to Waller, Barrie's literary executor Lady Cynthia Asquith practically went down on her knees to beg him to do it. Waller's instinct told him to whip up interest by starting a 'Find a Star' campaign in the national press. Someone, somewhere, would be discovered and become the leading lady of his new musical. The winner turned out to be Valerie Miller, who was pleasing enough and served her time in the short-lived production, and quietly vanished.

In our own times, television has taken Waller's old showmanship tricks to undreamed-of levels with searches for the 'new Joseph', the new 'Oliver', the new 'Nancy', and (for the American entries) the 'new Maria'. Such opportunities for free advertising have usually only been granted to revivals of the tried and tested musical success, and in collaboration with the composer Andrew Lloyd Webber and impresario Cameron Mackintosh. What a paradise if this facility was offered to all, the struggling and the modest, the hopeful and the meek, and what opportunities have been missed. There really is no end to the possibilities that have been overlooked. Along the lines of the BBC's 'Any Dream Will Do' (the search for a new young buck to play the lead in *Joseph and the Amazing Technicolor Dreamcoat*) or 'I'll Do Anything' (the search for the next actress to sing 'As Long as He Needs Me'), we might have had 'Moo!', a series to discover the most suitable cow for the title-role in Slade and Reynolds' *Hooray for Daisy!*, or 'Rise above It' ('Can you sing? Dance? Levitate? You could be the next star of Sandy Wilson's *The Clapham Wonder!*')

What variety, what surprises the public has missed as it has been force-fed countless versions of Nancy's torch-song. Television has no concern (why should it?) for the great archive of stuff that has piled up through the twentieth century, in a world where the British musical has been regarded merely as a sub-culture, inferior to its American counterpart and deserving almost total neglect.

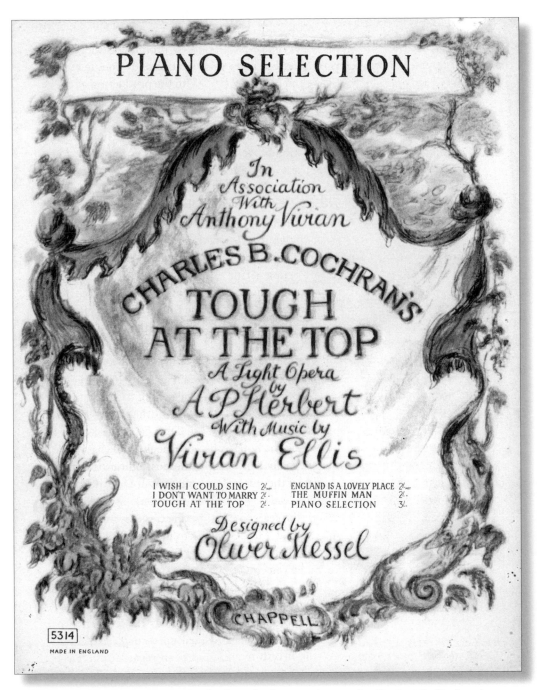

2   Celebrating England as a lovely place: the sheet music cover for *Tough at the Top* (1949)

Vivian Ellis and the heyday of British operetta

The BBC producers would never have got Vivian Ellis into that television booth. Although Ellis never committed his opinion of Ronald Cass to paper we may imagine it would not have been complimentary. Ellis distanced himself from many other composers of light music. During preparations for the Bobby Howes–Cicely Courtneidge show *Hide and Seek* (1937) he was asked to 'pool my resources' with the American 'song-writers' Lerner, Goodhart and Hoffman. Mark his use of words, *song-writers*, by a *composer* who was by this time 'sick of the subservience of practically everybody connected with our musical stage to the might of American superiority in this field'.[9] Gervase Hughes, not a writer to mince words, wrote that 'Vivian Ellis, whatever his shortcomings, is at least a *composer*'. Hughes doesn't leave it there, but continues,

> His musical comedies show awareness of classical operetta, but even his post-war collaborations with A. P. Herbert ... are regrettably tarnished with the harmonic clichés which riddled popular light music during the thirties. He has a flair for rhythmic aptness in word-setting, however, which raises his work above the level of most contemporaries in the same field.[10]

Hughes at least hits two nails on the head. 'This Is My Lovely Day', the principal song from *Bless the Bride*, his greatest post-war success, was often greeted with groans from the bands who had to play it, scornful of its progression of notes. The mildness of that score has something to do with the problem, although Herbert's lyric glimpses the empyrean in the immortal line 'This is the day I shall remember the day I'm dying'. Hughes may be unaware of Ellis's harmonic ingenuity in his songs, notably in the verses, but he is right to celebrate Ellis's word-setting abilities. Listen to any of his songs, and the fall of words to music is striking. Listen to any of his songs, and you will also think the man an absolute pussy-cat.

Lerner, Goodhart and Hoffman came to discover otherwise, as did his collaborator for *Listen to the Wind*, Angela Ainley Jeans, who one day when Ellis was absent from rehearsals agreed to a slight change in the music. Ellis was furious. The pussy-cat had claws when it came to protecting his work, and as a professional he was more than the equal of the fellow giants of his era, Coward and Novello. There is, indeed, a case to be made for his superiority, for the spread and quality of his work was consistent throughout a long career. Unlike Coward and Novello, when he tired of writing British musicals (perhaps influenced by the fact that he had lost his great patron, Charles B. Cochran) he simply withdrew from the field, recognising that his day was past. Earlier in his career, he wrote four novels,[11] and when it faded, busied himself by writing a series of lightly amusing books, among them *How to Enjoy your Operation*,[12] from which you will learn his opinion of the bed-pan: 'If the patient is at all sensitive, he feels as ridiculous as a red-capped pixie perched on a toadstool in a suburban front garden.'[13]

Although he worked with, and knew the value of, good lyricists – he would have insisted on working with no other – he was their equal. In fact, from 1936 on, apart from his collaboration with A. P. Herbert, Ellis wrote all his own lyrics. His lyric for the song 'Stock Exchange Art' is a brilliant conception, the idea that people might as well hang shares in frames because paintings have come to represent only money. The lightness of touch, the charm (and Ellis was surely the master charmer of his generation of composers), can be heard on a 1960 studio recording of him singing a selection of his songs.[14] Astoundingly, this genteel long-player gave Ellis a dash of undeserved notoriety when four of the numbers were banned by the BBC, who found the lyrics 'undesirable – in part they are downright objectionable'.

3 Vivian Ellis in satirical mood for the cover of his scandalous long-player

From the beginning of his career, we can detect certain other qualities in Ellis that have perhaps never received due attention, and these are distinguishing marks which stamp his music, no matter the period, no matter the collaborator. One is his almost unique ability to suit the song to the artist. When Georges Guétary first heard the songs Ellis had written for him to sing in *Bless the Bride*, Guétary was impressed but said (in French) 'They are not Guétary.' Ellis said, 'They will be', and made sure they were. When Sophie Tucker arrived in Britain to begin work on *Follow a Star*,[15] Ellis played her the score. Tucker listened and said 'And now let's see about *my* songs.' Ellis understood what she meant, and what she needed, and was a shrewd judge of character: he saw the hard-bitten side of Tucker, and admired it and wanted to serve it. He was able to *fashion* the material to the artist, and fashion it, in this case, with no hint of the bad Broadway imitation that so many other British composers served up.[16] Ellis was by now a past master at this, having appreciated the very different needs of such artists as June, Jack Hulbert, Cicely Courtneidge, Bobby Howes and Binnie Hale. This was a skill Coward and Novello undoubtedly possessed, but perhaps it was not so obviously exercised as with Ellis. No wonder that Ellis was able to come up with such a stellar collection of songs for the great Frances Day; he knew her elliptical talent, and wrote to it, and then set to in another vein for a number for Jack and Cis. While the musicals of Coward and Novello and their stars were pretty well interchangeable, Ellis cut the cloth after, as it were, a private fitting in which every measurement and nuance of a particular talent had been measured. Furthermore, Ellis achieved this trick without ever seeming to descend to musical commercialism. This was a lesson that more British composers might have learned from him.

There is another quality in Ellis which has largely been overlooked. A well-read man, he would have heeded the necessity to 'always keep a-hold of Nurse / For fear of finding something worse'.[17] Ellis, despite various attempts in his early career to promote himself as a Coward or Novello-like creature of elegance, never really escaped the nursery. In 1927 he wrote 'Little Boy Blues' for June to sing in *Clowns in Clover*, another happy coupling with Desmond Carter, a thing of trite innocence, innocence that will surely be unable to tiptoe into adulthood and disillusion. This atmosphere of untrammelled childhood sunniness and hope permeated his work early and late, pre- and post-war. When he worked with lyricists, they seemed constantly to be handing him lyrics that brought out the nursery in him. Nurse would surely have approved of A. P. Herbert's 'Other People's Babies', from the 1934 revue *Streamline*: this, after all, was a song *about* Nurse. Similarly, she would have smiled at 'Ducky' from *Bless the Bride*. Both numbers support the theory that Ellis had, if you like, total recall of lavish nursery teas, starched aprons, the maid's approbations, every rigour of middle- (perhaps even upper middle-) class childhood.

We must remember that the composer was reacting to the words delivered by his lyricist or, as with *Streamline*,[18] writers like Ronald Jeans. Why, then, is it that so much else of Ellis's output has this unsullied, crumpets by the crackling fire, quality? It is there in 'I'm on a See-Saw', one of many good songs in the 1934 musical *Jill Darling*. Adults do not generally lark about on see-saws; the whole idea belongs to infancy, and, though the words are once again Carter's, the music responds with typical Ellis simplicity. In 1937 he recorded a song about the young Princess Elizabeth and Princess Margaret Rose, 'Two Little Princesses', another dainty offering straight from the Ellis nursery, and what could be more child-like than the sublimely uncomplicated 'Spread a Little Happiness' from his 1920s success *Mr Cinders*,[19] this time with words by Clifford Grey? As if in obedience to Shakespeare's Seven Ages of Man, Ellis at the last surrendered to childhood's pleasure with *Listen to the Wind*, writing both music and lyrics for Angela Ainley Jean's book. One of its songs, 'It's Nice to Be Home Again' possibly encapsulates Ellis's basic philosophy. Another, 'When I Grow Up', tells us as much, for, unbearably whimsical as it may sound, there was something of Barrie's Peter Pan in Ellis. If it was not too mawkish, we might say that his Wendy was his sister Hermione, with whom Ellis lived through to old age.

It was Hermione who kick-started her brother's professional reincarnation after the end of the war, the point at which this book supposedly begins to sit up and pay attention. Seeing a piece in a newspaper about a new musical that A. P. Herbert had written and that C. B. Cochran was to present in London, she noted that it made no mention of any composer. Why didn't Vivian write to Herbert and Cochran, with both of whom he had worked before the war? Cochran had already approached William Walton and Spike Hughes to compose the music for the new work, and both had declined. Thus it was that Ellis rediscovered his skills. He took the script of *Big Ben* to Margate on the train (another enchantment that may have happened in childhood, and which he expressed so nostalgically in his orchestral *Coronation Scot*), and by the time the train reached the resort the main melodies were running through his head. He knew that in Herbert he had a collaborator with whose work he was in complete sympathy.

The 1946 *Big Ben* seemed to have the perfect *tone* for its time, if not the perfect book – the war done with, and Herbert's hope for Britain's future as its back-bone. The heroine sang 'I Want to See the People Happy', a patriotic wish which Herbert and Ellis made sincere. Ellis himself was moved when, at the end of the show, the cast turned upstage to look at Big Ben as it chimed out once again. Here was the post-war British musical as celebration, as national expression of the country's identity. This was the pair's contribution to the health of the nation, that 'subject of national interest' that D'Oyly Carte had sought to offer the public in *Ivanhoe*, although *Big Ben*'s success was mild, not helped by having been billed as 'a light opera'. After a sticky beginning the 1947 *Bless the Bride* took flight and could have run even longer than its original 886 performances. Ellis said he wrote most of the songs while he was gardening, and for this score he had inspiration from his maternal grandmother's score for a nineteenth-century operetta, *Carina*.[20] At a time when *Oklahoma!* was said to be breaking bounds, he and Herbert seemed to be taking British musicals back to operetta, *purpose-fully* back in a way that Coward and Novello did not. When Cochran withdrew *Bless the Bride* in 1949 it was only to present what he hoped would be their greatest hit of all, *Tough at the Top*. Ellis didn't like the title, perhaps fearing it would be unlucky, and had preferred the working *Kiss in the Ring*. Neither critics nor audiences warmed to it, although its score is one of Ellis and Herbert's best, not least when its heroine explains her reasons for thinking that 'England Is a Lovely Place'. Only in 1955 did the pair return, with an adaptation of Herbert's novel *The Water Gipsies*. A ballot of readers in the London *Evening Standard* showed that the most popular shows of that year were

1   *Salad Days*
2   *Sailor Beware*
3   *The Water Gipsies*
4   *The Boy Friend*
5   *The Buccaneer*

Promising as those results were, *The Water Gipsies* took Ellis and Herbert into a very different world, the *modern* world, or at least the modern world as seen by them. A gentle story of river people, 'a play with music' according to its authors, *The Water Gipsies* did attempt to fix itself to modern Britain, and some of the old Ellis–Herbert qualities are still to be found, as in the hero's hymn to bucolic pleasure 'Clip-Clop', but Herbert in a sense was trapped by the time in which he was writing, and by his own past, and the class to which he belonged, just as the social structures in Britain were about to reshape. What Herbert and Ellis avoid is any sense of cynicism in a score that inhabits three distinct purlieus, the pastoral ('Ah, Little Boat'; 'Clip-Clop'), the operatic ('This Is Our Secret'; 'Jane's Prayer') and the more lowly environs of Tin Pan Alley, as if Ellis had at last got muddled up with a jukebox. Before, Ellis's *And So to Bed* proved that there need never again be another musical about Pepys, and – wait! – didn't Pepys fall into line and give Ellis yet another perfect title that somehow evokes happy childhood, the refuge of being safely stowed, tucked in, replete with the happiness of the day, and Nurse coming up the stairs with a glass of hot milk?

One of Ellis's last pieces, *Half in Earnest*, an adaptation of Oscar Wilde's *The Importance of Being Earnest*, had to travel to Bucks County Playhouse, New Hope, Pennsylvania, for its premiere and tour in 1957, reappearing as the opening production at the Belgrade Theatre, Coventry, the following year. 'I had always wanted to do this show in America first,' Ellis wrote for the Bucks' programme. 'The British, bless them, are not too keen on innovation.' In fact, and Ellis must have known it, the time was done, although no less a beast than Kenneth Tynan, reviewing the British production, wrote that 'Despite a tendency to sacrifice sense and syntax for a crafty rhyme, Mr Ellis kept me pleased and gently amused throughout. The transitions from speech to song are most liltingly managed, and one cannot help admiring a man who rhymes "St Pancras" with "cantankerous".'[21]

Ellis remains one of the leading British composers of musical theatre in the twentieth century, but I have excluded him from the body of the book for two reasons. First, much of his finest work was done before the official starting point of this book, and I would not do justice to his contribution. Second, it seems to me that Ellis's post-war work is strangely unrelated to anything that came after it; there has been no after-burn. His name probably has been of little help to him. The British would naturally distrust a man called Vivian. Had he been christened Evelyn, they would not have been able to cope with it at all.

A purpose and manifesto

Those who have written about the British musical must bear some of the blame for its perceived reputation. Too many of them have adopted Gertrude Stein's way of thinking, believing that 'A flop is a flop is a flop.' In books, too, there has been much repetition of received opinion. The fact that a musical flopped should not blind us to its interest; it has not done so here. Some operas which now play throughout the world had disastrous first nights: don't mention *Carmen* to Bizet. Benjamin Britten's *Gloriana* had a subdued first night, not least because its toff audience wore gloves. It has been opera's good fortune that it has sometimes been given another chance, the opportunity to show itself worthy of consideration. Such a courtesy is not extended to the flop musical; once down the pan and flushed away for ever, along with any critical reappraisal. Perhaps perversely, the accent in this book is on those shows that have crept into the theatrical shadows. It is sometimes the most successful and best known British musicals of the period that receive scant attention here. This is not from any prejudice against them, but from a natural inclination away from those works towards those that seem to me to have qualities we need to reconsider. Consequently, there is less about *Pickwick* and more about *Joey Joey*.

The book does not attempt to be comprehensive, or chronological. No attempt has been made to list or discuss every British musical, or to give a complete overview of the period. By concentrating on prominent composers and writers, and on certain types of musical, the intention is to reawaken a debate about the value of the British musical, and hopefully to offer a new perspective. I have avoided any protracted discussion of the Broadway musical.

The main period treated in the book (from the end of World War II up to the coming of Andrew Lloyd Webber) is not sacrosanct. Where necessary, and it has often proved so, works under discussion both precede and follow this period. No attempt has been made to mention every composer and writer working in the genre, or to litter the page with dates. This sometimes precludes the inclusion of those whose work has been almost completely ignored, but the reader should be aware that we are dealing with an iceberg of material, of which only some is visible above the surface.

2 Delusions of Grandeur
Ivor Novello

One of the most surprising facts about the Ivor Novello musicals between 1935 and 1951 is that they had so good a critical response. Even those who found much to criticise in Novello's playwriting and compositions acknowledged the skill and theatrical cunning with which they were assembled. Gervase Hughes has crushingly suggested that 'his gift of superficial melody, backed by rudimentary technique, furnished a repletion of sentimental effusions which could be plugged *ad nauseum*' and 'Any intrinsic merit his operettas may have possessed has been inflated beyond reason in the panegyrics of undiscriminating eulogists; it is high time the bubble was pricked.'[1] Hughes' criticism may or may not be valid, and it may be that a declining interest in Novello has seen the bubble burst. This critic is percipient enough to see that while the Edwardian musical theatre had celebrated the female form (one has only to remember all those 'Girl' musicals), Novello, while giving audiences a regular diet of female stars who could sing his songs, himself personified a celebration of a certain type of male beauty. This stately manifestation could only be strengthened by the fact that Novello did not (except on one occasion) break into song; dignity was preserved. Novello, possibly even more so than Coward, depended on a public image, and one that had long been implanted into the public consciousness.

The qualities of his work may be up for discussion, but Novello's success was a much more subtle achievement than Hughes may have realised. The briefest acquaintance with some of the musicals' dialogue has the flavour of that found in his plays, and in the scenes which Novello writes for himself and his leading lady there is a definite flippancy, a skittishness, a lack of wit and a dash of the puerile, dusted over with a sort of languorous romanticism. Such a style may have been almost a reflex action by Novello, a way of distancing himself from the necessary heterosexual overtones demanded by the romantic situations into which his plays forced him. As a playwright, he subliminally may have had to radically adjust the subtext of such scenes simply to make them playable, night after night. He was not the first, and will not be the last, matinee idol to need all his acting abilities to make the possibility of heterosexual sex convincing. Contrarily, Novello's appeal on stage put no reliance on such a deceit. If Novello brought a whiff of effeminacy to his stage appearances, for some he brought the same gift to his music, although it is often not without a distinct muscularity. Whatever the nature of his appeal, Novello's place in British theatre remains unique; there really has never been another. That appeal is complex, and perhaps at no time in his career was it so accentuated as during the string of musicals that began with *Glamorous Night*.

More than ever before, Novello was exposed as a theatrical phenomenon. It is not simply that he devised, wrote the book and music and starred in his own musicals; others have taken on as much, although nobody with so consistent a success. This is a trick that Novello managed consistently for fifteen years, with no hint of decline. Where else could audiences go to see a composer sitting each night listening to his own melodies? And looking so pleased to hear them again! The very man responsible for their happiness was there, in front of them. His presence brought not only the voice, the manner, the profile, the accumulated reputations of brilliant boy composer, film star, playwright, but a sense of taste. A visit to a Novello musical guaranteed spectacle and music, but Novello's presence brought in its train the assurance that he was a man who understood not only spectacle and music but poetry and beauty, the ballet, the opera – a man who in some way was putting his audience in touch with the higher arts. He was not doing so, but there is the hint of that trick being played. In an article for the journal *Band Waggon* Novello wrote, 'I was brought up on the classics, nurtured as a chorister with dollops of Bach, Beethoven, Haydn, Handel, Mozart, Byrd, Purcell, Gibbons.' Now, he retained a liking only for Mozart. He could no longer bear any of the others, 'too full of form and lacking in emotion. They go on and on; those old boys didn't know when to stop.'[2] Now, he enjoyed anything from Mendelssohn on, especially Wagner, Arthur Bliss (he loved his Piano Concerto), Walton, Edward German and Richard Addinsell. This was enough to convince audiences that Novello *knew* about music; he *understood* the importance of music and its possible effects on the ordinary man. More importantly, he was able to bring a sense of this understanding (and his understanding of art and beauty and everything that emanated from this) to his very appearance on stage.

While never claiming a sophistication, the various components of these works stood in stead of sitting through *Aida* or *La Bohème*. *Arc de Triomphe* contained a mini-opera within itself. Novello's music for dance interludes effectively stood in for *Giselle* and *La Bayadère* (distinctly recalled in his dance music for *King's Rhapsody*). His leading female singers were not popular, but operatic. One of the most remembered, Mary Ellis, had triumphed in higher art, creating a Puccini role at the Metropolitan Opera in New York. Another, the Welsh soprano Olive Gilbert, who appeared consistently in Novello's featured roles, brought with her shreds of past glories with the Carl Rosa Opera. Employing such devices, Novello presented material in lieu of Puccini (the 'Bridge of Lovers' and 'The Miracle of Nichaow' standing in for *Madama Butterfly*'s 'Humming Chorus'). In such a way, the Novello shows were built on considerable foundations.

Novello versus Coward

No doubt Noel Coward wagged his finger at Ivor Novello over the subject of the musical play. Both men bestrode the revue and musical play almost simultaneously, until Novello's early death in 1951 left his friend and competitor to claim the crown. Although dealt with in some seriousness by two books (James Harding's Novello biography and Sandy Wilson's invaluable *Ivor*) in recent years Novello's musical works have been poorly dealt with by biographers. Coward has been much more fulsomely treated, in a range of biographies, editions of his diary writings and letters, and various studies, but his work in musical theatre has mostly been discussed by those who know little of the context into which they fit. Some of these supposedly authoritative writers betray an almost total lack of original thought or, even more unforgivably, sound research. More than one notable biographer has missed the point when it comes to understanding Coward's musical theatre career. In truth, there is a mountain to climb if we are to consider his musicals (and indeed those of 'darling' Ivor) properly, an Everest of a challenge, for the preparatory slopes scarred by so many ill-equipped writers and commentators have made the way forward slippery and difficult.

So, let us begin with a few facts about Coward and Novello, those two giants of the British musical, some of which are more factual (in the sense that they cannot be argued against) than others. Fact: Coward and Novello both wrote revues. Correction: Coward wrote revues, and contributed to others, while Novello made substantial contributions to revues but did not specialise in compiling an entire entertainment for that medium. Of these revue songs, Coward wrote lyrics as well as music, while Novello never professed to be a lyricist, although he could turn his hand to it. A great number of Coward's revue songs have endured, while only one or two of Novello's (the best known perhaps 'And Her Mother Came Too') have outlived their beginnings.

Novello was barely fifteen when his first composition – one of many 'platform' songs, among them 'Fairy Laughter' and 'The Little Damozel', whose flavour was to imbue his later work – was professionally performed, and twenty-one when worldwide success as a songwriter came with 'Till the Boys Come Home' (later known as 'Keep the Home Fires Burning'). Written in twenty minutes with a little assistance from its credited lyricist Lena Guilbert Ford (who may only have written a couple of its lines), this became the British anthem of the Great War. When the score was compiled for the Theatre Workshop's *Oh, What a Lovely War!* in 1963 it was unthinkable that the song should not have a central place. After Novello's death an old soldier sent a donation to the King George Pension Fund for Actors, explaining 'I marched to the tune of "Keep the Home Fires Burning" in France many times and I am sure that tune helped us to win the war.' The letter was signed 'An old Buff'.[3] He was not the only roughly educated to value Novello's music.

The song had first been heard (pianist Novello, singer Sybil Vane) at a National

Sunday League Concert at the Alhambra Theatre. The composer's doting mother was not in the hall to hear the chorus repeated nine times. By the autumn of 1916 the *Musical Standard* stated that Novello 'may safely be described as *the most popular of the younger English composers*'.[4] Novello was keen to follow up with another patriotic pleaser. At the end of November 1915 the *Daily Mirror* urged its readers to assist him in tracing a certain Mrs Huggins, who had sent Novello a lyric entitled 'Just a Jack or Tommy'; all he knew of her was that she was a widow residing in Manchester. The song was published the same year, as was 'Laddie in Khaki', this time with Novello providing both melody and lyric.

At Christmas 1915 the *Daily Mail* gave over its whole front page to the song,[5] informing readers that 'Keep the Home Fires Burning' was the favourite panto-mime number of the season, rendered by such artistes as the redoubtable Dor-othy Ward (who would be mentioned in dispatches in Novello's *Gay's the Word*) at the Grand Theatre, Leeds, by the Sisters Cora at Glasgow, and Miss Pearl Grey at the Theatre Royal, Edinburgh. According to the *Huddersfield Daily Chronicle* the song had 'got down even to the errand boy'.[6] Novello went to France with one of Miss Lena Ashwell's concert parties and during a period of twenty-seven days sang his song over 300 times to the enthusiastic reception of men at the Front. Writing of this time, the biographer W. Macqueen-Pope alerts us to an essential component of Novello's appeal. Never mind that Mam was tucked up in bed with a head cold; the first enormous success had

> happened in the afternoon, at a music hall, before an audience of ordinary worka-day people of the middle and lower middle class: just men and women of all ages in ordinary clothes and mainly on the shabby side [...] But that audience was the one for which Ivor wrote then and always afterwards, and that audience was the first to acclaim him and to remain true always.[7]

In musical plays, the distinction between Coward and Novello is strong. Cow-ard did not contribute songs that might seamlessly (or with the seams showing) be interpolated into scores by other hands, while Novello was constantly doing so in the shows that preceded *Glamorous Night*. More often, it was others who were interpolating their songs into scores that were principally by Novello. He began contributing songs to London musicals in 1916, making an auspicious debut in *Theodore and Co*, the score a collaboration between Jerome Kern and Novello's thirteen numbers. The same year there were four songs in the André Charlot revue *See-Saw*, for one of which ('Dream Boat') Novello also wrote lyrics. With the lyricist Clifford Grey he wrote seven songs for the 1917 *Arlette*, and in 1918 ten songs with lyricist Ronald Jeans for the revue *Tabs*. 1919 brought the musi-cal comedy *Who's Hooper?* based on a play by Arthur Wing Pinero, for which Novello set ten lyrics by Grey, and one by himself ('If You Were King in Babylon'), the rest of the music being by Howard Talbot. Two of his best remembered songs from this early period were heard in George Edwardes' production of the Harold Fraser-Simpson composed *A Southern Maid*, starring the legendary José Collins:

'Every Bit of Loving in the World' and 'I Want the Sun and the Moon', both lyrics by Douglas Furber. Neither melody gives much hint of the lush romanticism he introduced into the Novello musicals of the 1930s and 1940s.

In 1921 came the first London musical with a completely Novello score, *The Golden Moth*, its lyrics predominantly by P. G. Wodehouse. Almost forgotten today, *The Golden Moth*'s score reveals an easy charm, music full of lilt, explicitly charming; its numbers might have been reused for any of the post-1935 Novello scores. For the Gertrude Lawrence–Jack Buchanan vehicular revue *A–Z* Novello shared the music with Philip Braham. There were three other productions to which Novello made major contributions: another Charlot revue, *Puppets* (1924); Harold Fraser-Simpson's 1924 musical play *Our Nell* (José Collins now impersonating Nell Gwyn) for which Novello wrote three songs including 'The Land of Might Have Been', and the Jack Hulbert–Cicely Courtneidge revue *The House that Jack Built* in 1929, for which Novello set eight lyrics, mostly by Donovan Parsons. After this came some individual songs worked into various productions, and in 1935 'Keep the Peace Fires Burning', with a lyric by Novello's mother, an attempt at another 'Till the Boys Come Home'.

Then there was Novello the film actor, celluloid celebrations of his matinee idol days, in which his striking looks threatened to make him the English Valentino, or at least the British Ramon Navarro – something Coward, with a limited acting ability and lack of classic male beauty, could never have aspired to. Even for the very first of his many silents, *The Call of the Blood*, shot in Sicily, Novello was leading man, and always remained at the top of the bill throughout his substantial career in pictures. Novello was never 'featured' or relegated to 'guest artist'. Storylines involving gypsies were at the heart of *Carnival* (1921) and *The Bohemian Girl* (Balfe's opera without the music or, indeed, any sound at all) in 1922. Images of Romany romance and Ruritanian nonsense were already crowding in, to be stored up for later.

His visit to America in 1923 produced his starring role in D. W. Griffith's 'great love epic' *The White Rose*. When an American reporter threatened to describe Novello as the most handsome man in England, Novello pleaded to be spared the embarrassment. Griffith's run of success was almost ended, but Novello was launched on a string of enormous screen popularity, as a dashingly good-looking Young Pretender in *Bonnie Prince Charlie* (1923), then two hits – *The Rat* and *The Triumph of the Rat* – both based on plays he had co-written with Constance Collier. Novello again played the title-role in a third 'Rat' film, *The Return of the Rat*, made as a silent and adapted into a part-talkie in 1928. For Alfred Hitchcock Novello starred in the 'Jack the Ripper' silent *The Lodger* (1926) and *Downhill* (1927), the latter based on another Novello–Collier play. His links with Coward were strengthened when he played Nicky Lancaster in the film version of Coward's *The Vortex*, a role Coward had originally played on stage, and in 1929 he took Coward's stage role of Lewis Dodd for the film of *The Constant Nymph*. Novello's career in talkies was less long, including films of his plays *Symphony in*

* *

Every Sunday you can meet him,
because every Sunday in the Sunday Pictorial . . . .

Ivor Novello

Talks to you

SUNDAY

PICTORIAL

Every Sunday, Ivor Novello writes an intimate message to
Sunday Pictorial readers. No mere catalogue of people and
events, but a brilliant and sincere commentary on life as he finds
it. Ivor Novello ! every Sunday Pictorial.

4 Getting close to Ivor Novello in the *Sunday Pictorial*, an advertisement in *Theatre World*

Two Flats (1930) and the gloriously funny *I Lived With You* (1933) with its memorable tea-party scene in which Novello's mischievous Russian prince scandalises the guests, all females of a certain age, and forces them to down large doses of vodka.

After *Autumn Crocus* (1934), in which he played the inn-keeper Steiner ('rather too exquisite to be running a village inn' according to Sandy Wilson),[8] Novello was done with moving pictures, and did not appear in those fashioned from his musicals. This was a wise decision. Apart from other considerations, the camera would have revealed his age in a way that Leichner[9] and stage lighting did not. The actors chosen to tackle his roles on screen only proved how essential Novello had been to their success on stage: stodgy Barry Mackay, who had galumphed about in some Jessie Matthews' films, in *Glamorous Night* (1937), and lifeless Dennis Price bringing none of the Novello magic (how could he?) to *The Dancing Years* (1949). At least Novello was spared the experience of Herbert Wilcox's film version of *King's Rhapsody* (1955), with an exhausted Errol Flynn in the Novello part and Anna Neagle as a suburban leading lady.

Just as vital to Novello's British reputation was his career as the playwright of light comedies, although their quality and runs seldom threatened Coward's supremacy. Novello's scripts for his musicals and plays show a light gift for light dialogue; come to think of it, that pretty well covers much of Coward as well. As with the series of Novello musicals in 1935, Novello's plays were made the more appealing to the public by his presence as their leading man. Those that lacked his name in the cast list tended to do less well, and without him they have markedly faded. While Coward's plays continue to play all over the world, Novello's are forgotten, and there seems little prospect of these trifles being resurrected.

But in 1935 it was as a film and stage actor, mostly in his own plays, and as the boy wonder-composer of 'Till the Boys Come Home' that Novello had worked his way into the British consciousness. From that time on, his concentration was almost solely on the current and next Novello musical romance, at which point all the experience and flavour of what had gone before came into play. Looking at the films and plays the overwhelming sense is of romance, of a playful lightness, a lack of consequence, the air of a Venetian masked ball, the sexual dubiousness of smirking highwaymen with heaven knows what kind of ransom in mind, the whispered secrets of French alleyways known to the Rat, the swirl of kilt, the sudden piercing Novello look to camera and audience, the sculptured brilliantined hair lopping suggestively over his eyes, and – to be remarked on again and again by critics as he sat at a grand piano on stage among his musicals – the profile. These disparate factors were somehow melded and heightened by the glamour musicals he invented in 1935. Already, we can see that Novello's was a unique achievement in musical theatre. Being able to watch the composer (and film star and playwright and boy wonder) as singers performed his works – of course audiences flocked!

The Coward musicals were spread over a long period: from *Bitter-Sweet* in

1929 to *The Girl who Came to Supper* in 1962. Coward was in complete charge of his works: book, music and lyrics, except for the last show to which he did not contribute the book. His musicals were slipped in between the ongoing queue of plays; they would pop up every five years or so, while the Novello musicals after 1935 formed an orderly queue at the box-office, punctuated by his plays *Full House* (1936), *Comedienne* (1938), *Ladies into Action* (1940) and *We Proudly Present* (1947).

Novello's career in musical theatre from 1935 was a pretty sustained attack, whereas Coward's had always been intermittent. Novello wrote book and music, preferring to leave the lyrics to other hands. The authorship might have read 'Book, music and Novello by Ivor Novello' since there was one supreme ingredient that Novello's musicals had that Coward's did not: the composer. As in the most effective of his 'straight' plays, Novello was the pivot. This was exploited throughout the big Novello musicals: the profile coming down the stairs in Act I, the figure seated at the grand piano in Act II tinkering with one of his own melodies, the husky, smoke-induced voice whispering with alarming clarity to the back of the gallery his love for whichever soprano he was playing opposite. Coward was away from his own musicals, while Novello was there, emerging from the train smash of *Crest of the Wave*, evading the earthquake of *Careless Rapture*, managing not to be drowned during the shipwreck of *Glamorous Night*.

These bare facts may alone help to distinguish some of the ground we need to consider if we are to take Coward or Novello seriously as composers of the musical play. But we must go deeper, for at the very least there is the matter of style. The earlier use of the word 'simultaneously' gives us a hint, for both men came from not dissimilar social backgrounds. Both enjoyed genteel poverty, and were to an unavoidable extent open to the same influence and suggestion. Their natural *milieu* did not prevent, but perhaps exaggerated, their fondness for what we might call a romantic theatrical opulence. This was exploited by both men in revue, but in musical theatre that opulence transmuted into what we might call operetta, or operette, or (at a push) opera. 'Operetta' and 'operette' seem slightly indecent words for those who cannot stomach musical plays or genuine opera, whatever that may be. Operetta, too, almost promises the decorous, the unoffendable. No: we must regard Coward and Novello's excursions into musical theatre as musical plays or operas. That leaves us with descriptions dangerously close to absurdity, but we are not so far off the mark as the casual onlooker might think. Both men embraced opera while concocting their musical plays, but one of them with very much more commercial success than the other.

It is strange that Coward didn't attempt more in the musical play. Considering the breadth and potency of his straight plays, the musicals are remarkably tame. All the musicals which followed the first (except *Sail Away*) suggest that he unsuccessfully exploited the opera-induced valentine throughout his long career. And, before we move on, surely *Pacific 1860*, *Ace of Clubs* and *The Girl who Came to Supper* are almost completely lacking in any real feeling? This is not necessarily a bad thing, and may even be refreshing to present-day audiences soaked in the highly charged atmosphere of the modern musical. Most Andrew Lloyd Webber musicals exist in a state of fever-pitch emotion, made ridiculous by the modest feelings they dabble in. Novello also tiptoes across that high-wire, but with the support of a lyricist capable of poetic expression.

Whereas Coward's shows were stretched over thirty-four years, the most remembered and successful Novello musicals spanned only sixteen. In effect, Novello went for a continuous run: he wasn't writing his light comedies when he was doing the musicals, he wasn't starring in films. The musical became his full-time occupation, clinging to his belief in the opera-induced valentine, a style he used for every one of his shows, with the possible exception of *Gay's the Word*. The policy succeeded; most had good runs and made money at the box-office.

While Coward was unable to fill the smaller Globe and Cambridge Theatres, Novello was packing them in at the much larger houses of Theatre Royal, Drury Lane and the London Hippodrome. The runs speak for themselves: *Glamorous Night* (still attracting audiences and only taken off after a modest run of 243 performances because the management had already booked a pantomime), *The Dancing Years* (nearly 200 performances before the outbreak of war cut it short, and then a run of almost 1,000 during the war); *Perchance to Dream* (1,022 performances); *King's Rhapsody* (881, and might have been more if Novello had not died during its run). Even the less long running of Novello's shows mostly outstripped Coward's tallies: *Careless Rapture* (295), *Gay's the Word* (504), *Crest of the Wave* (203). Wag his finger at Novello as he might, it was Novello who went home counting the box-office takings, not Coward, but it is Coward who has proved the survivor, bolstered by an almost industrial promotion of his work.

This has been denied Novello, who left no great store of correspondence or diaries, and whose biographies have not always aged well. Peter Noble describes the curtain-call for the last performance of *Glamorous Night*.

> As he stood there, stumbling through his few words of thanks, the audience seemed to realise that this was a highly important emotional moment in his life, and a strange, tense quietude descended upon the house. When he had finished speaking the curtain came down very slowly to the tumultuous crash of cheers and applause. Again and again they shouted for Ivor. They just would not leave the theatre. Half an hour later, with the grease-paint removed, Ivor in his street-clothes stepped out through the stage-door, where he literally had to fight to get to his car [...] As he drove up through Covent Garden he looked back at that great and wonderful theatre. His eyes were moist.[10]

Writing in 1987, Sheridan Morley wrote of *Glamorous Night* that its plot 'given one or two minor changes of detail and locale'[11] is essentially reused for almost all Novello's later shows. This is nonsense, as is his assertion that Novello was 'never a lyricist'.[12] (Intermittently over the years he had written lyrics, and was lyricist for *Perchance to Dream.*) The air of dismissiveness is unmistakable. Morley thought the works 'to some extent a cynical operation [...] indicated by the alternative titles that he and his gay circle gave these lavish romantic spectacles ('The Prancing Queers', 'Careless Rupture', 'Perchance to Scream' or 'A Chance to Dream').'[13] Novello's attitude in writing the works was in no way sardonic; had they been, no audience would have been fooled by them. One might as well say that Jules Massenet, who had no religious conviction, wrote cynical works in *Thaïs* or *Le Jongleur de Notre Dame*, operas in which the overlay of religious fervour is paramount. Morley does not tell us if Coward's 'gay circle' had alternative titles for *his* works: 'Constipation Piece'? 'Ace of Drubs'? 'Fail Away'? Novello manipulated and engineered the stuff he presented to his audiences, and may have had a wry wink at it, but Morley barks up a misleading tree.

Listening to the earliest of the 'glamour' musicals Morley notes the similarities between Novello and Kalman and the 'countless minor Lehárs of the period: though Hassall's lyrics tend to have a plodding banality which makes these works largely unrevivable today, the music does swoop and soar in all the right places'.[14] Is Morley seriously suggesting that Hassall's lyrics are responsible for the lack of revivals? This is an extraordinary assertion, when Christopher Hassall was the true poet of British musical theatre; perhaps the English Oscar Hammerstein II. To what 'plodding banality' of lyric does Morley refer? Charged with writing lyrics that wore hearts on the sleeve, Hassall wrote words that often need no music to sing them.

Hassall's brief was constricted. We see that his lyrics were not led by character; Novello needed only words of love, general expressions of rapture, for the majority of his songs. The sort of songs which occur because of character in *Oklahoma!* ('I Cain't Say No', 'The Surrey with a Fringe on Top', 'Poor Jud Is Dead') are seldom found in Novello. Most of the songs are not *needed*. A great many of the Novello show songs seem interchangeable: if the leading lady of *Glamorous Night* does not fancy singing the title-song, she might just as well sing 'Music in May' from *Careless Rapture*. But even this is misleading when one examines the Novello–Hassall scores, for it is only the more 'romantic' songs that have found their way into the public consciousness. Hassall and Novello were equally adept in the minor corners of their scores, and here and there are 'point numbers' which attach themselves to a specific character. The lack of 'specific' lyrics is accentuated by the fact that several of the songs take place in a show within the show. Morley continues

One of the enduring problems about Novello's music was that because he always cast himself as a non-singing hero, and because his experience of heterosexual love was, to say the least, limited, he could only ever write love songs for a single female voice: the duets were something else altogether, and something he never entirely conquered until the very end of his life when, with Alan Melville as lyricist, he suddenly wrote instead a wickedly funny backstage musical called *Gay's the Word* which suggested [...] that he was about to embark on a whole new style of songwriting, one that owed more to *42nd Street* than to the Vienna Woods.[15]

Could it be said of Coward or Stephen Sondheim that because their 'experience of heterosexual love was, to say the least, limited' they 'could only ever write love songs for a single female voice'? As for Novello's duets, what can Morley mean that they were 'something else altogether' and that Novello only conquered

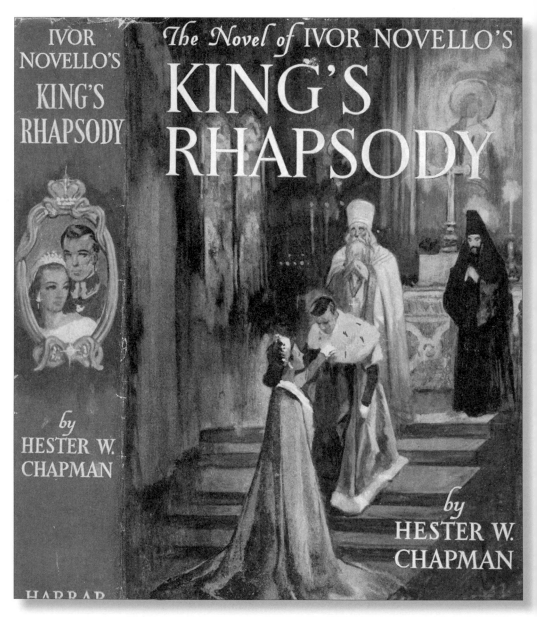

5 Merchandise exploitation: the novel of *King's Rhapsody*

that 'something' with *Gay's the Word*? For a start, *Gay's the Word* contains not a single duet. Novello had written and played countless intimate romantic scenes with his leading ladies; only the fact that he was not in any real sense a singer prevented him incorporating duets for himself and his co-stars in his musicals. To have written duets involving his supporting men would have been suicidal; as the non-singing lead, Novello was not about to write duets that would hand subsidiary males the crown. Duets were mostly reserved for 'show within a show' extracts.

There have been various attempts to revive the Novello magic, with rumours that the Novello estate hopes to revise and update his musicals, to make them ready and palatable for modern audiences, for there is no doubt that, long-runners and adored as they may have been, they have fallen into complete disuse. Such ambitions face a very considerable problem. Do what you will to update an Ivor Novello musical and it will still be missing one crucial ingredient: Ivor Novello. The songs may be luscious, the costumes gorgeous and the sets breath-taking, but all centred around the shows' male star, who never sang but only entered and emoted, and never more than when the orchestra struck up with one of his melodies.

Glamorous Night ✳ *Careless Rapture*

Many of the facts surrounding the creation of **Glamorous Night** (Theatre Royal, Drury Lane, 2 May 1935; 243) remain a mystery; it may never be possible to fully understand Novello's sudden emergence as (didn't they say?) the British Lehár, no more or less than an exiled Viennese. From the start, there was no doubt of Novello's intention. The vocabulary of his titles gives the hint: *Glamorous, Rapture, Dancing, Dream, Rhapsody, Triomphe*. The Trades Description Act would not have found Novello wanting. Such expressions of joy seem to promise nothing beyond an escape from real life in Britain just before, during and after World War II; the words themselves allure, with not a note heard of the music attached to them. Within this seemingly constricted context, Novello introduced factors that exercised his material in a way few other writer-composers of British musical theatre managed.

From 1935 his relish for theatrical effect was not the least of his armoury. For the first three of his four Drury Lane musicals Novello fully exploited the mechanics and historical achievement of Drury Lane by incorporating sensation drama into each production. 'Sensation drama' had been so-named in the 1860s, identified as a play containing a cataclysmic event, usually a fire, earthquake, train crash, shipwreck or avalanche, and Drury Lane, with its sophisticated and enduring stage machinery, was a prime exponent of the art, its first sensation drama, *The World*,[16] seen in 1880, featuring a shipwreck, with characters adrift on a raft, and a deadly lift to crush one of its seven villains. Two years later at the Lane *Pluck*[17] contained not one but two train crashes, the smashing of glass windows, a terrific snowstorm in Piccadilly Circus (1881 was notable for its hard winter), and a villain-started fire from which the heroine and her baby are rescued. G. A. Sala complained that 'if the playwrights and the managers do not take care they will create, ere long, a feeling of positive nausea among audiences who have become satiated with a class of entertainment which wavers between the grotesque and the revolting'.[18]

The incorporation of sensation drama into Novello's Drury Lane musicals shows Novello's awareness of several factors: the place of that theatre in the history of sensation drama and the exploitation of stage machinery which by 1935 had grown a little dusty with disuse; the ability to bring a filmic quality to theatre (indeed, how much had the advent of cinema, with its first stumbling silent steps in which house fires and similar disasters thrilled audiences, put a stop to sensation drama in the theatre?); the importance of the set-piece. While Victorians had presumably thrilled with genuine wonder at the sinking ship or collapsing buildings, by 1935 audiences could enjoy the same effects with a smile on their lips. The addition of the sensational ingredient to Novello's musicals (a shipwreck in *Glamorous Night*, an earthquake in *Careless Rapture* and a train crash in *Crest of the Wave*) was completely gratuitous. The sensationalism was nothing less than an indulgence on Novello's part, and one that audiences relished. To some the use of such trickery must seem absurd, but Novello knew how to entertain and amuse, and the visual thrill (much more sparingly used than in sensation drama's heyday) was part of the concoction. Even when the physics was abandoned, each of the Novello musicals (except *Gay's the Word*) had its grossly exaggerated moment, be it the all-white Bridge of Lovers in *Careless Rapture*, the ghostly descendents of Gantry Castle in *Crest of the Wave* (shades of the spectres summoned by W. S. Gilbert for *Ruddigore*), the Joan of Arc sequence in *Arc de Triomphe* or the coronation finale of *King's Rhapsody*.

The first of the 'Novello' shows (ignoring those that had flourished in the 1920s) set a pattern that, with various adjustments, was adhered to until his death, although it might be argued that a chasm of approach and taste separates the first from the last. *Glamorous Night* told its audience what to expect, as did that year's other successes, *This'll Make You Whistle* (guaranteed to get the lips puckering because it starred Jack Buchanan and his whispering sidekick Elsie Randolph), *Twenty to One* (a sporty frolic with mainly forgettable music by Billy Mayerl), and a Waller and Tunbridge farce, *Please Teacher!* In this company, and with its towering score and mammoth cast, *Glamorous Night* came out of the mist as something quite new, although there were other spectacular musicals of the time such as *White Horse Inn* and *Casanova*. That newness was not altogether illusory, and much of it may have been down to Novello's score. Too much has been made of Novello as the new Lehár, the reawakened Kalman, Novello leaning heavily on the Viennese tradition, echoing Sidney Jones and Paul Rubens and Lionel Monckton. In writing of *Glamorous Night* Novello's biographer James Harding finds traces of Brahms and Liszt (presumably not inebriated) in Militza's Romany hymn 'When the Gypsy Played', memories of the Edwardian Sydney Barnes in 'Fold Your Wings' and Puccini in the opera sequence.

From the beginning Novello's reputation never nudges those of his American counterparts, but there is something in his music more akin to Kern than to any of those composers from an earlier age with whom Novello is compared. Despite the British composers lined up for comparison, there is little sign of any of them in a Novello song, and not a shred of Sullivan or, in his lyricist, of Gilbert. Whatever corsetry of the past encased him, Novello evolved a voice very much his own. While Coward's operettas stuck seriously to their task, Novello proves himself from *Glamorous Night* onwards to be much the more flexible, incorporating musical comedy as well as cabaret. Novello was less a descendent of other operetta composers than the creator of a new form, in which a unique attitude to casting and the melding of the sensational with the *vin ordinaire*, the absurd with the emotionally stirring, resulted in entertainments that few have surpassed, and none have parodied.

The preposterousness of *Glamorous Night*'s plot may have had little to do with the fact that Novello thought it up on the spot in conversation with the impresario Harry Tennent. Anthony Allen, the handsome hero (naturally, as Novello wrote the role for himself), is the inventor of a new television process. To many in the Drury Lane audience 'television' would probably have been unknown. Only in August 1936 did the BBC risk some closed-circuit showings at the Radiolympia Exhibition, and in November broadcasts began from Alexandra Palace although there were only 300 television sets in existence to view them. Lehár's librettists had never introduced anything so revolutionary. The elderly operettas had never been so conscious of the filmic possibilities that Novello saw: the prelude in a shabby suburban street before the show opened to its unimagined (save by Novello) splendour, the opulent scenes of the opera within the play (a *mélange* of Arcadian fantasy), outside the opera house where Allen foils an assassination attempt on its star singer Militza (Mary Ellis), a gypsy wedding, the court of Krasnia to whose king Anthony eventually loses his adored Militza, who has bravely chosen duty above the pull of love.

Thus does *Glamorous Night* end with the same conviction found in *King's Rhapsody*. Just as Nikki's love for his country forces his separation from the woman he loves, so Anthony's patriotism obliges him to part from Militza. Along the way, Anthony and Militza's trip on the *SS Silver Star* is upset by a shipwreck, marked by bombs, fire and smoke, falling bodies and choral chaos – and then the ship sank beneath the stage of old Drury. This sensation was at the end of Act II, giving the stage hands the interval to clear it up. After successfully reaching a desert island, Anthony and Militza realise they are even more in love, but nevertheless have to part. Through the wonder of his new invention, Anthony and the audience are able to watch the marriage of his lover to her beleaguered king. In effect, something else which Novello never fought shy of: the unhappy ending.

The score of *Glamorous Night* is strong, and Hassall (only twenty-three at the time) writes with passionate conviction. Where words of love are required (as they so often are in a Novello score) he comes up with memorable lines and images, as for 'Shine through My Dreams' ('Make all my dreams reality'). The title-song of *Glamorous Night* is a perfect example of this, immortalised in Ellis's 78 rpm recording, one of the great mementoes of British musical theatre. For Elisabeth Welch's role of Cleo Wellington, a cabaret singer on board the *Silver Star*, Novello and Hassall wrote two numbers in a style that those old operetta fellows would not have recognised, and possibly would not have approved of. 'Shanty Town' has the sincerity of a negro spiritual, and a strongly sexual undertow as Welch longs for her black lover across the seas, and 'The Girl I Knew' reaches the world-weary cynicism of Lorenz Hart. With these two songs, Novello was once again able to exploit the possibilities of placing songs 'outside' the plot and beyond the reach of the main characters.

Careless Rapture (Theatre Royal, Drury Lane, 11 September 1936; 295) takes its title from Robert Browning, who cannot have imagined his words would have led so many to such a concoction of the old, the new, the frankly ridiculous and enjoyable. Just as Gilbert misrepresented Japan in *The Mikado* Novello turned to China, setting much of the play there. A major reason why the new piece was less of an operatic burden than *Glamorous Night* was its leading lady, Dorothy Dickson, from the land of musical comedy, with only her main solo 'Music in May' making demands on her voice. Everything surrounding Dickson, playing a singer called Penelope Lee, was up to the moment, removing the need for any cabaret insertions to bring audiences back to something like a real world, often a remote planet in Novello's geography. Hassall is again reaching for Hart in his lyrics for 'Thanks to Phyllida Frame' (Phyllis Dare playing the owner of a beauty parlour) and 'Wait for Me', performed by Dickson in fetching lamé to a stage crammed with chorus boys, top-hatted and caned, against a background of futuristic skyscrapers. In fact, this is one of the moments from another show-within-a-show, this time *The Rose Girl* with which Penny tours to China, presumably a Number One date. Novello ensures that while China is in our thoughts, the songs are more occidental than accidental.

Penny's love for Michael (Novello), and his unhappy relationship with her half-brother to whom Penny is engaged, gives the entertainment some sort of shape, but really the fun begins when the story is forgotten. Sensation drama intrudes when the city of Fu-Chin is hit by an earthquake (another pre-interval disaster, with twenty minutes to clear the debris). The earthquake gives Penny and Michael the chance to shelter in a ruin of a temple, where they conjure up images of an old legend about a beautiful princess and her sacrificed lover (shades, here, of Rider Haggard's *She*).

The exoticism persists throughout the Temple Ballet, one of Novello's most brilliant dance music items; audiences were also offered the 'Rose Ballet'. For some weeks at the beginning of the run, Novello fulfilled a long held ambition to appear in the Temple scene, dressed in what may be described as an Aztec-look halter, Wellington boots, Automobile Association gauntlets and an oversized black nappy. The effect was striking rather than fetching. Photographs of this event suggest that his legs were not in the same class as his profile, and after some performances his ballet debut was cut from the production. This was regrettable, as it can only have added to the gaiety of the occasion. Also cut from *Careless Rapture* after a few performances was the 'Singing Lesson' in which Novello burst into the studio of Mme Simonetti (Gilbert) to banter with Penelope and try his hand at some serious operatic pastiche. Fortunately, the number and its preceding dialogue was recorded before being excised from the show. It was evidence, and there would be more before the end of his career, that Novello was willing to turn his hand to anything, and that he was happy not to take himself too seriously.

There is no shortage of opulence in *Careless Rapture*, visual (not least, René Hubert's stunning costume for Dickson in the Temple scene, and its all-white finale on that bridge) and aural. Its diversity does not prevent it from providing one of Novello's most vibrant scores. Lightness breaks in not only because Dickson knows how to bring it and Novello knows how to write it. It is there in the Hampstead Heath sequence, when Michael whisks Penny away for a Bank Holiday spree, consolidating his fondness for her on a roundabout (another indulgence for Novello, who had a passion for candy-floss). Novello provides a trio of songs that outclasses Coward's similar attempt at a Cockney singalong in *The Girl who Came to Supper*. Novello's versions are 'Hi-Ti-Tiddly-Eye', 'Winnie, Get off the Colonel's Knee' and 'Take a Trip to Hampstead' – one feels that their composer would happily have gone on the charabanc so long as there was the possibility of some candy floss. Unlike Coward, Novello somehow avoids being patronising to the lower orders.

There is nothing disingenuous, either, in the principal love music (the one type for which Novello is remembered) of *Careless Rapture*, confined as it is to two numbers. The melancholic 'Why Is There Ever Good-Bye?' responded well to Gilbert's sonorous rendition, and best of all was a duet supposedly from *The Rose Girl* 'Love Made the Song I Sing to You'. The epic thrust of *Careless Rapture* has its summation in/on 'The Bridge of Lovers', with Gilbert proclaiming its final cry of 'A little suffering and then a life eternal', a rare moment when Hassall and Novello come within spitting distance to some sort of sub-text about the meaning of life itself.

Crest of the Wave ❖ *The Dancing Years* ❖ *Arc de Triomphe*

The third of the Novello spectaculars, **Crest of the Wave** (Theatre Royal, Drury Lane Theatre, 1 September 1937; 203)[19] is generally reckoned as one of the least interesting of the canon, but it almost transcended theatre to present as a filmic portmanteau extravaganza. The starting point of its plot was the public and press fascination with the exploits of the 7th Earl of Warwick, Charles Guy Fulke Greville, who went to Hollywood to find fame as an actor at the end of the 1920s. Only by 1937 was he beginning to achieve some small success. Novello's genteel origins and subsequent flirtation with the higher orders chimed with the public's interest in how the other half lived; courtesy of *Crest of the Wave* the public did not need to belong to the National Trust to discover. Novello rang up the curtain as Don Gantry, lording it at Gantry Castle which has fallen on hard times despite its ancestors declaring their love of their country in 'Rose of England'. Don needs £500,000 to keep the old ruin going, and tickets are available to visit it. Trippers trail through the private rooms, happening on the breakfasting family who pretend to be waxworks halfway through their kedgeree. A similar plight for the upper classes occurs two decades later in *The World of Paul Slickey*.

Back at Gantry, after being shot four times but surviving with barely a scratch, the Duke of Cheviot goes to Hollywood (à la Earl of Warwick) to get himself into films. Novello's plots, often verging on the infantile, are nevertheless sometimes convoluted, and *Crest of the Wave* is no exception. There is much to-do about two females with the same initials – Honey Wortle (good, and Don gets engaged to her) and Helen Winter (bad, and she shoots him four times). Another villain is a scowling film-star Otto Fresch, rather like Conrad Veidt in a bad mood, and played by Novello in a sort of reprise of his *The Happy Hypocrite* role. It is Fresch who organises the colossal train crash meant to finish off Don. The only inconvenience was to the Drury Lane stage-hands who had another huge mess to clear up in the interval. At the end of the evening Don is back at a Gantry suffused with seasonal sentiment as the family and its well-wishers celebrate Christmas with a round of carolling.

In the *Tatler* Alan Bott showed an acute appreciation of Novello's new work.

> Once a year he delivers the formula, the story, the script, the tunes, the ideas for spectacle, the personality, the profile, the archness, the attitudes and the variegated goods; and that once is enough to fill London's Largest Theatre until halfway through the next year. He draws to the Lane thousands who enter a theatre hardly ever. As for his formula, it has given pleasure to a million or two; and as for the queer doings which it involves, they can be enjoyed even by the minority, as ho-hum or the stuff of luscious day-dreams. There is no malice in my memories of *Crest of the Wave*.[20]

Novello is as much the architect as the devisor and composer of *Crest of the Wave*. To those unable to discriminate, it may seem that the potpourri is merely a meeting place for what is tossed in: big dance routines, including 'The Venezuela' danced by Dickson and Walter Crisham, possibly an attempt at the sort of stuff Astaire was doing in his new film *Shall We Dance?*, and here co-choreographed by Hilda Munnings, known more eminently as Lydia Sokolova; set-pieces used to warehouse a selection of musical numbers ('Versailles in Tinsel', in effect a film sequence incorporating more dance music and yet another lament for Gilbert, 'Haven of My Heart'); scenic delights as when a cruise liner fronted by bell-bottomed sailors turned, by some Drury Lane chicanery with a series of flaps, into a battleship. Having taken his audience to Hollywood, Novello ends with the rosy glow of a heart-warming Christmas, boiling the whole thing down to simple domesticity. There must have been something reassuring about the holding out of such cosiness in the autumn of 1937. There had been reason enough to celebrate the coronation of George VI in May, and that same month some hope was generated when Neville Chamberlain became Prime Minister, although in his first speech as PM he thanked Hitler for showing military restraint. In July the Nazis opened Buchenwald concentration camp, and in September began taking over Jewish property. Although these and other events were to work themselves into the fabric of Novello's next work, *The Dancing Years*, they were nevertheless in the background of Novello's consciousness for *Crest of the Wave*. If only by providing escapism, he was reacting to the world around him.

The world situation brought a new relevance to Novello's next appearance at Drury Lane, as Shakespeare's *Henry V*. It seems extraordinary that so gossamer an actor should have had the opportunity. Remarkable, too, that for his Katherine he should cast his *Crest of the Wave* leading lady, Dickson. The magnificence of the affair again brought the Lane's machinery into service, as with the departure of the ship for France and the Battle of Agincourt. Lewis Casson's production opened on 16 September 1938.

In the *Manchester Guardian* Alan Dent wrote that 'Mr Novello plays the king with far more zest and poetry than his more serious admirers could have anticipated', but everywhere the talk was of war. Two weeks later Chamberlain arrived at Heston Aerodrome waving the agreement between himself and the Führer that Britain and Germany would never again go to war with one another. That night outside Downing Street the PM declared 'I believe it is peace for our time [...] And now I recommend you to go home and sleep quietly in your beds.' *Henry V* closed; according to the play's Chorus, Gwen Ffrangcon-Davies 'no one wanted to know about militarism. The thing that impressed me was that Ivor never let out a squeak of disappointment, and it was not only his money; it was his most cherished ambition to make a success as a serious actor.'[21]

In the Novello lexicography 'serious' may not occur so much as other words, but a seriousness was becoming apparent even in the musicals, most prominent in the last to play Novello's best-loved theatre, **The Dancing Years** (Theatre Royal, Drury Lane, 23 March 1939; 187 / reproduced at the Adelphi Theatre 14 March 1942; 969). Note the timing of that original production. Five months later,

Britain would be at war. On 13 March the Nazis took control of Austria, the Anschluss, flouting agreements set down in the Treaty of Versailles. Despite having been given parts of Czechoslovakia by the British and French the previous year, in March Hitler took what remained of Czechoslovakia. On the very day *The Dancing Years* opened, German forces worked their way towards East Prussia and Lithuania, and Poland warned that any attempt by Germany to grab Danzig would result in war. The building of concentration camps continued. A few weeks after Mary Ellis first sang 'I Can Give You the Starlight' on stage at the Lane, Ravensbrück, a concentration camp designed for women, opened its doors in the North of Germany. Over 90,000 people were exterminated there.

The Dancing Years began with its hero Rudi Kleber as an old man, condemned to die by the Nazis for helping Jews escape their clutches, after which the story unfolded as a flashback. This was too much for the Lane's management. Nervous of dipping the musical's toe into anything so politically topical, a milder version of the scene was removed to the show's finale. (It is excised altogether in acting editions available today.) The struggling younger Rudi (the forty-six-year-old Novello chancing it in knee-high white socks and lederhosen) is fascinated by two women, the young country girl Grete and the opera singer Maria Ziegler. He has promised marriage to the first, but falls in love with the second. Love blossoms, but Rudi proposes to Grete, and Maria flies back to her protector-lover. At the last, Maria and Rudi, now older, meet and know they love one another still. When Rudi sees her young son, the boy he has fathered, he realises he cannot break up Maria's marriage. He has to make up for this disappointment by hearing her tell him that he has made the whole world dance.

There is no sensation drama in *The Dancing Years*, although the Austrian locale would have been ideal for the odd avalanche. The trickery is distilled into something more organic; even the dancing, including the feathery 'Leap Year Waltz', is less abandoned. The mood extends to the rest of the score, more languid than those that preceded it. There are not the liberal dashes of pastiche, no cabaret intrusions beyond the numbers made possible because Grete becomes a star in musical comedy, giving Novello an excuse to lighten up with 'Primrose'. The show within the show is an operetta, *Lorelei*, yielding a song that might have come from any of those Russian-egg segments, 'My Life Belongs to You'. An urgent ring to its lyric and a firmness of melody place it among the best of the songs. Elsewhere, the score has two numbers that have retained their popularity, 'Waltz of My Heart' and 'My Dearest Dear'.

Despite its brighter moments, *The Dancing Years*, if it is to work at all, rises or falls at its most reflective. 'The Wings of Sleep', a duet for Ellis and Gilbert (still on the Novello payroll, now as Cäcilie Kurt), spreads itself like a cooling ointment across the susceptible senses, and on its opening night caused a sensation when doing so: the applause lasted so long that the next scene could not begin. To convey the spread of time Novello uses three different 'Masques of Vienna', for 1911, 1914 and 1927, rather in the manner of those movies flashing up dates on calendars to show how time is moving on.

Several professional attempts have been made to revive *The Dancing Years*. Barry Sinclair (a Novello understudy) did it at the Casino Theatre in 1947 with Jessica James as Maria. The 1949 film is probably the work's most dreary manifestation, preposterously directed and acted in grisly Technicolor. As a reminder of Novello's plots and dialogue it brings the viewer up short; was its author always so cloth-eared? There is barely a line that sounds or feels right, and the amusement the film offers is unintentional. (Rudi to his lover: 'Yesterday was yesterday. This is today!') Its only saving grace is Robert Farnon's orchestration, giving the seven-year-old score a new lick, but the songs are sucked under by the noveletish inanity of the whole. Surely Mills & Boon, avid publishers of romantic fiction for the suburban housewife, made a bid for the book rights? The film is nevertheless invaluable in containing excerpts from *Lorelei* (where the contralto, absurdly, is only dubbed by Olive Gilbert, who is seen in the film in a tiny non-singing role), and a protracted 'Leap Year Waltz'. This is enlivened by being danced principally by Pamela Foster, a remarkable and eccentric ballerina whom I knew well. One evening I accompanied her to an art exhibition exhibiting a full length nude for which, in her eighties, she had recently posed. She at least lends the film a sense of mischief which is otherwise missing, as is any sign of those Nazis with which Novello tried to give the original play some bite.

John Hanson's Rudi sang most of the other character's songs in a 1975 tour. In 1984 the lesser-known Robert Swann made a more convincing and masculine Rudi in what was billed as 'Ivor Novello's Bubbling and Charming Musical'. In 1968, while Hanson was back in the West End as *The Student Prince*, a revival of *The Dancing Years* with David Knight and June Bronhill made it into London, but was off in a matter of weeks. For Michael Billington, 'even if David Knight rather overdoes the gauche boyish charm of the waltz-king, I certainly prefer a little bit of roguey-poguey to too much mimsy-whimsy'. Anyway, Billington found the whole thing 'irredeemably mushy and sentimental [...] In its time (just before the war) it may have satisfied the public appetite for glamorous nonsense.'[22]

The relative modesty of **Arc de Triomphe** (Phoenix Theatre, 9 November 1943; 222) has helped pale its reputation. Beginning with *The Dancing Years* sensation drama played no part in the musicals, although *Arc de Triomphe* hoped to make up for the loss with an opera within the musical, *Jeanne d'Arc*. Based vaguely on the life of the opera singer Mary Garden,[23] the new piece served not only as a vehicle for Mary Ellis but as a recognition of France itself, now occupied by Germany. For the plot, in Paris the singer Marie Forêt falls in love with a struggling composer, Pierre Bachelet: their duet 'Easy to Live With', sung against a backdrop of Paris rooftops, obviously recalls the opening scenes of Gustav Charpentier's *Louise*;[24] Novello would have known that Ellis and Garden had played the role in Paris. As so often before, the Novello heroine is romantically entangled with another, her impresario. While the impresario guides Marie to success,

Pierre emigrates and becomes a film star. Reunited, just as Rudi and Maria are in *The Dancing Years*, Pierre and Marie are still in love, but Pierre knows he cannot come between her and her career, goes to the Great War's trenches and is killed. A heartbroken Marie triumphs as an operatic Maid of Orleans.

The score is appealing if not as distinctive as some of its predecessors, with two of Ellis's solos, 'Man of my Heart' and 'Sleeping or Waking' showing Novello at his most languorous. Following her cabaret spots in *Glamorous Night*, Elisabeth Welch played Josephine, for whom Novello wrote both music and lyrics for the best of the songs, 'Dark Music', the melody creamy and dusky, the words crackling with sombre allure. There was nothing discreditable about *Arc de Triomphe*, and it did not altogether avoid Novello's lurch into seriousness with *The Dancing Years*. The rest of the 1943 offerings were a pretty desperate collection of concoctions meant to cheer up the populace, including *The Lisbon Story*, whose main attraction seemed to be a song about a donkey.[25] Despite air-raids and blackouts *Arc de Triomphe* managed six months, even with audiences having to make do with another actor, Peter Graves, in what would have been the Novello role.

Perchance to Dream ❊ *King's Rhapsody* ❊ *Gay's the Word*

While *Arc de Triomphe* saluted a foreign country's wartime subservience, **Perchance to Dream** (London Hippodrome, 21 April 1945; 1,022) had the background of national celebration. Of course it had; the world had been born anew. It was in the grim years when the Nazis came to world prominence that Novello had begun the shows; as war began he had provided *The Dancing Years*, and as it progressed *Arc de Triomphe*. *Perchance to Dream* marked an end to the conflict. The day before it opened the Soviets attacked Berlin. In early May, Germany unconditionally surrendered. There was a feeling in Britain that a political newness was needed; at the General Election in July the Conservatives under Churchill were swept aside with the Labour Party's landslide victory. The surrender of Japanese forces on 15 August marked the absolute end to international hostilities. Nine days after *Perchance to Dream* opened came the announcement on 30 April of Hitler's suicide. Perhaps Novello had chosen his title (Shakespeare's *Hamlet*) because of the Shakespearean magnitude of the events that were having such an impact on Britain, still holding out promises of glamorous nights while conscious of the fact that what was ahead was years of austerity. As the war ended, rationing did not end; it increased. Despite all the privations, a sense of release was in the air. Novello's response to it was in the mellow reflectiveness of his new work. The idea came to him as he walked through the Royal Pavilion at Brighton. Some might think that the lack of architectural taste was a fitting inspiration for his new work.

Telling the story of a noble house, Huntersmoon (the sort of property Novello's audiences would only come across if they bought a ticket) *Perchance to Dream* is cousin to *Crest of the Wave* and its fascination with that white elephant,

Gantry Castle. Like the earlier piece, *Perchance to Dream* presents as another portmanteau filmic entertainment minus the sensation drama and musical comedy elements. While Gantry necessarily faded into the background of *Crest of the Wave*, Huntersmoon is the real hero of *Perchance to Dream*, making itself available for the sometimes preposterous events that Novello's three generations enact there. Like the impoverished Duke of Gantry, Huntersmoon's Sir Rodney (Novello) is hard pressed to keep the place going, but (the period being Regency and movies not invented) takes to highway robbery rather than Hollywood. Robbing the wealthy to improve the already rich was popular in 1945; at the end of the year a Gainsborough film *The Wicked Lady*, with Margaret Lockwood as a highway*woman*, caught the public imagination. Through time, those who inhabit Huntersmoon are sometimes descendants and sometimes reincarnations. There is something other-worldy about the power of the house itself, a question or mystery summed up in its 'Meeting Theme'. The suspicion that it is time meeting itself is emphasised in the extended choral and ballet sequence 'The Triumph of Spring', with Novello encompassing the four seasons with a broad flourish.

Shadows of war cast over *Arc de Triomphe* and *The Dancing Years* are set aside for what is certainly Novello's softest, most nostalgic score, a marked difference from *Glamorous Night* and *Careless Rapture*. One reason for the shift may be that Hassall was serving in the armed forces, forcing Novello to provide his own lyrics. He proves a good enough Hassall impersonator, but left completely to his own devices Novello's style coagulates into something hitherto unheard. There is a simple elegance to the soprano songs, 'A Woman's Heart' and 'Love Is My Reason', a sort of paring-down, as if the elegance has started to be stripped away. There is pastiche in a comic duet 'The Elopement' and in one of the juvenile females celebrating a risqué dance brought from France 'The Glo-Glo', and both have a daintiness that affects much of the rest of the music. 'Highwayman Love', relished by Gilbert's cavernous contralto, comes as a relief, more musically and lyrically abandoned than usual; one wonders if Miss Gilbert realised the homosexual connotations that imbue it.

Most memorable is 'We'll Gather Lilacs', a duet for soprano and contralto that marks *Perchance to Dream*'s reason for being. At the end of war, the idea of scented arbours, where great armfuls of the stuff might be plucked, insisted on the existence of an utterly romanticised Britain, a stroll along an English lane until evening comes, when love settles by a glowing fireside. As the soldiers return to Blighty, the song vows another return, to contentment, and just as in 'Keep the Home Fires Burning' the words tell of homecoming. Unlike Coward's World War II pleaser 'London Pride', Novello extends his sentiment to the whole country, not just to the capital, but Novello had always taken the wider view.

Novello's response to his times is blatant here and more subtle elsewhere through the pages of script and score, rounding off with a ghostly finale (another reminder of those spectres of Gantry acclaiming the 'Rose of England'), the curtain falling not on characters but on Huntersmoon itself, standing in for all the homes of Britain, not only the castles and baronial halls but the timid terraces and two up two downs, the North Finchley bungalows and cottages and semi-detached dwellings and third floor backs to which its audiences returned at play's end. And there was Coward thinking he could catch a post-war mood with a costume drama called *Pacific 1860*, without any of the subtleties managed by Novello. Penny dreadful and tuppence coloured as *Perchance to Dream* is, it has the smack of the sort of literature maids were rumoured to read at night beneath their bedclothes, when the washing-up was done and the morning's blacking still a few hours off. Once again, Novello's reaction to the moment, perhaps as monumental as a return to civilisation, proved accurate. Huntersmoon, four walls, the safety of home, where time would do what it would. Absurd and lacking in *gravitas* as it all might be, the piece already seemed to say 'Revive me at your peril. And if you should attempt such a folly, spare nothing in lavishness and invention, and perform it with sincerity. Do not be deluded into thinking cut-price productions and theatrical posturing will do!'

But how long could Novello continue to turn the trick? Somewhere around the whole business of **King's Rhapsody** (Palace Theatre, 15 September 1949; 881) hovers the feeling that Novello knew the game was up. *Weldons Ladies' Journal* reported that a man in the audience at Manchester had stood up in the stalls at the end of the performance and shouted 'Best stop now, lad. Thou'll do nowt better than this.' If this was so, Novello determined to go not with a whimper but a bang. His mirror told him he was older, the matinee idol was hollow-cheeked; the American musical was gaining ground in London; the fact that Drury Lane had long been left behind must have coloured his feeling about the work he was capable of presenting, and after a non-stop run of successful musicals from 1935 sheer tiredness was playing its part.

The plot of *King's Rhapsody* reflects this: the ageing monarch of Murania abdicates to make way for his son, sliding only from the shadows at his son's curtain-fall coronation, to face who knows what unhappy and unsatisfactory future. There is no happiness in the last scene; the devastating effect of this on the audience would have been well known to its author. Reaching that point, many of the familiar Novello components are in place: a prolonged ballet, the 'Muranian Rhapsody', other dance sequences, no sensation drama (the lack of it accentuated the 'human' qualities of the piece) but a magnificently dressed Coronation finale.

The score of *King's Rhapsody* emphasises the stateliness of the occasion, bereft of such excesses as 'Highwayman Love'; here, Gilbert only gets to let her hair down in a frisky 'Take Your Girl', which still manages to be refined. Most of the score is Novello's music at its most statuesque: 'The Gates of Paradise', 'Fly Home, Little Heart', a National Anthem. Even at its most domestic, the score flies into the stratosphere. Within minutes of the curtain rising on the first night, Cristiane, a snow princess who is expected to mate with the dissolute Nikki of Murania, sang 'Someday My Heart Will Awake', ensuring stardom for Novello's latest 'discovery' Vanessa Lee (previously Ruby Moule, a Brixton telephonist). This is the song to which *King's Rhapsody* belongs, its title-refrain repeated when Novello, reducing his final appearance in the production to a walk-on, kneels at the cathedral altar to pick up the rose left on its steps by Cristiane. This is how the curtain falls on Novello's final romantic musical: the ageing Novello, the profile presumably turned to his audience, emoting silently as the orchestra's recollection of promise and hope works through its final strains. At that moment, perhaps, one may recall the words of John Drummond in the *Sunday Chronicle*: 'His followers are legion and loyal, yet he is the only star of the musical stage who does not sing, dance or "take care of the comedy spots," and his acting would scarcely jostle the immortals from their pedestals. [He is] unique in the theatre of our time, perhaps all time'. In a letter to Novello, Harold Hobson told him that *South Pacific* 'requires Rodgers, Michener, Logan and Hammerstein to do what you achieve single handed in "King's Rhapsody"; and then, in my opinion, they don't do it so well.'[26] And Hobson doesn't even mention that Rodgers never played a lead in any of his musicals, or sat at his piano on stage while his leading ladies sang 'I'm in Love with a Wonderful Guy'.

Only one blip marred the progress of *King's Rhapsody*. During the run, Novello was sentenced to two months imprisonment (reduced to one month after appeal)

6 Vanessa Lee, Harry Acres (musical director), Ivor Novello, Phyllis Dare, Olive Gilbert and Denis Martin at the recording session for *King's Rhapsody*

for a petrol ration offence. While Oscar Wilde's imprisonment had produced *The Ballad of Reading Gaol*, Novello felt only boredom. He thought the experience might awaken in him a deeper self, but did not discover it. At the time of *King's Rhapsody*'s premiere he said he wanted to write a straight play, 'But what about? Prewar is forgotten, the war years are too miserable, the present is so dreary. Escape lies in imagination and romance.'[27] And, presumably, a Novello musical. Interviewed for the journal *Illustrated*, he said, 'I loathe drabness in all its forms. To me spangles and glittering lights are truly inspiring. I don't believe that the theatre is a place for discussing reforms, politics and such like. The theatre is youthful, gay, and a child at heart.'[28] Novello regarded the American musical as 'highly salutary. It defies convention, teaching us to defy convention in our own way. Americans have infused a new feeling.' For his part, 'I have always tried in everything I have written to appeal first to the heart. The only thing that remains constant is an emotional quality that you can't nationalise.'[29]

A recent professional revival of *King's Rhapsody* with David McAlister as Nikki suggested that without huge sets, extravagant costumes and a brilliant cast the work has no legs. Here, the cavernous cathedral of the finale was reduced to the proportions of a Primitive Methodist chapel. Somehow even looking at the costumes one knew the material was wrong and the undergarments, if in place, were by Marks & Spencer. Worse, in an introductory note to a souvenir programme, the Managing Director of the Ivor Novello Charities endorsed this adaptation by Michael Pertwee: 'By incorporating songs from Ivor's other shows, this production is not simply just a revival of *King's Rhapsody* but also a celebration of Ivor Novello's music.'[30] This old trick seldom works; rather than doing the piece as Novello intended, hoping to spice it up by stuffing it with other of his best known songs.

Such trifling with Gilbert and Sullivan seems unthinkable (imagine *The Mikado* with a few plums from *The Pirates of Penzance* thrown in), but the British enjoy disfiguring their musicals by emasculating them and reassembling them à la Frankenstein. A 1972 revival of *The Maid of the Mountains*, rumoured to be thought a good idea because its producer still had the costumes from an earlier production, could not resist adding Friml's 'Song of the Vagabonds' and Harry Parr-Davies's 'Pedro the Fisherman'. Even so, considering the original *King's Rhapsody* had been such a commercial success it seems a bit thick to tamper with it. If it's such a good idea, why not revive *Oklahoma!* with a few choruses of *Carousel*'s 'You'll Never Walk Alone' (good for the football fan coach-trade), and pep up *Carousel* with a first-act closer of 'The Farmer and the Cowman'. While we're at it, why has no one yet dispensed with 'Be Back Soon' in *Oliver!*; it surely cries out to be replaced by Fagin and the boys singing 'Fings Ain't Wot They Used T'Be'? Then, *Oliver!* would be a celebration of Lionel Bart as much as a worn-through symbol of what we now consider the British musical to once have been. All things considered, it might be most sensible to let Novello's work retain its integrity. Rest it in peace.

Novello's last completed musical was a collaboration with the lyricist Alan Melville, Hassall having moved on to other projects, including *Dear Miss Phoebe*, an adaptation of J. M. Barrie's play *Quality Street*. Bringing Melville into the Novello circle may have had its origins in a laudatory 'Candid Cameo' Melville wrote for the *Sketch* in September 1949. Novello's response to Melville's tribute at the foot of the piece suggested that 'I am apparently a combination of St Francis of Assisi, Florence Nightingale and Flora MacDonald. But who am I to complain?' Novello went on to wish that

> some day Alan and I will collaborate in a musical play, where his Prince Astringent will counteract my Princess Saccharine (I really mean that, Alan – any ideas?) As for the Cameo itself: Alan Melville describes my profile as 'still enviable'. To quote one of my plays – 'I don't care for the *still*.' In fact, to use some of my imperishable dialogue of 'Tarzan of the Apes'[31] – 'Grrurgh,' 'Oooooh' and 'Barrh.'

Melville's reputation had been made in intimate revue, where his penchant for a theatrical wit had served such performers as the two Hermiones (Baddeley and Gingold), Henry Kendall and Walter Crisham. It was exercised in the theatre-based **Gay's the Word** (Saville Theatre, 16 February 1951; 504), in which an ageing actress Gay Daventry opens a theatrical academy in Folkestone and, by the play's end, finds herself back in a new musical in the provinces.

The piece was conceived as a vehicle for Cicely Courtneidge, in which Novello and Melville showed themselves adept at providing material that suited her broad, quirky style. Sheridan Morley hails *Gay's the Word* as 'an altogether new kind of Novello musical',[32] but it was nothing of the kind. The only newness of style was in the show's Act I closer, 'Vitality', a barnstorming catalogue of theatrical enthusiasm for Courtneidge, in which Melville saluted the great stars who by 1951 were being pasted into the theatrical scrapbook. The lyrics are lumpy and the setting uncomfortable, but for Courtneidge it was to prove a summation of her career. Far from being Novello's reply to *42nd Street*, as Morley insists, the score might have been mistaken for that of *Crest of the Wave* or *Arc de Triomphe*, hovering somewhere between those works and such pieces as *The Golden Moth*. Courtneidge's other stand-out number 'Bees Are Buzzin'' was cousin to *The Golden Moth*'s 'Nuts in May', written thirty years earlier, with Melville threatening to come up to the mark of that number's lyricist P. G. Wodehouse. He did not, and his subsequent assignments proved disappointing. Similarly, Courtneidge's contemplative torch-song 'If Only He'd Looked My Way' was firmly in the tradition of 'If You Only Knew' from *Crest of the Wave*. If sung full-throated by Mary Ellis the number would have been revealed as very much in the usual Novello style – it was merely Courtneidge's *non-singing* that suggested a new style.

'A Matter of Minutes' is an altogether brighter solo than that usually given to male singers in a Novello show, but this too recalls a Novello of the past, one who had worked alongside and taken on some of the zest of early Kern. The fact that in 'Ruritania' Melville has the male chorus explaining that the era of

GAY is the Word for **Sportswear**

BE <u>SURE</u> TO SAY IT . .
WHERE YOU BUY YOUR CLOTHES *!*

LONDON TAILORED

SKIRTS
SLACKS

IN FINEST MATERIALS

by GAY SPORTSWEAR
(LONDON) LTD.

Lyrics by . .
ALAN MELVILLE

Music by . .
IVOR
NOVELLO

Published by . .
CHAPPELL & Co. Ltd.,
50 New Bond Street,
London, W.1.

If Only He'd Looked My Way

Bees are Buzzin'

On Such a Night as This

A Matter of Minutes

Finder, Please Return

each **2/-** net

Piano Selection   **3/-** net

GAY'S
THE
WORD

∫
∫

*Available
from your
local music
shop or
from the
theatre
attendants*

7 Going gay via Ivor Novello's *Gay's the Word*: an advertising page from the theatre programme

glamorous nights is over and that 'The only fellow / Is Ivor Novello / Who still believes in us' shows the composer already disassociating himself from what he had done, recognising the fact that he had, in his own lifetime, become old-fashioned without ever going out of fashion. This, for any theatrical enterprise, is an exceptional achievement. Can one imagine any of our present-day British composers sanctioning such mockery from their librettists? What would there be to satirise?

From the beginning, although conceived as a platform for the star's particular talents, Novello decided on a considerable operetta content, a genre in which Courtneidge had no place. To achieve this, he wrote a secondary female lead on which he might hang the more traditionally 'Novello' pieces. Novello, still in his pyjamas, enjoyed going over 'On Such a Night' with Gilbert in Jamaica, but this, and the other 'operetta' numbers were not in the same class as those for *King's Rhapsody*. Novello would no doubt have incurred Courtneidge's displeasure had they been so. When she arrived at Novello's flat to hear the score, he asked his secretary Gordon Duttson to stay in the room throughout the meeting because he feared she would cause difficulties. Sensibly, she did not. *Gay's the Word*, one of the few British musicals to prove a tremendous personal success for its star as well as a critical and commercial winner, has not been revived. Its title has taken on an added meaning, which in today's theatre might prove to its advantage.

The last of Novello

A few hours after taking his curtain call at the end of another performance of *King's Rhapsody*, Novello died in his flat above the Strand Theatre at 2.15 on the morning of 6 March 1951. He was genuinely mourned, not least by the sort of ordinary people who had made up the audience at that first performance of 'Keep the Home Fires Burning'. His loss was to be keenly felt by the British musical theatre for the next twenty years. There had been, and would be, no other composer whose success was as consistent, his last shows as popular as the first, his work and songs still looked for. In many areas of his real life the constancy was as strong. Olive Gilbert, living in the flat below him, was an unofficial housekeeper as well as his constant ally, making a cheese omelette after the show as Novello sat playing cards with his secretary. 'What on earth is she doing?' Gordon Duttson would ask after too long had elapsed. 'Wait till the smoke starts coming under the door,' replied Novello. She kept his flat stocked with armfuls of gladioli or (if in season) Novello's favourite lily of the valley, and he never countenanced a musical after 1935 that didn't have a part for her. His valet Bill Wright was with him for years, as was his Welsh maid Edith Ellis. His late secretary Lloyd Williams served thirty years, as did the chauffeur Arthur Morgan. Professionally, Novello worked over and over again with the same colleagues, be they stars or chorus members. From 1935 his association with the impresario Tom Arnold never wavered. Neither did his association with the director

Leontine Sagan, responsible for *Glamorous Night, Careless Rapture, Crest of the Wave, The Dancing Years* and *Arc de Triomphe*, or with his musical directors and arrangers.

Novello's death not only had a profound impact on British theatre but on those close to him. His steadfast partner Bobbie Andrews, always in the shadow of Novello, receded into the darkness. When the staff was broken up, his secretary Duttson, still a young man, became personal assistant to Mary Martin, in London for *South Pacific*. Duttson's friendship with Novello was one of the closest, but he was effectively written out of the Novello history, and cut from the Novello circle. Many of the careers built around Novello went into the shadows: Roma Beaumont, Olive Gilbert (although there were still parts to be played, in *Man of La Mancha* and as a minor nun in *The Sound of Music*), Peter Graves, Dunstan Hart. Mary Ellis and Vanessa Lee appeared in one more musical, together, as the stars of Coward's *After the Ball*, a dismal disappointment after the Novello glory days. Presumably some of the ageing chorus members who had been employed time and again by their kindly employer retired to their gas-fired bed-sitting rooms in Barons Court. Hassall grew plumper and was made more distant from his Novello association by his librettos for *real* operas, Antony Hopkins' *The Man from Tuscany*, Franz Reizenstein's *Anna Kraus*, William Walton's *Troilus and Cressida*, and by his biographies and poems. His lyrics for the Sadler's Wells' *The Merry Widow* provided some of his most memorable verses, as in 'Vilja'. An overweight fifty-one years of age, he ran for a train; as he was pulled into the moving carriage by fellow passengers, he suffered a fatal heart attack. On hearing of this, Edith Evans remarked 'How wonderful! To leave for Crewe and to arrive in Heaven!'[33]

Just before Novello's death, he and Melville were about to start work on a new operetta, *Lily of the Valley*;[34] in the years after, Melville's fortunes with musicals would be fair to middling, providing words for an undistinguished Arthur Askey vehicle *Bet Your Life* and the winsome Scottish valentine *Marigold*. His authorship of a major clinker, *Mister Venus*, was forgotten when others were brought in to try to salvage the piece. This story of a visitor from outer-space – Anton Diffring in little more than a lamé posing pouch – who comes to earth to help out a postman, Frankie Howerd, was riddled with problems. Its director wanted his choice of leading lady, while Howerd insisted on the young Judy Bruce. As the show approached London, there was a major argument between Howerd and one of the composers, the soon-to-be Russ Conway. On the opening night of *Mister Venus* the audience threw vegetables on to the stage.

Once the man himself had departed, the Novello phenomenon was doomed. On the day of his death, the performance of *King's Rhapsody* was cancelled. The following night the understudy went on in his clothes. It was a ghostly experience, for something crucial had been lost. The national press was unanimous in its appreciation of Novello; the loftiest critics did not demur. Read by many of those ordinary admirers on their way to work, the *Daily Graphic* put it simply:

'His place in theatrical history is assured. Not because of his legendary success, not just because he is a great showman, but because, in an age of mediocrity, he gave common men and women an illusion.'

His old friend and business manager W. Macqueen-Pope or 'Popie', the author of many wordy and florid books, had his biography *Ivor* published in November 1951. As fulsome as his other works, it is nevertheless hugely informative, warmly appreciative of the man and critically astute about the work. Of the man, Popie considered 'He was, I think, the most completely happy person I ever knew [...] He created an atmosphere of beauty wherever he went.'[35] Let Popie, whose industry over a lifetime's work alongside Novello gives credence to his claim that 'I was his critic as well as his friend and the man who told the world about him. I knew (as well as he did), what he could and could not do' have some of the last words.

> If one tries to assess him, it must be this: he was complete in himself. His plays were never so good when he was not in them. He was seldom so good in other people's plays as in his own (*The Happy Hypocrite* was the exception, but, he made it his own as actor-manager). Very few of his comedies will endure for long.

8 Disaster for Frankie Howerd and Judith Bruce in *Mister Venus* (1954)

Very few of his musical plays will live long, as such. Some of his music will do so: it will go into the national repertoire as companion to that of Sidney Jones, Paul Rubens, Leslie Stuart, Lionel Monckton, Edward German and Sullivan [...] He will be remembered as some are remembered, for the result of what they did, rather than how they did it.[36]

3 Mastering Operetta
Noel Coward

> His knowledge of music being *nil*, the elementary fabrications which he fits to his own verses have to be written down, harmonised, jazzed-up and orchestrated by a corps of *entrepreneurs* . He only concerns us here because at one stage of his career he not only wrote, acted in and directed a handful of operettas or what-you-will, but also instigated their music. The cloying *Bitter-Sweet* (1929) and the more characteristic *Conversation Piece* (1934) were the most successful; a share of the credit belongs to his anonymous confederates.[1]

Gervase Hughes' judgement is harsh. There is no evidence that anybody else wrote Coward's music for him, although he certainly had assistants such as Elsie April and Robb Stewart who worked on his music with him. Perhaps it is simply that Coward was for all of his life much too *busy* to concentrate on his operettas, his musicals, his what-you-wills. It is perhaps too much to expect one man to write a catalogue of enduring plays, write and compose or 'instigate' popular songs and revues, write novels and short stories, and be a star of stage, screen, cabaret and gramophone records. There is the possibility that for Coward his musicals were of secondary importance, something to be picked up at regular intervals in his long life. Revues gave Coward his first very considerable successes, and some hit songs: in 1923 *London Calling!* ('Parisian Pierrot'), in 1925 *On with the Dance* ('Poor Little Rich Girl'), in 1928 *This Year of Grace* ('A Room with a View', 'Dance Little Lady').

Bitter-Sweet

The run of revues was followed by Coward's first 'operetta', **Bitter-Sweet** (His Majesty's Theatre, 12 July 1929; 697), written between 1928 and 1929. The title had an unexpected prescience about it, for there was a bitter sweetness about the fact that Coward was to suffer from the problem which affected many other British musical composers – his first musical provided a success he could not follow. The same happened to Julian Slade (*Salad Days*), Sandy Wilson (*The Boy Friend*), Lionel Bart (*Oliver!*) and David Heneker (*Half a Sixpence*). These composers moved into areas which they might not have been expected to inhabit, Slade with *Trelawny*, Wilson with his esoteric fantasies from Ronald Firbank, John Collier and Barbara Comyns, Bart with *Blitz!* and Heneker with the stuff he had already done with others before he got round to doing *Half a Sixpence*. This was not so with Coward. Thirty-four years after his first musical there is no sign of a radical shift in his approach to or understanding of the musical. Whatever he did to move away from the world of *Bitter-Sweet* he never managed to distance himself from it.

Even as the curtain first went up on *Bitter-Sweet* it was out of time. That year, London theatre was about frivolity and modernity. *Merry-Merry* was bound to cheer with a score from Waller and Tunbridge (one of its numbers, 'Bubbling Over with Joy', striking the mood that W & T liked to strike); friendly Lupino Lane in a musical farce *Love Lies*; *Open Your Eyes*, with a score by Vernon Duke including a few interpolations by Carroll Gibbons guaranteeing some degree of sophistication; the American Arthur Schwartz wrote the music for a Weston and Lee farce, *Here Comes the Bride*; Waller and Tunbridge, again, with help from Haydn Wood, writing the score for *Dear Love* with its three superb drolls, Vera Pearce, Sydney Howard and Claude Hulbert, and *Darling, I Love You*, the work of nine writers, among them composers Harry Acres, eventually to become Novello's musical director and arranger, Billy Mayerl and H. B. Hedley.

It isn't only that *Bitter-Sweet* seemed out of step with the current crop of British musicals; even as an operetta, it might have been on loan from a theatrical museum. It was free of transatlantic influences, and recent American operettas showed that the genre need not be immune to modern tastes. *The Blue Kitten* had Rudolf Friml pepping up a patently operetta score with the completely up to date 'I'm Head and Heels in Love' and 'Miaow-Miaow' and some charm numbers for a comedy lead, in this case Bobby Howes doing 'A Twelve O'Clock Girl in a Nine O'Clock Town'. Vincent Youmans' *Wildflower* qualified as an operetta but loosened its stays with 'I Can Always Find Another Partner' and the dance-crazy minimalism of 'Bambalina'. Even *Rose Marie* stopped off for 'Why Shouldn't We?' and 'Hard Boiled Herman', and *The Desert Song* leaves off taking itself seriously long enough to make room for 'It' celebrating Elinor Glyn's language of sex, but *Bitter-Sweet* is po-faced throughout. When it isn't, as when the effete male quartet sing their Oscar Wilde-inspired 'Green Carnations', something seems to have strayed in from another show.

If Offenbach made operetta fun, Coward takes it with a deadly seriousness. There is propriety without passion. When Coward's 'Ladies of the Town' go on parade we pinch ourselves to remember we are not on the streets of Harrogate but Les Halles. There is nothing joyous about these pleasure-seekers; compare them to Lehár/Viktor Léon/Leo Stein's grisettes in *The Merry Widow*, girls with real blood moving through them. Sentimentality aside, the lovers at the centre of *Bitter-Sweet* are milk-and-water, he with his mid-European accent (can it be true that Coward wanted to cast a singer called Hans Unterfucker in the role?), she making do and mending in a garret. When Britain and Hollywood made the musical into films, Jeanette MacDonald and Anna Neagle veered to the ludicrous. There is a contradiction in the fact that while Coward's best remembered plays are light-hearted comedies (*Hay Fever, Blithe Spirit*) in the main the musicals don't smile. It may be that Coward's skill as a playwright didn't extend to realising this salient fact; what, anyway, was there in any of his musicals to be serious about? And surely *Bitter-Sweet* is so lightly written that its characters can be of no real concern to anyone? There is more development in *Glamorous Night* than *Bitter-Sweet*, more excitement, more foolishness, more enjoyment. More shipwreck. In trying to be proper, *Bitter-Sweet* manages to be a largely sedentary affair, tipped towards the sensibility of the middle-classes.

The problem seems to be in Coward's *concept* of what an operetta should be, and this produces his peculiarly British style of what is principally pastiche. Listening to Lehár and Offenbach makes one aware of how the composers refused to let their lyricists hang about in lengthy introductory passages and verses that almost meet themselves coming back. If there was a point to a song, best to get almost straight down to it as in *The Land of Smiles'* 'Love, Let Me Dream Again' in Hassall's translations. Much operetta does not go in for the interminable verses that precede the meaty parts of 'If Love Were All' or 'I'll See You Again'. Nevertheless, those songs have proved the main legacy of *Bitter-Sweet*, as well as giving Coward the signature pieces that followed him through his career. 'If Love Were All' has come almost to stand for something else, but what? It shares with one of Coward's revue songs, 'Matelot', the feeling that certain sections of its audience are being excluded from the message it has to deliver. In the original production it was sung by a little beetle of a woman, Ivy St Helier, underrated as an actress and possibly as a composer,[2] and nobody has ever bettered the little beetle. Depressing as the song is, it is less bleak than 'I'll See You Again', that thick soup of a love song. At final curtain, the refrain is sung by the heroine to her dead lover, an effect used by Vincent Youmans and his lyricist Edward Heyman in the title-song of their 1932 musical *Through the Years*.

Conversation Piece

The episodic *Cavalcade* was seen at the Theatre Royal, Drury Lane in 1931, a panorama of Britain's twentieth century, and one of Coward's most memorable successes. 'After all,' the author told the first night audience at curtain-fall, 'it is a pretty exciting thing in these days to be English.'[3] One of its two songs, 'Twentieth Century Blues', introduced an enduring note of disillusion. Another revue, *Words and Music*, followed in 1932, with a clutch of remembered songs including 'Mad Dogs and Englishmen', 'Let's Say Goodbye', 'Mad about the Boy', 'Three White Feathers', 'Something to Do with Spring' and 'The Party's Over Now'.

Bitter-Sweet is an innocuous tale about a doomed love, but there is more bitterness than sweetness about Coward's next musical. In *Conversation Piece* (His Majesty's Theatre, 16 February 1934; 177) the machinations of sex are paramount, and the characters are obsessed with it. In some way this may distance them from us today, and the distance is wider because their sexual lives are hedged by the need to preserve respectability. The mother of the Marquis of Shere, the Duchess of Beneden (her title strangely reminiscent of a retired steam locomotive) positively bursts with it. The heroine, little French innocent Melanie, has to put up with it when her heart is burning with love for her protector (or should that be pimp?) Paul, the Duc (so he says) de Chaucigny-Varennes. Her so-called friends, two dubious ladies always on the look out for the next upright soldier, do not encourage an atmosphere of sweetness, but we have to remember we are in *Brighton*, Regency Brighton, and the Spirit of Brighton as portrayed in Rex Whistler's irreverent portrait of the Prince Regent awakening a supine nymph is being stirred up by Coward. He is writing of a bygone age, when morals were not what they were. And the old perfume is fading.

When Victoria and Albert inherited the Royal Pavilion as an official resi-dence, they put an end to such scandals. Come to that, they didn't appreciate the common people of Brighton staring into their windows from the too-close streets, and evacuated to the Isle of Wight. In its way, *Conversation Piece* allows us a glimpse over the garden-wall at another, pre-Victorian world of coquettes, horses dancing down the Old Steine, mistresses and guardians on questionable terms with their young wards. All of them flutter past in this version of a Pollocks' Theatre, tuppence coloured, Doris Zinkeisen-like canvas where all is cardboard. Even in reading the script, there is a sense in which one can feel them being trundled on, each in his turn, and then being pulled back to wait in the wings. Only stars of the quality of the first Melanie, Yvonne Printemps, could bring this to life, and this is possible because Coward writes the part with such sympathy. Paul is a dull dog as Coward discovered when he played the role for a time and loathed it; the originally cast Romney Brent told him he would. Perhaps none of it matters, for the goings-on in *Conversation Piece* are artificial and insubstan-tial. The characters who walk on and off are not so much characters as actors and actresses, their emotions stiffened by high collars, restricting waistcoats and tightened bodices.

James Agate considered the new piece 'not so good because of his bigger achievements, and people will not understand that genius need not, nay, must not always be at full stretch'. Agate thought the play too small for the theatre, and why did Act II end with the leading lady singing an aria in French? Possi-bly Coward thought it a clever touch; one which would exclude a good number of his audience. Agate believed that 'large sentiments loudly declared need a stronger backing of logic than Mr Coward in this play appears to have started out with. Last but one, it shall be remarked that Mr Coward had rationed himself too severely in the matter of wit, preferring to indulge in long passages of senti-ment which, between ourselves, is not his forte. Last, I am not too sure about the music. There was far too much of one cloying little tune ['I'll Follow My Secret Heart'] and not nearly enough of the witty, sparkling stuff whose top-line Mr Coward invents so happily.'[4]

Coward is put in his place as inventor rather than composer, but *Conversation Piece* is conspicuously lacking in anything like a full score; in effect, there are seven numbers. Two of those, 'Regency Rakes' and 'There's Always Something

Fishy about the French', are pure revue. Despite the sizeable cast, there is nothing for the chorus to do but stand around or stroll by. Melanie, her dubious lady friends and maid have two of the best items in 'Charming, Charming' and 'Dear Little Soldiers', and the delight is increased with Melanie's 'English Lesson' and 'Nevermore', as well as by Agate's 'cloying little tune'. Apart from that long-lived waltz this is a neat but largely incidental score. As the title suggests, it is there to talk as much as to sing, a platform for a conversazione. The lightness is typical of the quickly forgotten pleasantries that pass away such occasions between the pouring of the tea and the consumption of the sandwich. In this way, *Conversation Piece* describes itself impeccably.

This is not to say that the play is without moments of beauty, to which Printemps would have yielded. It is there as Melanie sings falteringly to practise her English grammar, as the voices of children at play come into the room. At such moments *Conversation Piece* seems better than *Bitter-Sweet*. That scene in particular has the ring of a scene Massenet wrote for Charlotte and the children in his opera *Werther*;[5] the conjunction of voices, Melanie's growing struggle into adult experience and the warble of the young at play, show Coward at his most relaxed. As a matter of fact, Massenet eschews a chorus as well; his chorus are only seen going off to church, not a word on their lips. Nobody even speaks about going to church in *Conversation Piece*. It might be better for all concerned if they did. Still, there is something of *Gounod fils* about 'I'll Follow My Secret Heart', with its swoops and long lyrical phrasing, and the song has stuck with the British public.

Operette ✻ *Pacific 1860*

Through 1935 and 1936 Coward wrote ten one-acters gathered together under the umbrella *To-night at 8.30*, presented in three different programmes. The most memorably non-musical of these was *Still Life* (a suburban housewife and a doctor falling in episodic love in a railway buffet), destined for more fame as the film *Brief Encounter*, and ultimately oblivion as one-half of the musical *Mr and Mrs*. Here and there the other playlets have a song or two, but two particularly are musical. *Red Peppers* is Coward's tribute to the 'wines and spirits' artistes of provincial music-hall ('wines and spirits' because their names were bottom of the bill with details of the supplying brewery), helped along by two pastiche routines which would have got the Peppers a slow hand-clap at Glasgow Empire first house Monday. *Family Album*, a sedate 'Victorian comedy with music', has more integration of character and music. Its compactness helps its pastiche to be more effective, and the songs have a genuine tenderness. *Family Album*, no doubt helped by its brevity, is a neat divertissement. A willingness to please had not deserted its author, but Coward's next musical, four years after *Conversation Piece*, showed he had paid little regard to Novello's outstanding successes at Drury Lane since 1935.

Stanley Parker's striking impressions of the stars of *Operette*, Noel Coward's Edwardian musical play at His Majesty's Theatre. (*Above*): Fritzi Massary as Liesl Haren, the worldly-wise Viennese actress. (*Right*): Griffith Jones as Lord Nigel Vaynham and Peggy Wood as Rozanne Gray; with Irene Vanbrugh as the Countess of Messiter. (*Below*): a fanciful all-Coward glimpse of the " Stately Homes of England " quartette.

OPERETTE

Sketches by **STANLEY PARKER**

9 Stanley Parker's impressions of Coward's operatic operetta *Operette* in *Theatre World*, June 1938, p. 278

Operette (His Majesty's Theatre, 16 March 1938; 133) carried the show-within-a-show format to excess, switching its real story with its on-stage story and listing many of the cast as two characters, sending customers away in a state of confusion. Reading the script today, one has the impression that its author spent much too much time in theatres, and cared little of the world outside the Stage Door. Even as an unabashed valentine to Edwardian musical comedy it may have dismayed its progenitors by its lack of energy. Too much time is spent on a seemingly endless revue lyric 'The Stately Homes of England', almost nothing to do with anything surrounding it. The two main love songs 'Dearest Love' and 'Where Are the Songs We Sung?' are mournfully lacking in ambition and theatrical lift if we compare them to the vulgar thrill of 'Glamorous Night'. Some of the songs are slotted into the musical-within-the-musical, *The Model Maid*. Coward was still up to this sort of thing in his final score for *The Girl who Came to Supper*. 'The Island of Bollamazoo' was to spawn other fanciful 'island' lyrics, as in *Pacific 1860*.

Today *Operette* seems not only pallid but exhausted and overshadowed by the more efficient *Bitter-Sweet*. There must be a question mark, too, over Coward's choice of leading ladies, a matter over which he regularly came to grief. The mature Peggy Wood playing Rozanne Gray was at the end of a long singing career, and Fritzi Massary, trying to cope with tongue-twisting lines, was barely intelligible ('Who ees these Piggy Wood?' she asked Coward), repeating the problems Coward had experienced with Printemps. Massary, like many of those on stage, was playing two people, the 'real' Liesl Haren and the 'on stage' Countess Mitzi. To further addle the audience's brain it was given a full cast list for *The Model Maid*. *Operette* probably qualifies as the most schizophrenic British musical of the twentieth century.

For war's end in 1945 a new revue played in London, *Sigh No More*, with some more good numbers, among them 'Matelot' and 'That Is the End of the News'. This was more than could be harvested from Coward's first post-war musical. Coward must have hoped that the new piece would celebrate an end to Austerity Britain. Hitler's suicide on 30 April 1945 wrote a line under the defeat of the Nazi terror, and the end of hostilities brought an exhalation of relief and joy which would all too soon be jolted back into a dull, ration-book reality with the overthrow of Winston Churchill's government, the declaration of the Cold War between the Soviet bloc and the West, and the Attlee government's decision to give Britain its own nuclear weapon. Anything happening in the world beyond the foyers of London's West End seemed irrelevant to what was being presented in British musical theatre of the period.

There was nothing in the least relevant or appropriate to the times in *Pacific 1860* (Theatre Royal, Drury Lane, 19 December 1946; 129) beyond a natural response to dreariness and uncertainty: escape. Coward offered a surfeit of extravagance. His play would take the audiences of Christmas 1946 from foggy, tinsel-happy London to the tropical South Pacific heat of the island of Samolo, an echo of the island of Bollamazoo sung of in *Operette*. He would import a famous leading lady from abroad as he had in the past. Graham Payn, Coward's partner, would be her leading man. A D'Oyly Carte and musical play veteran Sylvia Cecil would be the 'straight' 'mature' soprano. Gladys Calthrop's décor and costumes would be suitably lush as befitted the official reopening of the Theatre Royal, Drury Lane after being taken over for the duration by ENSA.[6]

Pacific 1860 started life as *Scarlet Lady*, with Coward wanting to import Printemps or Irene Dunne as the lady in question. When Coward decided on the American Mary Martin, Payn felt that something went fundamentally wrong. When Coward renamed the show *Pacific 1860*, Payn told him it sounded like a Canadian railroad: 'He was not amused.'[7] *Scarlet Lady* told the story of the opera singer Elena Salvador who in the 1860s is recuperating after an illness on Samolo and falls in love with one of the dashing sons of the island, Kerry Stirling. She leaves Samolo, but returns a year later to find that Kerry is to be married the next day. Alone on stage she manages a broken-hearted reprise of the score's anthem 'Bright Was the Day' as the play ends. Refashioned as *Pacific 1860*, the curtain came down on Elena and Kerry falling into each other's arms (silly Elena! – it was his brother who was getting married), but Payn felt that Coward's final version lacked the quality of the earlier draft.

After the long closure, the reopening of the Opera House Covent Garden and Theatre Royal Drury Lane were occasions for rejoicing, but for Drury Lane Coward's new piece proved a poor choice. His opinion of the operetta followed the usual trajectory: his play and score were superb and Martin a darling. The problems soon manifested themselves. Martin proved to be not only unsuitable for the role but difficult, refusing to countenance Gladys Calthrop's dresses, or to wear her hair up, or wear bows, and priggishly refusing to sing 'Alice Is At It Again' because it was 'off-colour'. By opening night Martin and Coward were not speaking. Offstage, Martin kept her distance from Payn: 'I believe that our distance showed on the stage: Two perfect strangers singing about the melody in their hearts just doesn't ring true. When I was out of the show for a couple of weeks with jaundice, there wasn't even a telephone call, or a "Welcome back" when I returned.'[8]

Pacific 1860 received a critical drubbing. Those seeking confirmation of this should be warned. Readers of Mander and Mitchenson's superbly researched *Theatrical Companion to Coward* may have been misled only in one thing – the pair's choice of newspaper review which follows each synopsis, cast and song lists. With Coward alive, when no praiseworthy reviews were available they veered to the polite. The *Pacific 1860* entry republishes a kindly notice from *The Times*, suggesting that Coward had caught the public mood by exporting it to the tropics and that 'This mild romance with its abundance of easy theatrical sentiment so gracefully expressed has precisely the same climate, and there are moments, as one pretty song succeeds another, when we rather hanker for a tropical storm.'[9] Scholars are slightly misdirected as to the critical reaction meted out to *Pacific*

1860, compounded by the revised Mander and Mitchenson ('updated' by Barry Day and Sheridan Morley in 2000) that merely reprints the original *Pacific 1860* entry.

The wider critical reception was less equivocal; even the *Theatre World* wasted no time on niceties. 'Mr Coward's muse deserted him when he sat down to pen *Pacific 1860* [...] The play is devoid of wit and humour, and there is not a single melody vivid enough to haunt the memory afterwards. Throughout the evening the music seems to be paving the way for the big number that never happens. It is never used to heighten the situations of the plot.'[10] Can this really be the well-mannered *Theatre World*? After praising both Martin ('sensational') and Payn ('one of our few leading men gifted with youth, ability and a passable singing voice') the review concludes

> We still cherish *Bitter-Sweet* with affection, and those of us who haunted the Lane in happier days enjoyed the emotional drama of *Cavalcade* and Novello's luscious novelettes. No wonder we are disappointed with the tame entertainment provided by Mr Coward for the re-opening of Garrick's playhouse and for the debut of so glamorous a star. 'I want to enjoy myself', says one of the bored bridesmaids in the last act. So do we, when we open a Drury Lane programme bearing so many talented names.[11]

In an effort to put some warmth into the thing (the cast and audience were already struggling through performances in a freezing cold theatre) alterations were made, a number taken out here, one put in there ('Uncle Harry', yet another 'point' number, of which the show already had too many). Coward was depressed by attending performances where the audience seemed totally uninterested, and became convinced that Martin was the problem. Now, he thought Calthrop's sets looked less like the South Pacific than Torquay. As the show's vigours dwindled he found it a bore. The Coward trajectory was played out – ecstasy at having written a great piece of theatre for which he would be acclaimed, and ultimate repudiation. But did the tired sensibilities of a Britain clambering into the new light of a grey peacetime deal Coward's work an unfair hand? No. It had surely been Coward's duty to welcome a young, hopeful age to London's best-loved theatre, to sound the trumpets and proclaim the brave hopes of the new order. There is no reason, perhaps, why an operetta might not have turned the trick, but the damp *Pacific 1860* wasn't it.

Its quick collapse at the box-office was followed by the arrival of *Oklahoma!*, making its predecessor at the Lane look even more of a dinosaur. The cleanliness of Hammerstein's work and the clear edges of Rodgers' melodies were a revelation, pointed by the endless rhyming and countless wordy verses of Coward through a string of songs that seemed largely irrelevant to the storytelling. The ensemble or groups of subsidiary characters in whom the audience had little interest battled its way through the trickiness of 'His Excellency', 'Pretty Little Bridesmaids', 'Invitation to the Waltz', 'Make Way for Their Excellencies' and other numbers whose tangled rhymes cannot have reached the upper balcony. Payn's tribute to the island's volcano, 'Fumfumbolo', goes on for ever, with Coward even providing a Samolan translation (he had invented the island's language), heard again in 'Ka Tahua', the servants' song of welcome to Samolo. A low point is reached with 'I Wish I Wasn't Quite Such a Big Girl', in which Penelope Stirling (Daphne Anderson) laments her size. It would hardly be allowed today, proclaimed as 'sizeist', and at the time must have put a brake on the proceedings.

The central romance of Elena and Kerry is too often removed to the sidelines, with only the main duet ('Bright Was the Day') necessary to its progress. Payn is involved in songs which are mainly incidental, and Martin's material is too often second-drawer. Of course, the prize for marking the end of the war had already been won by *Perchance to Dream*. It seemed that Novello could go on writing operetta to which audiences and (albeit reluctantly) critics succumbed; this facility was denied to Coward. Payn considered that since the success Coward had enjoyed with his patriotic epic *Cavalcade* 'much had changed in the intervening fifteen years. We were living in a strange new world.'[12] Nevertheless, it is difficult to see *Pacific 1860* as anything but self-indulgence on Coward's part. It had not been a happy experience, even, apparently for Miss Cecil, despite her successful aria 'This Is a Changing World'. The chorus took delight in singing 'This is your change of life, my dear' as they passed her dressing room door.[13]

Ace of Clubs

Cognisant of the fate of *Pacific 1860*, it is no surprise that Coward's next musical marked a change of direction, but success in this new cloak was just as elusive. Looking back to *Ace of Clubs* (Cambridge Theatre, 7 July 1950; 211) Coward pronounced it ahead of its time. For Coward it represented a particularly difficult struggle. It seems that the original storyline concerned the return of a young serviceman coming back to England after the war (and in 1950 this would have had some resonance with British audiences) but by the time the production opened Harry Hornby, bereft of any real characterisation or personal history, ended up as a lovesick sailor hanging around the 'Ace of Clubs' nightclub in Soho making eyes at its star singer Pinkie Leroy. By mischance (a mistakenly snatched mackintosh containing stolen jewellery) Harry and Pinkie become embroiled in the machinations of a local gangster. The plot, along with its cardboard *dramatis personae*, might just have done service for one of Butchers' quota quickie film scripts.[14] Reading the play today, one senses that Coward had no interest in these characters, no knowledge of their type, no sympathy for the Soho milieu, no passion available, nothing to tell.

Although he thought it masterly, managements didn't agree. Binkie Beaumont of H. M. Tennent offered constructive criticism but showed no further interest. Prince Littler, whose fingers had been burned by *Pacific 1860*, called for changes; Coward began work on a new version on Christmas Eve 1949. This was rejected

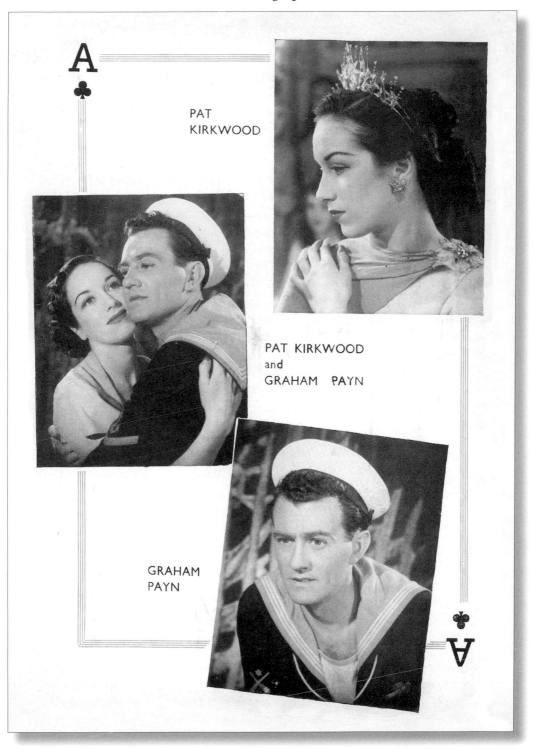

PAT
KIRKWOOD

PAT KIRKWOOD
and
GRAHAM PAYN

GRAHAM
PAYN

10 The stars of *Ace of Clubs* in the original theatre programme

by Val Parnell, thus denying Coward the use of the Hippodrome or Prince of Wales Theatre. The Tom Arnold management took notice but also wanted altera-tions, and it was under Arnold's banner that the show was staged. According to Gordon Duttson, Novello – troubled that his old colleague/friend/adversary was unable to get his musical produced – asked Arnold as a personal favour to Novello to take up *Ace of Clubs*. It seems that Coward was not aware of Novello's act of kindness.[15]

The show evolved through a string of working titles: *Over the Garden Wall* (presumably taken from the lyric of 'Chase Me, Charlie'), *Hoi Polloi* (does this tell us something about Coward's attitude to the people he was writing about?) and *Come out to Play*. Pat Kirkwood, best known as a variety and pantomime per-former, was cast as Pinkie, Graham Payn was shoe-horned into the leading male role, and Sylvia Cecil, a refugee from *Pacific 1860*, was brought in as the show's straight soprano, alias Mrs Rita Maybury, proprietor of the Ace of Clubs night-club. From the beginning there was something innately unambitious about this work. If Coward was serious about breaking with his operetta past, he needed a stronger will, better material, actors who were more skilled at making flesh and blood from cardboard. The horizons were limited. As the programme explained 'The action of the play takes place in the "Ace of Clubs", a night-club in Soho, and in Soho Square, London'. Coward's play seemed unable to even break out onto the *streets* of Soho; the action might as well have taken place in Stow-on-the-Wold. When a glimpse of the world beyond peeps through it is unreal; these people have no concerns, no interests, beyond getting to the next bit of plot or (rather more acceptable) the next song.

Having made his decision to be up to date, Coward seems hardly to have addressed his target, let alone hit it. Gladys Calthrop, brought in to design the production, was another who belonged to Coward's past. He found her first designs for the night-club 'not very good';[16] in fact, her costumes for the club scenes were hideous, making one more sympathetic to Mary Martin's com-plaints about Calthrop's work in *Pacific 1860*. On the fringes of this sat Robb Stewart, Coward's amanuensis, worked into the club scenes as the on-stage pian-ist Sammy Blake. Stewart's unhappiness at Coward's treatment of him struck a discordant note in the company; to the end, Stewart maintained that the extent of his contribution to Coward's music had never been acknowledged. Without doubt, Stewart was one of that 'corps of *entrepreneurs*' described by Hughes. The work of the show's musical director, Mantovani, was roundly attacked by Coward, as was Cecil when she asked to be billed alongside Kirkwood and Payn. There was much dissension in the purlieu of the Ace of Clubs night-club.

For Sheridan Morley, *Ace of Clubs* was Coward's 'answer to *Guys and Dolls*, a Damon Runyon text'.[17] Morley could hardly suggest that Coward's score comes anywhere near that of Frank Loesser. In fact, *Guys and Dolls* opened in New York in November 1950, several months after *Ace of Clubs*, meaning that Coward had given an 'answer' to Broadway before Broadway had asked the question. Perhaps

Morley was confusing *Guys and Dolls* with the 1940 *Pal Joey*, with its many night-club scenes and songs presented within the club's context. This, after all, was Coward's way in *Ace of Clubs*.

With one exception the musical numbers may be broken down into three categories:

1   Songs performed as part of the Ace of Clubs night-club floor show:
> Top of the Morning [Ace of Clubs girls]
> My Kind of Man [Pinkie]
> Josephine [Pinkie]
> Would You Like to Stick a Pin in My Balloon? [Ace of Clubs girls]
> In a Boat on a Lake [Ace of Clubs girls]
> Time for Baby's Bottle [Ace of Clubs girls]
> Chase Me, Charlie [Pinkie]

2   Songs for Pinkie and Harry outside the night-club context:
> This Could Be True [duet]
> I'd Never, Never Know [Pinkie]
> Why Does Love Get in the Way? [Pinkie]
> Something about a Sailor [Harry]
> Sail Away [Harry]
> I Like America [Harry]

3   'Operetta' songs for Rita Maybury
> Nothing Can Last Forever
> Evening in Summer

Never mind to which of these categories the songs belong; the songs are the best thing about *Ace of Clubs*, but this does not mean they are particularly appropriate or function well as part of the whole. Stephen Citron[18] has made the observation that Coward's songs work better outside the context of the shows in which they are contained; this is certainly true of the songs found here. The night-club songs for the chorines of the Ace of Clubs ('Top of the Morning', 'Would You Like to Stick a Pin in My Balloon?' and 'Time for Baby's Bottle') understandably have no 'point' in relation to the storyline. Rodgers and Hart's *Pal Joey* (1940) has similarly 'disassociated' numbers for the night-club girls, as in 'The Flower Garden of My Heart'. Pinkie's nightclub numbers, 'Josephine' and 'Chase me, Charlie' seem unlikely stuff to be found in a club frequented by gangsters, unless they are of the type that appreciate the finer points of complex rhyming and sophisticated lyrics stuffed with historical allusion.

Then there is the problem of 'Three Juvenile Delinquents', which seems marooned between 'real life' and the Ace of Clubs' floor show. The song displays as one of *Ace of Clubs'* best, but goes against the spirit of the enterprise. Juvenile delinquency has never been mentioned in the preceding scenes; the delinquencies up to this point in Act II are *adult*. Such a plum in the pudding is welcome, but the stance and tone of the lyric is wrong. Having taken no point of view about Soho, or modern life and its social problems, Coward suddenly decides to ridicule the idea of delinquency in present-day youth (although photographs of the three young man neatly dressed in smart suits and gay kipper ties do not present as very menacing), as if taste and style might for a moment be thrown out. As part of the Ace of Clubs floor-show it might just have worked, but marooned as it seems to be within the 'real' context of the play, it jars.

It may be that Coward's libretto of *Ace of Clubs* presents Soho and his characters just as they are, with no sort of explanation or perspective; as if the characters cry out 'Take us as we are!' But this is abandoned when the troublemakers break into song, using language no real delinquents would ('Then we cried vibrato, "How's your old Tomato?" – And the same to you!'). The delinquent who can rhyme tomato with vibrato is a rare find. Coward simply couldn't resist the urge to be clever. Listen to the young heroine of *West Side Story* sing 'I Feel Pretty' and she expresses herself in language that is right for her character; even one of the least successful British *verismo* musicals, *Johnny the Priest*, keeps control of the dictionary when depicting its delinquent youngsters. 'Three Juvenile Delinquents' is symptomatic of the wrong kind of cleverness.[19]

Beyond the floor show, Pinkie's two solos are both in reflective mood, as is her duet 'This Could Be True' with Harry. The songs do not celebrate their happiness. As for Harry, he is either thinking of abandoning emotional ship ('Sail Away') or keeping the girls backstage at the Ace of Clubs entertained for no reason ('There's Something about a Sailor' and 'I Like America'). In more serious mood, Rita Maybury, weary of the problems of running her night-club, has solos of quiet reflection, including 'Evening in Summer', one of the show's most effective songs with a lyric that brings Coward's feeling for London to the fore, even if it has reminders of Cecil's songs in *Pacific 1860*. If, as Morley suggests, the score is Coward's riposte to *Guys and Dolls*, we should note that nowhere in that score does Loesser revert to operetta. And there's another odd thing about *Ace of Clubs*. The cast list is long, but there is absolutely nothing for the chorus to sing. Of course, there is no storm for them to kick up.

At the premiere, Coward heard first night approbation for each of his stars. According to his diary Payn had a 'rip-snorting triumph', Cecil 'stopped the show', Kirkwood 'got them roaring' and the Three Delinquents 'tore the place up.'[20] Nevertheless, Coward's appearance at the curtain calls was booed, and at least one critic remembered the audience's polite applause. As the run progressed, Coward and the public lost interest in *Ace of Clubs*. It was acknowledged that Coward had made the attempt to bring his musical up to date, but it had been decidedly half-hearted. In his perceptive autobiography, Payn's recollections of the show are not especially happy. In her autobiography, Kirkwood writes of her disappointment on hearing her songs for the first time. To her ear 'My Kind of Man' was 'well below par'; 'Josephine' 'did not contain the master's usual wit'; 'Why Does Love Get in the Way?' was 'a sad little complaint which did not carry much weight'; 'Chase Me, Charlie' was 'not a show-stopper nor strong enough for the end of the show'.[21] Despite a company of almost seventy, there was not even a hint of any concerted numbers beyond those given to the Ace of Clubs chorines.

Comparing this with Novello's *King's Rhapsody*, which had opened eight months earlier, we see that Novello also had no compunction to overuse his substantial ensemble (32 choristers and 27 dancers), employing them sparingly, as in the Coronation finale, the Muranian Rhapsody and 'Take Your Girl'. Coward takes no such advantage of his large company; indeed, if *Ace of Clubs* is ever revived it may be as a chamber piece. Coward must have felt the fact that while *Pacific 1860* had been repudiated by critics and audiences, two years later Novello had brought off an operetta that was one of the glories of the London stage. By the time *Ace of Clubs* opened, Novello was, like Coward, turning his thoughts away from operetta in the preparation of *Gay's the Word*, and – as Coward had done – worked elements of operetta into what some saw as a 'modern' musical (but it wasn't).

It could be said that *Gay's the Word* is Novello's riposte to Coward's *Ace of Clubs*, but Novello had no need to offer a riposte of any kind; his work needed no apology. There is a thrill and majesty in Novello's 'Someday My Heart Will Awake' and 'The Gates of Paradise' that cannot be found in the mundane *Ace of Clubs*. Alan Dent in the *News Chronicle* considered that 'It is not the ace of trumps. But it will serve to take a trick.'[22] He concluded that the author had 'put out his witty tongue three or four times, but for the rest he keeps it in either cheek, alternately'. Mander and Mitchenson found this review inoffensive enough to include in their theatrical companion. Meanwhile, *Theatre World* was no more impressed than it had been by *Pacific 1860*. The editor, Frances Stephens, thought that 'After our recent experience of the modern type of American musical in the shape of *Oklahoma!*, *Annie, Get Your Gun*, *Carousel* etc., Mr Coward's latest work seems to be very much dated, and the really bright spots few and far between.' She saw that 'Three Juvenile Delinquents' was 'redolent of the old Coward satirical wit. But since this item had little to do with the play proper [actually, nothing at all], it was not enough to infuse the piece with the speed and variety which seem inseparable from the current fashion in musicals.'[23]

After the Ball

If Coward's next musical was anything to go by, he did not easily learn lessons, at least when it came to musical theatre. *After the Ball* (Globe Theatre, 10 June 1954; 188), an adaptation of Oscar Wilde's play *Lady Windermere's Fan*, was put through the Coward mincer: confidence that he had written a masterpiece, anger at its reception, and a slow but steady slide into a complete lack of interest in its fate. There was his usual joy at his choice of leading ladies: the veteran of several Novello musicals Mary Ellis (whom he eventually could not bear to listen to) and Novello's 'discovery' for *King's Rhapsody*, Vanessa Lee (whom he eventually decided could not act). There was dissatisfaction with the director (Robert Helpmann), arrangements and conductor (Norman Hackforth, apparently a 'stick of asparagus' in the pit). Again, Mander and Mitchenson veer on the side of pleasantry by repeating Eric Keown's respectful review for *Punch* in which 'the tincture of Wilde is a very uncertain asset, but if one can forget it there is still a good deal in *After the Ball* to be enjoyed simply as musical comedy. Mr Coward has written pleasing music and a number of extremely nimble lyrics.'[24] For *Plays and Players*, however, it was time for plain speaking. Pointing out Coward's lack of success in musical theatre over the previous decade, the reviewer notes that Coward had mistakenly turned to Wilde and to Novello's leftovers for his leading ladies. The result was 'provincial mediocrity, a musical play, incredibly old-fashioned, of the type which died in the twenties before *Bitter-Sweet* was written'. The review continued:

> It lasts for three long hours. There is not one memorable tune in it, though some of the lyrics show that Coward is still capable of deliciously funny lines – if only they were audible. The cast are modern and completely lacking in any sense of period style. Both men and women move badly. Only Mary Ellis and Irene Browne know how to wear their costumes. The rest of the cast looked as though they were in fancy dress. [...] Mary Ellis looked lovely and we wished she had a tune to sing to remind us of the past. Vanessa Lee showed us clearly once and for all that Ruritania and Mayfair do not mix. She had a lot of notes to sing. [...] Coward in the past has given us some of the most exquisite musical entertainments this century has seen. He is also one of the masters of theatrical technique. It is for these reasons, and the admiration I have for his work, that I am unable to accept this ordinary, provincial musical. Coward must show us that he is still the master and not just a name.[25]

The notice is devastating, although it suggests that condemnation is as much due to the lack of style in production as to the lack of quality in Coward's writing. Originally intended for production by H. M. Tennent at the Lyric Opera House, Hammersmith, an initial script for the musical reworking of the play was prepared by Coward's secretary Cole Lesley, who modestly neglects to mention this in his *Life of Noel Coward*. Coward felt he could bend Wilde's play to his will; Coward's skill at operetta could only be supported by Wilde's melodrama.

By the beginning of October 1953 it was 'coming along a fair treat', with 'a lovely song' in 'I Come from a Faraway Land', and a 'charming' 'Stay on the Side of the Angels'.[26] On 16 January 1954 he put the finishing touches to words and music. 'Now all is done and the relief is immense, particularly as I know that it is very good indeed. I have been very much *en veine* and have turned out some of the best lyrics I have ever written.'[27] Coward was still in Jamaica when *After the Ball* set out on an extensive pre-London tour in March 1955, but already had wind that 'there is obviously something not quite right'.[28] Coming face to face with his creation at the Bristol Hippodrome in April, he was appalled. Having expected to make several minor changes, he was faced with a major overhaul. When the show reached Newcastle he felt he had saved the day by increasing the Coward and cutting the Wilde. Such disregard for his source might have sounded alarm bells.

There remained the fact that only when Ellis arrived for rehearsals did Coward realise her voice was shot. By the time of the London opening, he had cut a substantial amount of Mrs Erlynne's music because Ellis could not sing it. The original cast recording offers only two solos for Mrs Erlynne, delivered by Ellis in the ghost of a voice. Lost to sight was an introductory song with the chorus 'Good evening, Lady Windermere', her solo 'What Can It Mean?' and her dramatic duet with Lady Windermere, 'Go, I Beg You, Go'. There is some confusion about how much of the play's music was jettisoned by Coward. He regretted the fact that almost a third of the score had to be cut. Although 'Go, I Beg You, Go' remained listed in the London programme, its vocal demands were clearly beyond Ellis's reach. How could the Mary Ellis heard on the original cast recording have coped with this demanding ten-minute sing?

Coward's score was expertly restored by John McGlinn for a Coward Centenary concert version, highlighting the troublesome co-mixture of Coward's songs and Wilde's story and text. There is no denying the brisk cleverness of the opening 'Oh What a Century It's Been', setting the scene for the play to follow, and the number's efficient reworking throughout the score, but the words go on and on. Elsewhere, Coward veers away from necessity for numbers that seem as fit for revue as for a musical play ('Why Is It the Woman who Pays?' and 'Something on a Tray'). The three songs for Mr Hopper ('Mr Hopper's Chanty', 'May I Have the Pleasure?' and 'Faraway Land') are superfluous to the proceedings. On the other hand, Lord Darlington's 'Letter Song' is so passionate that one wonders why it was cut while the more subsidiary Mr Hopper retained his unnecessary intrusions. Too often the songs pop up like unexpected plums in the pudding; one can hear the play slam on its brakes to make room for 'London at Night'. Good as it is, it needn't *be* there.

And yet, and yet … there is at the heart of *After the Ball* something that is missing from much else that Coward wrote for musical theatre. McGlinn's restoration for the Peacock Theatre's revival revealed the substantial qualities of the score, despite some deplorable performances. There seems no doubt that in his writing for Mrs Erlynne, Coward's emotions are at full pelt. The music for Lady Windermere is unremittingly bland (her aria cries out to be done in front of French windows through which a depressingly weak sun struggles, as do 'Clear Bright Morning' and 'Sweet Day'), while all the tension in the music and most of the drama in the play centres on Mrs Erlynne. She has the best entrance, with Coward anticipating the audience's warm reception of his leading lady. She has the best dialogue, the best end of scene lines, the most exciting exit music. By the play's end, we have willingly said goodnight to Lady Windermere and see Mrs

Erlynne, alone on stage, about to leave for a brave new life. This is the pearl of a part in all of Coward's musicals, the one Coward role that demands a diva.

As *After the Ball* sickened and died at the box office, Coward could hardly bear to look at it. One imagines, perhaps between a matinee and evening performance, Miss Ellis and Miss Lee behind a closed dressing-room door lowering their voices to regret the passing of Novello: 'Oh, darling! How different it all was in Ivor's day!'

Sail Away ❄ *The Girl who Came to Supper*

Following the failures of his most recent musicals, it may or may not have been Coward's 'choice' that his two final works in the genre had their premieres on Broadway. The first of these subsequently came to London: *Sail Away* (Savoy Theatre, 21 June 1962; 252), outrunning its Broadway version by almost one hundred performances. Listening to an original cast recording of Coward's score suggests that at last Coward had deserted the operetta, but an understanding of the show's history spoils the theory. His original script, with which the American company set out towards New York, had three sets of lovers. Coward hitched some old numbers to his original 'straight' lead: audiences were once again to be offered the opportunity to listen to 'This Is a Night for Lovers' and 'This Is a Changing World', but obviously not changed enough to prevent Coward from repeating stuff he had used thirteen years ago in *Pacific 1860*. As it was, the show already gave a second chance to another earlier song, 'Sail Away' from *Ace of Clubs*. The main character was to be yet another revival, Mrs Wentworth-Brewster, to whom Coward now intended to give more flesh and blood than had been possible in 'her' song, 'In a Bar on the Piccola Marina'. By the time the pre-Broadway tour opened, Mrs W-B had been replaced as the leading role by a character called Verity Craig (played by Jean Fenn) who falls in love with a younger man, attempts to kill herself and finally returns to her husband (shades of *Still Life*).

As the show played out its time in Philadelphia and Boston, it became obvious that the paying customers were uninterested in Miss Craig's or Miss Fenn's emotional affairs, preferring the company of the second female, comedy, lead, Elaine Stritch, as Mimi Paragon, a wise and canny hostess on board a cruise ship. Anyway, Coward was playing true to form. Tiring of Miss Fenn's nuisances, he sent her packing. With Stritch now the star, for a time *Sail Away* looked as if it might become that rare thing, a Coward musical success that *would* set sail. Stritch was the first and only one of his musical leading ladies to be funny; most of them could not have made a cat laugh. In effect, Stritch was the female representation of Coward himself, one of the very few females to be entrusted with his lyrics, often much too smart for the characters to whom they were assigned.

His intention in *Sail Away* was to focus on the score and play down the script, possibly in recognition that in the past it was his dialogue which had come in for

11 Waving goodbye to operetta in *Sail Away*

most criticism. There was little more than a thread of story, with Coward using what he described as a 'revue formula' to lengthen the entertainment. Those revue elements are well disguised in the score because they fit in well. 'Useless Useful Phrases' is a prime example: it seems to come naturally out of Mimi's character, but is in effect a list of Coward witticisms built around the phrase book used by travellers. Essentially, there is no *need* for it. The same applies to 'Bronxville Darby and Joan', a duet of mutual detestation for an elderly married couple. 'Why Do the Wrong People Travel?' is another self-indulgence, and one that seems to go into endless verses. Another number, 'You're a Long, Long Way from America', also outstays its welcome, perhaps forgetting that London (and probably even more so, Broadway) might not be all that interested in Coward's obsession with the absurdities of globe-trotting Americans. Of course, Coward was to an extent rootless when it came to writing either British or American musicals, having decamped to a splendid isolation in Jamaica. His antennae for what was current and fashionable and interesting was probably not as attuned as it might have been.

Nevertheless there is much about the score of *Sail Away* in Coward's best and most familiar style, notably the romantic numbers, which incline to melancholy. 'Later than Spring' and 'Something Very Strange' spring naturally from the theme of the older world-weary woman falling for a man half her age, a theme to which Coward must have warmed. One of the finest moments comes in Johnny's 'Don't Turn away from Love', its passion sharpened by the orchestrations. (In London, these were ascribed to Wally Stott, Ken Thorne and Roland Shaw.) The newer generation is represented by the play's secondary lovers, Nancy Foyle and Barnaby Slade, for whom Coward wrote what he considered modern lyrics, although lyrically both 'Beatnik Love Affair' (did Coward know what a beatnik was?) and 'When You Want Me' suggest a sophistication completely at odds with their characters. As so often before, characterisation is put aside to make room for wit.

Everything about *Sail Away* tells of a certain Coward restlessness, of an endless journey. That sense of moving on, of the suitcase always at the ready, had permeated Coward's music from the beginning of his writing days; homelessness is at the heart of 'Twentieth Century Blues'. Questing is the very reason of *Bitter-Sweet*'s 'I'll See You Again' and *Conversation Piece*'s 'I'll Follow My Secret Heart', of *Private Lives*' 'Someday I'll Find You'. In *Sail Away*, audiences had to take Coward's innate patriotism for the country of his birth for granted as he focused on the American; that old love of things British (where the finer print concentrated on London) would resurface again in his very last musical, **The Girl who Came to Supper**, adapted from Terence Rattigan's play *The Prince and the Showgirl*, originally seen in London with Laurence Olivier and Vivien Leigh in 1953.

Rattigan's story had a young American girl (Elsie Marina) coming to London at the time of George V's coronation in 1911 and falling in love with Charles, Prince Regent of Carpathia. As untutored Elsie – renamed Mary Morgan for

Harry Kurnitz's adaptation – is made ready for the royal circles in which she will be moving, and falls in love with a much older, difficult man (the Prince), the similarities between *The Girl who Came to Supper* (1963) and *My Fair Lady* (1956) are noted, and not to the *Girl's* advantage. Rex Harrison and Christopher Plummer, both of whom could not sing, turned down the chance to play the Regent, and Keith Michell who *could* was cast, only to be replaced before rehearsals with a patently non-singing José Ferrer. John Gielgud told Coward he should have played it himself. (Surely he cannot have been serious.) The forty-one-year-old Ferrer obliged not only by looking almost as old as Coward but by sounding uncannily like him.

Coward's opinion of his songs was as high as ever, but the note of supreme confidence dulled as it always did. He had thought of the piece as a *Passing Fancy,* the title he tried to convince Kurnitz to use, but soon Kurnitz was to blame for the show's ills. Then its director Joe Layton was at fault, Ferrer was all wrong, and Florence Henderson as the girl who came to supper wasn't right. The audience roused itself for a medley of London songs performed by Britain's Tessie O'Shea as Ada Cockle. The very name gives the clue as to what her songs might be, and you would not be wrong. Coward turns up with a string of Cockney pastiches, from 'Saturday Night at the Rose and Crown' to 'Don't Take Our Charlie for the Army'. With the various references to colds on the chest, cosy East End pubs where tinkers and tailors rubbed shoulders with soldiers and sailors, and portly old dears from Hackney longing to dip their toes in the briny, Coward is back among the lower orders he had written so patronisingly of in *This Happy Breed.* Ada Cockle's star turn is really the *Girl's* only patronising moment, but it lasts for several moments. Elsewhere, the *Girl* reverts to operetta, and works in several other well-used Coward tricks, including the invention of some Carpathian language, and wordy lyrics.

The composer is at his happiest in another medley (this time for Henderson) in which the entire plot and score of Mary's London musical, *The Coconut Girl,* is breathlessly performed. From 'Paddy MacNeill and his Automobile', through a 'swing' song (almost obligatory in operetta), via an ensemble number manfully performed by Mary solo ('Six Lilies of the Valley') to the show's novelty dance craze number 'The Walla Walla Boola', *The Coconut Girl* sequence has Coward inhabiting territory he had mapped out in *Operette* and with which he felt comfortable. On the other hand, the 'real' numbers intended to bring a closer understanding of his characters are mostly ineffective. Less forgivably, the songs go on endlessly about court etiquette and the way to behave when in the presence of lordlier beings, as in 'Curt, Clear and Concise', 'When Foreign Princes Come to Visit Us' and 'Sir or Ma'am'. The obsession with protocol and the overdose of what Pooh-Bah might have called 'the deference due to a man of pedigree' pander to Coward's fascination with royalty and smelt of obsequiousness. Rattigan may have been at much at fault as anyone, but *The Girl who Came to Supper* has the air of being written by elderly gentlemen who have lost touch.

The show was never produced in London, but British audiences were given the opportunity to hear it when the BBC broadcast a radio adaptation by Alan Melville. At last Michell got to play the Regent, his performance suggesting he should never have been replaced for the stage production. Melville's tinkering accentuated the worst aspects of Kurnitz and Coward's work, with interminable scenes in those snug old London boozers with cosy old Ada Cockle (Doris Hare) calling everyone ducks before being urged by wheezy Londoners to oblige them with another Cockney knees-up. Melville was even further up to his neck in jellied eels than Coward. Meanwhile, someone at the BBC forgot to hire a leading lady who could sing, but she was spared the demanding *Coconut Girl* sequence. In New York, the curtain came down on Coward's last musical after 112 performances.

Musicals from Coward: *High Spirits* ❉ *Mr and Mrs*

Coward was paid the dubious compliment of having *two* musicals by other hands adapted from *three* of his plays. The American composer Hugh Martin sought Coward's permission to make a musical of *Hay Fever*; permission granted, the project ground to a halt. In 1963 Martin presented Coward with a musical version of *Blithe Spirit*, renamed for the occasion *High Spirits*, and co-written with the actor-writer Timothy Gray, who had appeared in London the previous year in the disastrous *Scapa!* Coward thought the songs skilful, the treatment of his play beyond reproach. He mapped out a cast: Kay Thompson as Madame Arcati, Keith Michell as Charles Condomine, Celeste Holm as Ruth and Gwen Verdon as Elvira. By the time the show went into production, the cast was Beatrice Lillie as Arcati, Britain's Edward Woodward as Charles, Louise Troy as Ruth and Tammy Grimes as Elvira. Coward's enthusiasm went through many moods. The show's ultimate Broadway success owed most to Lillie, who turned the show into 'An Evening With', thereby infuriating the play's original author but delighting the customers.

The score rarely rises above a general competence, and shows no advance on Martin's *Make a Wish* and *Love from Judy*. When **High Spirits** (Savoy Theatre, 3 November 1963; 93) showed up in London, it had a cast that filled Coward with confidence: Cicely Courtneidge as Arcati, Denis Quilley as Charles, Jan Waters as Ruth and Fenella Fielding as Elvira. Coward's confidence in Fielding was quickly eroded, and she was replaced by the American Marti Stevens. Rehearsals did not bode well. The production was 'supervised by Noel Coward' but directed by Timothy Gray and Graham Payn. One can only feel for Payn's impossible position, sandwiched between Coward and Gray, and the cast seemed to know the game was up from the beginning. Before the opening, Coward reduced Courtneidge to tears, making her time as Arcati a misery.

Although Coward had no authorship in *High Spirits* it is awarded an entry in the 'revised' Mander and Mitchenson *Theatrical Companion to Coward*, but the *other*, *British* musical fashioned from Coward is for some reason missing. Indeed, it is absent from almost every book about Coward; few Coward scholars seem to have even heard of it, or perhaps having heard of it decide it is more tactful to pretend they haven't. They clearly have no time for sheer unadulterated enjoyment. Brash, vulgar, and unstoppably loud, **Mr and Mrs** (Palace Theatre, 11 December 1968; 44) is nevertheless a much better work than the trundling mish-mash that is *High Spirits*. In effect two separate musicals, the first half of the production, 'Mr', is based on Coward's one-act playlet *Fumed Oak*, 'an unpleasant comedy in two scenes' in which the hen-pecked Henry Gow (originally played by Coward) finally turns on his nagging wife, interfering mother-in-law and adenoidal daughter, telling them that after years of unhappiness he is about to walk out on them to start a new life. After the interval, audiences were presented with 'Mrs', a musical version of another of Coward's *To-night at 8.30* plays, *Still Life*, best known in its 1946 David Lean film version *Brief Encounter* with Trevor Howard as the doctor Alec Harvey and Celia Johnson as Laura Jesson. Happily married to their spouses, they nevertheless find themselves falling in love with one another. In a railway station buffet, the affair begins and blossoms but can only be doomed, and at the end of the play the pair return to their respective spouses.

Leonard Bernstein had once had Coward's permission to turn *Brief Encounter* into a musical, but the transformation of the play eventually fell to the British, with John Taylor's book, music and lyrics, and the 'adaptation' credited to Ross Taylor. The casting was more interesting and more accurate than for *High Spirits*. A decade earlier, the leading man John Neville had distinguished himself as a Shakespearean actor, once sharing the roles of Othello and Iago with Richard Burton. *Mr and Mrs* proved that Neville was as good a singer as actor. His leading lady, Honor Blackman, less assured in the vocal department, was already famous for her role as Pussy Galore in the James Bond film *Goldfinger* of four years before, and for playing Cathy Gale in the TV series *The Avengers*. The comedienne Hylda Baker, who had just begun a six-year stint as the star of a TV comedy series *Nearest and Dearest*, was in both halves of the entertainment, while the singer Alan Breeze appeared in 'Mrs'. Best known for his many years on radio's *Billy Cotton Band Show*, Breeze suffered from a crippling stammer, which may account for this being his only known stage role.

Mr and Mrs took the plays out of their original mid-1930s settings into the present day, effectively removing Coward's period pieces of thirty years before, kicking and all but screaming (listen to the recording), into the heart of swinging London, energised by Johnnie Spence's full-throttle orchestration. The intimate nature of both plays is radically altered by the introduction of a chorus only used in 'Mr' during the scene-setting 'Millions of People', a sort of hymn to suburbia introducing the Gow family, but used extensively throughout 'Mrs'. There is no opening-out of Coward's *Fumed Oak*, with the Taylors' adaptation faithful to Coward's script, especially well integrated in Doris's celebration of her 'Happy

Family'. The negligible role of the snivelling Doris is allowed a big dance number, 'I Want to Dance', before Coward's original script is deftly worked into Henry's 'And So We Got Married' and 'No More Money', before Henry finally walks away in triumph towards his new life in 'Big Wide World'. That world outside is obviously the modern one, because Doris mockingly refers to Henry as 'South London's swinging Sunny Jim'.

'Mrs' also broke faith with the period of *Still Life*. At Milford Junction's refreshment buffet, modernisation is on the rampage, and steam locomotives are giving way to diesels, although this station has obviously escaped the axing of Dr Richard Beeching.[29] Just as well, since Laura Jesson stumbles into the tea-room and thence into the arms of doctor Alec Harvey. Essentially, their relationship, their *tragedy*, is the only thing that need concern the emotions, but the Taylors' adaptation interrupts the inevitable progress of their still-born affair with a plethora of songs, mostly doled out to Miss Baker playing Myrtle Bagot, manageress of the buffet, and Mr Breeze as the ticket collector Albert Godby. As well as a knockabout title-song, Baker tells of her hopes for a married life in 'If the Right Man Should Ask Me', the song proper preceded by Myrtle's explanation that she had once worked in the theatre, going on stage every night, in Coward's own words, 'to sing *selections* from *Our Miss Gibbs*'. Baker, famous for her malapropisms ('and I can say that without fear of contraception') offered her own version, 'to sing *exceptions* from *Our Miss Gibbs.*' In another scene, she did her 'tottering down stairs in high heels' routine, to the obvious delight of the audience. Coward, never one for low comedy, was unamused.

Breeze showed his worth in the roof-raising 'Give us a Kiss'. Even Miss Bagot's young assistant Beryl's boyfriend Stanley had his moment, whisking Beryl off to a discotheque in 'The Electric Circus'. One of the few psychedelic moments in British musicals, this was another insistence that audiences were experiencing something completely *now* and swinging, taken into the heaving mass of humanity where there was a dark room in which couples could make love to one another for hours and hours. In its way, this strengthened the apparent theme of the different attitudes to relationships and love exhibited in Coward's original, made different by the ages and social standing of the three couples, Alec and Laura, Myrtle and Albert, and Beryl and Stanley. This is a not inconsiderable, although possibly unintentional, achievement by the Taylors. Along the way, the male chorus makes another assault on the senses with their thirsty 'I Want to Wet My Whistle'; all through these numbers Taylor's insistent music and Spence's spacious orchestration leave no doubt that *Mr and Mrs* means to be invigorating.

Between, around, beneath, above all this is the central dilemma of Alec and Laura, and it is here that John Taylor's songs are most effective; one cannot imagine their relationship better delineated than by their four duets.

1   'Father of Two, Mother of Three'. Alec tells Laura there is nothing wrong in their meeting. What could be more normal, less wrong than this innocence,

with nothing foolish or sly? Each time they part, he remains the respectable father of two, and she the loyal mother of three. They do not wish to lose self-respect. The music is assuredly happy, breezy, carefree, expressing their confidence.

2 'Come Thursday'. As time goes by, Alec and Laura look forward to meeting on Thursdays; it is the only day of the week they feel alive. Taylor's melody catches an almost metronomic expression of time passing. The chorus join in with a great burst of energy. Love is not necessarily in the air, but an extraordinary happiness is.

3 'Before Today'. The lovers admit how each has changed the other's life. They no longer know the world as before. An enchantment hovers over all, and the world becomes a bewitched wonderland containing only them. All lightness and delicacy, Taylor catches the quiet tragedy that we know is closing in.

4 'I'll Be Always Loving You'. The inevitable knowledge that they must part closes in on Alec and Laura. Taylor's simplistic melody and unremarkable lyric convey the depth of this unending love as the orchestra and chorus contribute to an overwhelming crescendo.

Coward, having sanctioned *Mr and Mrs* before production, cut it adrift at its opening night. One wonders what Coward might have made of making a musical from his own work. He would certainly not have come up with anything so attention-grabbing as John Taylor's songs. With not even a hint of a backward glance at operetta, and with all shades of Gilbert and Sullivan expunged, John Taylor's work is so much stronger here than in the anaemic *Charlie Girl*. *Mr and Mrs* blazed momentarily at one of London's biggest theatres, and almost as quickly was done with. The best that Taylor could manage after this was a musical version of Charles Kingsley's *The Water-Babies*, performed in the West End for matinees only, with the unlikeliest of stars, Jessie Matthews. In its way, *Mr and Mrs* is a good example of a show which is not brilliant, original, or memorable. It could not, however, be slept through. In 2009, André Previn's opera *Brief Encounter* premiered in Houston. No matter how skilful and musically interesting that work may be, I doubt if it offers the innocent enjoyment to be discovered in *Mr and Mrs*.

4 Pastiche and Esoteric
Sandy Wilson

Even in 1956 the shadow cast across British musical theatre by the death of Novello was long. Under the headline 'Genius of Novello' *Plays and Players* warned that 'Recently, it is true, there has been a movement afoot to elevate the musical show into a "significant modern art-form", but this can have little hope of success. The Public would never accept long-faced Musicals, and rightly so'. Here, at least, *Plays and Players* had it wrong. Twenty years later, musicals started trying to be as long-faced as possible. The journal continued:

> No one appreciated the need for colour and romance in musicals more than Ivor Novello. He knew that even the most serious playgoer enjoyed an occasional change, an escape from his own London, Bradford or Worthing environment. And Ivor offered the ideal form of escape, the Ruritanian musical.
>
> There was less sheer vitality in Ivor's musicals than in the popular American product of today, and less noise for noise's sake. His characters were unreal, their situations unlikely, and their sentimentality occasionally on the ripe side. But these musicals had glamour and an irresistible magic of their own. They also had lilting tunes that required singing, not mere bawling – tunes that lingered obstinately in the mind years after one had seen the show.
>
> British composers who complain today that they cannot get a fair hearing might look back on Ivor's successes and learn some valuable lessons. Their own shows often have a brilliant type of university wit, but university wit is generally accompanied by undergraduate cynicism. What they would learn from the books and scores of *Careless Rapture*, *Perchance to Dream* and *King's Rhapsody* is that enchantment is all. And until they have learned this lesson they should not try to compete with their streamlined American rivals.[1]

The first major new British musical theatre writer to emerge from the Novello shadow was Alexander [Sandy] Galbraith Wilson, so great an admirer of Novello that he would go on to write one of the best books about him. Surprisingly, there is not a shred of evidence that Novello exercised any influence over Wilson's work. Even when *The Boy Friend* had its first modest showing at the Players' Theatre in Villiers Street, Charing Cross, London in April 1953, two years after Novello's death, there was something completely fresh in the voice that Wilson brought to the genre. His earlier dalliance with musical comedy and operetta had never really been his doing, more the responsibility of his collaborator-composer Geoffrey Wright. One wonders how Wilson would have prospered had he continued along that rose-laden path instead of wandering alone into fields of pastiche and esoteric in which, looking around, he would find himself the only occupant.

On the face of it, the career seems slim. Contributions to intimate revues, a number here and there, and one whole revue to himself. One completely original musical. Two pastiches, one of them a success that literally went, and is still going, around the world. Three esoterics. There is a great deal more, of which the public knows little. Rather than hiding those works away in the body of the rest, let us consider them at the outset, if only because they give us an idea of the industry and range of the man. If Fate and Kander and Ebb had not intervened, we might even now be celebrating Wilson's musicalisation of Christopher Isherwood's Sally Bowles stories and *Mr Norris Changes Trains*: *Goodbye to Berlin*. This was commissioned in 1963 by the Broadway producer David Black. Wilson set to work. He met with Julie Andrews, who agreed to play Sally. 'But Sandy,' she said, 'you will keep in the abortion, won't you?' Later that year, Wilson was in New York, taken out to dine by Hal Prince. Wilson told him of his new piece. Prince was astonished, telling Wilson that he, not Black, was in the process of acquiring the rights to the Isherwood musical. He already had a librettist, Joe Masteroff, on board, but as yet no composer. This was hopeful. Would Wilson play Masteroff and Prince the songs he had already written for his Isherwood musical? Wilson played them. Masteroff thought they sounded too much like *The Boy Friend*. Returning to Britain, Wilson put his abandoned project back in the drawer.

The completed songs suggest that Wilson's treatment was much closer to Isherwood than was Kander and Ebb's *Cabaret*.[2] There is the familiar Weimar Republic Kurt Weill-like drawl undercutting the score, but Wilson gives his Sally five songs of her own. There is introspection in each of them, and notably in Christopher's 'In This Room'. What can Masteroff have heard as he listened? Wilson's *Goodbye to Berlin* has no trace of any of the atmosphere of *The Boy Friend*. Not for the first time, Wilson's work was misunderstood.

There is a deal of Wilson's work in the drawer. He wrote book and lyrics for a musical of Sheridan's *The Rivals*, but the composer Geoffrey Wright's interest may have languished, and *Lydia Languish* was stillborn. An extant recording of Wright playing its melodies emphasises the score's old-fashioned sweetness. There was to be a musical about the aviator Amy Johnson, co-written with John Morley. Another show in the offing was *Oh, Henry!*, inspired by the Charles Laughton British film *The Private Life of Henry VIII* with meaty roles for six leading ladies. As a source, Compton Mackenzie's novel *Extraordinary Women* veered to the esoteric. A satire on lesbians written in the wake of Radclyffe Hall's infamous 1928 novel *The Well of Loneliness*, the extraordinary women included Hall and her lover Una Troubridge, disporting themselves on Capri during World War I. They were behaving in a way that Mackenzie claimed would make 'Freud blush, Adler blench, Jung lower his eyes and Dr Ernest Jones write his next book in Latin'.[3] This sounded ideal material for Wilson, for whom 'queerness' was to be a component of his best work, but Wilson's adaptation was not taken up. Another candidate for a musical was Cecil Beaton's *My Royal Past*, a pastiche memoir apparently written by Baroness von Bülop *née* Princess Theodora Louise Alexina Ludmilla Sophie von Eckermann-Waldstein. No less a star than Jeanette MacDonald was to sing the big waltz song in this production. Wilson admits that 'When I wrote *My Royal Past* Novello helped me.'[4]

Wilson's first intention was to leave Oxford University and become an actor. A talent for song-writing persuaded him otherwise. The originality of his ideas, the cleanliness of his lyrics and simplicity of his music made him a natural for revue material when revue was about to embark on the last phase of its golden age. It now seems extraordinary that revues were so much a part of the London theatre that audiences were hungry to attend whole *series* of them. Wilson wrote items for *Slings and Arrows* (1948) and *Oranges and Lemons* (1949), and revues for the tiny Watergate Theatre, a breeding-ground of intimate revue, coming in at the tail end of the little shows that had populated London in the 1940s and continued to be popular through the next decade. In between, Wilson was lyricist for an adaptation of *French for Love*, a play by Marguerite Steen and Derek Patmore. *Caprice* (Alhambra, Glasgow, 24 October 1950; closed on road) was an old-fashioned concoction with music by Geoffrey Wright, an alcoholic director in William Mollison, a hoary plot about romantic complications in France, and additional songs foisted on it by its producer Jack Waller and the aged composer and conductor Joseph Tunbridge. This was musical making of the old school, even by 1950 standards. A number had to be written to explain the appearance of six lamé dresses which Waller had in his wardrobe and was determined to use. *Caprice* also imported its juvenile male lead from Paris, but considering he could barely make himself intelligible in English it was unfortunate to open in Glasgow. It closed in Birmingham a month later.

The Boy Friend

Nothing much more came of Wilson's collaboration with Wright, and anyway Wilson was about to be given the opportunity of going solo with book, music and lyrics. In 1952 he was invited by the Players' Theatre to write a short, two-act musical entertainment to be presented at their Villiers Street club. This was ***The Boy Friend*** (Wyndham's Theatre, 14 January 1954; 2,084), a musical that would share with *Salad Days* the reputation of being the flagship British show of the mid-1950s. The reception at the Players' was terrific, but the taste of its members, used to a diet of highly stylised Victorian music hall pastiche, was known to be indulgent and even faintly esoteric. (Strange to find that word again, especially as there is nothing remotely esoteric about *The Boy Friend*, even if Wilson later made a habit of esotericism.)

Whatever the reasons, managements were wary of taking *The Boy Friend* up, but the Players' persisted. Wilson tinkered with the score and libretto and made his small show into a slightly bigger one. Eventually, managers fought to present it in London. By March 1954 Wilson found himself 'Personality of the Month' in *Plays and Players*. There was much to celebrate. Plans to take *The Boy Friend* to Broadway had just been finalised. Incredibly, this would be the first British musical to cross the Atlantic since Coward's *Conversation Piece* twenty years earlier. Come to that, 'Wilson may well be the Coward of the present generation, for he not only composes music and writes his own scripts, but acts, produces, has his own cabaret act, and is now writing and illustrating a humorous book', a very feline one called *This is Sylvia*. As it happened, Britain was in no mood to welcome a new Coward, having grown a little tired of the old one. Now, however, Wilson seemed to stand alone: 'At the moment there are no writers of musicals of Wilson's age [29] to compete with him.'[5]

There is no mention of Vincent Youmans in Sandy Wilson's autobiography, but the songs of *The Boy Friend* directly reflect the mood, intention and spirit of several of those in the 1925 *No, No, Nanette*, with lyrics by Irving Caesar and Otto Harbach. The list below gives the title of *The Boy Friend*'s songs followed by details of the shows and the specific numbers by which they most seem to be inspired.

'Perfect Young Ladies'
No, No Nanette: Opening Chorus ('Flappers Are We')

'The Boy Friend'
The Girl Friend (1926), music by Richard Rodgers; lyrics by Lorenz Hart: 'The Girl Friend'

'Won't You Charleston with Me?'
No, No, Nanette: 'You Can Dance with Any Girl At All'

'I Could Be Happy with You'
No, No, Nanette: 'I Want to Be Happy'

'Sur le Plage'
No, No, Nanette: 'The Call of the Sea'

'A Room in Bloomsbury'
No, No, Nanette: 'Tea for Two'

'The You-Don't-Want-To-Play-With-Me-Blues'
No, No, Nanette: 'Where Has My Hubby Gone Blues?'

'Safety in Numbers'
No, No, Nanette: 'Too Many Rings around Rosie'

'The Riviera'
Oh, Kay! (1926), music by George Gershwin; lyrics by Ira Gershwin: 'Clap Yo' Hands'

12 *The Boy Friend*: one of the few remembered post-war British musicals
in its fortieth anniversary London production

One of the curiosities of *The Boy Friend* is that its score relies entirely on America for its inspiration. One of its tricks is to make it seem British. Some of those inspirations have little more than the *flavour* of their possible models. Sometimes the parody is more obvious, as in the title-song, for which Rodgers was happy for Wilson to follow the pattern of his 'The Girl Friend'. The particular domesticity of 'A Room in Bloomsbury' is matched to 'Tea for Two', with Wilson's melody hinting at the restrictive use of notes which was one of Youman's trademarks. This is even more true of 'I Could Be Happy with You', unmistakably mirroring 'I Want to Be Happy', even if Wilson's lyric is a little more uncertain about the need for happiness.

So it is that *The Boy Friend* has more of Uncle Sam than the British bulldog about it. When it comes to influences, British musical theatre composers such as Joseph Tunbridge, Philip Braham, Jack Strachey, Carroll Gibbons or Billy Mayerl are overlooked. There is no hint that Wilson pays any notice to Vivian Ellis's best score of the period, *Mr Cinders*. There is no trace of earlier influences, as found in so many British shows of the twenties, no hint of Novello, of Monckton, and nothing of Gilbert and Sullivan for whom Wilson professes a loathing. The achievement is to fashion a new British musical of the 1920s from transatlantic sources, an extraordinary achievement in itself. The surprise is that the transatlantic flavour seems not to extend much beyond *No, No, Nanette*. There is no regard for something as bucolic as Youmans' score for *Wildflower*, where there is room for a deeply-felt title-song beside the jollity, but of course *Wildflower* is operetta while *No, No, Nanette* stands proud as musical comedy. And yet, to whatever category *The Boy Friend* is consigned, it remains above all pastiche, with all the emotional restrictions that genre places on those who write it. Is it inevitable that *The Boy Friend* has always seemed a little lacking in the heart department? – the price to be paid for pastiche. Heartstrings may be touched, but it is from afar. Even so, Wilson achieves more feeling than might be expected. When just before curtain fall Pierrot meets his Pierette, and Polly and Tony share the announcement of their engagement with the other boys and girls, we are moved. As its director Vida Hope wrote, 'Nightly at Wyndham's the house is enraptured with ... what? They are not quite sure themselves.'[6]

There is something else that has always slightly bothered me about *The Boy Friend*: the manner in which it is done. For the first Players' Theatre production Hope insisted on an accurate representation of 1920s stagecraft. Guying in any form was not tolerated. This admirable ideal was shared with Wilson, but subsequent productions often failed to live up to it. Although the show was a solid Broadway hit with Julie Andrews as Polly, Wilson, as he makes clear in his autobiography, was unhappy with it. There is a suspicion that Hope is trying to calm the waters in a piece she wrote after returning from (supposedly) directing the New York production. Both she and Wilson had been banned from the theatre during rehearsals. Comparing it to the London version, she decided that 'not only are comparisons odious – in this case they just do not exist'. In New York

How, the poor things ask, *can* we be different? It is a credit to them that in some amazing way they did manage to bridge this horrible chasm and retain the sincerity and realism of the London production.

What are the differences, then? An important one is the much larger orchestra used [...] Another is that the tempo of the show is much faster and crisper than here. Small points are sharpened and heightened, as witness the nineteen-twenties make-up they use, more lavishly applied than at Wyndham's. Numbers are brisker in interpretation, and the big chorus song *The Riviera* in Act 3, is danced with a fanatical precision and accuracy that would do justice to the Rockettes at Radio City Music Hall!

In other words the whole show is performed with all the high gloss and efficiency of the modern American musical [...] But inevitably some of the tenderness has vanished.[7]

Freed from the Players' taste for accuracy it has been left to a myriad of directors, choreographers and artists, professional and amateur, to interpret the work as they wish. Wilson rebelled against Ken Russell's rag-bag film version, and for the Cameron Mackintosh production in 1984 was again banned from rehearsals. Goodness knows what is made of the piece in countless village halls where its popularity shows no sign of decline. It is almost certain that *The Boy Friend* will go on well beyond *Salad Days*. One of the reasons may be that in checking our theatrical histories we can confirm that *Salad Days* belongs to the 1950s, but we instinctively *know* that *The Boy Friend* belongs to the 1920s.

The Buccaneer

Like *The Boy Friend*, Wilson's next musical, **The Buccaneer** (Lyric Theatre, Hammersmith, 8 September 1955; 170 / Apollo Theatre, 22 February 1956; 29) is behind the times. Perhaps it suffers from having become a period piece, its world having faded so much away, but at the time it was contemporary. The word could not be used of the two characters mainly responsible for the continued publication of the boys' comic, the *Buccaneer*, founded years before by the kindly Mr Barraclough and now run by his widow. Sales are plummeting. It seems that British boys no longer have an appetite for the wholesome fare offered in its pages, preferring the new atomic age American comics that are flooding the market. Frail old Mr Donkin, the creator of the daredevil Captain Fairbrother, delivers episode 2,483 of his hero's adventures, and is told it may be the last. A brash American publisher of the new-style comics, Walter Maximus, wants to buy up the *Buccaneer*. He thinks Captain Fairbrother needs sex-appeal, and isn't it odd that the Captain seems to have no girl-friend? – won't readers think that's a bit funny? In his place, Maximus suggests something along the lines of Belinda Blast-Off, Space-Age Super-Girl. What's more, the *Buccaneer* will become the *Jumbo Jet* and set the kiddies' heartbeats racing.

Mrs Barraclough's secretary Mabel involves her schoolteacher fiancé Peter in a plan to interest the mother of one of his pupils in financing the future of the *Buccaneer*. The pupil is a precocious twelve-year-old, Montgomery Winterton, who tells Peter he thinks Napoleon was a woman and that algebra is mere sex symbolism. Montgomery's mother proves to be worldly, with an eye always open for the next husband, or lover. Maximus's young daughter, Marilyn, proves a match for Montgomery. In a dream sequence, Mr Donkin conjures up Captain Fairbrother, who insists that they can yet save the day and the *Buccaneer*. The *Buccaneer is* saved, to everyone's satisfaction, with more than a little help from Peter taking the manly form of the Captain in Trafalgar Square, supported by a gaggle of young children. Mrs Barraclough and Mr Donkin will carry on producing the comic, Maximus and Mrs Winterton pair up, Mabel has the added thrill of seeing her fiancé as a national hero, and the priggish Montgomery and Marilyn will in the years ahead become more than just pals.

Wilson's only truly original musical outside the pastiche of *The Boy Friend* and *Divorce Me, Darling!* is one of the most sharply defined of the genre. The definition is apparent in the generational grouping of its characters:

The Old:	Mrs Barraclough and Mr Donkin
The Middle-Aged:	Mr Maximus and Mrs Winterton
The Young:	Mabel Gray and Peter Curtis
The Children:	Montgomery Winterton and Marilyn Maximus

The divisions between these generations are stark. In *The Buccaneer* The Old live to preserve the decencies of the past. Mrs Barraclough's anthem 'Good Clean Fun' establishes her belief in all things pure, a virtue that she sees as completely British. (British boys will never, she assures us, tire of it.) To this, Mr Donkin adds a dash of adventuring in the line of G. A. Henty; presumably, Captain Fairbrother is a cousin of Biggles, that air pioneer whose relationship with his sidekick Ginger may even have lifted a few eyebrows when the character first appeared in 1932. In fact, The Old have not a self-regarding bone in their bodies; they wish only to keep up standards, and to go on providing British wholesomeness.

The Middle-Aged in *The Buccaneer* do not have these qualities. The pace of modern life, in Britain and in American, has produced Mrs Winterton and Mr Maximus, she acquisitively over-sexed, he ruthlessly ambitious. (But then he *is* from the good old USA.) In finally deciding to make a go of it together, one hopes they may recognise and limit each other's vulgarities. Both are harmless and appealing, because we know that basically they probably subscribe to the same values as The Old, values which they will slowly learn to value. They have merely gone astray. Wilson is as kindly to these wayward souls as to his other inventions.

The Young are, of course, climbing the ladder to The Middle-Aged and The Old. Mabel and Peter are good eggs. Although their romance is never central to *The Buccaneer*, it helps bring about the *volte-face* in the paper's fortunes. Their concerns here are not for the Middle-Aged (except that Peter owes some of his livelihood to Mrs Winterton), but for the Old. Mabel lives only to keep Mrs Barraclough and Mr Donkin from losing everything that is important to them. Peter obliges by turning himself into Captain Fairbrother. One feels that when things get too much for Mrs Barraclough and Mr Donkin, Mabel will happily slide into the editor's chair and Peter will take up Mr Donkin's pen.

The Children of *The Buccaneer* are, in the main, unseen – its (sadly dwindling) thousands of readers. There would be no reason for the comic without them, and no reason for Wilson's play. In any generally normal sense, neither Montgomery nor Marilyn are children. Montgomery is twelve, but wears spectacles, is impeccably dressed, has read far too many books, and has too high an opinion of his own intelligence. Marilyn suffers from being American, too outside the British way of life to enter into the spirit of it, but, thanks to her regard for Montgomery, does just that. At the beginning of the play, it is obvious that Montgomery's intellect repudiates the inanities of Mrs Barraclough's comic, but by the end he is one of its saviours. The Children have responded to the needs of The Old, come to terms with the idiocies of The Middle-Aged, worked with The Young to save the old values.

It is difficult to imagine any other British musical theatre writer coming up with any of this, and then writing a score that seems perfectly formed. We think of Wilson's fondness for the big American shows of an earlier age, and in the 1950s he was a regular visitor to those showing in London, but here we have something that owes them no debt of any kind. No standout numbers. Nothing pluggable. No chorus. No one is going to remark on the settings or costumes. No big effects, only a reincarnation of Captain Fairbrother (a gauze might help). No romantic duet for Mabel and Peter, except one called 'Unromantic Us' because its references lack romance. In Wilson's score, nobody momentarily shrugs off the real world to sing vaguely of love. Montgomery would squirm to be involved in anything faintly romantic, but in the sub-text of his duet with Marilyn, 'Just Pals', we discern a cerebral approach. Mabel shrugs off her feelings for Peter in 'Just Another Man', reprised when Montgomery repudiates any 'feeling' he might have for Marilyn. Love is not to be spoken of. Marilyn doesn't get moony about Montgomery, but sees him in purely cerebral terms. It isn't a beefcake body she's after in 'Oh What a Beautiful Brain'.

If we look for the deeper emotions, we find them in The Old. 'Good Clean Fun' conveys all we need to know about Mrs Barraclough's passion not only for her late husband but for her threatened newspaper and the faceless thousands of little boys bequeathed to her by Mr Barraclough on his deathbed. Ditto Mr Donkin and his hymn to 'Captain Fairbrother'. Has there, we wonder, ever been a *Mrs* Donkin? Then, late in the day when their comic seems doomed to oblivion, The Old confess that they are indeed 'Behind the Times'. One of Wilson's most poignant songs, this stands at the heart of a score that touches on perfection. The coolness of its tone, the guard on emotion, is of course the absolute antithesis of

13 Sandy Wilson looking forward to a unique career in British musicals

what we now perceive as the British musical. Emotion is Mrs Barraclough snuffling into a lace handkerchief, not lovers tearing themselves to tatters. Wilson shows the old British values, threatens them, and ends by upholding them. Some may see in this some sort of reflection of the way British musicals battled with their American counterparts. Captain Fairbrother may not be quite muscular enough for our present day, but *The Buccaneer* cries out for revival, at which point a director might look for inspiration to the final scene of Humperdinck's *Hansel and Gretel*, when the stage is filled with 'lost' children. Bringing on unexpected hordes of little tots to cheer on the Captain at the end of *The Buccaneer* might prove a *coup de théâtre*. *The Buccaneer*, after all, is about the co-operation between different generations. Its core is eternal.

The Buccaneer seemed to confirm the arrival of the small British musical, broken free from the moorings of Novello and Coward and all that had gone before. A train of more timid offerings followed in its wake, none smaller or more timid than Allon Bacon's one West End show *She Smiled at Me*, his adaptation of Tom Robertson's Victorian favourite *Caste*. From shy beginnings at the Connaught Theatre, Worthing it transferred to the St Martin's Theatre in 1956, offering the film star Jean Kent as its heroine Esther Eccles. Her leading man Peter Byrne recalled that 'We knew it was a disaster. On the afternoon of the opening I went round to see Jean. We just knew we had to get through the evening, so decided to have a nap. She went to bed and I slept on her sofa. And we went to the theatre and did it.'[8] But only for four performances.

Valmouth ✳ *Call it Love?*

Neither Mrs Barraclough nor Mr Donkin would have recognised the world that is **Valmouth** (Lyric Theatre, Hammersmith, 16 September 1958; 84 / Saville Theatre, 27 January 1959; 102). It is doubtful if schoolchildren have ever been directed towards the highly perfumed, sexually questionable town with its reputation for geriatric hedonism. Ronald Firbank's novel is most unlikely ever to find itself on the National Curriculum reading list. It is unthinkable that Madame Dubonnet would have urged her young ladies to hurry to their classroom for a lesson in *petit point*, after which she would read them a chapter from another of Mr Firbank's novels, *Prancing Nigger*. *The Boy Friend* had appealed to the sophisticate as well as proving eminently suitable for a night-out with Aunt Edna, liable to be offended by any hint of vulgarity. Even the most subtle niceties might be missed by some of the audience, but up to now Wilson had never offended. Booking a ticket for Aunt Edna to sit through Sandy Wilson's version of *Valmouth* might have resulted in a less comfortable evening. After the pastiche at the Villa Caprice, and the good clean fun of Mrs Barraclough and Co., Wilson's lurch to the esoteric was daring, brilliant and perhaps fatal for his subsequent career. Wilson presented the public with an identity crisis.

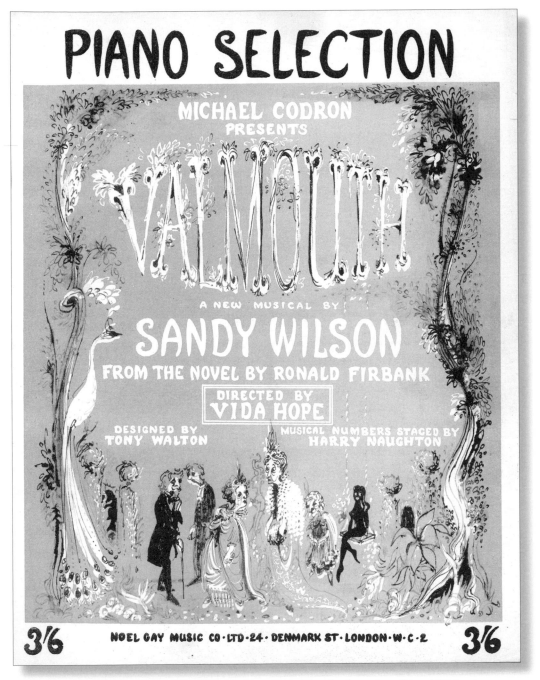

14 Gambling with the esoteric: *Valmouth*, Sandy Wilson's adaptation of Ronald Firbank

A glimpse into the pages of Firbank's novel gives a flavour to those unacquainted with his work. The spa town of Valmouth is enlivened by the return of Lady Parvula de Panzoust via the Valmouth cab.

> Alighting like some graceful exotic bird from the captivity of a dingy cage, Lady Parvula de Panzoust hovered a moment before the portal as much to manipulate her draperies, it seemed, as to imbreathe the soft sweet air.
> The sky was abloom with stars ...
> In the faint elusive light flitter-mice were whirling about the mask-capped windows, hurtling the wind-sown wall-flowers embedded in the fissure of each saturnine-hewn face.

Lady Parvula enters Hare-Hatch House. Its mistress, Mrs Thoroughfare, is not at home. 'The mistress, I presume, is with the scourge,' says the butler. Mrs Thoroughfare is devoted to Catholicism and self-flagellation. 'I know of no joy,' she announces, 'greater than a cool white dress after the sweetness of confession.' She mourns a priest from her past, although 'he had too many ultramontane habits. There was really no joy in pouring out one's sins while he sat assiduously picking his nose.' Eulalia Hurstpierpoint, an ancient crone whose interest in sex remains unaffected by her advanced years, has just acquired a new relic, the tooth of St Automona Meris, to be set as jewellery.

The very air of Valmouth is exotic, beguiling, a balm to its citizens. The capacity for illicit enjoyment is enhanced by a black masseuse, Mrs Yajñavalkya, bringing promises of muscular relief and sexual pleasures. Old as the hills Grannie Took, from the lower end of the Valmouth social scale, readies herself for a 'Vibro' day in Mrs Yaj's hands. Grannie Took's granddaughter Thetis paddles in the River Val, dreaming of the day when she will be married to Dick Thoroughfare, the seafaring heir of Hare-Hatch. She is likely to be disappointed, for Dick is married to Mrs Yaj's niece, Niri-Esther (a savage in the eyes of the Valmouth elite). Dick, meanwhile, is lusted after by his fellow-sailor Jack Whorwood. Lady Parvula lusts after the brawny David Tooke, one of the few Valmouth citizens who does not seem interested in sex. Cardinal Pirelli is brought in to consolidate Niri-Esther's conversion to the Roman church, but his excommunication precedes the destruction of Valmouth itself. The world it represented is simply swept away. Only Mrs Jaj and Niri-Esther escape, to a tropical island where they dream of the vanished Valmouth.

The embellishment, the translation, and indeed the denouement (Firbank leaves things quite unsettled in the book) is Wilson's. The adaptation is a skilful reduction, concentration, disciplining of Firbank's *papillon*-prose original. It recreates the artifice that is Firbank's unique voice, with all its queerness, its lack of moral delineation, its welcoming of the licentious and irreligious. In what is almost certainly his finest score, Wilson manages to find a convincingly Firbankian musical voice. This can be folkish, as in 'I Loved a Man' and David Tooke's 'What Do I Know of Love?' (telling us that what is important to him is not bodily love but a love of landscape), or 'Where the Trees Are Green with Parrots': all these have a musical 'lift' in their refrains that remains peculiar to *Valmouth*. Sexual profanity is well to the fore, not least in Lady Parvula's two revue-like numbers, but it is in the music for Mrs Yaj that the deeper emotions abide. Searching for emotional depths in Firbank is not easy, but Wilson finds them, just as he does, even more remarkably, in the ghastly circumstances of Barbara Comyns' *The Vet's Daughter*. Perhaps one would not expect to find such feeling in the esoteric, but it is here, in the dreadful old ladies remembering their past in 'All the Girls were Pretty' and in Mrs Yaj and Grannie Took's painful parting 'I Will Miss You'.

Call it Love? (Wyndham's Theatre, 22 June 1960; 5) was a Robert Tanitch play with five Wilson songs linking four elongated sketches about love and marriage through the ages, from 1880 to the then present. Just after the first night's interval, the gallery started booing. Unusually, the more sedate stalls joined in. Bernard Levin expressed surprise that 'it waited so long. Between scenes, there are songs by Mr Sandy Wilson. They are terrible, too.' Perhaps the songs, including a cha-cha and a rag, *are* terrible. They are certainly insipid and strangely half-hearted. There was something faintly depressing about having Wilson on the periphery of such a project, and though very few sat through *Call it Love?* it served the theory that he was confined to the era and tastes of *The Boy Friend*. If Wilson had been proclaimed the new Coward, *Call it Love?* did not live up to expectations.

Divorce Me, Darling!

It was five years after *Valmouth* that the next major work reached London. Only the fact that it was an *anniversary* of the creation of Polly Browne and *The Boy Friend* made it happen. The idea may have seemed irresistible. Of course! A musical sequel, taking the plot ten years forward, back to Nice, and the characters who are now older, more world-weary. Now, in the 1930s, it is not young love in the air but divorce. Any hint of cynicism or serious doubt hardly obtrudes into *The Boy Friend*, but is essential to its sequel. There is no doubt that Wilson had examples of 1930s musicals as his inspiration. *The Gay Divorce. Anything Goes.* This was much more Wilson's period than the 1920s; he had been six when that decade had ended; he had begun to grow up through the 1930s. His ability to pastiche the 1930s was as strong as his ability to pastiche the 1920s. What was more, *The Boy Friend* was known to a multitude of the population; it had become an institution, the characters already in existence.

When it came to it, the critical reception for *Divorce Me, Darling!* (Globe Theatre, 1 February 1965; 91) was fainthearted. Comparing it to *The Boy Friend* (reviewers could hardly do otherwise) W. A. Darlington for the *Daily Telegraph* found it gave him 'no touch of nostalgia. I don't even recognise it as a particularly close take-off of anything I actually saw in 1936', but this was 'light, bright entertainment in a remembered idiom'. *The Times* understood that those who could recall the originals that Wilson had made his pastiche from were in for an evening of unmixed delight

> but from a general point of view the impression is a good deal less satisfying. A great many people saw *The Boy Friend* during its five-year run, but Mr Wilson is over-bold in assuming that everyone coming to his new show will instantly recall the tangled circumstances of Polly's romance with Tony at Mme. Dubonnet's finishing school ...Mr Wilson's particular talent (displayed better in *Valmouth* than in *The Boy Friend*) is to recreate a vanished style while simultaneously making fun of it. This involves him in writing at least as well as the subjects he is parodying: and in *Divorce Me, Darling!* the quality of writing is not high. It is often hard to tell whether the fossilized dialogue is meant to be taken as pastiche or witty in itself: and Mr Wilson has used the loose construction of his musical comedy models as a pretext for poor construction himself ...[9]

R. B. Marriott in the *Stage* had similar reservations, considering the new work 'despite moments of gaiety, scraps of neat parody and a couple of good numbers, is not to be compared to the witty, deft, light-hearted show that ran for years and made Mr Wilson's name in the theatre'. Marriott expanded his point.

> Possibly the Thirties do not so readily respond to parody and pastiche as the Twenties; possibly Mr Wilson has missed the essence of them in their musical comedy manifestation in a deliberate attempt to follow-up *The Boy Friend* with a similar type of production. It is difficult to tell, there being no really distinctive pattern or atmosphere in *Divorce Me, Darling!*. It is certain, however, that with *The Boy Friend* Mr Wilson wrote a book and composed numbers that seemed to belong to the Twenties and nowhere else, several of the songs being as good as the well-known originals which inspired Mr Wilson. In *Divorce Me, Darling!* nothing is quite good enough. The best songs, 'No Harm Done' and 'Together Again' fall below the least in *The Boy Friend*, though quite charming, while the story of marital complications and plots of husbands and wives to make each other jealous is much too devious and becomes a bit of a bore. If the show had a strong driving impetus of its own and was not so diffuse, defects would be less noticeable.[10]

Harold Hobson in the *Sunday Times* reminded readers that in *The Boy Friend* Wilson had 'made no specific parody: despite the similarity of title it had no connection with *The Girl Friend*. What Mr Wilson captured was the whole spirit of an epoch of entertainment. In the thirties that spirit was tattered and weakened, and Mr Wilson has thrown it aside for particular evocations and recollections.'[11]

Taking a mean of 800 patrons at each performance of *The Boy Friend* at Wyndham's and multiplying this by the number of performances gives a total of 1,667,200 patrons. Add to this the incalculable numbers who had seen the touring version, and one might imagine the Globe box-office swamped with demands for tickets for the sequel. A cursory glance at American musicals gives us pause.

New York took to the off-Broadway *Little Mary Sunshine*, Rick Besoyan's pastiche of American operetta, but another bite at the same cherry, *The Student Gypsy*, packed up in three weeks. Perhaps the public needs to be in the mood for pastiche, at an exactly appropriate moment. Perhaps there is some scientifically calculable distance of years that has to elapse between the original and the pastiche.

One of the accusations against *The Student Gypsy* was that the pot-shots taken at original songs and styles were not as precise as those in *Little Mary Sunshine*, and there were those who accused *Divorce Me, Darling!* of the same scatter-gun approach. There was another warning for Wilson in the 1962 British production of *Little Mary Sunshine*.[12] Better cast, orchestrated, sunnier and less little than its American counterpart, the critics were bored. After a couple of dismal weeks at the box-office the cast generously gave their salaries back to the management, but nothing changed and the show closed after a month. Years after Wilson's works, whenever American musicals tried to reincarnate original hits in a second manifestation, disaster lurked. *Annie* (not the Moral Re-Armament *Annie*) was reborn as *Annie 2*; *Bye Bye Birdie* returned as *Bring Back Birdie*. (Interestingly, he was brought back twenty years older, so perhaps its authors should have taken a warning from *Divorce Me, Darling!*)

So, why were the 1,667,200+ patrons not jamming the lines of the Globe box-office to get tickets for *Divorce Me, Darling!*? Looking back, Wilson thought

> The winter of 1965 really wasn't the moment for an affectionate look at the Thirties; it was the year of the Rolling Stones' worldwide hit 'Satisfaction', and Julie Christie in the film *Darling* ... it was too soon. It wasn't until the late Sixties that people began to take a serious interest in 1930s style, with the first Art Deco exhibition and the huge wave of interest in Thirties movies, especially those of Busby Berkeley.[13]

There is something in this beyond the usual excuses of why British musicals flopped (the weather was too hot, the weather was too cold, the tubes were on strike, the title was wrong), and maybe even the funeral of Winston Churchill had its effect. The country may have been looking ahead rather than looking back. Having interred its greatest elder statesman of the 1930s, the public simply may not have been in the mood, or feeling the need to go, as one of the liveliest numbers had it 'On the Loose'.

Divorce Me, Darling!'s programme announced 'A new musical comedy of the 1930s', but never confessed to being a sequel. Perhaps some who wandered innocently into the Globe experienced *déjà vu* as the characters arrived to sign in at the Hotel du Paradis. Many would have been in the know, but many would not. One of the problems was that *Divorce Me, Darling!* might be approached from two directions: (1) from knowing everything it was possible to know about *The Boy Friend* or (2) from not knowing the first thing about *The Boy Friend*. The Number 1s were going to compare it with *The Boy Friend*, the Number 2s were going to wonder what all the fuss was about. Sadly, there were not enough of either 1 or 2 to keep the new piece going beyond a few weeks.

The 1930s couldn't be blamed for the show's collapse, any more than Mick Jagger or Joseph Losey. If *The Boy Friend* suggested there might be a magic formula gap of thirty years needed between original and pastiche, *Divorce Me, Darling!* suggested otherwise, despite the same equidistance it put between itself and its model. But by the 1930s (the *mid*-1930s, for *Divorce Me, Darling!* is set in 1936) there was as much awareness of film as of the stage. Hollywood was beginning to exploit Broadway. The echoes we find in Wilson's sequel are of Fred Astaire and Ginger Rogers, the Buddy Bradley dance routines recall those of the better-known Busby Berkeley, the highly respectable Madame Dubonnet has transmuted into the cabaret star Madame K (in effect Marlene Dietrich), and a newcomer to the original cast list, Hannah Van Husen, obviously thinks she is Ethel Merman. The preponderance of film references brought problems; perhaps it is more difficult to recreate film personalities than stage personalities on stage. For obvious reasons, film references were hardly available to *The Boy Friend*. (Had they been, by rights the cast should have done the whole thing in silence, silent films only dying out in 1930.)

The effect in *The Boy Friend* is purely British, and of British purity. Purity is no longer possible when we come to *Divorce Me, Darling!*, because Wilson is picking and choosing types and songs, manipulating the characters so that it may be possible for them to sing particular numbers. *The Boy Friend* too has its types – the innocent heroine, the chaste hero, the worldly glamorous older woman, the French maid – but Wilson never ties them in to a specific impersonation as he does in *Divorce Me, Darling!* That specificity is a bit of a millstone.

I think this is essential in understanding both works. In *The Boy Friend* we don't look at Polly Browne and think Jessie Matthews, Sepha Treble, Binnie Hale. Polly is *Polly*, a sort of embodiment of something we can't pin down to any individual. We have a vague idea that she is somehow typical of a 1920s heroine, even though some of them had a great deal more pluck than Miss Browne. Tony is a clean-cut, heavily made up young juvenile of the period.

In *Divorce Me, Darling!* it is sometimes difficult to locate the country that has inspired the songs. Some of the numbers sound as if they might have come from a British 1930s musical. (How about 'Back Where We Started' or 'Back to Nature' or 'Together Again' or 'Maisie'?) Unlike those of *The Boy Friend*, many of the songs are definitely transatlantic. Polly and Co. have either been travelling a great deal or watching too many Hollywood musicals. On the face of it, there doesn't seem a good reason why Polly should suddenly turn into Gertrude Lawrence or even, here and there, Ginger Rogers, or why Maisie should now throw over a simple Charleston for a conga. Wilson does not specify a 'new *British* musical of the 1930s'. The Britishness at the very heart of *The Boy Friend* is gone, never mind that Tony has now been lobotomised into being Coward.

15 Patricia Michael and Philip Gilbert reminding us of Gertie and Noel
in the original London production of *Divorce Me, Darling!* (1965)

The Boy Friend's greatest trick is to use American models and turn them into something the Saturday matinee at Frinton will lap up as British. This doesn't happen in *Divorce Me, Darling!* Perhaps it is a matter for regret that Wilson didn't turn away from America for that show. In the 1930s Britain offered a multitude of memorable artists, but the show has no hint of a Jessie Matthews, or of a Jack Buchanan (and certainly none of his whispering sidekick Elsie Randolph), no agreeable, flat-footed but facially nimble and wholly engaging comic actor like Stanley Lupino, no buxom self-deprecating comedienne like Vera Pearce, no prim horse-faced elderly actress like Bertha Belmore ('A man once proposed to me on the telephone … but it was a wrong number'), no tiny nonsense-loving little actor like Bobby Howes. The sort of humour – even, much more vulgarly, gags – that permeated the works of Waller and Tunbridge, have no place here. *Divorce Me, Darling!* has none of the madcap wit of *Please Teacher!* Nothing is quite preposterous enough to tie it into the British thirties.

This is hardly surprising, for beyond his admiration of Novello Wilson has never claimed much interest in other British musicals. So it is that Wilson works in an Ethel Merman–Martha Raye character Hannah Van Husen, there to belt out 'Here Am I (But Where's the Guy?)' and be one half of the show's best song, 'You're Absolutely Me' (Wilson's parody of Porter's 'You're the Tops'). What if Wilson had taken the domestic line and gone for Cicely Courtneidge rather than Merman? New songs that had the gentle comic edge of a Vivian Ellis rather than Porter? Listening to some of the songs Ellis wrote specifically for Courtneidge in the 1930s suggests something along such lines might have been much more fun: a tilt at 'Mrs Bartholomew' ('Come to Mrs Bartholomew and she'll bath all of you'). But no, *Divorce Me, Darling!* throughout almost all its length, except for those Coward sequences, wants to be American, not British.

There is something absolute about our general perception of the 1920s. We think we can spot the trademarks – the long pearl necklaces, the flappers, the bow lips, the cloche hats, the white flannels, the defined and artificial finales, the Charleston (even if most of us would be pressed to distinguish it from the Black Bottom). These accumulated absurdities have been absorbed into the public consciousness. When we get to the 1930s, our vision starts to blur, growing more blurred because some of the 1920s characteristics linger into the next decade. That Porter take-off is distinctly in period, but the period rightness of 'On the Loose' is questionable, and it seems almost inevitable that the squeaking hit of *The Boy Friend*, Dulcie, should ten years later boop-a-doop her way through 'Back Where We Started', a number that has just been sung by Polly and Tony in their 1930s style.

On stage at the Globe, the relative weakness of the book (relative, that is, to *The Boy Friend*) was striking, but it was impossible for Wilson to achieve the extraordinary neatness and precision of his earlier pastiche. Steven Vinaver's production did well, amid sets by Reginald Woolley that bordered on the stark, and at least in 1965 Joan Heal and the company seemed aware of the niceties that might make it all work. The Chichester revival of 1997 lacked something. One prayed for Vida Hope to come down and give the cast a jolly good talking to about style. Some, Sheridan Morley among them, lavished their praise and demanded a West End transfer, but if the time had been wrong in 1965 it was plainly not right in 1997.

One of the sorrows of this is that *Divorce Me, Darling!* is a very fine score, much more enjoyable than *The Boy Friend*. Perhaps *The Boy Friend* suffers from over-familiarity, or one has heard recording after recording that never quite seems to catch it right. Can one really *enjoy* the brittle original London cast recording, all ten inches of its long-play? It always sounds to me as if the cast was doing it in a very cold studio, and nobody bothered to take their coats off. It may be that the recording truthfully preserves the precision and integrity of the original stage production, and it may be a simple injustice that the Globe cast's recording of *Divorce Me, Darling!* is so much more enjoyable. Even so, just as the failure of *Vanity Fair* sent Julian Slade back to the provinces, the closure of *Divorce Me, Darling!* effectively ended Wilson's ongoing West End career, consigning him to the fringe of British musical theatre. This was a real injustice for a man who only ten years before was seen as the successor to Coward; especially so, when Wilson had so much more diversity and invention than Coward to offer the genre. While Slade managed to go on composing on commission because of his strong links with the Bristol Old Vic and the Everyman, Cheltenham, Wilson was left to wander in search of the esoteric.

As Dorothy Parker Once Said ✳ *His Monkey Wife*

Whatever was attempted now seemed out of the time when it might have attracted interest. Wilson provided the music for *As Dorothy Parker Once Said*, a musical entertainment written by Leslie Lawton around the works of the American wit, first for a season at Watford and subsequently at the Fortune Theatre in 1969, on both occasions starring Libby Morris, a quirky performer in search of stardom. She did not find it here. According to the *Stage*, it seemed at times like *The Boy Friend* with teeth. The reviews were not encouraging. R. B. Marriott thought Parker was hidden behind the 'sentimentally drooling music by Sandy Wilson', but Wilson had never really been lucky with his collaborators.

The final London musical, **His Monkey Wife** (Hampstead Theatre Club, 20 December 1971; season), is a distinctive esoteric ill deserving of the neglect into which it has fallen. Those ready to take offence at *Valmouth* might scarcely venture beyond the new work's title. The plain truth is that here was a musical about a man who marries a chimpanzee. Not, of course, any old chimpanzee, although any old would probably be as intelligent as many any old *Homo sapiens*. Emily is special. At the play's opening, she is maid and general attendant to Alfred Fatigay in his Congo jungle outpost of Boboma. Wilson's tropical sounds pronounce the place a sort of cousin to Valmouth. Alfred is engaged to Miss Fern Flint (her heart, it turns out, as stony as her moniker) awaiting him in Haverstock

Hill. When Alfred returns to London, he presents Emily to his fiancé as a maid, whom Fern renames Smithers. Eager to improve herself, Emily studies Darwin's *Origin of Species* at the British Museum. When Fern's wedding day arrives, Emily forces her to hand over her bridal veil. Unaware of this, Alfred finds himself married to his chimpanzee, and understandably flees. A heartbroken Emily falls on hard times, working with an organ-grinder, but her talents are recognised by a show-business agent who offers her a contract in a C. B. Cochran revue. Alfred, reduced to the gutter, is rescued by Emily's kindness, and when Fern attempts a reconciliation he realises that his happiness lies with Emily. Alfred and his monkey wife return to the jungle of Boboma to who knows what married bliss.

Oddly, this was not the first British musical to be written around an amiable chimp. *Mr Burke, M.P.* (Mermaid Theatre, 6 October 1960; season), written and composed by Gerald Frow, was a satire on the possibility of a primate becoming a Parliamentarian. *His Monkey Wife* is the more subtle in Wilson's chamber piece for eight actors. John Collier's novel was suggested to Wilson as a subject for musical adaptation by the playwright Rodney Ackland. Just as *Valmouth* is essentially about the loss of innocence rather than the sort of sexual liberalism of which it has been accused, *His Monkey Wife* is underpinned by the same philosophy. It is a celebration of domestic happiness, not bestiality; we can only be moved by looking on at the developing affection between Alfred and his mate. Emily might be expected to display only animal instincts, but she has her Reader's Ticket for the British Museum as an open sesame to knowledge. If there can be any doubt of her charms, the Librarian of the Reading Room is bewitched by her ('Who Is She?').

After the jungle calls of the opening, there is the chant of 'In Boboma Tonight', after which no more jungle beat is heard until Emily's show-stopping number for Cochran, 'Doing the Chimpanzee', this score's answer to 'The Riviera'. Of all the male characters in Wilson's shows, Alfred is the most developed. It is noticeable that while he is the only one of them to have to deal with an emotional relationship with a primate, he is also far and away the most feeling. From the first, in 'Emily's Waltz', when he is carvorting gently around his jungle hut with his primate, we know of his fondness, his capacity for kindness, his need for simple domesticity. He is willing to extend all this to his much-missed fiancé, and anyway she is associated with England, for which he yearns ('Home and Beauty and You'). In fact, England brings only frustration ('Don't Rush Me') as Fern procrastinates about naming the day. Finally, when recognition dawns, Wilson has Alfred deliver a hymn to the future now within his grasp, 'Live Like the Blessed Angels'.

Is it another achievement of Wilson's skill that we feel perhaps more moved by this because it is sung to a monkey rather than to a human? After all, Wilson's scores are not known for their love songs. There are really none to speak of in *The Boy Friend* where all is conjecture, and *Divorce Me, Darling!* hasn't a love song that one may take seriously; the main love song in *The Buccaneer* stays, as its title tells us, unromantic. No, it is in *His Monkey Wife* and *The Clapham Wonder* that the love songs are at their strongest.

In *His Monkey Wife* all is economy of lyric and simplicity of music, but this is all Wilson needs to distinguish the two worlds, Emily's and Fern's, the one colourful and magical, the other vacuous and dull. There is a moment in the play when Fern makes some sort of confession about the competition she has faced ('His Monkey Wife'), which finds Wilson at his most subtle. We can feel for Fern because she feels the power and serenity of Emily, who on a visit to the zoo meets up with a caged chimp; we get their view of the outside world in 'Dear Human Race'. Ultimately, of course, the only thing to matter to Emily is Alfred's feeling for her. The reward is in the acknowledgement that Alfred knows they will live like the blessed angels. All is reduced to normality. 'Who Is She?' is the question that Emily leaves behind her.

In 1971, the year of *His Monkey Wife*, the British musical was in a dismal way. A Pinero adaptation, *The Amazons*, barely lived out its premiere at Nottingham Playhouse. There was a hapless chamber piece, *Romance!*, which despite its encouraging exclamation mark collapsed at the end of its first week; the never-heard-of-since *Saturnalia* by Ron Moody at Coventry; a dreary spectacle called *What a Way to Run a Revolution* (not, presumably, a revolution in musical theatre), and *Good Time Johnny*, a musical about Sir John Falstaff by Julian More and James Gilbert. In 1956 their *Grab me a Gondola* had lit up the town, but by 1971 the game was done. Seven years later, it is a wonder in itself that Wilson's new musical *The Clapham Wonder* received even a provincial production. 1978 was just another disastrous year for the British musical. Consider *Once More, Darling*, an attempt to musicalise a contemporary British farce; to his credit, even its composer Cyril Ornadel admitted it was a dud. *Troubadol* was an expensive folly, out of time and place, the semi-American *Bar Mitzvah Boy* out of tune with its time. Triumphing unchallenged was Andrew Lloyd Webber and Tim Rice's expansive *Evita*. It seemed now that the British musical was personified by a biomusical about the mistress of an Argentinian dictator.

The Clapham Wonder

Against this sort of stuff **The Clapham Wonder** (Marlowe Theatre, Canterbury, 26 April 1978; season) had no commercial currency. Provincial, under-cast, under-reviewed, there was no hope that the miracle of *The Boy Friend* (little show gets taken up and becomes big) would reoccur, and in a way *The Boy Friend* itself was part of the new show's problem. When the curtain went up on *The Clapham Wonder* some must have wondered what had happened to the creator of Polly Browne. No one could have imagined that the creator of so sunny and light a heroine would now be offering a British musical set in *Wales*. As if this was not bravery enough, it was adapted from a desperately dark 1959 novel by Barbara Comyns, *The Vet's Daughter*. Years after the death of Novello, it had seemed to some unthinkable that the British (or Americans, come to that) would ever accept a 'serious' musical. Anyway, what was serious? To some, the fact that there was No Dancing might qualify as 'serious'. Or did the theme have to be historical? Of social significance? How serious was 'serious'? In the mid-1960s *The Matchgirls* and even *Strike a Light!* had 'serious' themes. By 1978 managements would present those sort of shows at their peril. (There had been peril enough in doing so in the 1960s!) Perhaps one could not get more serious a theme than *Jesus Christ Superstar*. Its hero, of course, was not British.

The emotional excess that was by now characterising the most eminently successful British musicals was not in Wilson's armoury. Neither was it in the armoury of Coward, Novello, Ellis, Slade or Bart, in all of whose work there is a sense of corseting emotions. Some, naturally, tie the stays tighter than others. Novello might be accused of treading the highest emotional tight-rope in his effusively romantic songs, but his (and Hassall's) work is tempered in a way that the new wave of British musicals arriving in the 1970s is not. Puccini knew that the best effects came from not playing out emotions on a constant high-pitch of feeling. Part of the problem with the international musicals the British turned to is that their subjects and librettos and scores could sometimes barely support such an approach. This seldom proved a bar to their commercial success. A public had grown that wanted to hear again and again about a woman crying for Argentina, whereas Slade's cry of understanding for Bromley and Bude was dismissed. Audiences wanted to leave theatres with their emotions in tatters. *The Clapham Wonder* was assuredly an assault on the emotions, but not of the type the audiences at Coventry in 1978 might have been hoping for. Wilson's new piece had been put on by the management because their production of *The Boy Friend* had been so conspicuously successful, but audiences settling down to some heart-warming escapism were confronted by unremitting misery. Most of them would never have even heard of *Valmouth* or *His Monkey Wife*, and were quite unprepared for the fare set before them.

Time, then, to tell Comyn's story of *The Vet's Daughter*. Alice Rowlands is the unhappy child of an animal-torturing, wife-beating and abusive father. The family move to London. The new abode is seedy and dark. Mr Rowlands' work as a vet is made up of terrible moments – living animals put into sacks and sold to the vivisectionist; a cat brought half-baked to the surgery because it has got into an oven. Alice's pathetic mother, her body already broken by the vet, dies in agony. Mr Rowlands brings the barmaid Rosa, the strumpet from The Trumpet, into the house as his mistress. Sometimes there is almost a sense of Valmouthian splendour as Alice describes her home: 'the dreary brown things in the kitchen would turn into great exotic flowers and I'd be in a kind of jungle, and, when the parrot called from his lavatory prison, he wasn't the parrot, but a great white peacock crying out'.[14]

Rosa introduces Alice to a greasy waiter. He tries to rape Alice. Rosa, who seems to Alice like 'a white negress' (a whiff of *Valmouth* is in this), leaves Rowlands. Alice's only friends are the deaf-mute Lucy, the servant Mrs Churchill and a young locum, 'Blinkers', who obviously cares about her. She sees his fondness but cannot return the love. Her father turns her out of the house, never wishing to see her again. Alice goes as companion to Blinkers' kindly but frail mother Mrs Peebles at 'The Burnt House' on an island in Hampshire. Mrs Peebles is known to have failed to hang herself, the marks still on her neck. Alice is besotted with a handsome young man, Nicholas, who exudes an 'easy happiness'. She has slowly developed a capacity for 'floating' – lifting herself into the air, first in her room, then in a wood. When she levitates in front of Nicholas, he is appalled. Mrs Peebles drowns herself, and Alice is sent back to Battersea to live with her father, who recommences his physical and mental abuse of her. Rosa has now moved back in with him. When Alice levitates in front of her father, he and Rosa realise the commercial possibilities of so freakish a gift and organise a display on Clapham Common. Alice rises above the Common, but falls to the ground. In the trampling of the crowds that have watched the spectacle, she and Rosa are killed.

This was never going to be popular. The bloodthirsty musical is not necessarily doomed to failure (remember *Jack the Ripper* or Sondheim's *Sweeney Todd*) but Comyns' total introspection in *The Vet's Daughter* provided Wilson with no wider context in which to make the work digestible. Both *Jack the Ripper* and *Sweeney Todd* have a moral framework; *The Clapham Wonder*, dependant on Comyn's novel, has none. The critic Desmond Connolly decided that 'Finding the right music for such a melodramatic story is not without its pitfalls, many of which Mr Wilson falls into. Some of the tunes have great charm but often get bogged down by the overladen story, which sticks to the music like dramatic treacle. The tale is not a suitable case for musical treatment.'[15] In 1979 the Lyric Theatre, Hammersmith, commissioned Wilson to write *Aladdin*, a pantomime forced to be a musical and a musical trying to avoid being a pantomime, with a score below the best of Wilson's work.

It would be disappointing to end on such a note, and there is no need to do so, for Wilson's contribution to the post-war British musical is one of the most distinctive and interesting. There has, of course, been far too much focus on *The Boy Friend*, and much tosh talked about it. Set it aside, and let us rediscover the several joys of *The Buccaneer*, *His Monkey Wife* and, yes, *The Clapham Wonder*. Bring in an accomplished illusionist to effect Alice's levitation, banishing the memory of the Canterbury production which at such moments resorted to a blackout, and spare nothing in production. No British musical ever deserved 1978, but – thirty years on – there may yet be a place for *The Clapham Wonder*, into which Wilson injects such energy and feeling. It seems extraordinary that such a daring British musical shares its author with *The Boy Friend*. When Alice sings of 'Our Golden Afternoon' we are conjured back to a sound-world created and inhabited only by Sandy Wilson. Perhaps the man who brought intelligence, subtlety, the neatest of lyrics and sympathetic scores to everything he wrote deserves to be remembered for what is most forgotten.

5 Resounding Tinkles
The *plein air* Musicals of Julian Slade and Dorothy Reynolds, Geoffrey Wright and Donald Swann

Vinegar, along with soap, bacon, clothes, meat, candles, petrol, and a wearying list of other necessaries, was in short supply from the outbreak of war in 1939. Only in 1948 did the British government begin to lift the restrictions. The clothing ration was stopped in March 1949. Petrol rationing ended in 1950, not in time to prevent Novello being sent to prison for breaking its rules. Food rationing, which had then lasted for an astonishing fourteen years, came to an end on 4 July 1954, the very month that *Salad Days* came to life. A general sense of celebration was not too distant, needed not least because of the nuclear shadow that haunted 1950s Britain. Britain, after all, still had living memories of the great 1951 Festival of Britain, and the coronation of its young Queen in June 1953. With a new youthful face on its postage stamps, the only way was ahead. Julian Slade and Dorothy Reynolds were about to beckon the way to a new Elizabethan age.

Salad Days

Central to the immediate potency of **Salad Days** (Vaudeville Theatre, 5 August 1954; 2,288) Slade and Reynolds promulgated a philosophy of dancing in the streets, an expression of what the writer Barbara Ehrenreich has named 'collective joy'.[1] Coronations, jubilees and street parties provide the occasional excuses for it in Britain, and all over the world festivals of dancing in the streets abound. Celebration may, of course, emanate from the misfortune of others: the joy in the streets of Iraq that greeted the toppling of their dictator's statue, and the execution of Saddam Hussein in December 2006. The most popular form of collective happiness, the most obvious expression of emotional release: pick a person up and dance with them. On this bedrock of elemental happy behaviour was Slade and Reynolds' best known, if not best, work to be built.

Between matinees of *Salad Days* at the Vaudeville Theatre, when its composer was playing in the pit at each performance, he and the Vaudeville's owner Jack Gatti sat chatting at the back of the stalls. 'You know, Julian,' said Gatti, 'I've always thought that opening number, 'The Things That Are Done by a Don', is a work of genius.' Slade expressed surprise. 'Really, Jack?' 'Oh, yes. It's the most wonderful opening number. Sheer brilliance. I mean, after hearing it the audience can only think it's got to get better than this.'[2]

At its first night in London in 1954, when the show had been dusted off for London after its rapturous reception at the Bristol Old Vic, the first half was decidedly sticky. Slade remembered that 'I went into Dorothy Reynolds' dressing room during the interval. She was doing her hair in the mirror and looked back at me. I said, "I don't know what to think, Dorothy. Do you think it's going well?"' Dorothy settled a curl. 'Oh, I shouldn't worry, darling,' she said, 'I think we'll get three weeks out of it.'[3] *Salad Days* went on to run for 2,288 performances, establishing the reputation of its composer (if not his collaborator) and opening a door to tireless condemnatory responses. Another British musical, *Harmony Close*, even had the cheek to sneer at it, and a London revue had a sketch in which Slade and Reynolds and their work were mercilessly lampooned. Almost certainly unwittingly, the team had begun the little school of *plein air* musicals that distinguish British musical theatre in the second half of the 1950s.

There was little in Slade's previous work to suggest he would take this path. His first scores, *Lady May* and *Bang Goes the Meringue!*, written and performed when he was a Cambridge undergraduate, show little sense of greeting the day.

16 Dorothy Reynolds, Denis Carey and Julian Slade at a dress rehearsal for *Salad Days*

The works that followed, *Christmas in King Street* and *The Merry Gentleman*, were seasonal pieces in lieu of pantomime for the Bristol Old Vic, where Slade had been taken on as bit-actor and part-time composer. His score for Sheridan's *The Duenna* showed a knack for pastiche, a proper grasp of period and tunefulness, and was greeted with some critical applause when produced at the Westminster Theatre in June 1954. Its 'Fandango' has a touch of Sullivan's 'Cachucha' from *The Gondoliers*, and Slade, brought up on regular visits to Gilbert and Sullivan operas performed by D'Oyly Carte, always acknowledged the influence of these works on his own. *Lady May* has its own Gilbertian patter song, 'A Gypsy Earl'.

Once, when Slade addressed a group of theatrically interested women in the 1950s, he mildly criticised D'Oyly Carte's intransigent productions, still following the directions given by Gilbert. News of this reached the ears of Dame Bridget D'Oyly Carte who sent off a stinging letter. Slade was more than happy to leave her in no doubt that he was a life-long lover of Gilbert and Sullivan, and conveyed his affection for D'Oyly Carte. Had Dame Bridget taken the trouble to listen to his music she may have understood how strong those bonds were. Although evident in the earlier work, the influence of G & S in *Salad Days* and beyond is barely noticeable, for by this time Slade and Reynolds had developed a style very much their own. Slade frequently uses the G & S double-chorus, as heard in 'Out of Breath' (the Act I finale for *Salad Days*), 'The Girl from London' (a sort of 'This Is the House that Jack Built' ensemble Act I finale for *Free as Air*), 'Song and Dance' (the Act I finale for *Follow That Girl*), and again in the Act I finale 'Back to The Wells' in *Trelawny*.

For Slade, Act I finales *demand* the double chorus, but these are essentially an expression of the choral tradition in which Slade worked. The influence of Sullivan is obvious in the frequent chorales spread throughout the Slade Reynolds works (all the above-mentioned finales as well as such examples as 'Solitary Stranger' in *Follow That Girl*, 'Testudo' in *Free as Air*, 'Going Up' – the Act I finale of *Hooray for Daisy!* – 'The Days Go By' and 'Red or White' in *Wildest Dreams*). Even Novello had not much explored the choral tradition, despite his own formative training as a choirboy, but in Slade the choral is always lurking. This, indeed, is one of the strands separating him from any of the post-Sullivan composers until Lloyd Webber. Beyond these Act I finales, just before the matinee customers were handed their trays of tea and Fuller's walnut cake along the rows of the stalls, G & S had been expunged, although in *Salad Days* shreds remain in such 'patter' numbers as 'Hush-Hush' and 'We're Looking for a Piano'.

The world of opera, although never in its 'serious' form, is also evident in Slade's work, and the influences here may be heard from the beginning, not least in the material he wrote for several Shakespeare plays at the Bristol Old Vic, including an extended score for *The Comedy of Errors*. Slade considered such almost totally forgotten work his best, and the few recordings of such incidental music argue the point. Here, especially in what we may see as its love songs, are the influences of Lionel Monckton and Vivian Ellis. On the first occasion Slade and Ellis met, they shared a taxi from some function, and Slade plucked up the courage to tell Ellis how much his music had influenced him. 'He looked absolutely appalled.'[4] The melancholia that imbues much of Ellis's work is very evident in much of Slade: it threads through *Salad Days*, *Free as Air* and *Wildest Dreams*. That air of happiness mingles with doom in the love duet from the Ellis – A. P. Herbert *Bless the Bride*, 'This is my Lovely Day'. Even the inhabitants of Nelderham, the village at the centre of *Wildest Dreams*, recognise that death is part of all, describing their happiness in terms of living and dying.

But is this Slade's lyric? Is this awareness of death, elemental facts of life in a British musical, Slade's work, or is it the work of his co-lyricist and co-librettist? Their works sign off with 'Lyrics and book by Dorothy Reynolds and Julian Slade'. Does that order recognise the fact that Reynolds was the main force behind book and lyrics? Which ideas were hers, and which his? Was it merely gentlemanly to put her name before his? This is a mystery that cannot be answered. To the end, Slade never revealed what part each played, and who wrote what. Did she write the love songs? Did she write the comedy songs? Did they share all between them? Some light may be thrown on this by listening to the scores of Slade's Cambridge musicals for which he was solely responsible, but in these he seems adept at writing both romantic and comical material, and we are little the wiser. In a way, the very fact that he perceived his collaboration with Reynolds as indivisible offers a clue as to how vital she was to his work, and one of the reasons his future career was so chequered. There seems little doubt that Reynolds was the driving force, and driving would anyway not be a word to easily affix to Slade. Several years his senior, Reynolds had years of theatrical experience behind her, and was an established actress at the Bristol Old Vic. Slade's nursery upbringing bowed to the stronger force. A photograph of the pair, Slade at the piano with Reynolds standing over him, somehow typifies the relationship. Jean Marion Taylor, who played one of the island girls in *Free as Air*, recalls how during breaks in rehearsal he would ask Reynolds for his sixpence to get a cup of tea.[5] There have been suggestions that when *Salad Days* was prepared it was Reynolds who added vinegar to the salad; we will never know how the tossing was managed.

With no intended intellectual context or any obvious reference to all of this, the moment was ripe for *Salad Days* when it opened for a three-week season at Bristol Old Vic and subsequently at the Vaudeville Theatre, London in August 1954. Its format, somewhere between reality and fantasy, with more than a dash of revue, was that which had already worked for the writers of *Christmas in King Street* and *The Merry Gentleman*. The story might have been written on the back of one of the new Queen's stamps. Tim and Jane meet up as they prepare to leave university (unspecified, but obviously Cambridge). Tim is being sent to see several uncles who might find him a career (the excuse for some revue-like scenes, including a diplomat's office and a flying saucer) and Jane's mother is lining her

17 Bob Harris (Troppo) and Joe Greig (PC Boot) enjoy innocent fun
in the original London production of *Salad Days*

up for a husband. Tim and Jane decide to marry and hopefully later to fall in love, and take on the job of looking after a piano wheeled by a tramp (actually, Tim's 'lost' uncle). The piano, Minnie, proves to have magical qualities. It makes people dance in the park. Soon, London is in blissful pandemonium. Wanted by the authorities, the lovers escape capture, eventually handing over the piano after their own month of happiness to their friends Nigel and Fiona, who will presumably find their own enchantment.

The *plein air* musical – the musical that seemed to thrive on, would be impossible without, the great British outdoors – had arrived. Although there is almost no reference in *Salad Days* to the weather, it is the sense of outdoor exhilaration that pervades it. The work also came with its built-in nostalgia; if anything, it almost seemed to look back on itself, even as the lovers promised, in 'We Said We Wouldn't Look Back', never to regress. The potency of this has lasted far beyond its first performance. At (what age?) twenty, twenty-one, the lovers are already saying they will look to the future, not the past. It is a sort of realisation that life must be played out; an awareness of mortality. It is surely this underlying and almost undetected philosophy which makes the lyric so memorable. Melancholia is there in 'The Time of My Life' (never be mistaken into thinking that happiness stops the inevitability of prevailing sadness) and in Jane's other *plein air* aria, 'I Sit in the Sun', there is even the threat of eventual loss; time may carry away the opportunity to find the lover.

The comical elements in *Salad Days* (a scene in a beauty salon, a visit to Ambrose's camp dress shop, flat-footed policemen with a closet penchant for ballet) may be little more than revue sketches squeezed into the hastily-assembled script, but even beyond the pages of *Punch* the audiences of 1954 recognised these types. Laughter at such things had been a staple of W. S. Gilbert. The capering coppers of *Salad Days* are descendents of the constables who so ineffectively pursued the pirates of Penzance. The Bishop whose legs lose control when he hears Minnie's music in the park is an extension of the ready-made comical vicar so beloved of *Punch*. If there is any threat to the *plein air* ecstasy, it is the Minister for Pleasure and Pastime, whose dour duty it is to catch Jane and Tim and Minnie and put an end to both pleasure and pastime, a plot device of which A. P. Herbert would surely have approved. We must know, of course, that by the end of the proceedings, the Minister himself will succumb. He is, after all, one of Tim's uncles. When all is done, and Tim and Jane leave their life with Minnie to start out anew, they are left alone on stage to sing a single refrain of the show's anthem. The summer is over, but has changed them for ever. They will, so they say, never look back.

Free as Air * *Follow That Girl*

The *plein air* that permeates the second Slade and Reynolds' London musical *Free as Air* (Savoy Theatre, 6 June 1957; 417) blows from the Channel Islands. The play's theme of escape shadowed the feelings they experienced after *Salad Days* had propelled them into the limelight. Its heroine Geraldine Melford is a wealthy young heiress who takes a boat to the remote Channel island of Terhou to escape the attentions of the popular press. The fact that Slade spent a little time on Sark writing the songs had its impact on this most expansively 'greenery' musical. The ocean and the island are hymns to wide open space, where Molly, the unsophisticated island girl who longs to escape *from* Terhou *to* the mainland responds to the arrival of Geraldine with 'If she's as pretty as all that, just think what the men must be like!' On Terhou, the pace of life is slow, the day passes in ordinary pursuits, in the case of the island's 'Parliament' (three old codgers) in sitting still and watching the world go by in 'Let the Grass Grow'. There is little for the islanders to do but arrange the coronation of the island's queen, and virginity may or may not be an issue. They sing the coronation song about everything including love being free, and gaze at the ocean, as Molly does in 'Terhou'. This acceptability of the natural world, and the longed for freedom of expression that the celebrations of May will bring is challenged by the threatened changes which contact with the mainland will introduce.

A persistent reporter from the big city, Ivy Crush, arrives with ideas to turn the island into a giant Butlins. Modernity is on the doorstep. A more muscular attraction arrives in the shape of a sexy racing-driver, for whom Molly inevitably falls. Geraldine, meanwhile, is attracted to one of the local lads. Their relationships are settled by curtain-fall, along the way bringing an acute awareness of Slade and Reynolds' attitude to love and sex. Their work is frequently associated with a defining primness, which is not altogether justified, although Reynolds' view of sexual matters may have been old-fashioned. Slade once told me that she 'strongly disapproved of homosexuality'. Could the dress-shop scene in *Salad Days*, with its mincing proprietor, have been Slade's own work?

The treatment of love in the team's songs bears close examination. The romantic duet is almost eschewed. It does not exist in *Salad Days*, where the only love song, 'The Time of My Life', is a solo carol to the summer, not a lover. There are four duets in *Free as Air*, sung by the three sets of lovers, Geraldine and Albert, Molly and racing-driver Jack, and the established spinster Miss Catamole and her long-time admirer Mr Potter. Only the eldest of these have a duet that speaks of love, 'We're Holding Hands'. Lyrically, the other 'love' duets are either jolly or wry. Geraldine and Albert get together for the carefree coronation song 'Free as Air' and again in 'I'd Like to Be Like You'. The latter is a supreme example of Slade's obsession with the necessity for another person to make oneself complete; there is a need to almost transmogrify into the other person, surely a unique feature in British musical plays. This is a theme that reoccurs throughout the canon. Meanwhile, Jack and Molly have a duet in which each exists in a separate world. Jack sings 'I've got my feet on the ground' just as Molly steps on his words with 'I've got my head in the clouds.' Love is around, but not fully expressed; there is not even a hint of anything like passion. Only in the final duet from *Wildest Dreams* does love seem to find some sort of satisfactory expression, but even this is not as clear as it seems. This emotional reticence may make way for something of rather more depth, an intense longing to be made complete.

It is too easy, perhaps, to see in Geraldine's contempt for the paparazzi (the word would have meant little to British audiences of 1957) links to a dominating royal story of our own time, but in its own way *Free as Air* holds up a mirror to the times. The Elizabethan release of dancing in the park is missing, and critics generally attacked the piece for what might be summed up as its calculated whimsy. There is some justification in this, but the philosophy is potent. The major recommendations for happy life are laziness, the need to observe tradition, prevent incursion from outside influences and to accept that contentment comes through simple living. Letting weeds grow under your feet is essential.

The commercial history of *Free as Air* is not completely happy. A long pre-London tour had audiences refusing to leave the theatre until the cast reprised song after song, but the first night at the Savoy proved a damp squib. Slade blamed this on the director, Denis Carey, who directed all the Slade–Reynolds works except *Wildest Dreams*. On the morning of the Savoy premiere Carey told the cast to 'play down', because he felt the forceful playing that had been in place throughout the tour would be unsuitable for London. Slade felt this was a decision from which the piece never recovered. Carey's last-minute fright may have been a reaction to the air of amateurism that had always attached itself to his production of the original *Salad Days*. Some, indeed, thought that quality was *necessary*. It was the amateur element, in its playing and presentation, which gave the piece its mystique. It is almost as if too professional an approach would send the work to bed with a malaise from which it would not rally. If audiences had responded to the end-of-term japes, 'let's let our hair down and put on a musical' atmosphere of *Salad Days*, with a largely non-musical cast having a go, it seemed sensible for the cast of *Free as Air* to try the same trick.

There was always the suspicion that audiences warmed to *Salad Days* because they went out thinking 'I could do that!' This is a mistaken philosophy when applied to *Free as Air*, which needs sensitive and highly professional treatment. However damaging Slade may have thought Carey's intervention, Carey directed the next two Slade–Reynolds works, but beyond these directed only one other musical, the 1955 *A Girl Called Jo*, based on the novels of Louisa M. Alcott. According to one of that show's authors, Peter Myers, Carey arrived for the first morning of rehearsal and after a few minutes said 'Oh, I didn't realise it was a musical!'[6] On such professionalism was the British musical built.

The team's preoccupation with *plein air* was interrupted by ***Follow That Girl***

(Vaudeville Theatre, 17 March 1960; 211) a reworking of *Christmas in King Street* with Christmas now forgotten, and its Bristolian setting switched to London. The programme politely acknowledged the contribution James Cairncross had made to the work as co-librettist for the Bristol version. By 1960 the kitchen sink had moved across from straight theatre to the British musical; audiences seemed more interested in Soho than the leafier parts of Kensington. Six years after *Salad Days* and three years after *Free as Air* Slade and Reynolds might have come up with something new, but *Follow That Girl* (never mind the fact that it was helped a little by an attractive new title-song which reminded some of the old standard 'Peg o' My Heart')[7] was yesterday's dish warmed through. One wonders whose decision it was to pursue it; it suggests that the writers were incapable of coming up with a strong, even startling, new subject, although the new show was slightly off-formula. Delightfully designed by Hutchinson Scott, its production values were secure, and the casting gave some young performers (Susan Hampshire, Patricia Routledge, Peter Gilmore) a leg-up to highly success-ful careers, but musically the work is thin, a skinniness reflected in its modest orchestrations.

There is a promising hint of *plein air* in the polka celebration of 'I'm Away', in which a Pre-Raphaelite painter and his modelling wife extol the joys of being in Battersea Park, and the plot hinges on a baby snatched from outside a shop in Kensington, but despite some invigorating moments on a bridge from which the heroine jumps into the Aquarium and meets three Victorian mermaids, the work is not of the greenery school. Describing the adventure with mermaids, the critic Milton Shulman told his *Evening Standard* readers that

> Should you be misled by this description into thinking this might be an Ionesco[8] musical, let me assure you that not an ironic, subtle or stimulating thought creeps into the entire evening ... In the name of wholesomeness and simplicity, the evening is deprived of wit, logic, consistency of mood, maturity of approach or subtlety of style. In short, anything that would give any semi-sophisticated adult any pleasure.

The revue elements worked into *Follow That Girl* – the mermaids, Routledge in a corset shop, she and Cairncross doing a pastiche Victorian parlour song – have dashes of fantasy but little hint of originality. Of melancholia there is some sign, as in 'Shopping in Kensington',[9] the hero's love lament 'Lovely Meeting You at Last' and his final duet with the fleeing heroine 'One, Two, Three, One'. All of these have a drooping sadness. Slade played at the piano among the tiny band that accompanied the proceedings. He told me 'I remember looking up at it all and thinking, Oh I am so bored!' In a climate where anything emanating from the Theatre Workshop at Stratford East was taking the critical and public attention, when the British musical was making room for the prostitute rather than the do-gooder, and six years after *Salad Days* the critic Irving Wardle, who had never seen *Salad Days*, considered *Follow That Girl*.

18 Marion Grimaldi and Newton Blick in the original London production of *Follow That Girl*

Perhaps the new piece is not the equal of the first, but the hard things that have been said about it seem to stem largely from a feeling that Mr Slade should have been scattered to the winds by Joan Littlewood's chill Eastern blast. But how incompatible are the two genres? In the appeal they make to an audience I can detect only one crucial difference between the Soho idyll of *Fings Ain't Wot They Used T'Be* and the Battersea idyll of *Follow That Girl* – the difference being that in its writing, and even more in its direction, *Follow That Girl* is built to withstand the wear and tear of a long run. Despite vociferous opposition from a Logue-rolling faction on the first night, I see no reason why it shouldn't.

... from the first waxwork group assembled at a *soirée musicale* the show possesses an immaculately pointed style that breaks down the distinction between satire and whimsicality ... The music, leaning alternately on Offenbach and Novello, has a spirit and turn of phrase that rescues even the scenes of insipid romance; and Susan Hampshire, bobbing a head of blonde curls before the pursuing crowd, gave the title a conclusive justification.[10]

Hooray for Daisy!

A return to Bristol and subsequently London came with *Hooray for Daisy!* (Lyric Theatre, Hammersmith, 20 December 1960; season), *plein air* at its most parochial, for which Slade reverted to the two-piano accompaniment of *Salad Days*, sliding back from *Free as Air*'s substantial orchestra and *Follow that Girl*'s modest ensemble. The milieu, indeed, is that of the village hall in the little village of Milbury, where the locals are preparing their Christmas pantomime. A tin of baked beans misbehaves at one of the rehearsals and the cast climb its beanstalk. The finale celebrates the actions of a local cow, Daisy. There is little doubt that an absolute lightness of touch is at work, and Bristol audiences responded enthusiastically to seeing some of the original players of *Salad Days* (Reynolds, Bob Harris and Joe Greig) recreating the yuletide spirit that Slade and Reynolds had introduced with *Christmas in King Street*. Eleanor Drew, the original leading lady of *Salad Days*, was taken on for the London production, replacing Bristol's Annette Crosbie, whose singing had to be heard to be disbelieved. *Hooray for Daisy!* attracted little but scorn during its brief spell at the Lyric, Hammersmith the following year.

The work has generally been dismissed as of no worth, but as proved by a live recording of one of the Bristol performances, if not by the eventual LP, it was a provincial hit. For those willing to discover, beyond its artlessness satire lurks. Here, for the first time, Slade and Reynolds hone their material, bringing the spotlight down to a pencil sharpness as they zoom in on the village. This is a technique that is continued and has its apogee in *Wildest Dreams*. The obsessions in *Hooray for Daisy!* are everyday: preparations for the panto, coffee mornings, whist drives, and coming across one another on the village green in 'Nice Day' to exchange inconsequentialities. How very different, one might say, and how insignificant compared to Oscar Hammerstein II's 'Oh What a Beautiful Morning', but Slade and Reynolds' description of a commonplace middle-class British community about its daily business is accurate, and as poetic, and we should not be deceived by its simplicity. This, after all, is the sort of conversation that may be overheard anywhere in Britain in our own times. The fact that Slade and Reynolds present it without artifice suggests that they employ an artifice all their own. The commonplace becomes a hymn as the weather knocks the villagers hither and thither.

They are excited at the return of a much missed beauty, Priscilla Vernon, who arrives on the 4.48 train and immediately recognises that Milbury is where she belongs. 'So this is Milbury!' she declares, 'and I've come home.' Those words commence her entrance song 'I Feel as If I'd Never Been Away', a catalogue of recognition as she matches her surroundings to her childhood. The atmosphere is wistful rather than passionate. The passion is sedentary; this applies as much to the love songs as to Priscilla's homecoming aria. Everything is under- rather than over-cooked. Compare 'I Feel as If I'd Never Been Away' with a Jerry Herman song from his 1979 Broadway musical *The Grand Tour*, where the heroine has a number 'I Belong Here'. The idea shared between Slade–Reynolds and Herman is more or less the same, the recognition of an adored landscape. In Herman's hands the idea takes flight with a knife clean lyric and strong, basic melody. Herman paints a picture, Slade and Reynolds make vague gestures. Herman has a strong female singer with a voice to shatter glass, and an orchestrator who knows how to make the best of a good job. Enough said.

One cannot imagine Priscilla or the population being happy to live in London, and she – like Geraldine in *Free as Air* – has made her decision as to where her life should be lived. She is content to be side by side with the balding, shy vicar (who manifests again, without a dog collar, in *Wildest Dreams*), the milky Camp coffee and petty concerns of the local community. The very idea of leaving this behind by climbing the beanstalk strikes home in 'When We Are Gone'. What, after all, had the audiences watching *Hooray for Daisy!*? been doing all week, except drinking too much coffee at mothers' meetings, and attending bridge parties? Far from being out of touch, *Hooray for Daisy!*, probably regarded with less seriousness than any of the Slade–Reynolds canon, reflects the sort of life still lived by a great part of the population at the beginning of the twenty-first century, forty years after it was written. Few other British musicals have held up so gleaming a mirror to middle-class audiences who came to the theatre and discovered themselves on stage.

The revue *On the Brighter Side* (Phoenix Theatre, April 1961) had a prominent sketch about Slade and Reynolds, an attack that came towards the very end of their partnership. *Follow That Girl* had not long departed, *Hooray for Daisy!* had recently been seen in London, and *Wildest Dreams* opened in London just as *On the Brighter Side* was playing out its final weeks. One might have expected such an attack to have been made earlier in the team's life, perhaps during the first years of *Salad Days*. The fact that the revue writers thought it worthwhile to go for the jugular seven years after *Salad Days* suggests that even in 1961 Slade and Reynolds had a currency. In the sketch, 'A Resounding Tinkle',[11] Stanley Baxter played Jolyon Blades, a gushing, painfully shy young composer, with Betty Marsden as Dottie Rowlands, a very theatrical actress of uncertain years with an excruciating singing voice: 'I'm Dottie!' she announces. 'In their time, Dottie and Jolyon have been called many things,' explains the tribute's host. 'Rodgers and Mrs Hammerstein; Learner and Lower ...'

He introduces the authors of 'Follow That Salad', as 'the most momentous partnership since Marks met Spencer'. They speak of their new show, 'Let's Make a Daisy Chain!'. Dottie breathlessly explains that 'It's about a magic cow and I play the leading role.' Jolyon takes up the story: 'The action takes place on an island. I wanted to make it the Isle of Man but Dottie thought that would be too suggestive ... Anyway it's all far, far from the mad horror of twentieth century life and revolves around the magic cow whose udders play "Chopsticks" when you milk her.' Since their first success, the narrator explains, 'hits have flowed like milk and water from the pens of Dottie and Jolyon. The first lasted five weeks, the second five months and the third one five years.' 'Well, actually,' Jolyon tells him, 'it was the other way round.' Clearly, at this time Slade and Reynolds were easy targets for mockery, and nobody was turning their works over in search of sub-text.

Wildest Dreams

Lyrically, over and again, *Hooray for Daisy!* hits its bullseye: the gimlet eye on parochialism. This idea is extended in the team's final collaboration, **Wildest Dreams** (Vaudeville Theatre, 3 August 1961; 76). It is at once their most interesting and misunderstood piece. Essentially a chamber work, the four principal roles were taken by performers seen in other Slade–Reynolds productions: beside Reynolds, Anna Dawson who had worked in wardrobe for *Free as Air* and understudied all the island girls, and played a small role in *Hooray for Daisy!*; John Baddeley from *Follow That Girl*, now replacing Denis Quilley who had played in *Wildest Dreams* for the original Cheltenham production, and Angus Mackay from *Hooray for Daisy!*. The sense of *en famille* was strong.

Wildest Dreams tells a story ('wafer-thin' according to one of the first-night notices) set in the dormant town of Nelderham, somewhere in the most middle of England. The very name is a sly reference to *Salad Days*. Throughout its long original run an elderly couple, Mr and Mrs Nelder, booked seats in the front row of the stalls for each Saturday matinee. One only hopes they knew of the tribute Slade and Reynolds paid them, and that they were able to attend the few matinees of *Wildest Dreams*. A young reporter Mark Raven (Baddeley) is sent by a popular newspaper to find out why the town of Nelderham has not responded to a questionnaire. 'What a hole! What a dump!' he declares on arrival. He is determined to wake the place up, 'make you or break you'. Ultimately, in true Slade–Reynolds *plein air* tradition, he submits to Nelderham's charms, and presumably never goes back to his tabloid masters.

The artistic pretensions of Nelderham are centred on the soirees held in Mrs Birdview's drawing-room with its bohemian oddities. One of the most prized is the stammering composer Stephen Bent played by Mackay (one may imagine audiences in 1960 feeling free to snigger at 'Bent') whose ineffectuality only leaves him when he is behind the steering wheel of a sports car. Another arrival to Nelderham is the young schoolgirl, Carol Arden (Dawson), sent to the care of her aunt, Harriet Gray (Reynolds). Harriet is made aware of Carol's burgeoning awakening to the opposite sex. The girl dreams (one of the several wild dreams

19 *Wildest Dreams*: Julian and Dorothy's last long-player (on record, at least)

that permeate the play) of being carried off into the desert by a sheikh on a white camel ('What are you doing? Isn't he *wonderful!*'). The sheikh, in effect Mark, is not reassuring, having turned others into mothers. He obviously derives from E. M. Hull's original sheikh and those beloved of the Mills & Boon novelist Violet Winspear, who penned her torrid tales of the Arabian sands in her suburban bungalow.

Harriet arranges a party for Carol, envisaging a night of pink lights and soft music, only to be greeted by a stomping 'pop' number as provided by the show's title-song. Harriet has a wild dream of her own, imagining a romantic liaison with the nerve-racked Stephen, magically transformed into a figure of almost Charles Boyer allure. In exploring the subconscious, the writers confirm the relevance of Freudian realities feared by the worried mothers in the *Salad Days*' 'We Don't Understand Our Children'. Harriet, of course, would sympathise with them, but all ends in unity, with the two pairs of lovers singing 'This Man Loves You' as the curtain descends. Even this tells us something about the Slade–Reynolds attitude to sexual expression, for it is Carol and Harriet who sing 'This *man* loves you' and Mark and Stephen who sing 'This *girl* loves you', putting the emotional onus on the other person. Emotions are always guarded in Slade and Reynolds, right up until the final notes of their final *Wildest Dreams*. Passion must at all cost be deflected.

Along the way, there is a clever tilt at Britten and the school of folk-song he plundered, when Stephen gives his song-cycle *The Waving Tendril*. The first song describes how 'the poet, meeting his ageing mistress in the glade, looks round at the trees and sees that they are green'. Aside from the effective wit of such material, the score of *Wildest Dreams* has moments of beauty when Slade's melancholia seems ready to overwhelm, not least in Carol's 'A Man's Room' in which, sitting in Mark's digs, she looks around at the discarded ties and shoes and disorganised books. Slade was possibly thinking of home. Carol's thoughts equate as yet another wild dream, of what it is like to be a man. Some critics found this embarrassingly naïve. Elsewhere, in the duet 'When You're Not There' the desolation of apartness, ever present in the team's work, is pronounced, and indeed may reveal to us that this is Slade's lyric, for it is a sentiment expressed again in *Trelawny*'s 'The One Who Isn't There'. Throughout the five London musicals of the team, 'When You're Not There' is possibly the only truly romantic duet about love, although even here the pair seem to be apart, each in their own thoughts. The intensity, married as it must be with Slade and Reynolds, to the every-day, is evident; for Mark, there seems no point in the daily round without Carol.

The Act I finale, 'Red or White' (wine) is another double-chorus, when at Harriet's party Mark gazes on Carol. The double-chorus accentuates the deep personal significance of a changing moment when relationships start to deepen, and is matched to one of Slade's most plaintive melodies. In its extension into the imagined (what is more, the sexually imagined), in its references to art-forms

20 Anna Dawson around the time of *Wildest Dreams*

beyond itself ('The Waving Tendril') and the general absurdity of modern culture, and its acknowledgement that a new sort of teenaged person is emerging, *Wildest Dreams* seems almost over-stuffed with relevance. Carol is a real advocate of female emancipation, declaring her independence in 'Here Am I'. If she wishes (and how unlike the heroine of those earlier Slade–Reynolds musicals) she will be a slattern.

In the more exposed expression of its passions, *Wildest Dreams* is light years away from *Salad Days*, but it never succumbs to the emotional grandeur that drives the Lloyd Webber and international school. It may be seen as a last collision of two worlds, which cannot co-exist. As the youngsters hop about for the 'pop' number, Harriet and Stephen are seen sedately waltzing, as if modernity has not happened. The waltzers are, in fact, dancing their way to oblivion. When *Wildest Dreams* closed after a few weeks, it took with it a body of work more ridiculed than appreciated, but few other British musicals of the future would bother to lift up a glass to certain aspects of British life with as much wit and sympathy.

At Cheltenham, where *Wildest Dreams* had its debut in September 1960, the *Stage* was enthusiastic. Its critic reported 'The presentation is brilliant in its economy', and went on to make the point that 'Dorothy Reynolds is not easy to forget. It is not just her beautiful accomplishment. It is something more, the something rare, that can only be called quality, a haunting thing, that stays in the memory.' R. B. Marriott was less impressed by the London production, but his review is perceptive. Under the banner 'Genteel goings-on in Gloucestershire' he thought it was done 'skilfully, tidily, gracefully, with craft and assurance' but that 'one is very much aware of a lack of certain rather important ingredients – vitality, imagination, theatricality, variety of feeling, gaiety, and wit among them'. This was 'entertainment of careful design with not a hair out of place, for those who like their theatre dull, or find the dull beguiling'. In that phrase 'find the dull beguiling' I think Marriott defines something essential about Slade and Reynolds. The best he could say was that 'There is an atmosphere of lightness of heart and a hint of fun. Purity reigns supreme. Everyone and everything seems totally wholesome.'

Reynolds did not wait until the closure of *Wildest Dreams* to end her collaboration with Slade. After the devastating notices, she told him that they had reached the end of the road, and that she wanted to pursue her career as an actress. This she successfully did, playing leading roles in many London productions, including that of the Matron in Alan Bennett's *Forty Years On*. She was not too proud to accept a modest role (thankfully non-singing) in Coward's *Sail Away*. After seeing her as the headmistress in *The Prime of Miss Jean Brodie* I wrote a letter of admiration. On tiny blue notepaper she replied 'I am so pleased you enjoyed all those musicals. The next time you come to see me in something do propose yourself.' Delighting in her turn of phrase but unsure as to the warmth of this response, I never did.

After Dorothy Reynolds: *Vanity Fair* ✲ *Trelawny*

At the end of their years of work Reynolds left with a sense of purpose; Slade had none. The pieces that followed seemed to have little of the relevance of his work with Reynolds. The disappointment of *Wildest Dreams* was compounded by his involvement with an ambitious adaptation of William Makepeace Thackeray's *Vanity Fair* (Queen's Theatre, 27 November 1962; 70). Parted from Reynolds, Slade was abandoned in an unsympathetic commercial milieu. All thoughts of the *plein air* were abandoned, as were any thoughts of ever again writing a completely original musical: all that followed were adaptations of novels or plays. Never before had he endured a pre-London tour such as that of *Vanity Fair* during which night after night was spent rewriting material which might prove more efficacious than that already tried.

The problems were legion. Staging was in the hands of Lionel Harris, who had directed *The Duenna*, but his work on *Vanity Fair* seemed antediluvian. At one stage he declared he was washing his hands of it and walked out. Slade was sent into the street and persuaded him to come back although 'I rather wish I hadn't.'[12] Unmanageably hefty sets slowed things down. The book by Alan Pryce-Jones (a newcomer to musicals, and he never tried again) took a linear approach to the novel, but the tone of Thackeray's prose proved elusive. The lyrics of Robin Miller were at best workmanlike, with more than a fair share of 'larks singing' and slack rhyming, and sometimes veered on the tasteless, as in the doxies and tarts giving 'The Chatham Farewell'. Time might have been better spent in opening out Thackeray's descriptions of war to the battlefields of Waterloo, taking advantage of theatrical possibility, and introducing a dash of *plein air*. *Gravitas* in any shape or form was missing.

Much of the casting was a mistake. Frances Cuka, who had established a name with her schoolgirl role in *A Taste of Honey*, was another Slade leading lady with limited singing abilities. The leap from kitchen sink to Julian Slade was too much. The real star appeared to be Dame Sybil Thorndike as Miss Crawley, making her first foray into musicals at the age of eighty. She had early on written to Slade to inform him that her voice veered to the baritone. The show suffered appalling vicissitudes during its first provincial performances, and its arrival in London coincided with one of the worst winters in memory. 'Oh my poor cast!' Slade lamented. 'I was so worried about them even getting to the theatre.'[13]

The notices were dismal, and dismissive of Slade's music. This was not unjustified. 'People forget that I'm a scholar', Slade once told me when he was bemoaning being regarded as an amateur, and perhaps, with other collaborators and at a less traumatic time in his career he might have reached to the greatness of the challenge. The truth is that his songs for Becky Sharp were impossibly weak, as were those for Miss Crawley. Beyond two staunch romantic outbursts whose style harked back to the Cambridge musicals, 'There She Is' and 'Someone to Believe In', and a passable attempt at a big dance tune 'The Waterloo Waltz' (and all of these had the advantage of Douglas Gamley's distinctive orchestration) the necessary weight and stature were missed. There is an almost apologetic entry in the score, 'Advice to Women', which strikes home. It has the aching quality of 'The Time of My Life' and 'I'd Like to Be Like You'. The melody had been written for the hero of *Wildest Dreams* but cut before London. *Vanity Fair* was a nemesis. At the moment when Slade needed to show his true mettle he was seen to fail, and this was a blow from which I think his reputation found no way back. When he needed to thunder, he tinkled. In a sense, he was never to find himself again.

The failure of *Vanity Fair* sent Slade back to the provinces. A string of attractive pieces followed, but a return to London had to wait until **Trelawny** (Sadler's Wells Theatre, 27 June 1972; transferred Prince of Wales Theatre, 3 August 1972; 177), for which Slade wrote music and lyrics. Commissioned for the opening of a revamped Bristol Old Vic, the show incorporated stage engineering that showed off the theatre's new gadgetry. Adapted from Arthur Wing Pinero's play *Trelawny of the Wells*, the musical was more successful in its reworking than *Vanity Fair*. In true Slade style, at Bristol the role of Rose was given to an inadequate singer, Hayley Mills, who had to be replaced for London by Gemma Craven, although she too found Slade's top notes unreachable. An air of seriousness was added by casting 'classic' actors Ian Richardson and Max Adrian in leading roles.

Slade's theatrically effective but lyrically weak score marked some return to form, with a few attempts at pastiche ('Ever of Thee'), a doleful aria for Rose ('The One Who Isn't There') and *two* numbers with double-choruses to prove the G & S influence had not weakened, the show's opener 'Pull Yourself Together' and the Act I finale 'Back to The Wells'. Before the Prince of Wales' first night, its producer Cameron Mackintosh took Slade in a taxi to see the marquee above the theatre. Slade looked up. 'But where's my name?' he asked. 'Julian,' Mackintosh replied, 'your name doesn't mean anything any more.'[14]

The last of Slade

The difficulties of early success and subsequent *dégringolade* are known to many artists, and Slade chose never in public and seldom in private to express his regret at the pattern of his career. There was no trace of bitterness in his conversation. I once asked which of his works he liked the best. 'Oh, I like all of them equally,' he said. 'They're all my children.' Beyond his work, he acquired a spurious immortality during the mid-sixties when Hugh Paddick let out his weekly cry in the BBC radio comedy series *Round the Horne*,[15] 'Oh hello. I'm Julian and this is my friend Sandy.' Those who had bothered to take an interest in the British musical were left in no doubt as to who this pair might be.

Even when his writing days were over, Slade remained interested in the works of other composers. In later years he telephoned Lionel Bart, whose career had also stalled, and thereafter they became friends. For a time the prospect of a new career came into view when Tim Waterstone commissioned him to write a novel. He had begun work on the book when at an airport he bought a Joanna Trollope novel and discovered that she had already conjured up the same plot and characters.

When *Vanity Fair* was revived for a few performances in London in 2001 Slade marked the occasion by writing a new song, 'La Vie Bohème', for that most irksome of heroines Becky Sharp. Presumably an attempt at introducing a much-needed showstopper, the Jerry Herman-like number only served to further lop-side an already dysfunctional score. In this sense, Slade was not being honest to his instinctive ability; if the modern world would not take him on as he was, he would put on new clothes. They did not suit. He appreciated the luxury he had been awarded of having had all his musicals commissioned, and knew he could not face the modern way of endless auditioning to managements, workshops, and interminable tinkering.

The past was all. Slade once told me of his last visit to Dorothy Reynolds, when she was dying. The tears rolled down his face. On another occasion I asked who he thought the most important person in his life. 'Oh, it must be Dorothy,' he replied. The label of amateurism that had long been attached to his reputation irked him, for his approach was balanced somewhere between a supposed dilettantism and supreme professionalism. We went together to an amateur celebration of his music mounted in Cheltenham by Humphrey Carpenter (a long-time devotee of Slade's work) and I remember Slade visibly squirming in his seat as one of the less adequate performers mangled one of his songs from *Salad Days*. He knew that this was what his detractors waited in the wings for. At the end of the performance the elderly character actress Damaris Hayman, supported by sticks, loomed up and said 'Oh Mr Slade. How we all loved *Salad Days*.' He must sometimes have felt the weight of that work's reputation too strongly. Asked to appear at some outdoor event attended by Princess Margaret, he was lined up to be introduced. 'Oh yes,' said the princess, 'you were once very famous, weren't you? Who knows, perhaps you will be again.'[16]

Towards the end of his life I wanted to commission him to write a short musical intended specifically to be issued as a recording. 'What could I do?' he asked. I had several ideas up my sleeve that I thought might appeal. What about C. H. B. Kitchin's novel *The Auction Sale*, an elegiac novella of autumnal love set around an old country house? I thought this would bring out all the good things that I knew to be in his mind and music. On a lighter note, what about an adaptation of Dane Chandos's witty 'Abbie' stories. I reminded him that Dorothy had read these inimitably on BBC radio. How about writing a little sequel to *Salad Days*, so that we might at last discover what had happened to Jane and Tim? Had their marriage, made before they had fallen in love in the *plein air* of the 1950s, endured? It soon became obvious that the ability, or perhaps the wish, to write again had left him, perhaps content with the pastorales for which he deserves to be remembered.

Slade's career might have taken a very different turn had his public school-induced sense of duty not stopped him. In early 1955, when he was still playing for *Salad Days* in the pit at the Vaudeville, he received a call from his agent who had been contacted by a young American composer, Leonard Bernstein, then in London for the opening of his musical *Wonderful Town*. Bernstein wanted to meet Slade, and arrangements were made for Slade to visit him at Claridges. The two young men got on well. Before long, Bernstein said 'Do you read French novels?' Slade said that he loved reading French novels. 'Do you know about V D?' asked Bernstein. 'As a matter of fact, I do know about V D,' Slade admitted. 'And *Candide*? Do you know that book?' asked Bernstein, by now warming to his visitor. 'Oh yes, I love Voltaire,' Slade replied. 'Great,' said Bernstein. 'You're exactly the guy I want for the musical we're doing. We start work in a few weeks. Lillian Hellman and you and I will be going away for a month to write it.' Slade explained that he couldn't possibly commit himself to such an enterprise as he had his show in London. 'Your show? What do you mean, *your* show?' asked Bernstein. 'I'm playing for it,' said Slade. 'I play the piano for it.' 'But what do you mean, *your* show?' asked Bernstein. 'I wrote the music for it,' explained Slade. 'You're a *composer*?' asked Bernstein, by now growing angry. 'My agent said you were a good lyric writer.' 'Well, I do write lyrics as well,' said Slade. 'A *composer*?' barked Bernstein. After he had calmed down, the two men shook hands and parted, but not before the American had agreed to go along to the Vaudeville to see *Salad Days*. Which he enjoyed.

As a small boy, the impresario Cameron Mackintosh, who would do so much to change British musical theatre, was taken by an aunt to see the original *Salad Days* at the Vaudeville, and afterwards was walked down to the pit to meet its composer seated at his piano. Aunts seem to have made a habit of taking highly impressionable young boys to see *Salad Days*; those aunts have a good deal to answer for. The experience changed Mackintosh's life. More recently he has said that the audiences for which Slade and Reynolds wrote their works no longer exist. Presumably they are sitting at home growing old. Nevertheless, he made a generous gesture when he mounted a lavish tribute to Slade at the Bristol Old Vic to mark the centenary of the premiere of *Salad Days*.[17] This occasion was the summation of Slade's career. Even Minnie, brought especially for the occasion from the Theatre Museum, was wheeled on to pay homage. As Slade stood speechless and profoundly moved, Mackintosh, one of those most responsible for ending the world of British musicals for which Slade had done so much, said 'Julian, thank you for my career.'

Geoffrey Wright and *The Burning Boat*

Reading critical comments of the 1950s it might be supposed that there was quite a collection of *plein air* musicals of that time, but in essence there are really only two others qualifying for membership, both unlike the work of Slade and

Reynolds. With no published script, no commercial recordings or sheet music, and a life span of a few days, ***The Burning Boat*** (Royal Court Theatre, 10 March 1955; 12) is all but lost, although in 1984 its composer Geoffrey Wright presided over an amateur revival at the Theatre Royal, Bury St Edmunds. Known for his prolific contributions to intimate revue and his best known composition 'Transatlantic Lullaby', Wright was the co-writer with Sandy Wilson of *Caprice* and *Lydia Languish* and was originally to have written the music for *The Boy Friend* for which Wright claimed to have given Wilson the title 'It's Nicer in Nice', and wrote other small musicals and songs for various films, as well as symphonic music. At one point Wright and Mabel Constanduros considered writing a musical about the British at play, *Holiday Camp*, but this materialised as a non-singing 1947 Gainsborough film. The writer Nancy Spain worked with Wright on a musical about her great aunt Isabella Beeton, but the work was abandoned when Wright lost enthusiasm for Spain's work. He subsequently worked on a revision of the musical with the novelist William Sansom, called *Sam and Bella*, which was considered for production by the director Frith Banbury (who had no experience of directing musicals) and even, it was said, by Hal Prince, with Julie Andrews as its leading lady. Wright, dissatisfied with Sansom, once more put the musical back in the drawer, until it was taken up again by a third collaborator, who wrote a new treatment and lyrics for the melodies Wright had already composed; the musical was now to be called *Bella*. This version also fell at the post when Geoffrey Wright the composer expressed his doubts about Adrian Wright the librettist. Such delights as 'Dance of the Afternoon', sung by the madam at a brothel visited by Isabella's wayward husband, have never been heard.

> Too much exposure's held to be unhealthy
> Pigments can play the deuce in sun.
> For the golden rule
> Is a room that's cool
> Where the sun can't creep in;
> A glass of wine
> From a potent vine
> And Elsie may pluck her mandolin.
> So why spend the day in life's dark corners?
> Soho at midnight has no moon,
> Much the safer ruse
> Is to choose a floozy who's
> Had a good lunch, so
> Come do the dusty dance of the afternoon!
>
> Dance of the afternoon, come join us
> Change partners once or twice, who cares?
> To go down the 'Dilly

And pick a filly's a
Pig in a poke, sir,
But *après midi*'s
A rhapsody
Of the pleasures of love but Elsie's bespoke, sir.
The hours between two and five are waiting
What do you think God made them for?
Every Tom or Dick
Likes to kick the prick
And not stick to the rules, so
Keep out the light, let's shoot the moon,
Darkness will fall all much too soon,
Come do the dusty dance of the afternoon!

The Burning Boat is set in Normouth, an imaginary seaside resort on the East coast of England, but, as confirmed by the ensemble in their Act II opener 'Normouth's Having a Festival', this is Aldeburgh, where Benjamin Britten and Peter Pears established their music festival in 1948. The people of Normouth (very few of them, as the play only has thirteen characters) are embarking on their annual festival, inspired as always by their own 'Benjy Britten' Sir Matthew, to whom several young locals bear an uncanny resemblance. (Sir Matthew was a hearty heterosexual.) The violinist, Leo Hartmann, arrives to play at a concert, beginning the play with the reflective 'Where Do We Go from Here?' The answer is, into a romance with the unhappily married festival supporter Jane Manson, plunging her into a maelstrom of doubt and unhappiness until she feels her marriage crumbling and herself 'Swimming against the Tide'.

Swimming against the tide
Fighting something stronger.
Swimming against the tide
Can it last much longer?

Faced with the occasion of the parochial music festival Nicholas Phipps's libretto might have been witty and satirical at its expense, and was to some extent, in the madrigal-like tribute to the festival's founder 'Sir Matthew', in 'Normouth's Having a Festival' and in the festival organiser's frantic patter-song 'Running a Festival', one of the score's weakest numbers, with much effortful Gilbertian rhyming. In effect, the accent is of an emotional domestic drama. The drama is not especially dramatic, but results in some of the score's best songs. Leo and Jane have two fine duets to bring the curtain down on Acts I and II: 'This Afternoon' and 'Now I Know'. Jane's serene celebration of living in Normouth, 'A Quiet Part of the World' seems perfectly to catch the small contentedness that imbues this part of Suffolk and its characters, expressed in Wright's warm, crystalline melodies.

The secondary love interest of a younger generation airman from a nearby American base and Frances Coleridge, daughter of the lady of the manor, prompts more good moments. A love song for Frances, 'Doesn't He Realise?', was a particularly liquid moment in Wright's score. This was utterly conventional, but a duet for the younger lovers, 'Twelve Tone Tune', had the composer expressing their feelings in a dodecaphony that might have interested Schoenberg. The pulsating title-song tells a parable of old Normouth remembered in a ritual about a burning boat, still enacted by the locals and now an allegory of the play's central dilemma. The play seemed to excite nobody, and almost before it drew breath was extinguished, but *The Burning Boat* deserves revival. It would certainly benefit from a new treatment which would include its change from the original three act version into two, especially as Act III is musically weak and reprise-heavy. The revision should benefit by being more wry than Phipps's script for the Royal Court, but would have to be no less affectionate or intent on the plight of its lovers.

Donald Swann and *Wild Thyme*

Wild Thyme (Duke of York's Theatre, 14 July 1955; 52) lives on through a few printed pieces of music, but theatrical historians will be cheered to know that its script, scores and orchestration survive, as does a private recording of the final London performance. *Salad Days*, although the first of the *plein air* musicals to reach London, had been predated by *Wild Thyme*. A demo recording of its songs was made by the composer Donald Swann and librettist Philip Guard in February 1953, when *Salad Days* was still undreamed of. The delay may have cost *Wild Thyme* dear. Coming in the wake of *Salad Days*, *Wild Thyme* was seen as just 'another' little British confection in the Slade–Reynolds style. The qualities of *Wild Thyme* might have been better appreciated if it had been at the top of the *plein air* queue. It was thus unfair of the *Sunday Express* to claim that the show was an attempt to 'cash in on the boom in saccharine simplicity'. It was also the first *plein air* to present as a fully integrated play, having none of the revue elements that had been slotted into *Salad Days*.

As it was, by the time the show opened the *Sunday Express* was quite worked up about it, with the headline 'Wake them up, Miss Toye!' Derek Monsey had run into *Wild Thyme*'s director Wendy Toye ('pretty, gay, invigorating, with the face of a wildly inquisitive bird') at the dress rehearsal. He considered that 'If the British musical is ever to be brought back to life it will probably be her doing.' Toye seemed to understand *Wild Thyme*'s innate modesty. 'I should like more than anything to do something really new in musicals' she told Monsey, adding (quietly) 'No, I don't think you can call *Wild Thyme* a revolutionary piece.'[18]

It was not, but its place in the British musical of the 1950s should not be underestimated. The plot is easily told. On a summer morning at the London terminus of St Padoria Cross the bored railway porter Geoff Morris (Denis Quilley), who longs to become a singer, meets the French opera singer Yvette Leroux (Betty Paul). She is restless and dissatisfied with her marriage to her husband-cum-manager, the pedantic, hypochondriac Seymour Verity (Colin Gordon). Geoff persuades Yvette to flee with him to the Devon resort of Wild Thyme, remembered as an idyll of his childhood. Diversion is offered by a group of knobbly-kneed hikers led by goofy Ernie Walker (Julian Orchard) and family, as well as two antique Devonshire yokels in Act II, and in Act III Ann's elderly aunt and uncle are brought in for what is really the only extraneous song in the score, 'The Beetle and the Butterfly', a number that might have qualified as one of Flanders and Swann's 'animal' songs. An essential ingredient of the piece was Guard's decision to write the script in rhyming couplets.[19]

On its first night *Wild Thyme* was rapturously received even by those who the previous evening had braved the blazing heat of the 1955 summer to attend the premiere of *Twenty Minutes South*. This double dose of the little British musical set some of the critics on their toes: Monsey declared it was 'morgue week in the West End musical world'.[20] Alan Dent for the *News Chronicle* considered *Wild Thyme* 'perfectly preposterous and unprecedentedly dull', and that some of Swann's music 'might have been written by the late Edward German in his school days'.[21]

Milton Shulman noted 'another milestone in the heavy trudge backwards of the British musical. Like *Salad Days*, *The Burning Boat*, *Twenty Minutes South* – what a cortège they make! – it admits that vitality, wit, colour and spectacle are something we must leave to the Americans.' Shulman betrays the paltry quality of his argument by stating that 'An incidental casualty of this trend is the chorus girl'. So *that* was what British musicals needed! Shulman's judgement defines the underlying problem with the critical reactions to the British musicals of the period: the denial to allow the genre to develop into something very different from the American models, to assume its own identity. Shulman goes on to complain that 'the characters are recruited from that strata of society needing little in the way of expensive clothing – railway porters, co-op shopkeepers, hikers, pub keepers and farmers'. In fact, Shulman's wish is to see the British musical ape its American counterpart, or perhaps to drag the British musical back to the extravagances of Novello and Coward, to plunder the wardrobe departments, to reharvest the lost sequins. As for the 'heavy trudge backwards' presented by the spectre of the little British musicals he lists, he cannot see that they represent a new thrust forward; and what, after all, did he think they were trudging backwards *from*? Finally, Shulman grudgingly admits that 'For those determined to support this brand of whimsical entertainment, *Wild Thyme* has more imagination and professionalism than most of its genre.'[22]

For Anthony Cookman in the *Tatler* the production owed much 'to the delightful settings by Mr Ronald Searle. His drop curtain, with its madly reckless birds and snails, is as good as a short preliminary scene putting us in the mood for the play. His later fantasticalities of a railway waiting-room, a seaside meadow and

21 *Wild Thyme* (1955), the first, forgotten greenery musical

a village inn are full of inventions as pictorially original as they are theatrically effective, and it helps with the country idyll [when Geoff and Yvette retire to their caravan in Wild Thyme bay] and the farcical chase that follows to see the moon going to bed in a tasselled night-cap and the sun rising with a straw boater and an eye alive with mischief.'²³

Fifty years on, the sense of affection around the creation of this chamber work remains almost palpable. Central to its character are Guard's rhyming script and Swann's music, romantic, lush, nervously energetic. In the music, too, is Swann's feeling for English landscape, established in Geoff's 'English Summer'. Geoff is blind to the love of his British rail colleague Ann, who berates him for his lack of feeling ('I Hate You'). The station master signals the approach of Yvette. Yvette, *en route* to Birmingham, admires the 'Lovely Day' while Ann can only see unhappiness and a 'Dreadful Day'. Yvette tells Seymour that she wants to escape from their present life. 'Where has your sense of responsibility gone?' he asks. Yvette replies, 'On its holiday' and tells of her wish, 'Even for a Day'.

When Geoff meets Yvette he is immediately attracted to her, tells her he wants to become a singer and of the many beautiful places in England that the train might take her to. Most special are his childhood memories of Wild Thyme Bay, with its painted caravan, rocks to explore, cormorant's nests to be plundered ('Only took one egg, Left the rest'), fishing, and cider and cream for tea – in 'I Can Remember'. The train for Wild Thyme is about to leave, and Geoff and Yvette jump aboard, leaving Seymour and Ann disconsolate and alone. In Act II Geoff and Yvette have arrived at Wild Thyme Bay and are entranced by the place. Even the caravan is still there, just as Geoff remembered it. He declares 'Yet here today, Yvette, I feel inclined, To think there's not much Heaven still to find' and begins their duet 'Heaven Is Here'.

Geoff and Yvette are obliged to share the caravan, but there is never a hint of impropriety. Even Seymour, who arrives in pursuit of Yvette, seems to have dismissed the faintest suspicion of infidelity. In Act III, Ann takes refuge in her aunt and uncle's public house, where the relationships are sorted out to everyone's satisfaction, and Seymour arranges for Geoff to do a telephone audition for the opera impresario who hires him to sing opposite Yvette in Paris. Some of the critics' seemed to agree (but not in the intended spirit) with Yvette's assertion as she reaffirms her love for Seymour that it was 'beyond the realms of all possibility'.

'Heaven Is Here' is in effect the anthem of *Wild Thyme*, Guard's lyric finding Swann at his most passionate. It sets the tone for most of Geoff and Yvette's duets: 'Sold for a Song' (in which they discuss renting the caravan) 'Two Is Company' and their fine Act III duet 'Long Before', a hymn to the pair's conviction that 'We were meant to sing together'. There is much to admire in the rest of the score, including the witty, scampering music for the hiking party and the brisk song and dance ('Kiss Me Like That Again') when Ann and Geoff are reunited, despite its somewhat Saint Vitus Dance quality. There are two other features of *Wild Thyme* that make this one of the best British *plein air* musicals. One comes when Yvette and Geoff retire to the caravan for the night. After the 'Lullaby', with Guard's lyric set by Swann almost entirely on one note, Searle's décor came to life, with creatures popping out of the undergrowth, and the moon rising in the ascendant. Matching this magical *coup de théâtre*, Swann's music rises to a wonderfully Palm Court crescendo (the most that may be expected of his little ensemble: piano, two violins, viola, cello, double-bass, flute, clarinet, piccolo), almost unbearable in its poignancy. It is a perfect fusion of some of the many elements that contribute to the rarified air and airs of *Wild Thyme*.

The second feature also marks out the score as something different from every other British musical of its, or any other, time. In its last quarter of an hour Swann's score erupts with ambitious choral arrangements of some of the principal numbers including 'Long Before', 'Lovely Day' and 'Heaven Is Here'. This is something especially joyful as the work ends, the whole driven along by Swann's frenetic flair. The libretto of *Wild Thyme* mostly sticks to the commonplace, but its style and the sincerity of its purpose are always evident, with Swann's music elevating the whole enterprise on to a different plane. There is perhaps nothing to match the quality of this score in the British musicals of the 1950s; if the *plein air* is exemplified in any work, it is here. Although musically more complex than it might appear, this is a piece that deserves revival. It was Swann's only London musical.

6 Away from Home
Adopted British Musicals

Works that emanated from other countries but premiered in Britain earn their own corner in the British musical's history. Some are more obviously British than others, less obviously 'adopted'. In some cases, their uncertain provenance has meant they have almost slipped out of the few books on the genre. These are not American musicals that were reproduced in Britain; those are obviously American, and beyond the scope of this book. The adopted British musical sometimes had American blood in it, or South African or Australian or Italian, but it won its theatrical nationalisation when it premiered not in the countries from which it in the main emanated, but in London. There is, of course, no cohesiveness in this disparate band of works. They do not form anything like a school, but as a group they offer up several interesting and often overlooked pieces.

Golden City

If London was to welcome 'foreign' shows to first reveal themselves in its theatres, the 'musical romance' **Golden City** (Saville Theatre, 15 June 1950; 140) set a high standard for the post-war period. With book, music and lyrics by the Southern Rhodesian John Toré, the play was directed by the Old Vic's Michael Benthall, with choreography by Robert Helpmann, designs by Audrey Cruddas, and orchestrations by Philip Green. These were distinguished forces to bring to the British musical of 1950, and indicated an intent to take the form seriously. In Benthall–Helpmann–Cruddas there was the feeling that a creative team, already in harmony with one another's work, meant business. There can have been no comparably warming spectacle in British musicals of the 1950s than the Cruddas sets and costumes. Compared to them, the rackety flats and backcloths of some of the most well-attended American musicals were inferior. As a series of stage pictures, *Golden City* knocked *Oklahoma!* back into the paint workshop. Cruddas had been born in Johannesburg, and at least brought some understanding of landscape and authentic culture to the framing of Toré's adventure, set in a Gold Rush Cape Town in 1886.

The plot centred on the romance between a young American telephone engineer Danny Martin (Norman Lawrence) and local beauty Sarie van Selm (Julia Shelley), alongside the efforts of Mabel Page (Eleanor Summerfield) to establish herself in Cape Town as a music-hall favourite. Sarie's sister Anna (Judith Whitaker) and sassy Dirk Marais (Ray Buckingham) conducted a secondary love affair, while a steadying hand was provided by the operatic tones of Tante de

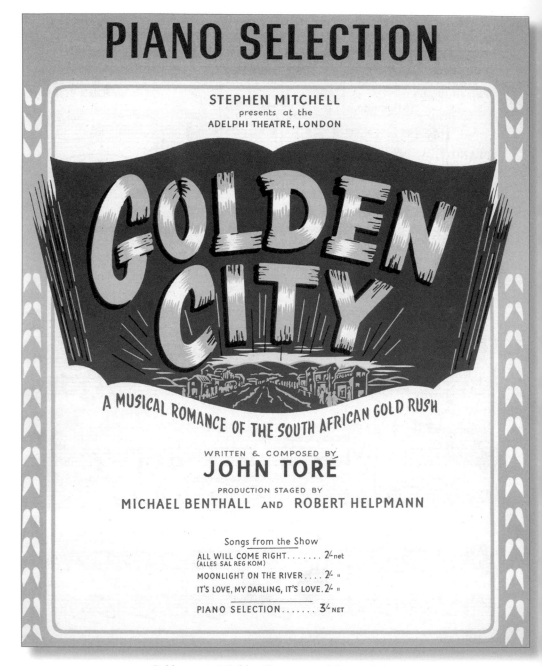

22 Gold or paste? *Golden City*, a taste of the exotic in 1950

Villiers (Muriel Brunskill), guardian of the van Selm sisters. This casting was artful: three handsome young leading men, a skilful leading soprano, a mature older lead in Brunskill (she had sung under Edward Elgar, Henry Wood, Thomas Beecham, and Malcolm Sargent), a broad musical comedy actress in Summerfield, two speciality dancers excelling in modern American ballet (Barry Ashton and Marion Crawford), and a witty dancer from both the classical and revue world, Moyra Fraser, on hand for 'The Girl in the Window'. A Coons' Carnival at the close of Act I, and a vibrant Zulu fire dance were dramatic highlights.

Such features were a faint reminder of the old sensation dramas, echoing the set-pieces so expertly used by Novello, whose final show to use such elements, *King's Rhapsody*, was running at the time of *Golden City*'s premiere. Much of Toré's score leans to Novello, but one of *Golden City*'s misfortunes was to have its score compared to *Oklahoma!*, as in the *Cambridge Companion to the Musical* which notes the similarities between Toré's 'It's a Great Occasion' and the song 'Oklahoma!' – similarities that may in fact only have been introduced when Philip Green made the show's vocal arrangements. The argument that Toré's score was a conscious effort to ape, or adapt, the American model of Rodgers and Hammerstein seems superficial, for there are elements in *Golden City* that mark it very much as an original. Toré is surely writing an operetta, and one with rather more meat than most of Coward's work in that medium, and in his own style.

The *Cambridge Companion* matches Rodgers and Hammerstein's 'People Will Say We're in Love' with Toré's 'One White Glove' but the comparison is meaningless; the theme of the songs is very different, and in the soprano's middle section Toré's soprano has a purely operatic section that would be quite foreign to the residents of Oklahoma. There is no equivalent in *Oklahoma!* to the presence in *Golden City* of the classically trained contralto brought in to deliver a couple of serious songs. *Golden City* has no Ado Annie, and no songs that fit that sort of character. Neither does *Oklahoma!* feature a character akin to Mabel Page, who is given the raunchy 'Gold Digging Digger' (its monotonous melody contributing to its steaminess), and (soon after arriving in Cape Town) 'What More Is There to Say?'.

Of course Toré's songs look to the past, and make the effort to add modern vigour, but this score has its own voice. Mabel's lament (according to *Theatre World* about a 'twirp' who had let her down) may more usefully be compared to Novello's 'If Only He'd Looked My Way', written for *Gay's the Word*. Interesting and visually compelling as it was, *Golden City*'s short stay in London set a pattern for almost all the 'foreign' British musicals that followed. Toré's future in British musicals was cut short by his death in London at the age of 35 in June 1959. That very month his new musical *Charlie Boy*, about Kentish hop-pickers, was scheduled to begin a pre-London tour, but seems not to have happened.

Love from Judy

Less foreign than *Golden City* and commercially successful, **Love from Judy** (Saville Theatre, 25 September 1952; 594) had British Eric Maschwitz[1] as librettist, with an American score from Hugh Martin and his co-lyricist Timothy Gray. Martin already had seven American scores to his credit when he and Gray were hired by Emile Littler for this adaptation of Jean Webster's 1912 American novel *Daddy-Long-Legs*. Maschwitz described the work as 'a young show, gay and happy';[2] he might have added 'sentimental', as probably suited a story originally published in the *Ladies' Home Journal*. As Judy, Littler produced a new star in Jean Carson, who was properly at the centre of the show's popularity. Everything for the show seemed to be in place: a string of happy songs, a colourful Mardi Gras opening, a beefy-voiced male lead, a black female role taking a leaf from *Show Boat's* book, and some bright dancing. Everybody and everything connected with it tried to act American except Carson who remained resolutely British. The play's good critical reception and long run, and the subsequent lengthy tour, suggested that this was just the sort of stuff British audiences wanted, but today the score seems ersatz Broadway, with no identifiable character of its own. Listening to other Martin scores,[3] one finds that much the same may be said of them, a collection of agreeably easy but not particularly interesting songs, but he was much more distinguished as a film composer. In no department did *Love from Judy* show any meaningful progress in the British musical; it diverted, and in doing so satisfied its patrons. Despite its score being American, and its substantial British run, *Love from Judy* did not chance its luck abroad. Having proved that Carson was a great asset to the British musical, *she* was allowed to slip away to America when the show closed.

The Crystal Heart

On the pre-London tour of **The Crystal Heart** (Saville Theatre, 19 February 1957; 7) its sixty-nine-year-old star Gladys Cooper suffered injury during a strenuous dance sequence. The boy dancers dropped her, and the sequence was cut from the production. A photograph of her caught in mid-air looks pretty perilous for a septuagenarian, and the costumes look like a touring production of *Sinbad the Sailor*. A dispiriting provincial reception seems not to have spurred the producers to make major amendments to the play, which was almost laughed off the stage on its London first night. Its libretto might have been by Pirandello or Genet or Anouilh or N. F. Simpson, but was by the American William Archibald, whose original story highlighted the plight of the rich widow Dame Phoebe Ricketts, obliged by the terms of her late husband's will to live out her life on a desolate island attended by her niece and other females. The plot takes off when a boatload of handsome men tip onto the island. Harold Hobson maintained that 'Mr Archibald and his composer Baldwin Bergersen have tried in this play to do

23 Innovative or foolish or made of crystal? *The Crystal Heart*, a famed 1950s flop

something more ambitious than the smug conventionalities of ordinary musicals [...] For myself, money aside, I would rather have written this failure than successes like *The King and I* and *South Pacific*.'

Despite the cackle of critical condemnation and the abuse heaped on Miss Cooper by the first night audience (emphasising her dignity, the *Stage* reported her final curtsy in the style of Marie Tempest), even her *attempt* at so extraordinary a role, the portrait of an elderly romantic somewhere between one of Tennessee Williams' Southern prettybelles and the Madwoman of Chaillot, should have been roundly applauded. After the final curtain had descended among chaos, the show's star emerged from the stage door and, elegant to the last, stepped into her little red sports car and roared away up Shaftesbury Avenue. The audience had apparently been unable to cope with such numbers as 'Handsome Husbands' in which Dame Phoebe explained how a man had asked her to tea and greeted her with leaves in his hair, chasing her across the garden ('his parsnips were lovely to see') until she fell into his soup tureen. It seemed for a moment that surrealism, arriving in the British art world in 1936, had only made it to the British musical theatre twenty years later. What other musical would have chanced its luck with a last-minute love song from the hero called 'D-O-G'?

> D-O-G spells dog
> C-A-T spells cat
> D-U-V spells dove
> So how does one spell love?

The Crystal Heart held its arms open to ridicule, and found its invitation readily accepted. The closing notice went up on the second night, and the show folded after its seventh performance. London's verdict seemed verified when the show was mounted off-Broadway in 1960, once again collapsing at the end of its first week, but *The Crystal Heart* had originality, a voice of its own, and a tone that no other London musical came near. The consistently inventive score offered such delights as the plangent lament 'How Strange the Silence' and 'I Wanted to See the World' with its broad melody and air of sea-faring heroism.

> I wanted to see the world
> Sail on the ocean blue.
> It brought me to you.
>
> Journey's end, with no warning
> Love came suddenly.
>
> I wanted to see the world
> How could I know that you'd
> Bring the world to me?

The heady blend of fierce longing and eccentricity that identified the work

proved unacceptable to the 1957 British musical sensibility. R. B. Marriott considered it 'the most feeble and inconclusive whimsy seen for many years'.[4] Uncomfortable at a suspicion that the absurdities of Ionesco had found their way into
the British musical, did audiences giggle at Dame Phoebe's closing speech? Was
there to be no pity for a heart made from crystal?

> Once upon a time, a few days ago, in the garden at Ricketts Folly into which I had
> come as a bride twenty years before, that garden where butterflies flew up like
> flowers that take to the sky: golden, red as fire, blue, green, of palest lavender, of
> deepest tangerine, that garden in which I had sat in moonlight, in sunlight, while
> woodpeckers pecked the moments away, like little clocks within the ferns – and I
> tried to look into my heart as if it were fashioned of crystal, as if I could see deep
> within its centre the face of love winking its eye at me.

Other adopted musicals of the 1950s

Could the Swiss do better? *Oh! My Papa!* (Garrick Theatre, 17 July 1957; 45) was
successful at the Bristol Old Vic, but London resisted it, despite its sterling cast,
colourful circus settings and routines. An appealing score included the plaintive
'My Pony Johnny', and a title-song made popular by the trumpet of Eddie Calvert,
although for one critic 'To have to listen to that theme song bellowed over and
over again is this reviewer's idea of torture.'[5] Charm, it seemed, could be overdone. Exactly one year later, the only 'adopted' attempt at British verismo arrived
with the French *Irma la Douce*, but this show marked the beginning and end of
any strongly French influences.

There was still, apparently, room enough for the musical as diversion, as when
the American team of Robert Wright and George Forrest, most well known for
their musicals based on the music of classical composers (among them *Song of
Norway* and *Kismet*), came to London with another 'charmer', *The Love Doctor*
(Piccadilly Theatre, 12 October 1959; 16). Their original score to a libretto based
on the medical comedies of Moliére had pretty enough songs, including 'The
Carefree Heart', 'Rich Man, Poor Man' and 'I Would Love You Still' but Wright
and Forrest were seldom at their best when not dependent on other composers. An American production of *The Love Doctor*, titled *The Carefree Heart*,
had headed for Broadway but closed on the road. Starring Joan Heal and Ian
Carmichael, the much reworked British production, with story-book designs
by the French designer Bernard Daydé, opened in Manchester to a mediocre
response, and the company was subjected to weeks of revisions, aggravated further when Michael Stewart was brought from America as a show (not necessarily
'love') doctor, and new directors were appointed. This, according to Carmichael,
'caused both Wright and Forrest to desert the, by then, fast sinking ship and to
vanish in their vast American automobile that they had brought over with them
on a tour of Scotland. We never saw them again.'[6] Carmichael pleaded with the

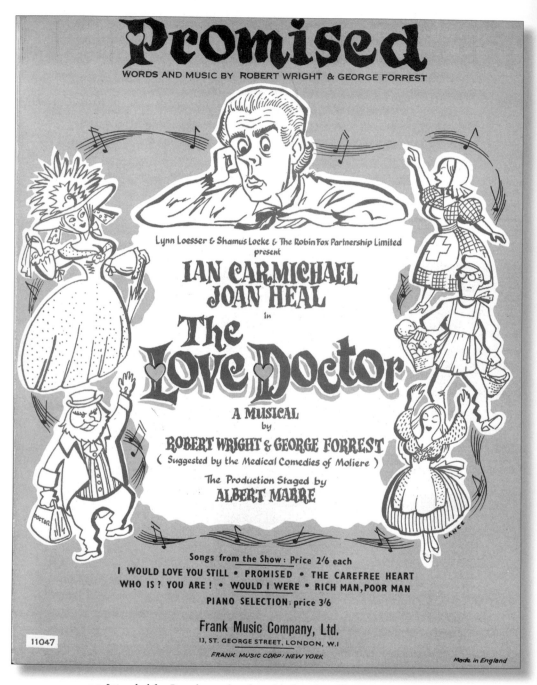

24 Intended for Broadway, abandoned in London: *The Love Doctor* (1959)

management on behalf of a debilitated company not to bring the show into London, but the deed was done. The scornful critical reception caused the management to shut up shop, but the second night's audience rose to the show. *Plays and Players* reflected

> If we use a 'touchstone' system of criticism, then this deserved to fail. But should every musical be compared with *Oklahoma* or *West Side Story*? By such standards, what modern drama would survive after comparison with *Hamlet* or *Macbeth*? The ethics of such criticism seem as unreasonable as to condemn the novels of Nevil Shute because they do not compare favourably with *War and Peace*. *The Love Doctor* was an unspectacular, unpretentious little musical which would have given pleasure to thousands had it not been killed off by the hyper-sensitive critics.[7]

Those who *wanted* unspectacular and unpretentious little musicals were heartened by the Australian ***Kookaburra*** (Princes Theatre, 26 November 1959; 44), a chamber piece of a musical set in the outback. 1959 also saw the first of three Italian musicals by Pietro Garinei and Sandro Giovannini to reach London. ***When in Rome*** (Adelphi Theatre, 26 December 1959; 298) was an undemanding but lively piece meant to help Dickie Henderson Junior to a hit musical. This was the sort of thing that was reputed to be suitable for the tired businessman. It found some response at the box office, but is now forgotten, as are the other Garinei and Giovannini shows that followed over the next two decades: ***Enrico*** (Piccadilly Theatre, 3 July 1963; 86) starring its composer Renato Rascel, and a musical about Noah, *Beyond the Rainbow*. When these productions closed, even after some commercial success, they took their reputations with them, leaving no perceptible trace of an Italian influence.

Adopted musicals of the 1960s

There seemed little reason for the 'new musical in ballet and song' ***The Princess*** (Strand Theatre, 23 August 1960; 44), newly presented in London following its American premiere at the Royal Poinciana Playhouse in Palm Beach, Florida. Its producer/director Ted Kneeland imported a company of seventy for the occasion, its programme promising how

> our various characters are affected by the symbolic qualities of LOVE, BEAUTY, WISDOM, LAUGHTER and TEARS ... and how joy and happiness once lost and replaced by TEARS can be restored.

Another programme note had Mr Kneeland explaining his

> belief that when attempting an art form in the creative field the important fact to bear in mind is the psychological definition of association of ideas. When this is not applied to interpretative and integrated mediums of setting, costume, music and choreography, the resultant lack of harmony comes as a shock to an audience.

Hmm. *The Princess*, a clumsy retelling of the Sleeping Beauty story in which the heroine suffers a life of tearfulness until restored to happiness by her prince, overlooked the fact that its audience might include some sophisticates. The singers and chorus did their stuff hidden in a box while dancers dominated the stage. After a disastrous debut and negligible box-office, the management generously allowed the public in free of charge for seven days, offering them the chance to pay for their entertainment after they had seen it. This ruse was tried in 1922 when Sir Alfred Butt hoped to whip up interest in a no-hoper called *Lass o' Laughter*. For *The Princess*, questionnaires were filled in and studied. 3,979 patrons reported they 'loved' the show, 320 could not make their mind up, and 129, probably making sure they would not be expected to pay, registered their dislike of it. The management suggested that the scheme should be expanded to all new productions with the results publicised outside theatres alongside the critics' comments. The stunt didn't work for *Lass o' Laughter*, and neither did it work for *The Princess*.

Another princess, this time Red Indian, was celebrated in **Pocahontas** (Lyric Theatre, 14 November 1963; 12). This was the work of the American writer-composer Kermit Goell, with an American performer Anita Gillette, making her only London appearance in the title-role. *Theatre World* thought the show would appeal to 'those who have never been to the theatre before in their lives, and those who have not seen a musical for about 35 years'. It found that most of the songs 'have the machine-made air of something especially composed for a provincial pantomime and are delivered as though Robin Hood were expected at any minute. The scenery also adds to this impression, being comprised chiefly of backcloths which look as though they were in Barnstaple last week and are due in Barnsley next.'[8]

This production could leave a lasting impression, as it did on Hugh Leonard. 'Pocahontas will always occupy a special and affectionate niche in my life: special, because it was the most diabolically putrid musical anyone ever saw anywhere; affectionate, because having sat through it and emerged into the Tyrol-sweet air of Shaftesbury Avenue, one knew that never again could life hold any terrors ... as in the case of a passed kidney stone, the worst had happened ...'.[9] It was noted by some that one of the dance routines took place in front of a backcloth showing London landmarks that had not even existed in 1616. An original cast recording was announced but Decca, possibly beginning to learn by experience, did not release it. It was left to a glossy-lipped popular singer of the day, Kathy Kirby, to record one of Miss Gillette's numbers, 'You Have to Want to Touch Him', the only shred of *Pocahontas* that seems to remain.

Adopted musicals of the 1970s

The Americans' bad luck continued with *Ambassador* (Her Majesty's Theatre, 19 October 1971; 86), a desultory attempt to make a starry musical from Henry James' novel *The Ambassadors*. The elements were promising: its director Stone Widney had been associate director on Broadway for *My Fair Lady*; the choreography was by Gillian Lynne; Peter Rice used his pretty style for the sets and costumes. Howard Keel headlined as the stolid, clock-accurate Lambert Strether, sent to 1908 Paris to rescue Jeanne de Vionnet from the clutches of an unsuitable lover, only to fall in love with the bewitching Countess Marie de Vionnet, played by the French actress Danielle Darrieux. Keel's manly presence and voice and Darrieux's Gallic glamour proved indispensable.

Don Ettlinger's book and Hal Hackady's lyrics failed to come up with anything noteworthy in an evening that had embarrassingly unfunny comedy numbers ('You Can Tell a Lady by her Hat' and 'What Can You Do with a Nude?'), a depressing aria for its ingénue Isobel Stuart ('Love Finds the Lonely'), and too many songs that strained to create a Parisian atmosphere. Despite this, there was something irresistible about two of the score's anthems, Keel's 'All of my Life' and Darrieux's 'Surprise' that made one overlook their unremarkable musicality. After the show's failure in London a revised production, cutting the opening scenes set in Strether's home town of Woolett, Massachusetts, but with the two stars intact, was seen on Broadway the following year. After the short run *Ambassador*'s composer, Don Gohman, killed himself.

A more prominent American collaboration was responsible for *I and Albert* (Piccadilly Theatre, 6 November 1972; 120), with music by Charles Strouse, lyrics by Lee Adams and book by Jay Allen. Strouse and Adams had an impressive list of scores behind them: *Bye Bye Birdie, All American, Golden Boy, It's a Bird, It's a Plane, It's Superman!* and *Applause*. All these had opened in New York, but *I and Albert*, a biomusical about Queen Victoria, seemed naturally destined for a British premiere. The play followed Victoria's career from her ascent to the throne in 1837 to the Golden Jubilee of 1897, but the sixty-year span brought its own problems. Albert's early death left the leading lady without a lover for Act II, although the writers did manage to make him last out until just after the Interval, by which time Albert had at least managed to organise the Great Exhibition. Act II was mostly spent with the Widow at Windsor in bombazine. With Albert gone, the spirit seemed to desert not only the heroine but the musical.

Prime Ministers Melbourne and Disraeli were prominently featured, each with a number of his own. Disraeli's 'When You Speak with a Lady' was delivered as he did conjuring tricks. The two men provided some threads through an episodic evening overburdened with costume and effect. As Victoria, the apparently frail Polly James had a personal success, erasing memories of Anna Neagle's earlier impersonation, and had a dashing consort in the Swedish actor Sven-Bertil Taube. The film director John Schlesinger, who had almost no experience of stage directing, oversaw a complex production, and there were reported extravagances such as on a whim ordering the replacement of specially designed kilts because he preferred another tartan. Brilliantly conceived designs by Luciana Arrighi exploited the concept of Victorian children's building blocks and back-projected images. The shape of the blocks was effective, but the musical's shape proved troublesome, and the writers had the disadvantage of no pre-London tour. They found every attempt to rewrite material hampered by decisions that had already been made. Despite a valiant try, difficulties with Allen's play were never satisfactorily resolved, and the Strouse and Adams score was well below their best, suggesting that singing queens might best be left to opera.

There were cultural reasons for staging an American musical about England's Queen in Britain, but economic reasons explained the debut of the American-written **Gone with the Wind** (Theatre Royal, Drury Lane, 3 May 1972; 398). Simply, the producers thought this musical of Margaret Mitchell's gargantuan novel with its so-so Harold Rome songs would be less of a risk in London. They were right. The British production was generally well received, with an outstanding performance from June Ritchie as Scarlett O'Hara, outclassing that of her Rhett Butler, Harve Presnell. Despite her bravura effort (and considering she had just finished playing a chimpanzee in Sandy Wilson's *His Monkey Wife*), Ritchie was unhappy during the London run and found nothing else to do in musicals. For America, Harold Fielding mounted a revised production which sank without trace on its pre-Broadway tour. Trevor Nunn was co-librettist and director of *another* **Gone with the Wind** (New London Theatre, 22 April 2008; 79) with a score by the Californian Margaret Martin. It was greeted with derision from its first four and a quarter hour-long performances. Everyone concerned seemed to have forgotten that Harold Rome had done it all before.

The 1970s offered two other 'foreign' British musicals, the first **Bar Mitzvah Boy** (Her Majesty's Theatre, 31 October 1978; 77). This had music by the Broadway composer Jule Styne, the only score he wrote expressly for London. His collaborators were librettist Jack Rosenthal, adapting his television play, and the lyricist Don Black. There seemed no reason why a theatre that had enjoyed such a success with *Fiddler on the Roof* should not repeat it with another heart-warming story of Jewish life, and this after all was *British* Jewish life. It involved teenage angst and doubt (always of concern in post-war Britain) as Eliot Green in Willesden is prepared for his Bar Mitzvah. He walks out on it but after almost killing his mother with the shock of wondering what she is going to do with the vol-au-vents, faces up to growing into a man. An advertisement for the CBS original cast recording explained '*Bar Mitzvah Boy* will be on the stage for a long time'. It wasn't. Perhaps the story, so well suited to television, shrank on stage, but if it had to be musicalised, it is hard to imagine it better done.

Styne, then in his seventies, wrote some of his best late music, enhanced by Irwin Kostal's orchestrations, and Black's lyrics were convincing. For the show's ingénue, Eliot's sister Lesley (Leonie Cosman), there are two effective numbers,

'You Wouldn't Be You' and (with its unmistakable Styne sound) 'Where Is the Music Coming From?', which probably deserved to be in a better show. The Jewish family dynamics are expressed in 'This Time Tomorrow', 'The Bar Mitzvah of Eliot Green' and as Eliot's parents reflect on their past together the unpretentious 'We've Done Alright'. 'The Sun Shines out of Your Eyes' brought the company together effectively in one of the show's best moments, and Ray C. Davis, in the sort of featured role he made a habit of playing in British musicals, made 'The Harolds of this World' poignant.

The American director Martin Charnin (himself the writer of Broadway musicals) turned down the suggestion that the leading role of Rita Green should be played by Maria Charles, who had played the role on television and appeared in two Sandy Wilson musicals. Instead, Joyce Blair was cast, but was not happily parted. The third-billed Vivienne Martin considered Blair was treated badly by the producers. By the time *Bar Mitzvah Boy* opened in London, Martin's one comedy scene had been cut along with her number, drastically reducing her role, and the credits listed no set or costume designer. Its closure was unmourned.

A few weeks after *Bar Mitzvah Boy* opened, the curiosity of **Troubador** (Cambridge Theatre, 19 December 1978; 76) proved that money alone could create a British musical. The driving forces behind the production were the American businessman Michael Lombardi and Success Motivation Institute of Japan. *Troubador* concerned itself with Courtly Love, not the name of a Mayfair couturier but of a curiously intricate medieval concept of the expression of deep emotional feeling, although not generally applicable to man and wife. Lombardi's libretto defied parody as it tried to convince audiences of its twelfth-century veracity. 'Woman – hath she a soul?' intoned a narrator as the scene transported us to Narbon in Southern France, a state ruled over by the Viscountess Ermengarde. In the opening scene, the young chauvinist Lupus delivered 'The Wife Beating Song', a hymn to the thrills of thrashing women as the chorus egged him on with 'Whack her till it hurts / Not in spurts but in avalanches.' Thrust into prison, Lupus is taken up by Ermengarde, who means to tutor him in the advantages of Courtly Love. The show charts Lupus's conversion to the politically correct troubadour of the time, although even by curtain fall his wife is gazing longingly at him as she agrees, 'If there is love, the hand that strikes is sweet.'

Why audiences in 1978 should have been interested in the grittier points of chivalric custom and acceptable domestic violence seems to have been a question the show's producers did not ask themselves. Lombardi's rhyming ('status'/'afflatus') qualifies him as the William McGonagall[10] of the British musical. Nevertheless, the bilge that was *Troubador* was luxuriously decked out with music by Ray Holder and undeserved rich orchestrations by Ken Thorne. Along the way, Holder pulled off a ludicrous aria for Ermengarde, 'The Loneliness of Power', the pressures of sovereignty causing her to 'take out my needlework and stew'. Wearying of his tenants, the Cambridge Theatre's owner Larry Parnes added to the fun by switching off the heating, further discouraging patrons from

MICHAEL LOMBARDI
in association with
Success Motivation Institute of Japan
and
General Entertainment Investments Limited
present

A Musical to fall in love with

Troubadour

Book and Lyrics by MICHAEL LOMBARDI
Music by RAY HOLDER

starring

KIM BRADEN   John watts

with
SANDRA BERKIN   GORDON WHITING
MICHAEL G. JONES   DUDLEY OWEN
SABA MILTON   IAN STEELE
and
ANDREW C. WADSWORTH

Directed by JAMES FORTUNE
Staged by DAVID DREW

Designed by TIM GOODCHILD
Lighting by DAVID HERSEY

Musical Director   Orchestrations by
DENYS RAWSON   KEN THORNE
Executive Producer JOHN F. OAKLEY
A MICHAEL LOMBARDI PRODUCTION

CAMBRIDGE THEATRE
Under the direction of LARRY PARNES
EARLHAM ST. CAMBRIDGE CIRCUS LONDON WC2 Telephone 01-836 6056
CREDIT CARDS WELCOME

25 'Courtly Love' at the Cambridge Theatre in the 1978 *Troubador*

sitting through Lombardi's work. There is something not inappropriate in ending this reflection on 'foreign' British musicals with such a folly as *Troubador*, for almost all these productions lost money, most suffered critical brickbats and short runs, but all, including *Troubador*, were relatively harmless. Perhaps the only one to offer a fresh perception of the musical was *The Crystal Heart* but, if this had ever been the intention of Archibald and Bergersen's fantasy, critics and audiences chose to ignore it. Adoption, so far as the British musical was concerned, was not always a sensible idea.

Unadopted musicals

More forgotten than these few adopted musicals are those that were promised, held up tantalisingly to excite the (limited) public interest and never heard of again. So fevered was the rush to generate British musicals throughout the 1950s and 1960s that productions announced in the press frequently never got beyond someone tipping a wink to the editor of a journal. At the time of writing, it seems improbable that such a state of affairs could be, but the delights held out to the supposedly eager devourer of the British musical contain some fascinators.

The revue and screen writer Diana Morgan had completed a libretto based on Coward's play *The Marquise*, presumably the project in which Evelyn Laye hoped to make a return to the stage. In January 1955, Vida Hope fought back tears as she informed the press that Sandy Wilson was busy on his new musical about Henry VIII. Jessie Matthews told a reporter she had decided against making her London comeback in a musical by Hubert Gregg about a cockney's rise to stardom, because she disagreed about how the part should be interpreted. By the mid-1960s the announcements for projects that seemed little more than pipe dreams reached flood level. Hubert Gregg was to be disappointed again, because the trumpeting of his musical about Nell Gwyn, to star Pat Kirkwood, came to nothing. Another musical on the same subject, *Nell!*, managed a brief tour in 1970. Bryan Forbes was one of the writers of an embryo musical about Dr Barnardo, to star Tommy Steele.

It was reported that John Morley had written book and lyrics for a Sandy Wilson musical about Amy Johnson which would be seen in the Spring of 1967. A musical version of Dickens' *A Tale of Two Cities* would star Keith Michell as Sydney Carton and Margaret Burton as Marie Antoinette. This one did eventually happen, but with Edward Woodward playing Carton, and no Marie Antoinette. In May 1966 came the news that Ray Galton and Alan Simpson were writing a musical about Noah for the comedian Tony Hancock. A few months later Bernard Delfont commissioned Leslie Bricusse and Anthony Newley to write a musical about Noah. The flood did not come. Harold Fielding would present a musical about Rosa Lewis written by David Heneker and John Taylor. Max Bygraves was to star in a musical about the comedian Sid Field.

Herbert Kretzmer was making a musical of Pinero's play *Trelawny of the Wells*.

Anna Quayle would star in the musical *Navvy*, a treatment of Terry Coleman's book about the railway navvies; this had music by Derrick Mason scored for cimbalon and percussion, and would be directed by Gillian Lynne. John Barry's musical of Graham Greene's *Brighton Rock*, directed by Joseph Losey, was ready for London. Lionel Bart's musical about the Hunchback of Notre Dame would star José Ferrer and open in autumn 1967, when Gavin Lambert and Kenneth Hume's musical about Napoleon's Josephine would also open, starring Shirley Bassey. It is just possible that some of these promised shows might have fared better than some of those that made it into production.

7 Community Singing
Realism and the British Verismo Musical

A separate volume should be written on 'Realism in the British Musical Play'. Part of that volume would indeed be about the genre's attempt to offer an accurate reflection of real life; a substantial part of the volume would be about the inability of the British musical play to do it. In opera we may recognise verismo as a heightened portrayal of a 'realistic' event, as in Giordano's *Andrea Chénier* or Cilea's *Adriana Lecouvreur* or Leoncavallo's *Pagliacci*. Verismo holds up the glass to life, the unflattering light of day, sordidity, pans across the drawing room with its chintzy cheeriness to the kitchen sink. The heightening itself is of course often courtesy of the music, and this is as true of the British musical as it is of opera. A comprehensive history of the British musical verismo would probably trail back to Gilbert and Sullivan. There would surely be someone prepared to argue that *Iolanthe* is a truthful representation of peers or indeed of the late nineteenth-century fairy, and that *Trial by Jury* offers an insight into what went on in a Victorian courtroom, even though the fantastical elements confuse. Looking through the titles of British musical plays presented in London in the twentieth century, their links with reality do not jump off the page, but in the mid-1950s there were definite movements, rather than *a* movement, to rectify the failing.

The death of Novello sharpened the perception of what the British musical lacked; without a comparatively significant figure, the genre's reliance on operetta seemed out of time, only emphasised by the fact that Novello's work had been supremely melodic and successful. By 1953, some rumblings of dissatisfaction of what the British musical had become were sounded. Seeing how important the contemporary was to modern life – 'Fabrics are contemporary; wallpapers are contemporary. Contemporary furniture occupies an honoured station on the first floor' – V. C. Clinton Baddeley considered it

> a curious fact that the British musical play is hardly ever in the fashion. Charming and romantic works are written about Grandmamma and the naughty 'nineties; about the Crimean war, the French Revolution, the '45, the Civil War, and Merrie England; indeed, about any time between Henry VIII and Edward VII, or about Paris in 1910, or Ruritania. Never about our own time.[1]

This, of course, is not quite right (what about such 'modern' British musicals as *The Kid from Stratford* or *Big Ben*?), but the sentiment is admirable, and Baddeley is right to recognise that those musicals set in the 'modern age' (even *The Kid from Stratford* and *Big Ben*) have little to do with modernity, or holding up any sort of mirror to life beyond the theatre foyer. He continues

This was not at all the custom of the old theatre. The ballad operas and the light operas of the 18th century were right up to date, from the sparkling satires and burlesques of John Gay and Henry Fielding to the domestic comedies of Isaac Bickerstaffe and Charles Dibdin. Later the burlettas and extravaganzas indulged a tediously prolonged flirtation with classical gods and goddesses, but when W. S. Gilbert rescued the musical play from that boring convention he recalled it to life by making it once again up to date. [...]

When will someone take the road that has always proved the right one in the past? When will someone follow the great masters of irony, the great observers of the contemporary scene, and give us a musical play with an edge to it? Gilbert could find in a passing affectation all the materials for *Patience*. Gay could satirise contemporary life and burlesque Italian opera in a work set in a thieves' kitchen. [Was Clinton Baddeley granted a prescience of *Fings Ain't Wot They Used T'Be* and *Oliver!*, both of which set their songs in such locations?] No doubt the seriousness of our times has depressed our writers. So many themes seem unsuitable for laughter. But as soon as we submit to that kind of censorship we shall all be on the road to the tomb. If American writers can invent a musical play about their diplomatic service[2] it is surely possible for our writers to find a likely subject in Britain [...] The high class English musical has been under a cloud far too long: it is not likely to emerge from the shadow until someone writes a contemporary work which is a true commentary on English life.[3]

Progenitors of Verismo:
Twenty Minutes South ❊ *Harmony Close*

The first signs that the British musical of the 1950s might be attempting some sort of realism resulted in some pretenders. *Twenty Minutes South* (St Martin's Theatre, 10 May 1955; 101) described itself as a story of ordinary suburbia. It stated its credentials from the start, with 'two typical suburban housewives waiting for the milkman'. Commissioned by the Players' Theatre, the idea came not from its actor-librettist Maurice Browning, but the theatre's musical director, the composer Peter Greenwell, who wanted to write a work that would catch the spirit of those people who every day 'From our suburban heaven / On six mornings out of seven' travelled up by train to their London offices. In the evenings they travelled back 'twenty minutes south' to their dances at the local hall and their prize chrysanthemums and romances. On the train the girls chatted about the latest way to do their hair and the men, according to Browning, complained 'Our wives don't understand us, we're afraid'.

In the very pattern of ordinariness, *Twenty Minutes South* establishes a sort of realism in its opening number; an ordinariness matched with contentedness. Ambition tends to be limited: for the man perhaps winning a cup for his prize dahlias, and for the girl a clean-living boy who will offer his hand in marriage, wear her home-knit cardigans and live uncomplainingly over a garage. These people know where they come from, and where they are going (nowhere much). Browning's play follows the adventures of the Banister family, happy in their suburban bolthole in Addison Park until the advent of an interfering cousin, Kitty Hemming (Daphne Anderson). The Banister sisters are having difficulties with their boyfriends. Susan adores the boy-next-door Roger, but he only thinks of his stringent exercise regime. Jane wants a long engagement and time to assemble her bottom drawer before marriage, but Bob wants her to marry him without delay. Even a kiss before marriage is risqué. The well-meaning Kitty gets these emotions even more tangled, and complicates matters when she becomes the boss's secretary at Susan and Jane's office. By curtain-fall, the outcast Kitty reunites the two pairs of lovers, and accepts a proposal of marriage from her boss. What better conclusion could there be than mass marriage?

To qualify as a British musical verismo, there must surely be the attempt at seriousness, and while Browning sticks to his suburban theme, there is a peppiness and vim to Greenwell's music that obscures the focus. Perhaps what is missing from Browning's libretto is a point of view. We are merely invited to look on an artificially heightened slice of modern life, but so far as *Twenty Minutes South* is concerned this is life with *The Grove Family*[4] with songs. Greenwell's music nevertheless takes us into their world, to which most of its audience belonged. The ensemble numbers are among the best: the office scenes with the chattering girls and musically clacking typewriters, as in 'Typing, Typing' and, when Kitty arrives in the office to take control, 'I'm Delighted'. The choral opening ('The 8.27') and the closing number when the company make its way home ('The 5.27') act as the musical envelope of the show. These and the livelier numbers are sharply characterised, as in 'I Like People' (Anderson's opening number on a railway platform, sung as she was wheeled around on a trolley by three young blades), 'One of the Family' (introducing Kitty to the unsuspecting Banisters), and the frenetic 'Having Ourselves a Wonderful Time'. Only in the show's fortunately few romantic numbers does the mood become soppy. Greenwell recalled

> I wrote what people expected to hear, and I didn't do my own thing. One or two bits in it are really me, but I didn't put myself into it, and I sort of saw what the critics meant. I was writing what I thought were the popular songs of the day. The show had a mambo ['The Addison Mambo'], which was all the rage at the time. I remember Sandy Wilson's agent Joan came to see the show at the Players'. We had written a song for Bob and Jane called 'Certainly No-One In Love' in which they sat in front of the television and decided it wasn't for them, and this we dropped and replaced with 'This Is Love'. Joan said 'You've removed a quality song and replaced it with a conventional pop song.' The truth is in those days one didn't realise.[5]

It may be that Browning and Greenwell were subconsciously constrained by writing a show for the Players' Theatre, an establishment demanding a very particular style, and a certain pertness of execution. Such restrictions did not hold

Greenwell back in the writing of a subsequent Players' commission, *The Crooked Mile*, but that show was never presented *at* the Players'. Its very slightness made *Twenty Minutes South* an unlikely verismo, but it was a piece that showed the way, crucially affected by its gentility and patronising tone to those whose lives it attempted to convey.

Harmony Close (Lyric Theatre, Hammersmith, 17 April 1957; 62) was another trailblazer and, like *Twenty Minutes South* but unlike almost all the British verismos which followed, it shone attention on the middle, not working, class. Verismo in the British musical would almost completely overlook the upper. The show set off for London in 1956 with Dennis Lotis in the leading role, but never reached its destination. The following year a revised production was launched with the less starry ('rugged', according to the show's publicity) Zack Matalon replacing Lotis. The authors described their work as 'That rare thing – a contemporary British musical. Charles Ross, the author and part-composer, has set his story in a London mews and peopled it with realistic characters, talking and singing in the modern idiom.'[6]

The older inhabitants of the mews are represented by the Indian Army (Retired) Colonel Carruthers and his daunting wife, the dull and timid Mr and Mrs Brown, and the retired prostitute Dolly Gander (Rose Hill), the only one of the older guard who seems able to bridge the gap between them and the younger generation. The younger inhabitants are all 'artistic': the tyro novelist Jim Sinclair (Zack Matalon), the ballet dancer Paula Scott (Louie Ramsay), the artist Tony Peters (Bernard Cribbins) and nightclub singer Robin Webster (Colin Croft) who extend a welcome to a new arrival, the hopeful young actress Jill Grant (Jo Ann Bayless). Mrs Carruthers, Mrs Brown and Dolly lament the presence of the young in the mews, labelling them 'Undesirable Elements'. When Mrs Carruthers derides their artistic pursuits ('I'd rather see a girl of mine on the streets') Dolly sensibly replies 'Oh, so would I. The work's more regular.' Artistically, the older women of the mews are reserved.

> We naturally like some books as well
> Which nobody here disputes
> But we'd rather believe they were written
> By the girls in the library at Boots.

With their selected reading from that chemist's subscription library they are confident that

> The only books we know that speak of acceptable social norms
> Are a few of the Angela Thirkells, and *some* of the Somerset Maughams.[7]

We can at once see that *Harmony Close* inhabits different territory from *Twenty Minutes South*. The easily-satisfied suburbans (a nice new hairdo or a giant marrow) seem ridiculously easy to please beside the sophisticated pretensions apparent in London W1, or, as Ross works into his lyric for 'London Is a Village', 'Double–U One / Won't trouble *you* one bit'.

Harmony Close is better at expressing itself than *Twenty Minutes South*, possibly because its librettist's background was in intimate revue, where a sharp lyric could win the battle. Ross had already contributed to *Airs on a Shoestring* and would go on to be the main contributor to two more intimate revues, *Look Who's Here!* and *4 to the Bar*. His aptitude for clever rhyming is at its best when Robin begins blackmailing the rest of the mews, for all have some sort of guilty secret. In the portmanteau number 'Robin's Dream' he imagines what the skeletons behind each door might be, allowing 'fantasy' sequences that show the author and composer at their best. Colonel Carruthers' respectability is shattered as Robin imagines him carolling 'Pale Hands I Loved by Amy Woodforde-Finden – where are you now?' The nubile Pale Hands obligingly appears, but insists that the Colonel's love for her can never be because 'You are white and I … I…' 'That's all right, old girl' replies the Colonel, 'I'm used to the old khaki drill.'

Robin dreams of Mr and Mrs Brown. *Mr* Brown is carrying on with one of the girls in his office, while at home *Mrs* Brown is obsessed with thoughts of Liberace; she tells him 'When you're a vandal and massacre Handel, you handle the keys to my heart.' She invites Liberace, via her TV set, to 'Give me A Flat and B Natural', a line that some percipient members of the audience would have recognised as a sly reference to Liberace's sexuality. Paula, too, is thought to have secret yearnings, imagined here as a passion for rock 'n' roll dancing 'in blue suede ballet shoes'. Thus, the writers are able to remind the audience that somewhere in the world outside Elvis Presley is already at work. The inhabitants of Harmony Close finally get together and demolish Robin's scheme by admitting their secrets to one another ('I Confess'). The emotional entanglements of the play result in the least successful of its songs in which Ross introduces vague romanticism. None of the songs persuade us that either Ronald Cass or Ross is a first-rate composer.

In later years Cass and Myers wrote much material for an increasingly tiresome series of films starring Cliff Richard, in which their work never rose above the pedestrian. Better music from Cass would have strengthened *Harmony Close* (*Plays and Players* considered it unforgivable that the piece didn't have a single memorable tune in it), and perhaps encouraged Ross to treat his 'contemporary British musical' to more serious intent. It is only in the romantic numbers, which are lyrically and musically the weakest, that anything remotely 'serious' is attempted. The wit is appreciated, but such injections of what is obviously revue material undermine the strides that the writers might have made in the development of the 'contemporary' musical that Baddeley longed for. Nevertheless, the play encourages the belief that community singing is better than disharmony, uniting the young and old of the mews in their views on English weather in the jolly 'Lovely Weather for Ducks' and bringing both sides together at the final curtain to agree that 'Life Should Be a Lively Thing', another Cass melody with too general an air about it. One of the best things is 'Goodbye to All That' in which

Dolly considers her former life on the streets, and the dreary interior comfort to which she has now been reduced.

Here, just for a moment or two, real life does seep into the show. The Wolfenden Report, published in September 1957 five months after *Harmony Close* opened in Hammersmith, noted an increase in street prostitution, and started a crackdown by the authorities. There is nothing condemnatory in Ross's lyric, which works because of Dolly's workmanlike attitude to her old way of life; there is regret, but no sentimentality. In this, there is a real attempt at verismo, and within another frame this song might have had more impact. Even so, it remains the show's best moment. Dolly's acceptance of what others might find 'tasteless' is more noticeable, too, because she seems to belong to the older, buttoned-up Harmony Close set, but in fact is more liberal than the youngest of its inhabitants. By her standards, they are mostly prudes. The following year, the revue *Living for Pleasure* had Dora Bryan singing a number by Arthur Macrae and Richard Addinsell, 'No Better than I Should Be', in which a streetwalker lamented her choice of profession. This caught some of the same tone as 'Goodbye to All That', celebrating and indeed immortalising that British myth, the tart with a heart of gold.

Issues for the British verismo musical

Harmony Close presented a collection of odd-balls, but there were no homo-sexuals and no blacks, elements of British society in the 1950s of which British musicals fought shy. None of the Jamaican immigrants who had come to Britain in search of work and prosperity had found a billet in Harmony Close; the trail-blazing immigrants who had arrived at Tilbury on the *SS Empire Windrush* in 1948 had been housed in a vast underground shelter. For all the British musical knew or cared, blacks barely existed; if they did, it was usually as versions of the comical plantation servants who inhabited old Hollywood films about the Deep South. Of course, there had to be the Hattie McDaniel-type faithful retainer in any adaptation of *Gone with the Wind*. More or less the same role was created for Adelaide Hall in *Love from Judy* and Edric Connor in *Summer Song*. As early as 1950 *Golden City* filled the stage with dancing Zulus, and as late as 1976 *Mardi Gras*, a tedious musical by Melvyn Bragg and others set in New Orleans, avoided any significant white–black issues. Elisabeth Welch was worked into Novello musicals as a cabaret turn in *Glamorous Night* and *Arc de Triomphe* but had nothing like a real part; for this, she had to wait for one of the verismos, *The Crooked Mile*, although even here there was no real attempt to tackle any prob-lems attaching to being black, issues that must have cropped up in Soho, and all over Britain, in the late 1950s. It was as if an unofficial apartheid ruled in Brit-ish musicals, confining blacks to variety, cabaret or their own shows, as in the revues *Calypso*[8] (1948), *The Jazz Train*[9] (1955), *Nymphs and Satires*[10] (1965) and the musical entertainment *Cindy-Ella*[11] (1962). The American musical *No Strings*, charting the love affair between a white man and black woman, failed to run in London in 1963.

Some of these musicals played out against the background of the ubiquitous *Black and White Minstrel Show*,[12] a BBC TV variety favourite from 1958 to 1978, and a crowd-pulling success at the Victoria Palace between 1962 and 1972, after which it toured up until 1987. Even since then, there have been attempts to revive the format of blacking-up white performers. Two years after the death throes of those minstrels saw the only performances, in Jamaica, of the essentially British *Battersea Calypso*,[13] a musical by James Bernard and Paul Dehn (authors of *Virtue in Danger*), and Ken McGregor. This followed the love affair between a black man and a white girl, the action switching between Battersea and Jamaica. All is multi-coloured and multi-racial, but, rather in the manner of *The Crooked Mile*, any tensions that exist do not really involve the central relationship of hero and heroine. Like Wildeblood, Bernard and his collaborators accept the white–black relationship; there is no shadow of the miscegenation that threads through *Show Boat*. Although outwardly heterosexual, *Battersea Calypso* barely conceals its gay subtext, perhaps at least unintentional in its praise of London ('Bugger it! It's Battersea!'), but obvious in its hymn of praise for one of Jamaica's glories.

> Banana, banana, Jamaican banana,
> Banana, banana, banana for me,
> A young one, an old one, a hot one, a cold one,
> I like it for breakfast, for lunch or for tea.
> A big one a small one,
> A short or a tall one,
> I want a Jamaican banana tonight.

Bernard and Dehn had already written probably the most daring 'gay' song in British musicals, *Virtue in Danger*'s 'Stand Back, Old Sodom' with its ancient and lecherous predator carolling a handsome young man ('Take your eye, sir, off my fly sir'). Here, homosexuality is played for comedy, the technique almost always used on the rare occasions when gayness crops up in the British verismo. We should reflect on the fact that most of these occasions occurred before the abolition of the Lord Chamberlain; afterwards, gay characters in British musicals become much rarer. Of course, the fey and ineffectual have sometimes slipped unwillingly into this category. Coward's effete young men of the Green Carnations in *Bitter-Sweet* must have been recognised in the 1920s, but it is not until the 1950s that the gay character becomes more 'obvious'.

If it was to reflect contemporary life, the British verismo musical didn't seem particularly interested: only *Fings* put up a character that might easily be identified. Wallas Eaton's interior decorator was flagged up by his campness, a characteristic that threaded through almost all the rest of the gay characters in British musicals, although none of these belonged to the verismo. In the 1950s *Salad Days* had its hysterical dress designer Ambrose ('I'm drained of all emotion. I'm a husk'), and *Valmouth* the emotionally-attached sea-faring Jack Whorwood and Dick Thoroughfare. Equally camp were the two Marriage Bureau managers in the 1964 *Instant Marriage*, a slap-happy 'Soho' musical that tried to cross low-life with a Brian Rix-type farce. When it came to blacks and gays, the British verismo would have none of it, or at least not much. Prostitution, on the other hand, was prominent in *Fings* and *The Crooked Mile*, usually played for laughs, with perhaps a catch of sentimentality to colour the palette.

Expresso Bongo

The starting pistol for the true British verismo was probably fired by **Expresso Bongo** (Saville Theatre, 23 April 1958; 316), the first sustained sour note in the British musical. In 1958 the critic J. W. Lambert wrote of 'that expert operator Wolf Mankowitz turning his sharp eye on some of the shoddier aspects of contemporary success – the teenage rock 'n' roll king, his seedy agent and their seedier milieu. With Paul Scofield turning on his most dreadful, strangely threatening, needling whine as the agent all should have been well. Some of the targets were well thumped, like the bongo – especially current Tin Pan Alley religiosity. Yet somehow the piece missed fire: in a field where professionalism is all, a touch of our old amateurish nonchalance seemed to have crept in, a slackness in timing.'[14]

The piece was compiled by four writers who would go on to have substantial careers in the genre. The book was based on his original story by Wolf Mankowitz, and Julian More, the music by David Heneker and Monty Norman. Permutations of this collaboration, often involving other writers, carried through to the mid-1980s. One wonders what sort of work *Expresso Bongo* would have been if either Heneker or Norman had been given sole responsibility for its music? It is, after all, with the composer that the true 'voice' of the musical is at its most intense. This may count as an imponderable, but future works written after Heneker and Norman parted company suggest that the sharpness of their first collaboration would have been even sharper (Norman) or less sharp (Heneker). The fact that neither Heneker or Norman claimed sole responsibility may have contributed to the work's accessibility in the climate of late 1950s Britain. The fact that both their names appeared as its composers probably worked against either of their names becoming what is laughingly called 'household'. The British public had enough problems remembering the name of even one composer, let alone two.

Of what did *Expresso Bongo*'s sourness tell? The setting seemed to be the real, modern, up-to-the-moment Britain, or at least Soho, and that ill-defined territory Tin Pan Alley. By the end of the 1950s the show-business milieu as the groundsheet for a musical had of course been done to death, and there were bound to be comparsions with *Pal Joey*, another piece that favoured the sour over the sweet. A down-at-heel chancer, Johnnie (Paul Scofield), looks to the Hit Parade to make his fortune, taking up Herbert Rudge, played by James Kenney, already expert at portraying troubled youth from his title-role in the British 'B' film *Cosh Boy*, and transforming him into pop-singer Bongo Herbert. A constant in Johnnie's life is the stripper Maisie King (Millicent Martin), a cue for the only 'show-within-the-show number' 'Spoil the Child', very much in the style of Coward's 'Won't You Stick a Pin in My Balloon?' in *Ace of Clubs*, and some of the chorines' numbers in *Pal Joey*.

Beyond this, *Expresso Bongo* is notable for its originality of theme and treatment. The romances, between Johnnie and Maisie, and Bongo and a rich woman of uncertain years, Dixie Collins (Hy Hazell), are not celebrated with love songs; such moments become laments: Dixie realising that age is not on her side ('Time'), and Maisie trying to explain where she stands with Johnnie in 'Seriously'. Rapture is not at the forefront of this agenda, although eventually Maisie is allowed to believe she may be in love with Johnnie ('I Am'). The hearts, with the exception of Maisie and, hopefully for Maisie's sake, Johnnie, are hard. This is a world populated by cunning music agents in sordid little rooms up staircases in Soho, acquisitive hangers-on, empty-headed debutantes, sleazy night-club owners, and Bongo's lamentable family, good reason for him to escape into an apparently glamorous world. In 'The Shrine on the Second Floor' the writers achieve a supreme irony; as Bongo emotes the sugar-sweet lyric, we have prior knowledge of the real background from which he has come: the slatternly mother, the wastrel father, the bug-ridden slum.

In 'Nothing Is for Nothing' it seems to be Norman speaking through Johnnie's understanding of how the world works. Dixie is perfectly willing to help a handsome young buck up the ladder of success providing he 'does his bit' in the free board and lodging she offers. Mr Mayer, an old hand on the lower rungs of the pop ladder, knows the benefits of giving record promoters backhanders. Johnnie looks to the world beyond. This is territory that we may imagine being inhabited by Kurt Weill and his collaborators, and throughout *Expresso Bongo* the satire runs alongside a flavour of ballad opera, with moments when we feel that the characters are giving us points of view about the human condition. Tellingly, when some of the leading characters get together to insist 'He's Got Something for the Public' they each let us know that Bongo also has 'that extra something special for me'. Selfishness, the need to leapfrog over the person in front, is all, and these are sentiments that we find again in Heneker and Norman's *Make Me an Offer*. By that time, however, the message is diluted; more than a little charm has been introduced to weaken the vinegar. Johnnie would never have been able to put in an appearance in *Make Me an Offer*, although he might have resurfaced a couple of decades later, for Johnnie is surely a prototype yuppy, although a yuppy who never achieves or manages to climb the greasy pole of success.

At the beginning of the British verismo, *Expresso Bongo* was setting a standard that would prove exacting for its followers. It lured a highly respected modern actor from the 'straight' side of the profession into its leading role, putting him alongside others (Martin, Hazell) who were practised hands in musical theatre, under the direction of William Chappell, whose long career had given no hint that he might be able to pull together such a ground-breaking piece. The success of *Expresso Bongo* was measured by the fact that it was subsequently made into a film, but one that has Laurence Harvey all at sea in the role to which Scofield had brought such distinction. The film also throws out almost every note of the score, leaving only 'The Shrine on the Second Floor' to be sung by the Bongo (Cliff Richard) as a straight number, effectively negating its parodic effectiveness. Denied a top-flight cast and its songs and a generous supply of all-round talent, *Expresso Bongo* turned into what it may have been in danger of becoming on stage, a black and white 'B' movie. When *Irma la Douce* was made into a film, the producers again decided that the best way to deal with a stage musical was to cut the songs. Heneker was at least fortunate in that Hollywood condescended to keep much of the score of *Half a Sixpence*.

The seedy and unglamorous was seen again when, three months after the premiere of *Expresso Bongo*, its writers presented their adaptation of the French *Irma la Douce*, with the original music of Marguérite Monnot and a translated and redressed book and lyrics by More, Norman and Heneker. *Irma la Douce*, undoubtedly verismo with its prostitute leading lady, low-lifes, prison scenes and alley-way Parisian argot, although snatched from the French, identifies absolutely with the first good works of those British writers, but has no qualifications as British verismo. However, it was the first musical attached to British verismo to put sex at its centre. In *Twenty Minutes South* sex is reduced to settling down with slippers, pipes and angora cardigans (for the women); in *Harmony Close* the satirical elements keep it at bay; in *Expresso Bongo* the reality of it has been broached. *Irma la Douce*, with its one female character a French girl of the streets, could be more concentrated in its approach, and the milieu of the adaptation was thoroughly convincing in the staging by one of British theatre's most prominent young directors, Peter Brook. The very serious intent of More, Norman and Heneker that made *Irma la Douce* so vibrant is all the more surprising when one considers much of the team's later work.

Fings Ain't Wot They Used T'Be

The roughest diamond, and perhaps the truest of the British verismos **Fings Ain't Wot They Used T'Be** (Theatre Royal, Stratford East 17 February 1959 for 63 performances. Revised version 22 December 1959; Garrick Theatre, 11 February 1960; 897) had the best of the titles. *Expresso Bongo* told you nothing except that, in its milk-bar way, it was modern. *The Crooked Mile* might have been a musical about Blackpool, *Johnny the Priest* a musical about an unlikely ordination, but there could be no mistake about *Fings*, which told it as it was. Things *were* no longer as they had been, either in modern Britain (to be more precise, Soho) or in the theatre. The thieves' kitchen of eighteenth-century ballad opera was back, its ceilin' comin' dahn, and now urgently in need of a limp-wristed interior

26 Judith Bruce with the boys in the 1961 Australian production of *Irma la Douce*

decorator to tart the place up and make it 'Contemporary'. The prostitutes that had hovered in earlier British musicals made no bones about it, still trying to find punters in the street, but aware that winds of change were blowing them indoors. In September 1959 Fenella Fielding sang a Sandy Wilson song 'Outdoor Girl' in the revue *Pieces of Eight*: a prostitute's lament for the loss of the outdoor life. Her attitudes and regrets show no advance on those of Dolly Gander in the 1957 *Harmony Close*.

In *Fings* the prostitutes, despite the efforts of its authors and director Joan Littlewood who sought an authentic recreation of Soho low-life, really belong to the same world as Wilson's harlot, although the bitter-sweet atmosphere of Wilson's lyric eludes the lyrics of Lionel Bart. If *Fings'* author Frank Norman had had his original way, Bart or any other composer would never have been involved, for what Norman handed in at the stage door was a straight play, not a song in it. Littlewood saw things otherwise; she wanted music, a bit of a knees-up, the sort of stuff that the Stratford audiences (or an element of it) might discover on a night out at the Belt and Braces. The result was a musical of sorts, perhaps a play with a good deal of music, perhaps something akin to verismo's beginnings in *The Beggar's Opera*, perhaps a hybrid.

Decca produced the original cast recording, one of very few to be done 'live' on stage. The result was not very satisfactory, and probably not Decca's fault. For a start one can imagine Littlewood putting her head round the dressing-room doors before curtain-up and saying 'They're recording the show tonight, but don't change anything.' It's a difficult listen. With the exception of the title-song the score is dull, and anyway the tune is too much like Rodgers and Hart's 'Mountain Greenery'. 'Contempery' is neat, and never more effective than in a version recorded by Bart himself. 'G'night Dearie' is standard stuff, written for an earlier Bart show *Wally Pone*. If *Fings* had real 'street cred' it was not because of Norman or Bart or Littlewood, but Littlewood's actors, her 'nuts': Barbara Windsor, Toni Palmer, Yootha Joyce, Glynn Edwards, Edward Caddick. Of course, Stratford believed them to be real people because in their modest way they were a new breed of actor, non-acting actors, most of whom had never walked past the doors of the Royal Academy of Dramatic Art in Gower Street. Not only were they very 'unactory' actors, but they were also non-singing actors. The warbling leading lady of *Twenty Minutes South* or *Harmony Close* belonged to a different age. She would probably have turned up for rehearsals of *Fings* in a Debenham and Freebody two-piece and chiffon scarf, and been horrified by Littlewood's efforts to help actors get at the truth.

Those antics encouraged the pursuit of truthful acting (whatever that might be), and in its way *Fings* offered it. The impression given is that there is no dressing-up of how things are out there in 1959 Soho. There is none of the sanitisation that affects *The Crooked Mile* or *Johnny the Priest*: *Fings* serves up raw. What *Fings* triumphantly achieved was capturing the moment, fixing itself at the fulcrum of change, with what seemed almost a certificate of reality. Littlewood had given the public exactly what was suited to the time, a work that almost perfectly *expressed* the period, just as *Salad Days*, mysterious as it may seem, had captured its own. The difference between the Slade and Reynolds' piece and *Fings* is that *Fings* was a musical token of the turn away from middle-class convention that had ruled so long in British theatre, straight or musical.

Other verismo musicals are less red-blooded than *Fings*, but they mostly have a social predicament at their core. *Fings* has none. *Expresso Bongo* makes a point of at least glancing at social responsibility, at what happens when integrity goes out of the window, the shallowness of fame; *The Crooked Mile* examines the problems of allegiances that spill over from the responsibilities of affection, and the inescapable pull of place; *The Lily White Boys* makes no secret of its parable nature, how climbing the social ladder and fitting in with society is in itself corrupting; *Johnny the Priest* wants to send you away wondering how on earth we will deal with rebellious youngsters who find no foothold in society. In each of these, and other works that might just as well be labelled verismos (there are elements of verismo in *Blitz!* and *Maggie May* may well be another contender), the characters have something to think about, options, conflicts rubbing at their consciences. It seems to me that the qualities of *Fings* spring from the fact that it simply *is*, simplistically representational of what it seeks to recreate on stage. It remains a matter of personal taste and judgement as to whether the show itself, within the context of the work other verismos were attempting, is their match. It may be a masterpiece, but then Leonardo da Vinci's *Mona Lisa* leaves me cold. On the other hand, I have been moved by looking at the work of much inferior, almost unknown, painters. Perhaps I came upon Mona Lisa at the wrong moment, the wrong time of day, the wrong time of life. Coming upon musicals is subject to the same chances. Perhaps I feel uncomfortable because what *Fings* offers as real life strikes me as patently artificial, just another theatre trick. It must be said, too, that its particular trick was never really repeated; with her next Stratford East musical, *Make Me an Offer*, Littlewood went respectable. None of the characters who inhabit *Fings* find a place in its world. Perhaps I am searching for a reason just enough to justify what probably amounts to a dislike of the piece. This probably puts me in the wrong, and disqualifies any lukewarm appreciation I have for *Fings Ain't Wot They Used T'Be*. As with every other production mentioned in this book, the reader's views will be as valid as mine. We are each entitled to our view. I admit that *Fings* may be the masterpiece of the 1950s, and king of the verismos, but I do not much care for it. The title is unbeatable, and the feeling the work engendered in its time must have been electric. The effect it had was more in wiping out what had gone before than in establishing any influence over what was to come.

The Crooked Mile

The BBC TV magazine programme *Tonight* marked the opening night of **The Crooked Mile** (Cambridge Theatre, 10 September 1959; 164) by inviting the singer Marion Grimaldi (who was not in the show) to sing a number that had already been cut from it, 'The Heart of London'. *Theatre World* was reserved in its praise of the 'two Peters' collaboration.

> A fury of discords by Peter Greenwell thrusts us into *The Crooked Mile* of Soho, a new 'musical' in which rival gangs present a pattern which threatens to become hackneyed. Many of Peter Wildeblood's characters have likeable human traits and his lyrics have point and there is humour in many of the situations. The work owes something to Theatre Workshop's Soho collation *Fings Ain't Wot They Used T'Be* and something more to Lysistrata and the borrowed parts are not very well integrated. People who saw Miss Millicent Martin's performance in *Expresso Bongo* – a more satiric and a more melodious affair – will need no urging to go and see her in *The Crooked Mile*, which allows her more and bigger opportunities. Her performance as Cora, a young hireling who collects gardening paraphernalia against retirement, is really something. Mr Jack MacGowran, remembered for good work in sterner stuff, appears unprofitably as a very gentle grafter for whom crime has not paid.[15]

27 Elisabeth Welch and Jack MacGowran making a paradise of Soho in *The Crooked Mile* (1959)

Reading *Theatre World*'s guarded welcome, it should be remembered that this journal frequently referred to 'tasteless' elements when shows introduced such aspects of real life as prostitution, homosexuality, sex outside marriage and single mothers. In 1960 it complained of the 'tasteless storyline' – a pregnant, unmarried princess in the American musical *Once upon a Mattress*. The *Stage* considered *The Crooked Mile*

> a great stride forward for British musicals. It was *Expresso Bongo* which first gave the hint that the British musical was at last absorbing those issues which the better American productions have been drumming into us for so long. Now an immense stride forward has been made with *The Crooked Mile* at the Cambridge. It has the pace, zest and vitality so lacking in the vast majority of home-grown pieces. To many, perhaps, this may be a retrograde step. The British musical stage has normally been all sweetness and light. Every character is either thoroughly 'nice' or wildly farcical, and there are no doubt those who think that *The Crooked Mile*, peopled almost entirely with small-time crooks and prostitutes, is aping the wrong aspects of the trans-Atlantic scene. But the fact must be faced that, if we want all of those qualities which go to make up an exciting musical, the seamy side of life provides the best material.

The Crooked Mile was the loudest proclamation of the new verismo, with the highest production values. This is the *Aida* of the verismo musicals, everything about it bigger than its fellows. The bigness extended to the score. Credit here is due to the adventurous spirit of the Players' Theatre, for whom Peter Greenwell was resident musical director. Greenwell and Peter Wildeblood met in 1958, the year Wildeblood published his novel *West End People*, and Greenwell agreed that this would be adapted for their first collaboration. *Theatre World*'s 'Looker-On' explained that

> Mr Wildeblood wanted to write about the contemporary scene and he has a theory that ordinary everyday folk 'don't work' when they break into song. According to him, characters in a musical must be exotic or removed in time and place. They must belong to another period or be set abroad. Even so, Mr Wildeblood still wanted this first musical to be about people of today, living in this country.

Wildeblood insisted that 'Soho is the only kind of contemporary myth we have. One can afford to be realistic about Soho and still produce unusual characters and an environment quite out of the ordinary.'

The Crooked Mile used Soho, sugaring the pill of prostitution, pulling comedy from the business of selling sex on the streets – even though Cora tells the girls that a new law about to come in will mean that they have to work indoors but fails to point out that its author had been instrumental in bringing about such changes. The show exulted in types, and was unafraid to stand sentimentality beside the earthiness. This was Soho made up to be what it probably never was.

Its hero, Jug Ears, is ageing and ineffectual and not physically attractive. Jug Ears is also on the wrong side of the law but he, like Cora the street-girl, has a heart of gold. In their way, these characters are children. But we have to scrape at the surface of *The Crooked Mile* to discover what it really is. Isn't it a story of middle-aged love (always difficult on stage) mixed up with a Gilbertian plot about misunderstandings about a child's age? There isn't even any love interest; only Elisabeth Welch foolishly *thinking* she is in love. (She is, but not with the person she thinks she is in love with.)

What elevates *The Crooked Mile* is its positive philosophy, the belief that aspirations may be unreachable but that happiness may be got from simply staying put, with being satisfied with what you've got, being content with where you are and who you're with. The Land of Oz is in the back yard of Soho. This is what makes Wildeblood and Greenwell's best song of the score, 'Free', effective; freedom, Wildeblood tells us, is not about just walking through a door. Perhaps the message of the show is that it's fine to fail. It's unlike the message given out by *Expresso Bongo*, whose reputation has outstripped that of *The Crooked Mile*. In *Expresso Bongo*, failure leads to sourness. In *The Crooked Mile*, not moving on becomes the only inevitability. Thus, when the chorus bellows the last lines 'Suddenly you feel you want to stay' we are stirred by the lack of ambition. These people will keep where they are because they see Soho as a ready-made Paradise. Wildeblood and Greenwell have granted Soho mythological status.

The power of *The Crooked Mile* is also dependent on the fact that this is a substantial piece of theatre, on a much bigger scale than any of the other British verismos. Much of this is Greenwell's achievement. For a moment it seemed there would be no going back for the British musical, for Greenwell brought a new confidence to the genre. Could this be the same composer who had written little musicals, polite and diverting, for the Players' Theatre? Could this be the man who had written *Twenty Minutes South*, the British musical's tribute to the drabness of suburbia, doing for Charlton what Bernstein had done for New York in *On the Town* and *Wonderful Town*? Where *Twenty Minutes South* is skittish and coy, *The Crooked Mile* is a musical with muscle, blazing its banner of verismo with a splendour that none of the other verismos of the period can match. The best of the score suggests a grandeur and depth that eludes almost everything else in the British verismo musical, and almost everything else in the whole canon. Sweet Ginger's 'If I Ever Fall in Love Again' is at least a minor classic. Welch complained to Greenwell of its 'Chinese harmonies' but this suited her voice, and MacGowran, less stable in his singing, welcomed the fluidity these harmonies allowed.

The Players' Theatre proved its serious intent to further the cause of the British musical in its support of *The Crooked Mile*. Its production values could not have been higher. The distinguished French director Jean Meyer was brought over from the Comédie-Française; designer Reginald Woolley had a natural sympathy for the Soho sets; and the glorious orchestrations were by Gordon Langford. The casting was top-notch, with acknowledged stars in Millicent Martin (the prostitute Cora) and Elisabeth Welch (Sweet Ginger), as well as the noted Irish actor Jack MacGowran as Jug Ears. Welch and Martin had fabulous entrances. Welch was announced by Jug Ears' gang and made her way down some stairs onto the stage (a perfect invitation to applause), and Martin burst into Sweet Ginger's ironmongery establishment and shouted 'Shop!' Wildeblood didn't bring issues to the fore, but accepted them without fuss. Cora speaks of money she's earned from 'that divorce-job in Brighton'. It is Sweet Ginger's dissatisfaction with Jug Ears, her devoted but dull dog of a not very satisfactory boy friend, which deludes her into thinking a handsome hunk wants to take her to America. One of Jug Ears' gang brings her down to earth.

> **Squeezy:** You belong here, Sweet Ginger.
> **Sweet Ginger:** I could have belonged there just as well, given half a chance.
> **Squeezy:** Ah, but would they have given you half a chance? Them Yanks can be very funny, you know, about … well, foreigners. It's not like here, you know, where you either like a person or don't, and it don't matter tuppence about what colour they are.
> *(Sweet Ginger's hand goes up to her face.)*
> Say what you like about Soho, that's one good thing in its favour. *(A pause)* Sweet Ginger?
> **Sweet Ginger:** I was just thinking. All the years Jug Ears and me have been together, he's never even mentioned it.
> **Squeezy:** Bless your heart, I don't suppose he's even noticed.

Squeezy suggests Jug Ears' innocence, and Sweet Ginger betrays her own. Neither of them, it seems, has ever thought about colour. It is merely a difference. It may be too easy to detect in this a coded message from Wildeblood, as in Jug Ears' hymn 'Free'. Of course Jug Ears is singing of his time in prison, when

> You look through the bars
> And tell yourself that one day
> You'll fly away, up through the stars
> As free as the wind you'll be, as free as the air
> But deep down inside you, you know you belong right there.

It is too easy to discover something other, something more meaningful, in Wildeblood's hymn to freedom; to what use is Wildeblood putting his lyric? There were those who felt the whole had been too washed over with sentimentality, and the script lacks the sort of steeliness that Wildeblood might have been expected to bring to it. The green-fingered Cora is storing up gardening implements against her retirement, and in her introductory song 'Horticulture' goes for a string of innuendos which would surely have passed Gertrude Jekyll by. It's a long slow wink at the audience, but makes *Harmony Close*'s 'Goodbye to All That' seem almost forthright.

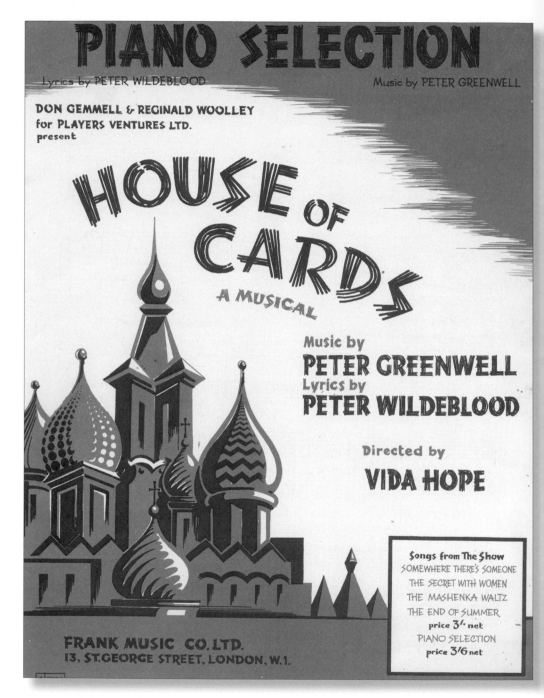

28 Russian adventure misfiring in Wildeblood and Greenwell's *House of Cards* (1963)

Although by the time of *The Crooked Mile* some of his notoriety had subsided, Wildeblood's personal history is reflected in his play. A tyro playwright, in 1954 he was working as a journalist when he was sentenced to 18 months imprisonment for homosexual offences in what came to be known as 'The Montagu Case'. In the dock, Wildeblood admitted to his sexuality, and in 1955 published *Against the Law*, an autobiographical account of the controversy and an explanation of what it was like to be a homosexual. The book also served as a powerful indictment of prison life. The *Daily Telegraph* considered it 'a very courageous, honest book which can do a great deal of good, even to the most prejudiced'. Wildeblood's honesty, his argument that 'the right which I claim for myself, and for all those like me, is the right to choose the person whom I love' had a profound effect on the British attitude to homosexuals. He was asked to brief the House of Lords, and gave evidence to the Wolfenden Committee, thus contributing to the reformation of the law in 1967. Wildeblood opened an afternoon drinking club in Soho where his clientele included prostitutes, pimps, gangsters and homosexuals. He began writing a book a year: *A Way of Life* (1956) based on the exploits of his club; *The Main Chance* (1957) and *West End People*. Wildeblood brought the openness, this awareness of human frailty that permeated his life and work, to *The Crooked Mile*, and with Greenwell found musical expression for it in this one show.

The next Wildeblood–Greenwell musical, *House of Cards*, removed itself from modern life by being a pleasant period piece based on a Russian play, with a much more apparently 'old-fashioned' musical comedy score than *The Crooked Mile*. First produced at the Players' Theatre before being revised and sent hastily into the West End, *House of Cards* caused barely a ruffle, and effectively ended the collaboration. Another project was abandoned. Wildeblood turned away from musical theatre, explaining that he couldn't afford to spend two years writing a show and two years getting it on only to have it come off after a few weeks. Greenwell carried on working, writing some original songs for a musical biography, *The Mitford Girls*, which fell back on popular songs of its period. Greenwell's contribution was inferior to his earlier work, and there didn't seem any reason for the show itself, beyond the ability to appeal to an audience at Chichester Festival Theatre. Almost before they had begun, the two Peters had become a footnote in the history of British musicals. Asked at the end of his life if he was disappointed that his role in the establishment of homosexual equality had been all but forgotten, Wildeblood answered 'Here is a quotation I have found consoling: You can achieve anything you want if you don't mind who gets the credit.'

Make Me an Offer ✳ *The Lily White Boys*

Wolf Mankowitz's play, and the songs of Heneker and Norman, made up their next collaboration, **Make Me an Offer** (Theatre Royal, Stratford East, 17 October 1959; season / New Theatre, 16 December 1959; 267) the second British verismo to begin life at Stratford East, again directed by Littlewood, although it is a very different beast from *Fings Ain't Wot They Used T'Be*. That show would never have countenanced the sentimentality of 'I Want a Lock-Up', nor the character (least of all a hero) capable of expressing such a longing, although there was more than a hint of regret in *Fings*' 'The Ceilin's Comin' Dahn'. *Fings* had no room for such obvious chorus numbers as 'Portobello Road', although Bart would later emulate that sort of Heneker knees-up number in *Blitz!*'s 'Down the Lane'. *Make Me an Offer* had none of the rough edges of *Fings*, a smoother libretto and score, a cast more adept at musicals and a more cohesive plot. It benefited from its central passion, Wedgwood china. Mankowitz was regarded by some as the intellectual voice of Soho, not least for his fable *A Kid for Two Farthings*, a work that cried out to be made into a musical but never was. Wedgwood is the spine that keeps *Make Me an Offer* strong; it is its hero, Charlie's, obsession, as it was Mankowitz's.

Considered as a score, this is one of the strongest of the British versimo school, and one of the most integrated. Heneker and Norman find the right voice for the story, but it is *two* voices. Listening to the score today, it does not seem particularly seamless; elements here and there tend to rub up against one another. As a product of Littlewood's Theatre Workshop it disappoints: it lacks any sort of rawness, and seems over-fashioned to please. One can imagine Littlewood not bothering to stay around for the second part of the show she had directed, or indeed not making it to the interval. As a Littlewood product, it doesn't ring true, the dialogue doesn't seem to have been through the processes that *Fings* had endured. What we get is a neat, tuneful and pleasingly inventive little musical, but nothing is shaken. Verismo at its most polite, or perhaps, as a music-hall comic might have said, re*fained*.

On the last night of **The Lily White Boys** (Royal Court Theatre, 27 January 1960; 45), its lyricist Christopher Logue and director Lindsay Anderson joined the cast on stage to sing the Lily Boys' final verses.

> Time to go now, time to tell you,
> Life is short and men are fools.
> Fall in love, but ask no questions,
> Pay your taxes, keep the rules.
>
> When the future finds you wearing
> Plastic teeth while counting shares
> And you're begging God for mercy,
> Don't forget us in your prayers.

Enough here to tell us that this is no ordinary piece, not a work that strains for popularity. Those words are not the product of a Julian More or a Dorothy Reynolds; they don't belong in a British musical at all, or should not. Logue had no qualifications as a lyricist for musicals, only as a poet, another Angry Young Man who had spent time marching at Aldermaston and was still seething. In its way, *The Lily White Boys* is the British verismo that John Osborne wanted to write in the previous year's *The World of Paul Slickey*. Osborne, of course, does not qualify as a verismo writer because Slickey's world is too fantastic, too artificial, too outside its subject matters, too intent on sending up theatrical conventions and cocking the snook, to qualify. Osborne is savage, as is Logue and his librettist Harry Cookson, but Cookson the playwright and Logue the poet-cum-lyricist have a piece which belongs inside the world it represents, satirises, reflects.

While Slickey's eyes are set *upwards* (the upper classes and their preponderance for casual sex changes, diplomatic blackmail and debutante gossip), *The Lily White Boys* looks to the housing estate, the underprivileged dockland boys and their girlfriends, fixes its eye on a lack of education and opportunity, and only upwards to the greasy pole that is the only way out of it all. Those boys decide to turn their backs on juvenile delinquency, the coshings and burglaries they live by, and turn to respectability. They go for careers. They become pillars of the community, a policeman, a lawyer, a Parliamentarian. Having achieved their gaols, they are only dissatisfied, grimly unhappy. The message is not helpful; the lily white boys do not point a way to fulfilment and happiness through good intention.

'Experimental' is a word too often attached to *The Lily White Boys*, not that many words have ever been attached to it. Some of this may be excused on the grounds that it is described as a 'play with music' rather than a musical. In this and much else, it has the hallmark of ballad opera, allegory, parable. Is it experimental because Logue was 'experimenting' with poetry (isn't that what all poets do?) and becoming a lyricist; Cookson was an experimental playwright; its two composers, Bill Le Sage and Tony Kinsey, refugees from the world of experimental jazz, were experimenting with writing a score; Anderson was 'New Wave'; the Royal Court itself a hot-bed of agitprop drama and highbrow experimentation? All this was a world away from that inhabited by London managements searching for a new musical success; one can hear the managements running in the opposite direction. Those whiter than white boys stood no chance. R. B. Marriott in the *Stage* recognised the work's rough edges, but called it

> the most interesting of the British musical shows since attempts began to be made a few years ago to fashion something authentically our own in this form of theatre [...] it has roots going deep enough and sufficient flavour of its own to make an impact of originality and freshness. It is angry, satirical, uncompromising and alive.

29 The least known of the verismos – and the hardest edged?
The cover for a book of lyrics from *The Lily White Boys* (1960)

The Lily White Boys is perhaps the most solidly verismo of the whole British bunch. Cookson the playwright has no time for the colourful eccentrics into which Norman and Littlewood have turned the characters of *Fings*. If we were to revisit the characters of *Fings* twenty years later there's a fair chance that only one or two of them would have 'bettered themselves'; they have no wish to do so, and have probably never considered the attempt. As much probably goes for Sweet Ginger and Jug Ears in *The Crooked Mile*, and even the typists of *Twenty Minutes South*, but it is not true of those lily white boys, Ted (Albert Finney), Razzo (Monty Landis) and the inappropriately named Musclebound (Philip Locke), or their girlfriends Jeannie (Georgia Brown), Eth (Shirley Anne Field) and Liz (Ann Lynn).

There was nothing amateur about *The Lily White Boys*, and nothing experimental either. One has only to read the production credits: choreography by Eleanor Fazan, designs by Sean Kenny, direction by Lindsay Anderson, and to look at the cast list to feel the quality. Logue was satisfied that it was doing well enough for the Royal Court to be selling 60 per cent of the seats every night, but beyond Sloane Square, and perhaps nervous of another British musical lashing out at the Establishment, no one beyond seemed interested. Shaftesbury Avenue didn't want a musical that showed a society in which a desire for gain is all.

> Everyone wants bread with eyes,
> And cheese with no eyes in it,
> And wine that leaps into the eyes,
> Served by a bitch that makes men itch,
> It's a jungle son – go with it.

The last of the British verismo musical: *Johnny the Priest*

Probably the British verismo musical's last gasp, ***Johnny the Priest*** (Princes Theatre, 19 April 1960; 14), like *The Lily White Boys*, was about juvenile delinquency. In Maybury, somewhere in London's dockland, a young priest, the Revd Richard Highfield (Jeremy Brett), does his best in the pulpit of St Mary's and in the youth club to put the youth of the district on the straight and narrow. The amount of energy he uses in his crusade is of concern to the ageing members of the church council, but his wife Mary (Stephanie Voss) supports him in his endeavours. A young delinquent, Johnny (Bunny May), is one of the vicar's successes. Highfield gets Johnny into the Navy, but the boy steals a telescope and is accused of assault. Johnny asks Highfield to give the police a false alibi, but Highfield cannot find it in his conscience to do so, and Johnny faces an uncertain future.

Johnny the Priest was a production mounted by the Players' Theatre in the wake of such shows as *The Boy Friend*, *Twenty Minutes South* and *The Crooked Mile*, but *Johnny the Priest* was the only one of the verismos that supposedly dealt with the problems of the youth of the day. The libretto was by Peter Powell who after directing the premiere of R. C. Sherriff's straight play *The Telescope* decided to adapt it into a musical. The music was by the 'classical' composer Antony (Anthony in the original programme) Hopkins, making his one and only incursion into musicals. Decca announced the forthcoming long-playing record of *Johnny the Priest* in the theatre programme as having music by Malcolm Arnold.

The seasoned director Norman Marshall, brought in for the musical version, had a predilection for 'alternative' theatre within a defined British context as expressed in his 1947 book *The Other Theatre*. Unafraid of experimentation, he had encouraged an undermining of the Lord Chamberlain's influence, and his association with *Johnny the Priest* promised to benefit from his belief in a people's theatre. The principal roles were perfectly cast. Jeremy Brett had already been the leading man of two musicals, *Meet Me by Moonlight* (it used existing music, thereby disqualifying it as original) and *Marigold*; now, his young vicar would surely have had the spinsters of his parish fighting over the front pews. Stephanie Voss brought her kind soprano to the vicar's supportive wife, especially appreciated in her singing of 'Beyond These Narrow Streets', and the toothy Hope Jackman as Johnny's mother Mrs Palmer had two of the show's strongest numbers, 'The Little Box' and (the show's hit song, according to its co-orchestrator Gordon Langford) her Act II belter 'Johnny Earn Peanuts'.

There was a sureness of casting, too, when it came to the two younger roles, Johnny and his girlfriend Vi (Frances Buckeridge). The elfin-faced Bunny May, who had the distinction of being the first boy to play Enid Blyton's Noddy on stage, had created the role of Johnny in the premiere of Sherriff's original play *The Telescope* at Birmingham Repertory Theatre and was on the Players' Theatre payroll in *The Boy Friend* when they brought him back to London to take on the new role. May suggested all the vulnerability of the teenager without overdoing any of it, and was deeply moving in one of the score's most magical moments, 'Rooftops', when Johnny first looks at the heavens through a telescope: he wonders at 'A star … beautiful! … How can I … how can I express … how beautiful?' as the orchestra ascends scales.

How all of this came over on its first night in London we can only wonder. Bernard Levin declared that

> considered as Britain's answer to *West Side Story* – with which there are some uncanny parallels – *Johnny the Priest* is a hopeless failure. 'Charge Me' (the delinquents' song) does not bear thinking of in the same thought as 'Gee, Office Krupke', and the jiving in this show is about as abandoned as a gavotte. But taken for what it is, *Johnny the Priest* is musically more interesting than any such show for a very long time. This is because the music is by a 'real' composer (I am sorry about these distinctions, but it is the world that makes them, not I), Mr Anthony [*sic*] Hopkins. Mr Hopkins's musical thinking is very close indeed to that of Mr Benjamin Britten – there is the same clean lyricism, the same ingenuity, the same

handling of recitative. The result is that whenever Mr Hopkins is trying to write conventional musical comedy tunes he is weak; but when he takes the minor key between his teeth and writes what is in effect opera he is strong. He has thrown a bridge across the absurd and arbitrary gulf that divides one kind of art from another and for that, at least, he deserves praise.[16]

Levin's evaluation of what Hopkins (and, to be fair, Powell) had done shows considerable perception, for *Johnny the Priest* is one of the most intriguing works of the genre. W. A. Darlington felt that in Sherriff's original play

> the Vicar's dilemma was dramatic, the action was strong and clear. Set to music, it retains its sincerity but loses its edge. [...] The one real purpose that the music does serve is to give Johnny's companions, the boys and girls of the dockland streets, a chance to create some atmosphere. It is, however, the same atmosphere that has been created so often lately, the atmosphere of lawlessness in dingy surroundings. There is no novelty in it. For my own part, I do not believe that so serious a play as this is good material for a musical.[17]

Does *Johnny the Priest* live up to the expectation of 'a musical drama'? It is a challenging description. Surely the critics couldn't all have been wrong in their judgements? Why should we give it a second thought? This is that most difficult of things – the supposedly 'serious' British musical. In its way *Johnny the Priest* was at once a brave and modest show. At first sight, its horizons seem severely limited, a flimsy piece about a well-meaning vicar who wants to do good but can't bring himself to tell the lie that will take one of his protégés back to the straight and narrow, and a wisp of a teenage boy trying to get a grip on life. Of action there is hardly any. Action drama, anyway, had never been R. C. Sherriff's calling card; he veers to the suburban, to the kindly suburban. Of his plays, *Journey's End* is the one deserved and enduring classic, but even this depends not on the dramatic but on observation of character.

As much may be said of Sherriff's other works, often with the most commonplace of individuals at their centre. His novel *The Fortnight in September* (1931) follows a working-class family on their annual seaside holiday; the play *Home at Seven* (1950) with its amnesiac banker believing he may have committed a crime; *The Hopkins Manuscript*, a not quite science fiction novel of 1939, tells the story of a poultry-loving scientist who copes with the sun falling to earth. Edgar Hopkins faces the destruction of the world in a resigned, gentlemanly way; for Sherriff, it is decency and quiet intelligence that is essential if the dilemma is to be resolved.

So it is with the dilemma of *Johnny the Priest*. We are not dealing with weighty conflicts: this doesn't have the emotional dimension of a musical based on Romeo and Juliet; it isn't a costume piece about Robert Browning and Elizabeth Moulton-Barrett; there are no set-pieces or songs that press themselves on the consciousness, or monumental themes. This is a contemporary subject where

30 Can the vicar save him? The dejected *Johnny the Priest* (1960)

the quandary is eminently old-fashioned. It's about goodness, doing right instead of wrong. It tries to put the lives of the questioning young on stage, and it is hip and relentlessly modern for the West End of 1960.

The lyric, when Johnny's girlfriend Vi confesses her feelings for him, tells us so. In the coldness of print, Powell's words are terrible, a list of hopelessly rhymed expressions that might more judiciously have been left in the waste-paper basket. But they are artful in their naïveté. This, after all, is a young, not very well-educated, girl trying desperately to express herself, putting on the carapace of sophistication for her boy; what such lovers say to one another is probably not supposed to be heard by anyone else. Even *Salad Days* didn't get as artless as this, and here we are supposedly dealing with the rough and tumble youth of London's dockland. But there is something achieved, a straining towards adulthood, captured beautifully in the performances of May and Buckeridge, that Powell and Hopkins have recognised. This song, 'I'm Your Girl', is greatly helped, as is so much of the score, by the orchestration, which was shared by the composer and Gordon Langford. The score settles into four distinctive areas, each with its 'voice'.

1   Religious scenes
2   Delinquent scenes
3   Duets for Johnny and Vi
4   Songs for Mrs Palmer

When it came to orchestration Hopkins and Langford must have divided up the numbers between them. Hopkins surely orchestrated the 'religious' elements of the score, the numbers that remain chamber pieces and often take place within the confines of St Mary's Vicarage, while Langford penned the big-band arrangements which frequently lift *Johnny the Priest* into another sphere, notably in the scenes for the delinquents and the aggressive items for Mrs Palmer. The ensemble (all having named parts) is made up entirely of 'adolescent' youngsters. This Greek chorus, presenting the challenge to the Vicar's crusade of reform, has no adults in it, making this the closest British musicals come to the gangs of *West Side Story*. The adolescents are what the authors or the Players' Theatre management consider to be up-to-date. They slouch through the songs. They berate the playing of ping-pong in the church hall as a social distraction, and have a healthy suspicion of organised religion – and who can say that, by the time the curtain falls, they have not been proved right? But these are hardly delinquents in any frightening sense: a nice glass of lemonade would probably cool them down. They have, anyway, been introduced by the writers of the musical into Sherriff's play, which of course had no room for such a vocal chorus in its original version.

In the circumstances, it's not surprising that the matter of faith and belief throws itself across the play. And, in 1960, only fifteen years after the end of the war, when teenagers were being recognised as something more than people who had yet to grow up, there is a relevance to *Johnny the Priest*. Many of the numbers have 'faith' at their core. There is 'Vicarage Tea', an intriguingly shaped trio in which the new young vicar and his wife nervously entertain Miss Fortescue, a member of the church council, unimpressed by the fact that the handsome new vicar thinks too much about the plight of Maybury's teddy-boys, and may nurture Roman tendencies. In 'Be Not Afraid' (note the biblical arrangement of the title) the vicar and his wife support each other's ambition to do what is Christian and right. Subsequently, Mary Highfield has an impassioned vision of a better life for Johnny in 'Beyond These Narrow Streets', and how tellingly Hopkins makes his melody soar when necessary. Johnny realises there is something else he cannot reach beyond the 'Rooftops', and finally there is Highfield's recognition of 'A Boy Called Johnny', certainly melodramatic in its intensity, but moving. In all of these, Hopkins' music is more than hymnal, and there are moments of beauty, notably in the melos and brief lyric of Johnny's 'Rooftops'.

If, against Levin's advice, we compare *Johnny the Priest* to *West Side Story*, where is the depth of emotion in the British effort? Any emotion seems concentrated in what is going on in the vicar's mind. The tussle between good and what the vicar perceives as evil is the central dilemma, and the public has never got worked up about what goes on in vicar's minds. The love interest skips the vicar and his wife (perhaps an area the writers should have explored, extending the play's brief) and concentrates on the touching relationship between Johnny and Vi. Their duets, 'I'm Your Girl' and 'A Tanner's Worth of Tune', a jumpy, playful little song in which Johnny and Vi can't agree about the exact pattern of a wallpaper in a coffee bar, are gems. 'A Tanner's Worth of Tune' should be taken up by a wallpaper firm's advertising department, for – with its description of migraine-inducing patterns with bottles, bangers on forks, fishes and bottles – it reeks of its time, and the melody is too insistent to forget. How brilliantly, too, the song reinforces the strength of feeling between Johnny and Vi. It is an argument set to music, but the argument couldn't be happier. Then, there is always Hope Jackman on hand as the earthy Mrs Palmer, and she is a much-needed antidote to the holy musings back at the vicarage, notably in her abrasive opinion of the charitable work of the church in 'The Little Box'.

To more exotic rhythms, Mrs Palmer has more greedy advice for the young in 'Johnny Earn Peanuts', for she sees things in black and white. She has nothing but scorn for the well-meaning cleric, noting that such men earn next to nothing, and herself looking forward to a nice fat win on 'the Pools', although she strangely sings at one point that she is now upwardly mobile and 'we got an Aga where we had a grate'. She sums up her view on the church's charity with 'Now the far distant shore won't get my pennies any more, And you know what you can do with the plate ...' Mrs Palmer invigorates the play, much of which is quite grey in tone. 'Doin' the Burp', the first of the teenager's outbursts, is a sedentary jive, and in the youngsters' lament for ''The Foggy Foggy Blues' we can almost smell the mist coming in over the docks. 'Ping Pong' in which the teens deride the vicar's call to arms in the youth club, has the same dull edge to it; one can almost smell the musty old volumes of *Punch* with which the hopeless young vicar hopes to amuse his junior flock.

When, towards the end of the play, Richard and Mary Highfield with Johnny meet Miss Fortescue in the street, we have 'Stormy Night', another conversation put to music as in 'Vicarage Tea' with dramatic skill. The discomfort of all concerned is conveyed by the hesitant musical setting as the wind whistles around it. The final moments of the show are decidedly chilly, and 'Stormy Night' accentuates the brooding darkness at the heart of *Johnny the Priest*, which some might mistake for dullness. We should note, too, that St Mary's Vicarage is most probably not kitted out by the Ideal Home Exhibition; one suspects some hideous furniture, fumed oak knick-knacks, and a remarkable lack of mod cons.

To enliven things there is always the ensemble, who work hard only at being what actors mistakenly think of as adolescents. The teddyboys' girlfriends bawl about being expected to satisfy their needs by playing 'Ping-Pong' and moan their jive-like devotion to 'Doin' the Burp', but there is always the feeling that not one of the actresses would dream of going on stage without a nice string of pearls close by. When the young invade *Johnny the Priest* it is as if the twin-set brigade has met the seat-slashers. The boys in *West Side Story* had flick knives; in *Johnny the Priest* they simply wear too much Brylcreem. The several songs for the teenagers of Maybury jolly the show along, but they don't alter the bleak mood of *Johnny the Priest*. The days are drear in Maybury; there are no summer parks for the teenagers to cavort in; the light doesn't get about too much. Reginald Woolley's sets favoured dark corners, angles and doorways and backcloths that needed cheering up, but they were authentically artificial. For weeks, he had wandered around the docks of London with a sketchbook, presumably on dank November days when the light didn't get through. It seems no mistake that the show's sheet music cover is predominantly brown, and the programme cover the most deep of reds. The positive blocks of colour, a quality somehow missing from much of the show itself, accentuate the show's intended beauty. And of beauty there is a good deal here.

There is a slight chance that *Johnny the Priest* may be a real work of art. Perhaps, though, truthfulness for its own sake – and the triumph of goodness, at least when it means dropping a helpless kid like Johnny in the dirt – is not as potent as some vicars might have us believe. If Richard Highfield had told that helpful lie, we might have watched Johnny walk off into the hope of a new life, with – as Mary Highfield puts it – 'telescope to eye'. Perhaps by 1960 the sermonising of a vicar and his wife (just sparing time, no doubt, from making scones for the church fête) counted for nothing. A vicar, and what he stood for, could no longer be a hero. Perhaps, too, in the end *Johnny the Priest* didn't offer any answers to its moral dilemma. As it was, *Johnny the Priest* found itself at the very end of an era.

It can only have been a matter of weeks after its closure that Hope Jackman, unexpectedly out of work, found herself cast in yet another musical. She would play Widow Corney in an adaptation of Charles Dickens' novel *Oliver Twist*. Jackman cannot have known it, but she was perhaps the only link between the death of one of the most promising periods in the British musical – where musicals had tried, hand on heart, to tell a sort of truth about Britain – and the birth of a new era. Jackman's new musical would go on forever, eventually transmogrifying into little more than a commodity, but her involvement with poor little Johnny and his longing for a telescope was never bothered with again. The British musical was almost done with holding a mirror up to life.

8 Specifically British
David Heneker, Monty Norman, Julian More and Wolf Mankowitz

Following the 1965 opening of *Passion Flower Hotel* its book writer Wolf Mankowitz stated that

> Those of us who have been working for the musical theatre for some years would like to make it categorically clear we are not concerned to create pastiche American musicals. We are driving towards a specifically British musical theatre.[1]

Expresso Bongo was compiled by four writers who would go on to have substantial careers in the genre, to whom Mankowitz was referring with 'those of us who have been working for the musical theatre for some years'. The book for *Expresso Bongo* was based on his original story by Mankowitz, and Julian More, the music by David Heneker and Monty Norman. More was not involved with the next collaboration *Make Me an Offer* – book by Mankowitz, music and lyrics by Heneker and Norman. Important works of the verismo school, these singled out the four young writers as bright hopes for the future. Considered as a school of writers, their contribution to British musicals has been considerable.

David Heneker: *Half a Sixpence* ✱ *Charlie Girl*

After contributing with Monty Norman to the 1960 revue *The Art of Living*, David Heneker effectively struck out on a solo career in musicals, at once scoring a definite London and Broadway hit with an adaptation of H. G. Wells' novel *Kipps*. *Half a Sixpence* (Cambridge Theatre, 21 March 1963; 679) bore the mark of its commissioning impresario, Harold Fielding, whose presence was also to be felt in the creation of *Charlie Girl* and *Phil the Fluter*. Written to provide a vehicle for the pop-singer and sometime actor Tommy Steele, *Half a Sixpence* proved that Heneker, adrift from his former collaborators, was a dependable lyricist, able to turn out words appropriate to his task. Beverley Cross's book and Heneker's songs skilfully fashioned Wells' story to Steele's cheerful persona. There was no need for audiences to imagine that Steele was playing anyone other than himself. In Kipps's Act I solo 'She's Too Far Above Me' Heneker pandered to Steele's doe-eyed innocence (he would never again write so submissive a love song for a male character), while the plunkety-plunk brightness of 'Money to Burn' spoke of the vaudeville to which Steele's reputation was already linked.

Elsewhere, the score managed several characterful numbers, including 'All

WIMBLEDON   THEATRE,   S.W.19

Licensee: Audrey Lupton   Lessees: Wimbledon Theatre Ltd.

Commencing SATURDAY 9th MARCH FOR 6 DAYS ONLY

(Must End on Friday 15th March)

Nightly at 7.30   Saturday 9th March 2.30 and 7.30

Matinee Thursday 14th March at 2.30

HAROLD FIELDING presents

WORLD   PREMIERE

Prior to presentation at the Cambridge Theatre

TOMMY STEELE

AS

KIPPS

IN

HALF   A   SIXPENCE

A NEW MUSICAL   BASED ON THE FAMOUS H. G. WELLS NOVEL

Book by BEVERLEY CROSS   Music and Lyrics by DAVID HENEKER

Lighting by RICHARD PILBROW   Designed by LOUDON SAINTHILL

Choreography by EDMUND BALIN   Musical Director KENNETH ALWYN

Directed by JOHN DEXTER

BOX OFFICE OPEN 10 a.m. to 8 p.m.   Tel.: WIM 5211

Stalls and Circle: 10/6, 8/-, 5/6   Unreserved 2/6

31 Playbill for the premiere of *Half a Sixpence* (1963)

in the Cause of Economy', 'The Oak and the Ash', the item with most sense of period, and 'The Old Military Canal'. The title-song duetted by Kipps and his girlfriend Ann, and her touching lament 'Long Ago' were other highlights, but most attention focused on Act II's central number, 'Flash, Bang, Wallop!', sung by Kipps and company as they posed for a wedding photograph. Written during the very last days of the pre-London tour, the song was a descendant of *Make Me an Offer*'s 'Portobello Road', itself a distant relation of Noel Gay's 'The Lambeth Walk'. This was cockney territory, thumbs-in-the-waistcoat, lurching from side to side and giving out with an often repeated, happy-go-lucky refrain. In the context in which it found itself, 'Flash, Bang, Wallop!' was irrelevant, but became *Half a Sixpence*'s signature song and a precursor of other songs in Heneker's scores.

Heneker's next score for Fielding, **Charlie Girl** (Adelphi Theatre, 25 November 1965; 2,202), co-written with John Taylor, was a musical that tried to cross the most old-fashioned sort of musical comedy with the spirit of a swinging London. A retelling of the Cinderella story, with the tomboyish daughter (Charlie) of gracious Lady Hadwell falling into the arms of the family's cheeky sparrow of an estate manager Joe Studholme, who solves the financial problems of the Hadwells when he wins on the football pools, *Charlie Girl* was made up by several collaborators. Ross Taylor 'conceived' the story (possibly on the back of a postage stamp), and Hugh and Margaret Williams (the authors of some drawing-room comedies) wrote the book, with contributions from the farceur Ray Cooney. Hugh Williams described what a Frankenstein's monster a Harold Fielding British musical could be: 'The idea for the musical had already been set up and the numbers written when it was suggested to us that we might like to write the book. It's all about stately homes and we were supposed to know a lot about them because of *The Grass is Greener*.'[2]

Five orchestrators turned Taylor and Heneker's work into a score. With its high society settings and cockney japes, with Joe (like Kipps in *Half a Sixpence* and the butler in *Our Man Crichton* and, long before, Bill Snibson in *Me and My Girl*) proving himself the equal of the upper classes, *Charlie Girl* struck a chord with the public, skilfully engineered by Fielding. He aimed not at the audience that had already sat through Heneker's work in *Irma la Douce* or *Expresso Bongo*, but at the coach-trade audience that wanted an undemanding and pleasant night out at the theatre; nice enough while you sat through it, and forgotten by the time you got to Trafalgar Square. For the older members of that audience, Fielding cast Anna Neagle as Lady Hadwell; for the younger members, the cheeky sparrow Joe Brown; for both, the inoffensive comic actor Derek Nimmo. Taylor was sole writer of many of the songs: 'Bells Will Ring', 'I Love Him, I Love Him'; 'My Favourite Occupation', 'What's the Magic?', 'Like Love' and 'Fish and Chips' (obviously intended as the show's answer to 'Flash, Bang, Wallop!' but not by Heneker), with Heneker being solely responsible only for the dire 'I 'Ates Money' and collaborating with Taylor on the rest of the score.

32 Three stage designs for the original London production of *Half a Sixpence* (1963): *(above)* show cloth; *(opposite, top)* Kipps' bookshop; *(opposite, bottom)* the Martello Tower

After a critical thrashing, Fielding steered the production to commercial success, but its score cannot have brought Heneker artistic satisfaction. In a by no means unflattering review, the critic John Russell Taylor felt the whole thing had been done by a computer. This was what the British musical-going public liked. Perhaps, too, the mixing of the almost sainted Neagle with cor-blimey Brown instilled social cohesion in the stalls. In 1965 neither Neagle nor Brown could have been considered certainties for a West End success. After a finished career as a film actress, with her last musical appearances on stage in London in a variety of risible roles in *The Glorious Days*,[3] Neagle had been enduring a seemingly endless provincial tour in the courtroom drama *Person Unknown* when Fielding decided to fashion *Charlie Girl* around her. This was pretty brave, as Neagle's talents in the singing department (in most departments) were distinctly limited. It was not unusual to hear titters in the Adelphi's stalls when Miss Neagle opened her vocal chords. Brown's stage experience was negligible.

With its prissy, artificial depiction of a swinging Britain, *Charlie Girl* sounded and acted like a calculation, with Taylor and Heneker introducing a transatlantic twang that never sounded like the real thing. This is something Fielding would doubtless have approved of – writers who could make a new British musical sound vaguely like an old American one. Fielding also appreciated the fact that

Heneker was so pliable a composer and lyricist, willing and able to mould his material to the demands of his impresario. For Neagle, there was a gentle Act I finale 'I Was Young', through which she might glide with the sort of 'Mayfair in Maytime' blandness she had exhibited in her husband's films. When for *Charlie Girl*'s revival in 1986 Cyd Charisse was cast as Lady Hadwell, Heneker and Taylor came up with 'When I Hear Music, I Dance', a number with more Hollywood glitter and a heavenly chorus. The songs share an ersatz sophistication, as if they had been rescued from long-forgotten minor musicals of another age.

Heneker's *Jorrocks* ❋ *Phil the Fluter*

Heneker was solely responsible for the score of *Jorrocks* (New Theatre, 22 September 1966; 181), perhaps his finest achievement: he considered it his best work. Presented not by Fielding but by Donald Albery, *Jorrocks* succeeded Albery's production of *Oliver!* two weeks after the end of its run. The components were more promising than those of *Charlie Girl*. Beverley Cross was responsible for this adaptation of Surtees' warm-hearted, fox-hunting vulgarian John Jorrocks who forsakes his grocery emporium to become squire of the village of Handley Cross and, to the consternation of the local gentry, its larger-than-life Master of Foxhounds. It seemed to be open season for Surtees. Coincidentally, this was the year the BBC mounted a television production of his novels, starring Jimmy Edwards. The musical *Jorrocks* was impeccably cast, with not a pop singer or ageing star of yesteryear, first-rate orchestrations by Alyn Ainsworth and Grant Hossack that managed to sound as if they had been left over from *Oliver!*, a sound director with some experience of musicals, Val May, and atmospheric settings by Disley Jones. In its roof-raising ensembles, *Jorrocks* outclassed *Oliver!*, from the frenetic opening in Jorrocks' tea warehouse ('Ask Mr Jorrocks') through Cheryl Kennedy's entrance, 'Belinda' (so successful that the show's leading man, Joss Ackland, wanted it cut), to 'The Happiest Man Alive'. The sense of confidence in these opening passages is palpable, as is the sense of time and character, exemplified in the wittiest offerings. In 'Toasts of the Town' Mrs J and her hapless attendants remember her halcyon past in Tooting, while in 'I Well Recall the Day' Mrs J tells the bewildered Doleful the story of her marriage to her blood-sporting husband.

The critic Hugh Leonard's rooted objection to the show was that Cross and Heneker had written 'more than a musical: it is, unintentionally or not, unabashed propaganda for the joys of the chase, and of its seventeen musical numbers, no less than seven are dedicated to the pleasures of hounding a small animal until it is torn to pieces by dogs.'[4] Huntsmen proved a problem throughout the run, booking themselves into the theatre's boxes and blowing their horns. To many, it was unpalatable subject matter, and almost certainly played a part in forcing *Jorrocks* to go to ground, taking with it some of Heneker's best work. Finest of all was a song that contradicted the endless cry of 'halloah', 'The Midsummer Fox', sung by Jorrocks' hunting companion Charlie Stubbs and the chorus. Heneker's inspiration is the traditional air 'Among the Blue Flowers and the Yellow'; it is one of his most imaginative settings. In a rare moment of quietude, Stubbs tells of a day long gone, on a Midsummer's dawn, out of season when there was not a thought of a fox. The hounds of the Hillingdon Hunt were being walked when out of some hollyhocks stepped a dog fox. The hounds give chase, and, as the song takes off, gathering in speed and vigour, 'the hounds must have kill, must have kill!' When the hounds run the fox to ground the huntsman finds them sitting together; the moral – were it not for man, fox and hounds would play.

For Leonard *Jorrocks* confirmed his suspicion that the British musical was 'dying on its feet'. In the context of 1966, this was pretty accurate. He considered that 'Even by its own lights, *Jorrocks* is no earth-shaker. Its author, Beverley Cross, seems to subscribe to the belief that musicals are no more than out-of-season pantomimes in which plot development, character drawing and literate dialogue are not only intrusive but a positive burden to audiences' although 'no one in his right mind expects social realism in the musical theatre'. He exempted Heneker from blame: the music was always 'agreeable'. Nevertheless, Leonard decided that 'Prejudices aside, *Jorrocks* makes for an undemanding and not too painful evening. But it is an anachronism in its techniques and presentation: a little more daring and the presupposition of an audience with minimal intelligence might have made it worth seeing. The *genre* is dying, but not on its feet.'[5] Heneker and Cross were not the only writers in British musical theatre to draw such a reaction by 1966. Writing of another British musical of that year, *Strike a Light!*, the playwright and critic Frank Marcus asked 'do we really want more musicals? Isn't this whole genre on the wane, tottering to its grave? It's become so stereotyped, so predictable. All this phoney *joie de vivre*, all this prancing and posturing!'[6]

In a way, Heneker invited such criticism. He had been at the forefront of what seemed like the beginning of a movement to alter the character of the British musical, the establishment of the school which Mankowitz was perhaps forming, but by the time of Fielding's production of **Phil the Fluter** (Palace Theatre, 15 November 1969; 123) this was for Heneker a lost cause, unless the school was supposed to be producing the sort of not very good froth of which *Phil the Fluter* was a fair example. Fielding's interest, anyway, was never in establishing a school of British musicals. The problems with the new show were legion. For this period piece fantasy on the life of the Irish song-writer Percy French, Fielding used the *Charlie Girl* casting formula, with Evelyn Laye (who had replaced Neagle as Lady Hadwell) as his elder stateswoman of musicals co-starring with comic actor Stanley Baxter, and the by now apparently obligatory pop-singer, this time the appealing Mark Wynter as French.

Beverley Cross's book was worked up from an original play by Donal Giltinan, but presumably Cross had once again to shape his adaptation to Fielding's demands for appropriate parts and star material. Heneker was compromised by the decision to include several original songs by Percy French, including 'The

Mountains of Mourne', 'Are You Right There, Michael?' and 'Abdul Abulbul Amir'. Baxter's material was weak, including 'That's Why the Poor Man's Dead' (another attempt to do a 'Flash, Bang, Wallop!', and the sort of comedy song that so often mars Heneker's scores), while Wynter had to do with numbers that might just have got away with being the 'B' side of one of his pop singles. The Heneker of *Expresso Bongo* wasn't in it. His skill showed up in Laye's anthem, 'They Don't Make Them Like That Anymore', a sly lyric that told the audience everything it wanted to believe about the woman who was singing it. Her remembrances of the old Lyceum stage door johnnies, of lovers sending the Coldstream Band to serenade her, of accepting orchids by the dozen, conjured a vision of a world that was never to come again.

The effectiveness of the song, delivered with Laye's ineffable graciousness and vocal exaggeration, was welcome in the tawdry surroundings: 'knees-up' numbers such as 'Good Money' (another version of *Half a Sixpence*'s 'Money to Burn') and another of Baxter's comedy items, 'Follow Me'. It must have seemed strange to some that in 1969 a British musical could still be putting out such material. Did anyone ever find this stuff amusing? On the original cast recording, Mrs Fitzmaurice's daughters perform their songs with a seemingly permanent moue. Building up the entrance for Laye, Heneker has them sing (or pout) 'Mama'. Bearing in mind that Laye was now seventy years old, the lyric strikes an uncomfortable note as the girls tell of mama's endless flirtations with their young admirers.

Phil the Fluter emphasises another trait in Heneker's lyrics. The songs for his female characters too often sound like hymns to female submissiveness, as in 'How Would You Like Me?' in which one of the Fitzmaurice daughters offers herself up for a make-over to meet her lover's approval. Heneker can have had no second thoughts about this lyric, as the song was reused fifteen years later in *Peg*, by which time its thick coyness was even more evident. Only at the last, in the finale strains of 'Wonderful Woman' does everything fuse together as Baxter and Wynter and chorus join in salute of Mrs Fitzmaurice and thus subliminally of Laye. This is no more remarkable than anything that has gone before in *Phil the Fluter*, but it is testament to Heneker's feel for what would work on stage. Allied to its choral outburst and dramatic orchestration, it is guaranteed to bring down the curtain with an unquestionable grandeur, and Fielding would have been content to send the customers home feeling they had seen 'a good show'.

Heneker:
The Amazons ❊ *Popkiss* ❊ *The Biograph Girl* ❊ *Peg*

Phil the Fluter, although far from being Heneker's *Twang*, was the last of the glory days. From here on, his work was in more modest productions with their beginnings in regional theatres, and when they did respond London managements offered smaller productions. Heneker wrote only the lyrics for ***The Amazons***

(Nottingham Playhouse, 7 April 1971; season), with music by John Addison and book by the distinguished American librettist Michael Stewart. Adapted from Arthur Wing Pinero's farce, the score had some strong moments, including a ridiculously patriotic tongue-in-cheek opening in 'There's Nothing Wrong with England', and an effective love song in 'Don't Follow the Music'. Elsewhere, an air of busyness may have weakened the effect of Addison's music, especially enjoyable in its songs for a manly female sergeant-at-arms. Addison's music occasionally sounded as if it might be by Heneker, not least in 'She Hates Me', with its echoes of *Charlie Girl*'s 'That's It'.

Despite a certain charm, *The Amazons* joined the fate of many other period pieces of its time, perhaps regarded as a curiosity because its plot rested on three girls being brought up as boys. London didn't invite it in. Heneker worked again with Addison, sharing the music for **Popkiss** (Globe Theatre, 22 August 1972; 60), an adaptation from Ben Travers' farce *Rookery Nook*. Presented by the Cambridge Theatre Company, it seemed a brave venture at a time when Travers' work was unfashionable, and the adaptation proved again that inserting songs into well-constructed plays was a dangerous game. In any case, the score was thin, and an air of cheapness hung over it.

In its small scale manner *The Biograph Girl* (Phoenix Theatre, 19 November 1980; 57) – book by Warner Brown, songs by Heneker – was ambitious, with its story built around the careers of some silent film greats, the directors D. W. Griffith and Mack Sennett, and the actresses Mary Pickford and Lillian Gish. The transatlantic twang of *Charlie Girl*'s 'The Party of a Lifetime' and 'Let's Do a Deal' was well to the fore, but no more convincing here. A good number of hectic songs and some quite effective moments (Pickford's 'Working in Flickers' was one, sung by a leading lady with a Mickey Mouse voice) sometimes reached further, as in Griffith's soulful 'Beyond Babel', and the dilemma of the silent film industry was never out of focus. Lillian Gish turned out another of Heneker's submissive females in 'Every Lady Needs a Master'. Despite such lapses, *The Biograph Girl* was more demanding on its audiences than anything Heneker and his collaborators had offered since before *Half a Sixpence*, but inadequate casting and a certain coolness about the piece held back its potential. More importantly, it was plainly out of time in 1980 London, and the atmosphere of enforced economy didn't inspire confidence.

Heneker's final West End score was for **Peg** (Phoenix Theatre, 12 April 1984; 146), an adaptation of J. Hartley Manners' play *Peg o' My Heart*, with no credited book-writer. If it sounded like something out of the ark, it didn't disappoint. Written for ten performers, this 'romantic new musical' was adrift in a Britain to which it bore no relevance. Everything was laid on with a trowel, the charm, the below-stairs antics of the constantly jolly staff, the tomboyish demeanour of little Peg from the USA who stirs up the Chichester family at Simla Lodge in 1913 Sussex. Throughout, Heneker's old-fashioned music was the wrong sort of old-fashioned. There was enough chirpiness to open a chirping shop in the opening 'A Matter of Minutes', 'Three of a Kind' and in a particularly embarrassing duet for the show's young lovers 'Peg and Jerry'. Heneker's irritating transatlantic twang was back with a vengeance, overworked as the show tried to drum up excitement in the two and ninepennies. One of its strongest manifestations was in Peg's Act II 'Manhattan Hometown', another contrived dose of Americana which nevertheless proved to be one of the best things about *Peg*.

The first-named star Siân Phillips had a laborious point number, 'The Fishing Fleet', while Edward Duke had a P. G. Wodehouse moment with 'A Genuine Hall-Marked Alpha-Plus Little Brick'. Mrs Chichester's unmarried daughter was another in the line of Heneker ladies trapped in femininity, as she contemplated her future in 'When a Woman Has to Choose'. Ultimately, the only song most of the audience remembered on the way out was the interpolated 'Peg o' My Heart', music by Fred Fisher, lyric by Alfred Bryan. The fulsome orchestrations only served to emphasise the work's basic deficiencies.

Whatever criticisms were levelled at *Peg*, it was difficult to deny the professionalism of its score, and in its way it was an appropriate swansong to a career throughout which Heneker had increasingly tried to respond to commercial instincts, instincts that perhaps were not his own but those of his paymasters. Eager to please, *Peg* had no place in the climate it found itself marooned in, although it taught its American producer Louis Busch Hager that 'There is a definite sense of gentleness left in England's dramatic world.'[7] Whether this philosophy survived the drubbing *Peg* received from the critics is not known.

Mankowitz: *Pickwick* ❋ *Passion Flower Hotel*

For Mankowitz, 1963 offered financial and commercial success in his book for the Dickens' adaptation *Pickwick*, with none of the qualities Bart had worked into *Oliver!* Two years later came **Passion Flower Hotel** (Prince of Wales Theatre, 24 August 1965; 148), based on the novel by Rosalind Erskine (a pen-name of Roger Erskine Longrigg). Somehow, Mankowitz's mission to establish a new school of British musical had led him to this, London's first unashamedly 'permissive' musical. The upper-crust girls of Bryant House School decide to introduce the boys of Longcombe School to a sexual bully-off; in effect, opening a brothel in the school. The final line, with one of the girls making the point that she and her pals had yet to be 'finished', was typical of the endless innuendo with which Mankowitz bombarded the audience. Basically, this was sex without the sex, but with some songs. Actually, several of the songs were not bad, even promising, although they all sounded as if they needed more refinement. The music was up to the moment, genuinely popular in a way that Norman and Heneker's music never was or would be, although 'What Does This Country Need Today?' in which the over-sexed Lady Callender shocks the assembled parents by suggesting that what Britain needed was sex, sounds exactly like something Norman and Heneker would have written. (Compare it to 'He's Got Something for the Public' from *Expresso Bongo*.) The image of the composer John Barry[8] was ideally matched to swinging London, and in its way *Passion Flower Hotel* was a perfect offering for Britain's capital in the mid-1960s, the promise of something mucky on the hoardings and nothing doing in the stalls. It was an odd way to help promulgate that 'school' of specifically British musical. The production made the most of its swinging London credentials, op and pop art, but the old-fashioned air kept breaking through, even in the programme credits. (The men's shirts, far from being courtesy of Carnaby Street, were by Van Heusen.) No one doubted the energy pushing *Passion Flower Hotel* on, least of all its five young leading ladies who lined up each day for vitamin injections.

Mankowitz and Norman: *Belle*

On the evening of 10 April 1961 the audience at the King's Theatre, Southsea, was the first to sit through Wolf Mankowitz's book and Monty Norman's music and lyrics for their first shared collaboration, based on an original 'play with music' by Beverley Cross. The show marked Mankowitz and Norman's break with David Heneker and Julian More, accentuated by Mankowitz's assertion that he wanted to create a new 'school' of British musicals, and by the clear emergence of Norman's particular talent. While Heneker was contemplating *Half a Sixpence* (another book by Beverley Cross), Norman was creating a score that seemed intent on pushing the genre in new directions. In retrospect, we may see his as a sort of mission, laudable and almost unique in British musicals, but paying less dividends than the blatantly commercial road taken by Heneker and disappointingly, before too long, by Mankowitz. Norman, however, was not to be swayed from commendable endeavour, creating some of the more interesting and provocative scores in British musicals. Whether Southsea had any prescience of this is unknown, but all in that April evening the curtain came down on a British musical with a sardonic celebration of capital punishment. The attending *Stage* critic thought the authors had 'a sympathetic approach'.[9]

When a few weeks later the curtain fell on the first London night of **Belle, or the Ballad of Dr Crippen** (Strand Theatre, 4 May 1961; 44) the critical reaction was mixed, some praising but most condemning. R. B. Marriott considered the 'qualities of ballad and music hall are cleverly combined and produced in 'Belle', and in my view make a real contribution to the development of the intelligent musical show in this country.' He felt the authors' comedy 'pure music hall, owing something to Robb Wilton and his school of sketch geniuses'.[10] The condemnations were fierce. Few British musicals had been exposed to such virulent accusations of bad taste; headlines told of this 'sick joke with music'. Half a century later it is possible to see *Belle* as ahead of its time; musicals about murder, unacceptable in 1961, caused not a flicker of revulsion in subsequent years. Distance from the actual events helped these find a place. Jack the Ripper

33 Merging musical with music hall: the doomed *Belle* (1961)

is so popular a subject that any relation to real life seems almost incidental, and Sweeney Todd is little more than a fable.

For some, the problems with *Belle* began with the fact that this was a musical based on a real murder that had happened only fifty years before. A *play* might have been one thing, and, after all, in December 1962 a British film[11] about Crippen caused not a ripple of protest, despite its hopeful X-rating. The very fact that *Belle* was a *musical* was enough to cause offence. Those who wished to learn the details of the 1910 murder of the music hall artiste Belle Elmore by her husband, a shrinking violet of a man called Hawley Harvey Crippen, could look it up in an encyclopaedia, or read of it in books of the great trials. The idea that the story of his dispatching of her body, his escape on board the *SS Montrose* with his young secretary-lover Ethel le Neve disguised as a boy, his arrest, trial and hanging might be transmuted into song, into *comedy*, was too much. In turn, the critical onslaught was too much for Mankowitz, who took to getting up on stage after the performance and berating the critics – never a good idea.

His public appeal for sympathy for poor old *Belle* was in turn too much for Frances Stephens, the editor of *Theatre World*, in whose opinion

> Mr Mankowitz went to great lengths publicly, and perhaps none too wisely, to counteract the verdict of the majority of the critics that *Belle* [...] was not in the best of taste. Even those most sympathetically inclined were sorry that the show – so lively and clever in its re-creation of the late Victorian music hall atmosphere – should have had such a theme. [...] It was interesting, psychologically, to pose the question as to how many years must elapse before a notorious murder can be treated lightly or burlesqued on the stage, as, for instance, *Maria Marten*![12]

Stephens has a point. At the time of writing how *would* we react to a musical about the Yorkshire Ripper, thirty-two years after the first of his murders? A *play*, perhaps; certainly, if it treated the matter seriously, but how could a *musical* do so? In 1943, only thirty-three years after the Crippen murder, Ogden Nash wrote a substantial closing number for Act I of Kurt Weill's *One Touch of Venus*: 'Dr Crippen'. This told the whole Crippen story (presumably, as it was on Broadway, to audiences who knew nothing or very little about the man) with its insistence that Crippen was 'Lying in a felon's grave / When they tried him in court / He had one retort, / It was all for Ethel le Neve.' Such treatment for many murder cases will always be impossible, but there is something about the Crippen case which retains its comic edge in the public consciousness.

The *Belle* controversy was exaggerated by the fact that it was set in the context of Edwardian music hall. Something about Crippen nestled in that corner reserved for criminals for whom the British have a sneaking sympathy. As soon as the scandal broke, his name was part of music hall argot. Mankowitz sought to recreate the essential spirit of the British *music hall* within a British *musical*, and in Crippen found what he believed to be a perfect marriage of plot and style, a perfect reason/excuse for the sort of show he wanted to do. The Crippen murder was to be a 'music hall musical', with Norman supplying what amounted to a score of pastiche. This was a remarkable decision, made when rumbles of change and discontent were undermining the public's perception of what the British musical might be.

Only some of those rumblings were happening within the British musical itself. In May 1961 *Fings Ain't Wot They Used T'Be* was still running at the Garrick Theatre, but *Johnny the Priest* had been the last, brief manifestation of the British verismos in April 1960, following on *The Lily White Boys* which had struck a much harder note. *Oliver!* signalled a seismic shift. By now, the simplicity of the *plein air* musical was in terminal decline, marked by the repudiation of Slade and Reynolds' *Wildest Dreams* three months after the appearance of *Belle*. Two months after *Belle*, the Newley–Bricusse *Stop the World – I Want to Get Off* suggested the genre was taking a new direction, although its relevance to anything beyond the theatre's doors was always in doubt, unless it was to man's obsession with his inner self. *Stop the World* proved to be more of a cul-de-sac.

None of these productions seemed to have any bearing on *Belle*; hardly surprising, as they offered no challenge to taste. However, a week after *Belle*, the revue *Beyond the Fringe*[13] opened at the Fortune Theatre. Time was already running out for British revue, never mind the fact that three months later Peter Myers and his collaborators offered a new effort at the Saville Theatre, *The Lord Chamberlain Regrets*,[14] a title suggesting it was up-to-the-moment satire. It wasn't, except in patches. This was the old-fashioned Eton mess of sketches and songs that had served for all the Myers revues of the previous decade. It was obvious that, so far as revues went, an assorted box of fancies might no longer be enough. *Beyond the Fringe* bared its teeth, eschewed songs and the fripperies that had inhabited revue. At the same time, a new magazine, *Private Eye*, was launched. A nightclub, the Establishment, opened in London in October 1961 (not to be confused with 'The Establishment', a number in *The Lord Chamberlain Regrets*, satirising Britain's ruling class). The air was, if not suffused with change, starting to tingle with it. Questions were being asked about the way life in Britain was being lived. All this, of course, against the already repudiated background of such works as *The World of Paul Slickey* and *The Lily White Boys*.

Still unresolved was Britain's law on capital punishment. Although in March 1956 the House of Commons passed the Death Penalty (Abolition) Bill, the abolition was overthrown by the House of Lords. A year later, the 1957 Homicide Act limited the death penalty to what was designated 'capital' murder. Three months later John Vickers, convicted of 'capital' murder, was the first to be executed under the new law at Durham. The calls for abolition continued. Only six months before *Belle*, nineteen-year-old Anthony Miller was executed at Glasgow Prison – the last teenager to be hanged in Britain. Three weeks after *Belle* closed, Zsiga Pankotia, a 31-year-old Hungarian, was hanged for murder at Leeds.

Abolition came in 1965, a year after another British revue, *Hang Down Your*

Head and Die,[15] had done its bit to bring about a change in attitudes. Musicals remained mute on the subject, with the exception of *Belle*. *Belle* not only suggested (*sang*) that the hunt and the trial and 'the hanging all in style, is better than a pantomime', but *sympathised* with the convicted murderer. *Belle* had Crippen as the victim, not the perpetrator, and this was possibly another reason it proved so unacceptable to the 1961 sensibility. As the opening 'Fifty Years Ago' has it, in the public's eye Crippen becomes 'the hero and the villain'. This made him ideal material for a 'ballad' musical, with its recurring 'Ballad of Dr Crippen' charting his progress from insignificant dentist to condemned murderer. The hero-villain had found just such treatment in *The Beggar's Opera* and *The Threepenny Opera*, and that very word – opera – was to have some resonance when it came to *Belle*.

Mankowitz maintained that it was not the curse of Hilldrop Crescent that killed off *Belle*, but the curse of the prolific authoress Ursula Bloom,[16] responsible for 430 published books. One of these was *The Girl Who Loved Crippen* (1954). Only after the book was published did Bloom learn that Ethel le Neve was still alive and living as Ethel Smith. A meeting was arranged. Bloom made good use of her Crippen connection in numerous newspaper articles over many years, and popped up again when *Belle* was announced. 'Miss Bloom reminded the public that Ethel le Neve was still alive,' said Mankowitz, 'and that she might be pained to find herself the heroine of a musical which poked fun at the Crippen tragedy. As a result, there was a rush of sympathy for Ethel, and people stayed away from the theatre in droves.'[17] Bloom visited Ethel and informed her of the musical, 'sitting at tea in her room, with the cloth she embroidered herself and the cake she made with her own hands. No musical performance would coax her out of the quiet she has chosen. She asks only to stay as a shadow. For this poor woman does not forget. [...] Ethel le Neve has her own music about him, and it is the grand opera of very deep emotions.'[18]

Presumably neither le Neve or Bloom sneaked into a performance of *Belle*, but had they done so they might have recalled Bloom's words about le Neve's 'grand opera of very deep emotions'. Music hall parody may dominate Norman's score but the music for Ethel (played by Virginia Vernon) has those very elements of opera that Bloom so highly prized; it is in Ethel's role that the most dramatic music resides. Her first song, 'You Are Mine', an oasis of quiet in a resolutely cheerful and rumbustuous Act I, is a perfection of simplicity, as she delineates her passion for her dentist employer. After the disappearance of Belle Elmore (aka Cunegonde Crippen) Ethel expresses her ecstasy in 'I Can't Stop Singing', a high soprano aria in which she endlessly repeats the lyric's title. Reality bites whenever Ethel takes the stage; her character is never guyed. As the tragedy unfolds, her desperate cry, 'Don't Ever Leave Me', with its threatening drumbeats across her opening words, has Norman rising to almost Puccini-like heights through 'No matter what may happen / No matter what befalls us / I could withstand it all with you by my side.' Ethel's only duet with Crippen (George Benson), the 'Song of Our Future', has a Wagnerian drive and sweep about it as the couple dream of being together in Hilldrop Crescent. The love between Crippen and his mistress is never satirised, but heightened by the seriousness with which Norman describes it.

Belle herself is less kindly dealt with. We see that she is a third-rate music hall artiste from her very first number.[19] Out of tune, she hoots and makes vague stabs at her song 'Bird of Paradise', describing her feathered state to an extent that must surely have alerted the Lord Chamberlain to Norman's intentions; 'all the cocks' are waiting for her bird of paradise. Belle's vulgarity is confirmed when she encourages her fellow lady artistes to travel to the Colonies where the men are in urgent need of female consolation. This loud-mouthed vulgarian is the least sympathetic character in the play, and she is the *victim*. Beside her, Crippen is all gentle manners, only coming to life in song for his heartfelt 'Song of Our Future' with Ethel, and 'Coldwater, Michigan' in which Norman parodies the cross-talking double-act.

Those parodies are not difficult to spot, although they seem to have no direct antecedents. Chief among them is the rousing 'Meet Me at the Strand' sung by the male impersonator Jenny Pearl (Nicolette Roeg), an evocation of the about-town Lothario, haunting the stalls of every London theatre and taking his girls back to his private suite at the Savoy. This also serves as a celebration of the trousered females of the halls, the Vesta Tilleys, the Hetty Kings. Other more specific music hall parodies occur. The plodding copper, the butt of so many music hall jokes, surfaces in 'The Policeman's Song' in which Inspector Dew and his assistants review the nasty affair they are faced with. Here, Norman's lyric invokes the boys in blue of *The Pirates of Penzance*, complete with some Gilbertian rhyming: 'Though it's all circum*stantial*, I'm afraid the little *man shall* be sub*stantial*ly dangled by the hangman.'

Everywhere in *Belle* the parodies queue up for attention. In 'The Devil's Bandsmen' Norman exploited the unique talents of Davy Kaye, the actor playing Mighty Mick opposite Jerry Desmonde's George Lasher. Kaye's party piece one-man band is made up into a Salvationist number, providing a genuine music hall cameo inside its parody. Elsewhere, Kaye has the tongue-twisting 'Pills, Pills, Pills' (celebrating the fact that Crippen is procuring some hyoscine, with the intention of putting Belle out cold for a little while). Another skilful sequence, 'The Minstrel Show' incorporates several individual numbers, using the atmosphere of the blacked-up Kentucky entertainers to deliver Norman's description of the state of Britain in 1910. The sense of time and place is strengthened by 'The Bravest of Men', a swipe at Britain's blind patriotism ('The foe always crack when they see the Union Jack'; 'We conquered the Boers 'cos we never lose our wars'). Central to the plot is 'The Dit-Dit Song', conveying the turning-point in Crippen's story, when the message that Crippen and Ethel are on board the *Montrose* is sent by Morse code, courtesy of Marconi's invention, to the police. Norman has Crippen and Ethel tapping out a message of love, making this possibly the most ironic love song in British musicals. Its poignancy is emphasised when the song is reprised

34 *Belle*: a contemporary *Punch* cartoon depicting Davy Kaye and George Benson

towards the close of the show, as Crippen awaits his meeting with the public executioner.

Several elements of production were essential to the unique flavour of *Belle*. One of the paramount considerations of Harry Robinson's orchestration is to recreate the sound of a tired pit-band almost sleepwalking through the show. As the orchestra's conductor, Arthur Tatler convinces us that he has spent most of his life trying to get music out of such bands, perhaps at the 'old Mo' in the Edgware Road. He didn't. His credits include being music co-ordinator for the 1972 film *The Great Waltz* and playing an uncredited pianist in *A Clockwork Orange*. The Edwardian settings by Loudon Sainthill were also much praised, as was Val May's direction. The six leading performers were perfectly cast. It may be, though, that Mankowitz's conception of a show was not well thought out, just like *Passion Flower Hotel*. There could be clear distinction when 'show within a show' sequences were clearly divorced from a plot, but the distinctions between the real and music hall are blurred in *Belle*.

There may have been something in Mankowitz's book which put a brake on *Belle*: its director Val May remembers the show as 'a bit of a mess'.[20] As this is not detected in listening to Norman's songs, it suggests that Mankowitz may have been to blame, but, of course, Mankowitz must have been aware of the difficulties he faced in presenting Crippen's story to the public in such a form; he would have been sharply conscious of needing a context to make the story acceptable. His efforts were not widely appreciated. The mix of melodrama, history, music hall jokes and murder did not appeal to the critic Bernard Levin. As well as haranguing the public from the stage, five days after *Belle*'s opening Mankowitz took *Belle*'s showgirls through the streets with a small coffin which they delivered to Levin's office in Fleet Street. Messages attached to the coffin read: 'Dear Bernie. This is your size, not mine. Wolfie' and 'To Bernard Levin with best wishes from the Belle company.' Mankowitz was said to have remarked 'This is the moment we have all been waiting for. To send a midget coffin for a midget critic.'[21]

Levin carried on. *Belle* did not. There had been little to suggest in either Mankowitz's or Norman's past that this had been where the writers were heading, towards this strange conflagration of affection and satire, cruelty and love, this anarchic distortion of history, this effrontery. Just as nothing in British musicals preceded it, nothing followed. With its back turned towards *Belle*, the British musical carried on regardless, despite those who had spoken up for what it had tried to do. A leader in the *Stage* was in the forefront of support.

> Wolf Mankowitz may fairly plead that the story was translated into music hall terms at the time it took place, and that Crippen and his ménage have always excited sympathy, as well as an indulgent smile, along with sober reactions [...] the words 'Bad Taste' are usually shouted by people who are afraid of anything out of the common rut, or have no fresh ideas of their own.[22]

Mankowitz would have been interested to learn that in 2009 DNA evidence suggested that Crippen was innocent of his wife's murder.

Monty Norman after *Belle*

The discouragement of *Belle*'s failure had some compensation when its financial backer, Cubby Broccoli, commissioned Norman to write the score for a James Bond film. The resultant music would bring Norman more recognition than anything he did in musicals. The next one, a collaboration between Norman and Julian More, continued the air of experimentation. ***The Perils of Scobie Prilt*** (New Theatre, Oxford, 12 June 1963; season) was a satire about spies for ten performers. Interestingly cast, with the pop-singer Mike Sarne in the title-role, the production had *Irma la Douce*'s director, Peter Brook, but was abandoned after a few performances at the New Theatre, Oxford. A week before *Scobie* opened, Mankowitz's adaptation of Dickens' *Pickwick Papers*, *Pickwick*, opened successfully in Manchester, while Heneker had triumphed in March with his score for *Half a Sixpence*. Undeterred, Norman stuck to his enterprise, but commercial success was to prove elusive, and *Belle* had done damage to his chances.

Who's Pinkus, Where's Chelm? (Jeannetta Cochrane Theatre, London, 3 January 1967; season) was lumbered with a hopeless title by its librettist Cecil P. Taylor. Norman wrote the music and shared the lyrics with Taylor for this Charles Marowitz–London Traverse Theatre Company production. Norman may have seemed an obvious choice as composer for this piece of Yiddish theatre, but his songs made little impression, and the whole thing was done with in a few performances on the fringe of the West End. *Quick, Quick Slow* (Birmingham Repertory Theatre, 20 August 1969; season), for which he wrote music to More's lyrics, looked more hopeful. It cleverly exploited the public's fascination with amateur ballroom dancing as celebrated by BBC TV's *Come Dancing* which played from 1949 to 1998, but there was no afterlife. Like Heneker, Norman was seeing opportunities and productions shrivel.

More British musicals and diversions: *Grab Me a Gondola* * *The Golden Touch* * *Joie de Vivre* * *Bordello*

Meanwhile, More reverted to his collaborator James Gilbert for **The Golden Touch** (Piccadilly Theatre, 5 May 1960; 12), an obvious attempt to tap the audience that had responded so readily to their rather vacuous **Grab Me a Gondola** (Lyric Theatre, 26 December 1956; 673). Broadly based on the pouting and chest-expanding properties of the British actress Diana Dors, *Grab Me a Gondola* charted the adventures of Virginia Jones, at large in Venice for a film festival. Attempting a sort of sophistication, evident in such songs as 'Cravin' for the Avon' with its rash of Shakespearean allusions, *Grab Me a Gondola* caught the public mood and became a genuine success, fulfilling, in a spurious manner, the sort of need answered in our own times by glancing through *Hello!* or any of the celebrity-centred magazines. But then, in 1956, with *Salad Days* triumphing over all, British theatregoers were not looking for anything thought-provoking. *The Golden Touch* replaced the mindless Miss Jones with a fabulously rich Greek tycoon, and introduced the British musical to beatniks (and vice versa), but the Midas touch was missing.

Much of the attraction of *Grab Me a Gondola* was its star, Joan Heal, bursting with a star appeal that her future career didn't fulfil. She was obliged to play much the same part in another clinker, **Joie de Vivre** (Queen's Theatre, 14 July 1960; 4), an unfortunate adaptation of Terence Rattigan's 'French window' comedy *French Without Tears*. Rattigan adapted his play, now laced with lyrics by Paul Dehn and music by a veteran of musical theatre Robert Stolz.[23] One of the most disastrous offerings of 1960, its cast endured a long pre-London tour and constant changes to script and score. Its leading man, Donald Sinden, perfect material for a straight rendition of his role, was totally unsuited to a musical. Patricia Michael, in her first professional engagement in the chorus and understudying the leading role of Diana Lake, recalls that

Donald Sinden had never done a musical or sung on stage before. He had such difficulty holding a tune and keeping in time that in his solo number, 'I'm sorry but I'm happy,' we chorines all knelt in a line in front of him clicking our fingers to keep him on the beat.[24]

Sinden did not long have to endure his discomfort, as Michael remembers.

The final line of the show, delivered by Barrie Ingham, was 'Stop laughing, Venus you old bag, it's not funny, it's a bloody disaster!' I *think* the word was bloody or something similar. This was met with howls of agreement from mainly the 'Gallery First Nighters.' In my *naïveté* I thought they were cheering and that we were a hit but no one else was fooled.[25]

Indeed they were not. W. A. Darlington reported that 'The final curtain fell to a tempest of booing and did not rise again, and I am left to try to account for this sudden collapse.'[26]*Joie de Vivre* was one of the most bruised victims of the *fin de partie* that was happening to the British musical at the demise of the 1950s; in a sense, time would be called when *Oliver!* opened in June 1960. And yet, the catalogue of failures in 1960 reflected a certain vibrancy in British theatre, and – without doubt – a turnover that today we may only marvel at. Theatregoers were hardly home after one premiere before they had to grab hat and coat to take their seats for the next. Consider the shows of that year, and note for how little time they stayed around: *The Lily White Boys* (45 performances), *Johnny the Priest* (14), *The Golden Touch* (12), *Joie de Vivre* (4), *Follow that Girl* (211), *Hooray for Daisy!* (51), and the same year's Cheltenham offering *Wildest Dreams* would open in London in 1961 for seventy-six performances. In this company, *Joie de Vivre* (and *Johnny the Priest*) suggested that taking perfectly sound plays and adding some songs to them was not an infallible pathway to success.

Joan Heal was only one of the many musical actresses who suffered from the general malaise that affected British musicals of this period: the high hopes of a personal success (in *Grab Me a Gondola*) followed by a string of unsuitable roles in unsuccessful works, beginning with the leading role in *A Girl Called Jo* for which she was totally unsuited, no-hopers such as *The Love Doctor* and what amounted to cabaret vignettes in *Divorce Me, Darling!* and *Joie de Vivre*, in which she appeared as a character not found in Rattigan's original play. As Chi-Chi, Heal had two numbers, ''Allo Beeg Boy!' and 'Le West End', whose titles alone possibly tell us all we need to know. The interpolation did not succeed. According to Milton Shulman (who obviously left the theatre before the booing started) 'Joan Heal practically splits herself putting over two numbers with raucous effect.'[27]

The reception accorded to *Joie de Vivre* points up another aspect of those *fin de partie* productions: the power of the audience, not least the Gallery First Nighters who attended every first performance. Without their intervention as it drew to its close, *Joie de Vivre* might have endured a very different fate. Remember that

Shulman left *before* the gallery lost patience and seized its opportunity to strike back at what was on stage – and then consider his headline 'I find Rattigan with music is so out-of-touch – but it could be a success.' Before reading a word of the review, we know for a fact he was in a telephone booth or back in Fleet Street before Patricia Michael and her fellow artistes were struggling to cope with the overheated emotions of their audience. Shulman found much to criticise, but 'such minor matters ... may not preclude it from being a success'. W. A. Darlington admitted

> If something had happened to make me leave the Queen's Theatre last night, so that I should have been compelled to miss the last 15 to 20 minutes of *Joie de Vivre*, I should have written a notice quite different from this one.[28]

Just how different he makes clear. He would have said that

> Robert Stolz's music was gay and lively, that Paul Dehn's lyrics had quality and point, and that the dancing was spirited. I should have said that Terence Rattigan's book, though nothing like so funny as his play *French Without Tears* upon which it is based, seemed to be keeping its first night audience reasonably well entertained.[29]

Something of the Roman arena had got in through the theatre doors, the ability of the audience to give its thumbs up or down, the music hall audience's capacity to give the ovation or the bird as it wished. At this time in British musicals, displeasure and disappointment would often have been greeted with quiet disdain and polite applause, but at the first London night of *Hooray for Daisy!* a man in the front row shouted 'Rubbish' before the show finished and walked out. In *Joie de Vivre* and *The World of Paul Slickey* something like chaos permeated the theatre. Afterwards, writers, composers and producers must have wound their way homeward wondering what they had done wrong and how they could get it right next time. In most cases, few lessons were learned, and the recurring mistakes of judgement and taste were left to hapless casts to deal with. There is, so far as I know, no evidence that audiences booed *The Golden Touch* and its like, but it was probably a close call.

More was reunited with Gilbert for the Birmingham Repertory Theatre's *Good Time Johnny* (1971), which had Ronnie Barker as a modern-day John Falstaff playing opposite Joan Sims. Its chances of transferring to London dimmed when Barker had to relinquish his role. In 1973 More was lyricist for *R Loves J*, adapted from the Peter Ustinov play *Romanoff and Juliet*, with music by the conductor Alexander Faris. This failed to outgrow its season at the Chichester Festival. The following year one of More's projects, **Bordello** (Queen's Theatre, 18 April 1974; 41) did make it to the West End, but this small-scale attempt to make a musical around Toulouse-Lautrec and his fascination with ladies of the night was quickly ejected. No matter how permissive a society the London audience exemplified in 1974, it did not wish to spend time or money on a long evening in a Parisian brothel. In 2000, the little painter returned to the stage in the musical *Lautrec*, and in the same year London saw productions of two other 'French' musicals, *Notre-Dame de Paris* and *Napoleon*.

It should be noted that uncontrollable anger at the state of the British musical was not confined to 1960. As late as 1996, a non-British musical about the electric chair, *The Fields of Ambrosia*, had members of the audience threatening to invade the stage. There was rather more justice to the noisy walk-outs and contretemps with aisle attendants during performances of *Passion Flower Hotel* in 1965 – justified because audiences had been lured into the theatre thinking they were going to see a musical about sex. They weren't and it wasn't, and at a performance I saw second house Saturday a large number of testosterone-fuelled males made their displeasure known. Others of us quite enjoyed the songs and wondered why the set looked as if it had been put together with odd bits of plywood. More politely, members of the audience for Stephen Sondheim's *Passion*, seen in London in 1996, regularly tip-toed gently back into Shaftesbury Avenue even before the curtain had fallen on the first act. Long before, as the cast struggled to get through the first night of *The Crystal Heart* at the Saville Theatre in 1957, the audience had erupted, giving its much respected leading lady the music hall bird so familiar to poor Belle Elmore. Such outbreaks of passion have largely disappeared from our modern musical theatre, and even mutterings of displeasure from one audience member can result in threats of violence from another.

Norman with and without Mankowitz: *Stand and Deliver* ❋ *So Who Needs Marriage?*

For Norman, the disappointing run (or lack of one) continued with **Stand and Deliver** (Roundhouse, 24 October 1972; 14). Appearing at a dire moment in the timeline of the British musical, the show did not find favour. Here was 'a bawdy ballad in two acts' by Mankowitz, with story and songs credited to Norman, marking their first collaboration since *Belle*, with which it shared the 'ballad' label. The tribute to John Gay's *The Beggar's Opera* was unmistakable, for this was the story of the famed highwayman Jack Sheppard. The veteran director Wendy Toye was in charge. In the event, almost nothing about *Stand and Deliver* struck the right note, a wrong show at the wrong time in the wrong theatre (who would have dreamed of going to see a new British musical at the Roundhouse?) and the show folded. The critic Martin Esslin found himself at the almost deserted second performance.

> To say that *Stand and Deliver* is a dismally bad musical is an understatement. A witless pastiche of Gay's *Beggar's Opera* centred on cardboard reproductions of historical characters … with frantic but totally unoriginal music and cliché-infested lyrics, bereft of any good lines of dialogue or witty repartee, but stuffed with puerile naughtiness and revolting *double-entendres*, it presented these

gallant performers with a truly insuperable obstacle. The less said about it the better ...[30]

Those mentions of 'puerile naughtiness' and 'revolting *double-entendres*' do suggest that Mankowitz had learned nothing from *Passion Flower Hotel*. Esslin went on to make a very interesting point about the play and its location. He was chastened by the fact that the musical *might* have worked in a different setting, where a proscenium might have 'presented a far more coherently pretty picture'. The evening's gathered clichés might have 'looked less tatty, a little more convincing surrounded by cherubs and red plush boxes' in more appropriate, old West End theatres, those places where there was nowhere to put your long legs, nowhere to sit comfortably in the interval, smelly lavatories and expensive programmes. Esslin thought the show's chocolate box conventions belonged in a chocolate box setting, not in the starkness that was the Roundhouse. But then 'On the other hand, it would be better still if the whole hollow convention was finally abandoned altogether and thrown where it belongs, on the nearest rubbish dump.'[31]

British theatre of the 1970s had no sympathy for British musicals offered by any seasoned practitioners. By 1975 there was little of importance, including Andrew Lloyd Webber's Wodehouse musical *Jeeves*, which at least attracted some serious attention at Her Majesty's Theatre. This was Lloyd Webber's one attempt at writing the very sort of musical that was now dying on its feet, and it shared the same fate as most of the others. Norman made do with the more than modest *So Who Needs Marriage?* (Gardner Centre, Brighton, 8 May 1975; tour), another chamber piece – this time for six players – in the manner of *The Perils of Scobie Prilt*. The only show for which Norman wrote book, music and lyrics, it was heavily in the shadow of Sondheim's *Company*, a work with which it shared its central theme (basically 'Is marriage a good idea? Not necessarily.'). Interesting and sometimes penetrating in its insights, *So Who Needs Marriage?* was probably the most inventive British musical of its year. The *Stage* considered the score 'a compact affair. It quite lacks the acidity of Sondheim, and so sugars the bitter pill of the story's moral that marriage in this day and age is, or, at any rate, might best be dispensed with.'[32] At its final matinee performance in Norwich, one of its stars, Jon Pertwee (playing a multitude of parts) entered, looked out into the almost deserted theatre and said 'My God! It's like being on the *Titanic!*' It seemed that audiences did not want to go where Norman wished to lead them.

Norman and More: *Songbook*

Four years later, reunited with Julian More, with whom he shared all credits, Norman at last had another success with *Songbook* (Globe Theatre, 25 July 1979; 208). This 'new musical' chamber piece had the explanatory subtitle 'a tribute to Moony Shapiro', presented by its five performers, one of them Mr Shapiro himself. It was a good idea, and the sort of thing both writers understood: the life story of an imaginary composer of popular songs who had written for all sorts of genres and people from the 1920s through to the end of the 1970s before being electrocuted by his synthesizer. Norman and More's inspiration may have been *Side by Side by Sondheim*, an entertainment for three singers and a narrator celebrating the work of Sondheim, seen in London in 1976. In creating the purely fictional *Songbook* More and Norman took on the almost insuperable challenge of having to write an entire lifetime of a composer's music, incorporating style after changing style. For a score that aimed at so many targets (there were over thirty songs) it was likely that some of those targets would be missed; nevertheless it hit the bullseye with regularity.

On its pre-London tour *Songbook* opened with the excellent up-tempo 'Landin' Headfirst on My Feet' (supposedly from the 1948 movie *Baltimore Ballyhoo*), replaced in London by a new title-song. Act I took Shapiro's career up to the early 1950s, with the evocative 'East River Rhapsody' from *Feldman Follies of 1926*, giving way to the songs he wrote through the 1930s: the boop-de-boop frippery of 'Pretty Face' (from the movie *Pretty Faces of 1934*); a number that might have been written for Edith Piaf, 'Les Halles' (in its way a tribute to Monnot, the composer of *Irma la Douce*); songs written around the rise of Hitler ('Olympics Song' and 'Nazi Party Pooper'), these the British musical's answer to Mel Brooks' 'Springtime for Hitler' as originally heard in the 1967 film *The Producers*; an Andrews' Sisters take-off 'I'm Gonna Take Him Home to Momma', and a clutch of World War II numbers including the gutteral 'The Girl in the Window' for Marlene Dietrich, and a very irritating all-join-in-with-the-chorus song, 'Bumpity Bump' for Cicely Courtneidge.

The second half began with a protracted sequence on Shapiro's only work to reach Broadway, *Happy Hickory* – the sort of pastiche that Betty Comden and Adolph Green had been writing with Leonard Bernstein in their New York cabaret days. More and Norman did not have the edge of the American team Comden and Green's cod operetta in their skit on operetta, *The Baroness Bazooka*.[33] Here, the swarthy hero introduces himself with 'I'm a goat, goat, goat, goat, goatherd / And I herd, herd, herd, herd goats.' Nevertheless, More and Norman suggest why the public did not flock to see *Happy Hickory*. This took Shapiro's career to the mid-1950s, and to the heart of Act II, when another very different note creeps into *Songbook*. The mood darkens as age and disillusion take hold. We come to feel more for the man and his theatrical and personal failures as an autumnal sense of regret and realisation intrudes. Shapiro's playful way with dealing with the Nazi threat is transmuted into something much darker for 'I Accuse' (from his musical *Red White and Black*) with two oriental girls representing Shapiro's contribution to the Vietnam debate. 'If you can kill your kith and kin / When will you kill me?' … 'Yankee, go home'. The songwriter needs to convey a philosophy, but Shapiro has his doubts, shared in another number 'Messages'.

Time is passing for the old songsmith, and personal sadness hits him hard.

Now, More and Norman use a song first heard as one of the rejects from the score of *Happy Hickory*, but now sung straight. More and Norman tell us it had been penned in the twenties and stuffed in Shapiro's bottom drawer. Despite the 1920s provenance, 'Don't Play That Love Song Any More, Sam' has obvious references to *Casablanca*; whatever its origins, it is at the centre of *Songbook*, one of its rare 'real' moments. By the start of the 1970s, Shapiro is aware he is winding down ('Golden Oldie'), having tried every which way as a composer, including a desperate attempt at writing a Beatles number 'I Found Love', Norman and More at their most crude. One of the last songs, 'Nostalgia', written by Shapiro before his shocking death, sweeps all away with its repeated insistence that 'Nostalgia gets me down'.

Songbook demands something of its audiences: a little sophistication and a glancing knowledge of popular music of the twentieth century is necessary if the pastiches are to be appreciated. For a British musical to attempt such a feat would have been impressive at any time, but where was the audience for it? The casting of the celebrated actor Bob Hoskins, stumpy and belligerent and vulnerable, was an enormous help in making Shapiro come alive as a person as well as a songwriter, and Hoskins brought Tin Pan Alley credibility with him after his TV success in Dennis Potter's play *Pennies from Heaven*. When Hoskins left the cast before London something was lost. Nevertheless, *Songbook* found audiences enough in London to play out several months. Two years later, a new production opened and closed the same night in New York. The American critic Frank Rich praised the concept but felt that Norman and More had practised 'a toothless and unfocused, if affectionate, brand of satire. They aim too widely at their many targets and hit very few.'[34] *Songbook* would be the last British musical for More, who went on to write the libretto for the short-lived 1987 Broadway production *Roza*, with music by Gilbert Becaud.

Norman: *Poppy*

By the early 1980s it seemed unlikely that Norman would find another work to suit his particular qualities, but in September 1982 the Royal Shakespeare Company's Barbican production of **Poppy** (revised version at the Adelphi Theatre, 14 November 1982; 97) was a gift. The title suggested a Billy Mayerl musical from the 1930s, but this was a Peter Nichols' play about the Opium Wars, and Britain's treatment of the Chinese during the reign of Queen Victoria. Nichols' 1977 *Privates on Parade*, about an all-male army concert party, the Song and Dance Unit South East Asia, had disqualified itself as a musical by being billed as a 'play with songs', told through the medium of all-male concert party. *Poppy* had a principal boy played by a girl, a Dame played by a man, two randy pantomime horses, a pantomime opening chorus, and a song sheet to jog the audience into joining in, no matter that the words told of the rape and pillage done by the British forces in Peking.

The resulting score sounded so much of a piece that we have to remind ourselves that Nichols, not Norman, wrote the lyrics. Despite this, Norman is able to fashion the songs exactly to his style, and there is never a doubt that the score of *Poppy* is a direct descendant of *Belle*. In that show, Norman had the template of Edwardian music hall, but in *Poppy* he had the rather more difficult template of the British pantomime – more difficult because *musically* the British pantomime has less that is musically identifiable about it than music hall. There are obvious specifically pantomime elements in the score: that audience song-sheet, the song a friendly Jack might sing to his friendly old cow (or horse, in this case) before he ventures up the beanstalk, the opening scene on the village green, but these are soon exhausted. Musically, *Poppy* presents Norman with many problems; there are less targets to which pastiche may be applied, but Norman's reaction to Nichols' lyrics' is skilful. The pronounced echoes of *Belle* ('John Companee' could only be reminiscent of *Belle*'s 'The Bravest of Men', and there is plenty of *Belle*'s spirit in such pieces as 'If You Want to Make a Killing') serve Nichols' well, and Norman manages the play's shift to the orient with deftness and taste. Most memorable is a number that in itself recalled Dr Crippen's 'Dit-Dit Song', 'The Blessed Trinity', in which the company celebrate the virtues of the age.

9 To Whom it May Concern
The British Biomusical

The very thought that the British musical should be responsible for representing the lives of real people may induce uneasiness. Paradoxically, one of the most tremendous successes of the genre is a biomusical about Jesus Christ, which may have made its subject's life more real to its audiences. In essence, reality and the musical are not happy bedfellows, and the post-war British musical has come a fair share of croppers in offering up versions of lives that have been lived. The accent has always been on the historical, and the historical of rather long ago; the British musical has rarely tried to put a modern life at its centre, perhaps hoping that distance will lend enchantment. The contemporary has been almost ignored.

Ready-made music

The Broadway method of dealing with real lives brought some commercial and sometimes critical rewards with such works as *Fiorello!* (New York mayor Fiorello La Guardia), *The Unsinkable Molly Brown* (a *Titanic* survivor) and *Annie Get your Gun* (Annie Oakley). New York also had an occasional fancy for lives of famous composers set to their own music, as in George Forrest and Robert Wright's *Song of Norway* (Edvard Grieg) and *The Great Waltz* (the Strauss family). This vein was explored in Britain by Eric Maschwitz, one of the British musical's jobbing contributors. Despite having penned two noted lyrics in British song ('A Nightingale Sang in Berkeley Square' and 'These Foolish Things') and written prolifically for musical theatre, his work is seldom remembered. One of his earliest successes, **Waltz Without End** (Cambridge Theatre, 29 September 1942; 181), predated *Song of Norway* by two years. Perhaps, if audiences really wanted a musical based on the life of Frederic Chopin (1810–49), it was mere politeness to do it with Chopin's music. The result, a decent London run, long touring days and endless amateur productions, suggested this was a good idea, although James Agate in the *Sunday Times* considered 'To alter a composer's rhythms, key and tempi is to murder that composer. To make voices sing words that are the acme of tawdry nonsense is to destroy an exquisite reputation.'

The trick was repeated fourteen years later with **Summer Song** (Princes Theatre, 16 February 1956; 148), the life told through the music of Antonín Dvořák (1841–1904), the American writer Hy Kraft collaborating with Maschwitz on the book, Maschwitz's lyrics, and the artful musical adaptations by Bernard Grun. To the musical purist, this could be nothing but tosh. When Maschwitz applied to the Performing Right Society to register for royalties on the musical's songs, the composer and committee member William Alwyn was appalled. However ethically right or wrong their mangling might be, the collaborators went at it with a will, and at least audiences were spared the spectacle of a singing Dvořák. Rather, Laurence Naismith's Dvořák, visiting a Czech lumberjack community in 1893 Illinois, was at the edge of the musical in a non-singing capacity, in effect to get inspiration (according to the writers) for the 'New World' Symphony, probably the only piece of Dvořák patrons of *Summer Song* had ever heard of. This Dvořák was on hand to deliver heartening homilies about the human condition, to read aloud his homesick letters to his wife far across the seas (to some sympathetic underscoring), and to tell us he was about to conduct his great new work. Everything was, considering the circumstances, in the best taste. It was a good thing that Naismith was such a fine actor, able to convince audiences that he was something like the real thing.

There was strong casting throughout *Summer Song*: a fresh-voiced Sally Ann Howes, and the popular operatic singer David Hughes as the two lovers, with an American double-act, Bonita Primrose and Van Atkins, as the comedy leads. Primrose's return to the States was a loss to the British musical; voices to shatter glass were not two a penny in the years ahead. Much appreciated, too, was the honeyed sound of the Trinidadian singer Edric Connor, given two of the show's most memorable moments in 'Deep Blue Evening' and 'Cotton Tail'. Probably the biggest British musical production of its year, *Summer Song* was kindly received but failed to run. It was not that the 'life of the composer and his music' had run its course (*The Great Waltz* waited until 1970), but perhaps that the British did not want to know about Dvořák's inner workings. Maschwitz thought that revisions should have been made during its try-out at Manchester, but, blinded by its happy reception, the show went into London a little too long, and sometimes, as befitted its setting, lumbering. Philosophically, Maschwitz decided that 'In the theatre it is no good complaining; if the audience doesn't attend, then for some reason or another you have failed.'[1] The old-fashioned air of *Summer Song* did not necessarily disqualify it from approval, and in its choral and orchestral felicities it remains appealing. The fact that it was about Dvořák is mostly irrelevant.

Literary biomusicals

The British musical was content to venture into many different spheres in search of its 'real' subjects, into its own world of show-business, and notably into the worlds of murder and mayhem, industrial strife and royalty. One of the first post-war 'real life' works was also one of the very few to tackle the literary life, and certainly the most tasteful work of its year: ***And So to Bed*** (New Theatre, 17 October 1951; 323). Ultimately good taste probably did for it. Vivian Ellis's adaptation of J. B. Fagan's play about Samuel Pepys (1633–1703) proved successful enough to survive an early transfer to the Strand Theatre. Ellis's score, his first post-war solo effort without A. P. Herbert, had the advantage of Mantovani's ten-piece orchestra giving the illusion of a seventeenth-century sound, a technique later used in Douglas Gamley's orchestration for *Virtue in Danger*. Ellis produced a sustained pastiche, with no concession to the 1951 ear, finding melody through an exploitation of the sarabande, gigue and rigaudon, and even using a snatch of one of Pepys's own songs at the beginning of 'Beauty Retire'; the title-number had long ago been written for one of Ellis's 1930s shows.

All seemed to be achieved with the most delicate of strokes, not least a love song, 'Love Me Little, Love Me Long,' which now sounds dangerously faint. Of broadness, there is none, and no place was given for Pepys, the pop-eyed comic actor Leslie Henson, to play for easy laughs. *And So to Bed* was assured in tone and remained faithful to its context. Like almost all the real-life British musicals that would follow, it also existed as a costume piece, and costume pieces may have offered audiences comfort zones far removed from the aggressiveness of the world from which it had stepped. Above all, *And So to Bed* proved that the British musical could be small (long before *Salad Days* was blamed for this cutting down to size) and somewhat beautiful. It even survived a post-London tour starring the husband and wife team of Anne Ziegler and Webster Booth, but not necessarily in that order. Listening to the score today, its mildness seems almost overpowering.

The other dominantly literary British musical arrived a decade later with **Robert and Elizabeth** (Lyric Theatre, 20 October 1964; 948), based on the love affair of the Victorian poets Robert Browning (1812–89) and Elizabeth Barrett (1806–61), played by Keith Michell and June Bronhill. This blatantly romantic piece had a sturdy adaptation by Ronald Millar from Rudolph Besier's old play about the couple, and an unseen musical by Fred G. Moritt. Most importantly, it had music by the Australian Ron Grainer, proving himself expert at evocation of period and style, his score dealing sometimes in pastiche but always attuned to the modern taste. No matter if the work sent thousands of playgoers down the road to Foyles Bookshop in search of some Collected Poems, *Robert and Elizabeth* had an assurance and spirit that lifted it into the top echelons of the British musical, it had passion and humour, lashes of sentiment and a blazing partnership in Michell and Bronhill, joined at the top of the bill by the actor John Clements, making his only appearance in a musical as the domineering and sexually dubious Mr Barrett. The younger generation's attitude to their Victorian corset exemplified Millar and Grainer's skill in 'The Family Moulton-Barrett', with its reference to getting 'in the family way', a phrase that would have been meaningless to Victoria's subjects. This was a rare fall from grace. For most of its time, *Robert and Elizabeth* inhabited the world from which it had been taken. In its way it could not be and has not been bettered.

The most conventional of the score is found in Michell and Bronhill's duets, intended as mildly amusing ('In a Simple Way') or soaring ('I Know Now') but although essentially romantic it is not the love music which most impresses. The exception to this is the plangent 'You Only to Love Me' sung by Angela Richards as Elizabeth's sister Henrietta. Attention is naturally focused on the plight of the crippled heroine, and her plight calls Grainer to his best work. In her duet with Henrietta, 'The World Outside', the claustrophobic domesticity in which Elizabeth exists is brilliantly contrasted with the longed-for beyond the window. So much of the music here must have come from an understanding of Bronhill's timbre, and her innate quality as a storytelling singer. The same is true for 'The Real Thing', when at last Elizabeth is taken from her musty room into the garden. For Act II, there is Elizabeth's 'Soliloquy', a real *coup de théâtre* in the right hands (as were Bronhill's), as Elizabeth struggles for the first time to her feet at the song's close. The worm turns when she rejects her father's advances with the pelting 'Woman and Man', a great cry for natural heterosexual relationships. The songs for Barrett and the rest of the cast are less memorable, but the marriage of Grainer and Bronhill makes *Robert and Elizabeth* something extraordinary in British musicals. Surely Grainer and Millar were only at the beginning of a long and satisfying career? No; mostly disappointment.

Other British works to celebrate literary endeavour include Sandy Wilson's entertainment *As Dorothy Parker* (1893–1967) *Once Said* and John Dankworth's book, music and lyrics for *Colette*. Dankworth's original score told the story of Sidonie-Gabrielle Colette (1873–1954); it had sophistication and Cleo Laine in a rare stage role, managing forty-seven performances at the Comedy Theatre in 1980.

The showbusiness biomusical:
*Joey Joey * Man of Magic * Sing a Rude Song*

It was inevitable that the British musical would have an incestuous affair with show-business, but the experiment was not successful. How, for instance, might a musical be made from the life of a Regency clown? This was the problem faced by ***Joey Joey*** (Saville Theatre, 11 October 1966; 23). In its first manifestation as *Joey* at the Bristol Old Vic in 1962 the whole affair was by Ron Moody; by the time the much revised show resurfaced in London four years later, the credits read 'Story, music and lyrics by Ron Moody' and 'Book by Keith Waterhouse and Willis Hall'. At some point it had been deemed necessary to bring in playwrights Waterhouse and Hall to beef up Moody's original, a move hardly calculated to please Moody, and in the end it seems that none of the parties were happy with the result. There was another problem which turned a difficult situation into the impossible: Moody was playing the clown.

Today, Joseph Grimaldi (1778–1837), the monarch of all pantomime clowns from whom is derived the generic clown name of 'Joey', is almost unknown to most theatregoers, and so it probably was in the London of 1966. In a programme note, the historian David Mayer III wrote that 'Grimaldi was the dramatic satirist of his era, an actor with range and resource, a nimble tumbler, an inventive

35 A rare reminder of an overlooked charm show: Ron Moody's life of Grimaldi, *Joey Joey*

comic whose "tricks of construction" ridiculed ostentatious coaches and dandy-ish uniforms, the fashionable millinery and even the strange animals introduced in other Covent Garden entertainments.' It had indeed been at the theatres of Covent Garden and Sadler's Wells where the depressed Grimaldi ('I am grim all day, but I make you laugh at night') reigned supreme. Another of his gifts to posterity was the phrase 'Joey Joey', meaning backstage fun and larks, and in borrowing this phrase for its title *Joey Joey* set out its stall not only to divert and entertain but to inform.

This is one of the dilemmas associated with turning real lives into musicals. Of what, however, might the audience *be* informed? After his death, Charles Dickens had been hired to edit Grimaldi's unpublished memoirs, and declared them 'twaddle'. Despite his legendary status, Grimaldi had a somewhat uneventful life, storing up theatrical successes, giving birth to a son whom he hoped would follow in his steps (he briefly did, before becoming a degenerate and predeceasing his father) and, physically broken by his exertions, retiring heartbroken from the stage and dying at the age of fifty-eight. An honest précis of all this might read 'the classic sad clown'. Structuring a full entertainment around the man and his world had to survive some uncertain foundations.

Whatever the outcome, *Joey Joey* was the product of Moody's obsession with Grimaldi. To further it, Moody turned down the opportunity to go to New York with the original production of *Oliver!* He subsequently claimed that his Fagin had been based on Grimaldi. The new musical was five years in the making. Playing the sad clown might have provided Moody with the most satisfying theatrical achievement of his career, and his many appearances in revue, and indeed his Fagin, suggested he could bring the old comic back to life. The warning signs were already there in 1962, when the *Theatre World* critic wrote that 'Theatrical legends cannot be exhumed.' The main criticism was that Moody was incapable of *being* Grimaldi, of igniting the audience's belief that they were watching a great actor – should Moody have looked for a Norman Wisdom to step into Joey's old shoes? As it was, when *Joey Joey* turned up four years later the critics were unanimously of the same opinion. In the *Daily Telegraph* W. A. Darlington considered that 'In a rather uninspired way book, lyrics and music all served their purpose. It was rash of Mr Moody, in my view, to top off this not inconsiderable achievement by playing the part of Grimaldi himself [...] Probably he played the part about as well as anybody would who is not a born funny man.' *The Times* declared it 'a gay, heartening and extremely likeable show', in effect 'an act of homage to Grimaldi, the romantic clown, in the form of a free fantasia on his career and art little concerned with bibliographical accuracy'.

The inclusion of some of Grimaldi's original material, a beguiling notion, may not have been to its advantage, but there was something loyal and right about the fact that Moody performed two of Grimaldi's numbers, the show's opener 'Typitywitchet' and 'Hot Codlins'.[2] To his cry of 'Here we are again!' Grimaldi would leap on stage and harangue the pit.

A little old woman her living got
By selling codlins, hot, hot, hot;
And this little woman, who codlins sold,
Tho' her codlins were hot, she felt herself cold.
So to keep herself warm, she thought it no sin
To fetch for herself a quartern of ...

The Sadler's Wells presumably shook to its foundations as the audience shrieked out 'GIN!', heard Grimaldi's mock-shock as he cried 'Oh for shame!' and joined him in the 'Ri tol iddy, iddy, iddy, Ri tol iddy, iddy, Ri tol lay', scarcely able to wait for the next verse.

This little old woman set off in a trot,
To fetch her quartern of hot, hot, hot!
She swallowed one glass, and it was so nice,
She tipped off another in a trice;
The glass she filled till the bottle shrunk,
And this little woman they say got ...

with its inevitable reply. 'Hot Codlins' was first sung in 1819 as Grimaldi approached the end of his working life, but put on a London stage in 1966 proved a mystifying and almost embarrassing revival. Audiences (certainly the one at the ill-attended matinee I saw) seemed unwilling to be dragooned into community singing, and being treated as if they had wandered into a seaside summer show. Anyway, at the end of its first week, the producers put up the closing notice, and Moody seemed to pack up shop. Perhaps he was reminded of another of the stories around his hero. When Grimaldi thought life not worth living, he went to a physician, who advised a visit to see the great Grimaldi, the sure cure for all unhappiness. Facing the failure, Moody told the press that he was considering giving up the theatre, but by Christmas he was playing Mr Darling and Captain Hook in the annual Scala revival of *Peter Pan*.

It sounds as if *Joey Joey* had little to recommend it, but that is far from the truth. In its way, it was bewitching. There were compensations for the lack of a decent story, or a half-way decent plot, not least Timothy O'Brien's magical recreation of Regency London, sometimes black and white, against which the period costumes, and the garishness of the Commedianti's costumes, stood out. There can be no pretence that its score was in the first division, but it had charm and sentiment, including Moody's declaration of his unsatisfactory existence in 'The Life That I Lead' at the end of the first act. As his wife Mary (his first wife Maria Hughes and his second Mary Bristow here telescoped into one) Vivienne Martin had some of the best of the score: her duet with son Joey Samuel ('Our Place') all comfort and homeliness; a comedy number, 'Flowers', 'Mary' and her claim for some sort of recognition in Grimaldi's life, 'Let's Think About Me for a Change'. The other songs, sometimes involving two British drolls unused to musicals, Gordon

Rollings and Joe Baker, were less distinctive. For some, most pleasure was found in the recreation of some authentically Regency stage routines: a basket dance for Grimaldi's compatriot Jack Bologna (Teddy Green), but most especially the hectic 'Winter Harlequinade' which effectively provided the final highlight, with Johnny Hutch's troupe of gymnasts falling through doors and windows in a kaleidoscope of idiocy before Grimaldi and his little son Joey Samuel (who in this version of events had not yet grown into a man) looked ahead hopefully as 'Father And Son'. But who had once said 'There is nothing so dead as a dead clown'?

More modest and less pleasing than *Joey Joey* was Harold Fielding's production of a 'musical fantasy suggested by incidents in the life of Harry Houdini' (1874–1926), **Man of Magic** (Piccadilly Theatre, 15 November 1966; 135). In choosing a show-business legend who had been American (in fact Hungarian), the writers were challenged. Raymond Marriott in the *Stage* was encouraging:

> Fact and fiction are mingled, but several essentials of Houdini's character are strongly evident, to give the story and the man rather more interest than is usual with the hero in a musical show. Houdini's dedication to his work, which makes it a mission in life; his driving ambition to get away from small-time vaudeville and become a world star; his careful, long sustained cultivation of his individual personality and the glamour of showmanship – all these aspects of Houdini are extremely fascinating.

One of the positive appeals of *Man of Magic* was its recreation of several of Houdini's illusions, not least the Chinese Water Torture, provided on this occasion by C. F. Taylor (Metal Tanks) Ltd, who hopefully knew what they were about. Escapology was not forgotten, nor Houdini's suspension from the Brooklyn Bridge (cunningly achieved by the use of puppets in the first act closer), but the recreation of Houdini's tricks could be problematic. At one point, Judith Bruce as Houdini's wife Bess was strapped to a table as a circular saw descended on her. At the first technical rehearsal Bruce screamed 'Stop!' as it came closer and closer. An irritated Fielding told her to pull herself together: *he* would be strapped to the table and show her there was nothing to worry about. Before the whizzing saw reached him, the yellow-looking Fielding screamed 'Stop!' Meanwhile, in the stalls at a rehearsal, sat Bruce's little daughter Nancy, named because Bruce had played Bart's heroine in *Oliver!* in London and New York. The show's low comedian Stubby Kaye sat beside her in the stalls and tried to make a buddy of her. 'Are you ticklish?' he asked. 'No,' she replied, 'I'm British.' This was probably funnier than anything in *Man of Magic*. When audiences dwindled the cast was asked to take a salary reduction. Perhaps remembering the derisory amounts they were being paid, they declined the offer.

The debut libretto by John Morley (who had appeared in a small way in *Follow That Girl* and worked on an Amy Johnson bio-musical with Sandy Wilson) and Aubrey Cash had some strengths, and the psychology applied was probably as

36 Stuart Damon as Houdini and Judith Bruce as Bess conquering the world
in the original London production of *Man of Magic*

good as one was going to get in a British musical. A significant weakness was
the music of Wilfred Wylam, the 'classical' composer Wilfred Josephs hiding
behind a pseudonym. Wylam's only foray into musicals was undistinguished,
but catching the flavour of Coney Island side-show, of the New York gin pal-
aces, and conveying the European diversity of Houdini's locations, was perhaps
too much to expect. It was generally agreed that nothing could have eclipsed
Stuart Damon (tall, dark, handsome, good actor, excellent singer) as Houdini,
but there was nothing memorable for him to sing beyond a driving duet with
Bruce, 'Conquer the World'. One of the strongest leading ladies of the 1960s,
Judith Bruce, did her best with her numbers, but none stayed in the mind. It
may have been Fielding himself who insisted on hiring the American actor
Stubby Kaye, for ever associated in the public's mind with *Guys and Dolls*, to
play Houdini's manager, Toby Kester, but here and there Kaye's material verged
on the terrible, as in 'Kester's Crystal Cabbage'. The dramatic dimensions of the
story grew darker towards its close, and did not marry well with such schoolboy
humour.

At least *Joey Joey* and *Man of Magic* tried to incorporate genuine elements
of their original sources, but the creators of a musical about the music hall performer Marie Lloyd (1870–1922) turned away from her famous songs, among
them 'Don't Dilly-Dally' ('My Old Man Said Follow the Van'), 'A Bit of a Ruin
That Cromwell Knocked about a Bit', 'Oh, Mr Porter!' and, from her earlier more
innocent days, 'The Boy in the Gallery'. Her audiences were delighted by the
suggestiveness in which she specialised. The song titles tell about it: 'Every Little
Movement Has a Meaning of its Own', 'Rosie Had a Very Rosy Time', 'She Didn't
Like to Tell Him What She Wanted', 'She'd Never Had a Lesson in her Life', 'You
Can't Stop a Girl from Thinking'. Marie Lloyd is known to have had at least 140
songs in her repertoire. Their words and music are redolent of their times, and
the social divisions of the society, the relish of drink and sex. Always somewhere
in the subconscious of the British psyche, music hall spoke of glitter and artificial
splendour, as in the gaudy provincial theatres of Frank Matcham in which Lloyd
regularly appeared, and of the eerie magic caught on canvas by Walter Sickert.
The cupids and caryatids gazed down at a mass of varied vulgarity. The archive
of atmosphere and melody available to anyone wanting to recreate the British
music hall was massive.

Sing a Rude Song (Garrick Theatre, 26 May 1970; 71), mounted for the centenary of Lloyd's birth, had a literate book and lyrics by Caryl Brahms and Ned
Sherrin, some contributions by Alan Bennett, and music by *Robert and Elizabeth*'s Ron Grainer. The challenge facing them was considerable, as was Lloyd's
life, a rise from poverty to national fame (and sometimes infamy), three disastrous marriages (*Sing a Rude Song* dropped the first), physical exhaustion and
death at the age of 52. 'Nothing can be done for this little lady,' said the doctor
called to attend her, 'she's dying of a broken heart'.

It was to *Sing a Rude Song*'s credit that it eschewed all of Lloyd's original material, but this meant coming up with songs as good as the ones Lloyd had sung. This the score signally failed to do in a collection of numbers that sounded like a public house sing-a-long. Brahms and Sherrin's lyrics lacked character, simplicity and singability; even the titles were continued on the next page ('No One Knows What It's Like to Fall in Love at Forty' and 'I'm in a Mood to Get My Teeth into a Song'). The promise held out by Grainer's previous scores was dashed. The orchestrations, unlike *Belle*'s accurate pastiche of a bored pit-band, were scraggy. 'Theatrical legends cannot be exhumed': the *Theatre World* critic had it right. Barbara Windsor played Lloyd, but Windsor's particular vulgarity was wrong, too young and chirpy, as if her brassiere might be about to fly across the studio during a *Carry On* film, and the dollops of sentimentality seemed a long way from anything to do with the emotionally upholstered Lloyd. Something was wrong, especially from authors who must have had an innate understanding of what music hall was about. It was the underbelly of the beast that was needed, but there was never a glimpse of it here.

The casting was poor. Denis Quilley as Husband Number 2, the music hall performer Alec Hurley (1871–1913), was given a new song 'I'm Nobody in Particular' which was so similar to his most famous number 'I Ain't Nobody in Particuler' as to render it unnecessary; perhaps Brahms and Sherrin were simply concerned about correcting the grammar. A member of the Bee-Gees pop-group, Maurice Gibb, was cast as the most disastrous of the husbands (Number 3), Bernard Dillon (1888–1941); this may have been a calculated attempt to draw in a different sort of audience, to whom it did not matter that Gibb had strictly limited acting abilities. But in any case, *Sing a Rude Song* seemed to happen in a vacuum, almost unaware of the lost world it hoped to recreate.

It is possible that there was a better musical about Marie Lloyd that might have challenged *Sing a Rude Song*. Cecil Madden had spent long years working on one called *Don't Dilly Dally*. Then, *The Times* of 20 December 1967 announced that 'A recently completed musical on the life of Marie Lloyd is due for a large-scale London production next year.' The musical was *Thanks for Nothing* (a dangerous title, and a gift for critics), written by the journalist and music hall enthusiast Daniel Farson and Harry Moore, using some of Lloyd's original songs and a number of new ones with lyrics by Farson and music by Norman Kay. It was to be produced by Joan Littlewood at Stratford East. Farson recalled in 1972 that Littlewood had originally wanted Windsor to play it, but then chose Avis Bunnage, another of her Stratford 'nuts'. Wandering into a rehearsal of his play, now renamed *The Marie Lloyd Story*, Farson failed to recognise any of his dialogue; one of the actresses was being dragged, screaming, across the stage. The next day when Farson walked into the stalls, he heard Littlewood's assistant Bob Grant telling the cast to play it as if it were a ballet.

Kay confessed that the original music-hall songs could not be improved upon (a point that *Sing a Rude Song* seemed to confirm), but the Theatre Workshop production was not without its admirers, and Bunnage was a memorable heroine.

She had the right common touch, mature and guttural and elemental, especially potent as Lloyd grew older. This was certainly more like the Lloyd plagued by unhappy relationships, rotting teeth and ill-health, whose hacking cough may still be heard between verses on her recording of one of her World War I hits 'Now You've Got Your Khaki On'. For Farson, the most moving moment came at the end of the first act, when Bunnage sang 'Don't Dilly Dally' and, gradually, the whole theatre joined in. In its way, any musical about Lloyd was a luxury; her legacy would survive without such a reminder. In 1969 a revised version of *The Marie Lloyd Story* premiered at the Theatre Royal, Lincoln, using only Lloyd's original songs. Successful enough to be taken up for a West End production, plans for its revival were dropped because of the imminent production of *Sing a Rude Song*.

Later London musicals based on the real lives of show-business personalities suggested that those looking for long runs should look elsewhere for inspiration. Among these *The Biograph Girl* learned a lesson already learned on Broadway with Jerry Herman's *Mack and Mabel*, that the world of the silent film is perilous territory for musical treatment. Others attempting to revive dead stars were *Dean* and *Marilyn!* In the latter, all Stephanie Lawrence's hard work on stage to recreate the allure of Marilyn Monroe was ruined at the end of the evening by a full-screen film montage of original clips, making clear the magical ingredient that no stage recreation could hope to achieve. *Cockie!*, a short-lived 'musical on the career of Charles B. Cochran' the impresario, in effect a musical revue with no original numbers, was given no welcome from critics or audiences.

A trend for 'tributes' took off in the 1970s. An early example was *John, Paul, George, Ringo and Bert*, with a book concocted by Willy Russell. Managements realised that they did not need to risk an original show and score when hugely successful artists and their already world-known songs could be shoehorned into an evening's easy entertainment. Audiences walked *into* the theatre humming the tunes. Such diversions were often presented as or mistaken for British musicals. *Underneath the Arches*, a celebration of Bud Flanagan and Chesney Allen and therefore the Crazy Gang, had a title that immediately conveyed its subject to its middle-aged and elderly audiences, but no original songs. *The Travelling Music Show* of 1978 was a rare example of a tribute show to two of the British musical's own, Anthony Newley and Bricusse, but quickly failed. In the decades to follow there has been a flood of revue-biography-concert shows, mostly riding on the back of famous pop groups with reputations that guaranteed a healthy box-office. These works are usually only relevant to the managements who make great amounts of money from them, but at times London's theatres (and provincial theatres welcoming their touring productions) are almost suffocated by them. In a climate where the tribute show flourishes, the chances of any British musical breaking through into the public consciousness, let alone favour, are slim.

The British biomusical and dark deeds:
The Rector of Stiffkey and Jack the Ripper

The British musical had to find a way of coping with annals of crime, or at least notoriety. One of the finest, *Belle*, dealt with the case of Dr Crippen, adding dashes of pastiche and pantomime and grand opera, to general puzzlement. The Reverend Harold F. Davidson, Rector of Stiffkey (1875–1937) in Norfolk, would probably not have been surprised to find himself the subject of a musical entertainment. Before taking holy orders he had been a music hall turn. 'As an entertainer I belong to the era before jazz, bridge, and Noel Coward,' he told a reporter.[3] Much respected in his parish, Davidson caught the train after his Sunday services, spending the rest of the week in London or, more accurately, Soho. Here he became, for reasons that made national headlines, 'The Prostitute's Padre'. Perhaps he was the root of that age-old musical hall question and answer: 'God saves fallen women!' – 'Will he save one for me?' Adding to the gaiety of the nation, Davidson was accused of immoral conduct, summoned to an ecclesiastical court and defrocked in Norwich Cathedral, on which occasion he was late for the ceremony, and sent the Bishop a jocular note of apology. It was the end for the pyjama parties he had hosted at Stiffkey rectory, where working girls relaxed and took tea with Davidson and his compliant wife.

Without a Max Clifford to guide his future, the disgraced cleric was taken up by the 'Showman King of Blackpool', Luke Gannon, who made a living from what today we would regard as the politically incorrect. To Gannon, Davidson was a God-given gift. In the autumn of 1932 Davidson stepped into a barrel where he would stay without food for two weeks and a fee of £500. On the very first day of this exhibition 10,000 patrons paid their 2d. to visit. Three years later Davidson was back in Blackpool, this time in a glass-covered cabinet, looking comfy in a bed, wearing pyjamas and with a good book (hopefully of spiritual content) to read, but he was threatening to fast himself to death unless the council rejected its intention of closing down such lurid sideshows. The police took Davidson into custody, charging him with attempted suicide. The case was dismissed, and a doctor declared that the rest had done the rector good. However, a poetic justice awaited. In the summer of 1937 Davidson was a major attraction at Skegness Amusement Park, appearing in a cage with two lions, Freddie and Toto, as 'A Modern Daniel in a Lion's Den'. Jostling the sleepy animals into alertness, he was fatally mauled by Freddie. Onlookers managed to pull Davidson from the cage, but he expired at Skegness Cottage Hospital.

For any British musical, this was better than any show-business theme could ever have been. What is more, Davidson could be presented as an innocent with complete conviction, for many believed he had never indulged in any sexual activity with any of his girls, and those who did believe it were probably unconcerned. The music hall background, the scandal and its tawdry after-life provided strong meat for dramatisation. The first British musical to light on this fable was **God Made the Little Red Apple** (Stables Theatre Club, Manchester, 19 March 1969; season) written by Stuart Douglass, restaged three years later with a stronger cast as **The Vicar of Soho** (Gardner Centre, Brighton, 2 August 1972; season). George Benson was Davidson, Anna Barry one of his most prominent girls, and James Bolam in several roles, including that of Gannon, made his mark with a song and dance sequence. The lack of any cast recording or published music makes any meaningful commentary impossible; at the very least, the fact that this was the last score by Tony Russell, the composer of *The Matchgirls*, held interest.

Three months after *God Made the Little Red Apple* another Rector of Stiff-key musical managed to get into London. David Wright and David Wood's **The Stiffkey Scandals of 1932** (Queen's Theatre, 12 June 1969; 12) had first surfaced as **A Life in Bedrooms** (Traverse Theatre, Edinburgh, 11 April 1967; season) with Charles Lewsen as Davidson, a role he resumed for the London production. Wood based his script on the verbatim courtroom proceedings published in *The Times*, in a piece that had too much the air of a documentary. *The Stiffkey Scandals of 1932* had some good credentials: a cast that included the jazz singer Annie Ross, Terri Stevens, Peter Bowles, the Go-Jos and the Piccadilly Ten. As with so many British musicals, the production team was of the finest: director Patrick Garland, musical director Carl Davis, designs by Patrick Robertson, costumes by Rosemary Vercoe. In truth, the piece was as much a play with songs as a musical, but in either form it generated little interest. Furthermore, it had none of the daring of *Belle*. Its third manifestation was as **The Prostitute's Padre** (Norwich Playhouse, 20 March 1997; season), revised for the occasion by Wood. Jimmy Thompson promised to be an ideal leading man, but at the last moment withdrew. Badly cast, Henry Burke's production was a dismal reminder of Norfolk's naughtiest vicar, the auditorium filled with far fewer worshippers than attended the popular rector's sermons. At the very height of his fame it was almost impossible to get a pew.

The dubious heroism of highwayman Jack Sheppard was found in *Stand and Deliver*, but a critical drubbing, short run and lack of any recording has consigned it to total obscurity. There was more mayhem in **Jack the Ripper** (Ambassadors Theatre, 17 September 1974; 228), a work underappreciated at the time. Of the several musicals originating at the Players' Theatre, *Jack the Ripper* bore the most marks of the association, simply because of the form through which the work's authors (the libretto by Ron Pember and Dennis de Marne, the music by Pember) told their story: Victorian music hall. London's Players' Theatre in Villiers Street had long been the home of an allegedly ribald but distinctly polite, nightly recreation of that genre, and the authors, perhaps wanting to entice the management into taking their work on, set their play-within-a-play within the context of a night at the music hall, replete with the Players' usual loyal toast to Her Majesty ('God Bless Her!').

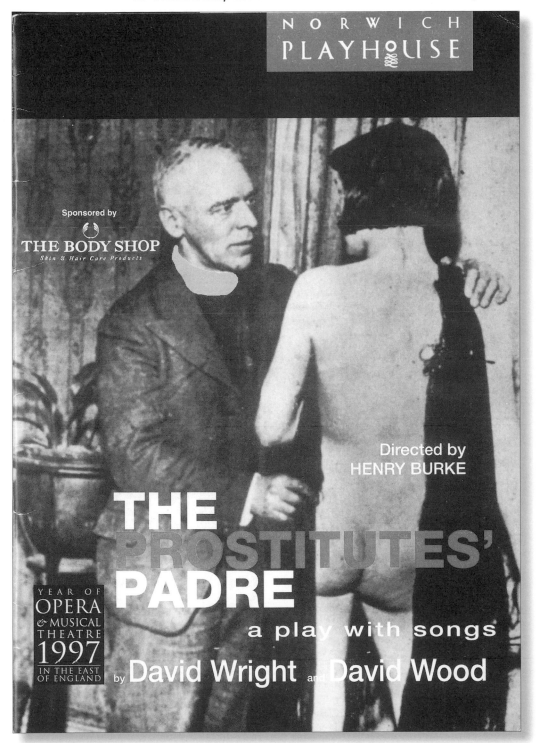

37 Another manifestation of the Stiffkey scandal of 1932

A jolly time was to be had by all, and then the music hall atmosphere was switched off and the audience spirited into the back streets of Soho, to face the 'real' elements of the evening, the prostitutes of Whitechapel, principally the doomed Marie Kelly, superbly played by Terri Stevens, who had already scored in the Stiffkey 'real' life musical. As the action went in and out of the music-hall proscenium into the dirt and chaos of the East End of 1888, *Jack the Ripper* turned into one of the most socially conscious musicals of the post-war period. There were moments when its intensity was almost overwhelming, and all achieved on a tiny stage with some stunning theatrical effects. All London seemed to stretch at the back of the stage at one point, through a deepening fog that spoke of misdeed and filth. The director and designer Reginald Woolley had long had an artists' eye for the alleyways and dim reaches of London, and in *Jack the Ripper* he may have reached a zenith.

Poor old *Belle* had struggled to retain public favour with *one* murder (never mind the fact that Sheridan Morley had described Crippen as a mass-murderer)[4] but *Jack the Ripper* had a handful. Pember and De Marne's trick was to marry the raucous music hall numbers alongside those that spoke of a reality beyond the echoes of brightly-lit theatres. Opening the programme, the audience could read a welcoming message from the Ambassadors' owner, Larry Parnes: 'In this day and age you all have very varied tastes, but I always like to think that these tastes will include a charming musical like *Jack the Ripper*.'[5]

This, of course, was nonsense; the writers and cast must have squirmed to read it. The dreadful deaths of the prostitutes, the removal of their internal organs, *charming*? In fact, by travelling the distance between its music hall setting and – if we think in a cinematic sense – of frequently dissolving into the 'real' drama, the play worked on the senses. Behind the seemingly endless ensemble numbers, *Jack the Ripper* provides two of the most haunting songs in British musicals of the 1970s, 'Goodbye, Day' and 'Step across the River'. Marie's description of her existence in 'Half a Dozen Pints' is almost as good, made almost unbearably real in Stevens' performance. Where *Belle* had intentionally muddled the murder with the comedy (there was a scene where Crippen took a huge saw to Belle's dead body) *Jack the Ripper* managed by turn to chill, thrill and be emotionally compelling, whereas *Belle* had never managed all of the above. When it seemed as if *Jack the Ripper* might be a success an original cast recording was made, but never published. Fortunately, the play has found an afterlife among amateur societies.

The British musical occasionally continued its experiment to deal with real crimes. In 1999 the case of Derek Bentley (1933–53), hanged at the age of nineteen for the murder of a policeman, was the subject of *Let Him Have Justice*, a work that had no time for the amusing diversions used by *Belle* or *Jack the Ripper*.

The British biomusical 'By Royal Appointment'

In its attempt to offer reality, the British musical has sometimes bowed the knee. For some writers, the By Royal Appointment label has promised much. Not everyone has heard of Joseph Grimaldi or Harry Houdini or Derek Bentley, but the obedient citizen knows his monarch. Sometimes, royalty has been not at the centre of the musical, but drops in sometime during the evening to add blue blood. *And So to Bed* had Charles II, as did *Wren*, 'a musical celebration of the seventeenth century' briefly seen in London in 1978. *Pocahontas* had King James I (1566–1625) and his queen, and French royalty was *de rigueur* for adaptations (of which there were a few) of Alexandre Dumas's *The Three Musketeers*. The appearance of Nell Gwyn (1650–87) necessitated the appearance of King Charles II (1630–85) in *Nell!* (Richmond Theatre, 8 April 1970; season and tour). One of its producers, Tony Hatch, presented his wife Jackie Trent as Gwyn, with Stuart Damon as Charles II and Hermione Baddeley as Nell's mother. The songs were by John Worth, already established as a writer of pop songs, but its failure to get into London or a recording studio has consigned them to history. From another time, Queen Victoria was about to enter just as the final curtain fell on Alan Melville and Charles Zwar's *Marigold*, and HM got the best number, 'The Blessed Trinity', in the 1982 *Poppy*, but it is only for the most brave to attempt a musical that puts royalty in the leading roles. Victoria and her consort were the reasons behind the American-written *I and Albert*, one of the more successful regal musicals. Those that followed were less fortunate.

Thomas and the King (Her Majesty's Theatre, 16 October 1975; 20), another American work but seen only in London, is sometimes referred to as one of the most visually stunning of musicals, possibly to take the mind off its content. In a way, it all rather resembled *Troubador*, its songs sounding as if they were lefto-vers from that score. The story of Henry II (1133–89) and his Archbishop of Canterbury, Thomas Becket (1118–70), ending in the murder of Becket in Canterbury Cathedral, is clearly dramatic. Henry's possibly rhetorical question 'Who will rid me of this meddlesome priest?' inspired four knights to murder his archbishop, an event that horrified Christendom and made Canterbury a place of pilgrimage for almost four centuries. Henry regretted the death, and was probably politically wise to do so. In 1174 he wore sack-cloth and was flogged by priests as he walked through the streets of the city.

The writers (Edward Anhalt book, James Harbert lyrics and John Williams music) had little option but to produce singing kings and a warbling archbishop, and an uneasy alliance was made by casting the musical actor James Smillie as Henry with the straight actor Richard Johnson as Thomas. The attempt to keep things serious was commendable, but most of the songs were mired in tortu-ous self-analysis (the heroine's 'Am I Beautiful?', 'The Question', 'What Choice Have I?), and too often the singers seemed to be addressing God rather than the four and ninepennies. Harbert's lyrics struggled to maintain dignity (at one point someone sings of Becket 'We'll ring his Canterbury bell'), although Williams' music was always professional. Reminiscent of the final moments of *Two Cities* with the curtain coming down on 'It's a far, far better thing I do than I have ever done', *Thomas and the King* was almost obliged to have an eleven o'clock number called 'Who Will Rid Me?'

It was inevitable that a musical about Henry VIII (1491–1547) should find its way into London, although a mooted version by Sandy Wilson had failed to do so in the 1950s. The temptation of having not one but six leading ladies in **Kings and Clowns** (Phoenix Theatre, 1 March 1978; 34) may have been irresistible, especially to Leslie Bricusse who with Anthony Newley had made a multi-woman out of the one leading lady of *Stop the World – I Want to Get Off*. A quick casualty, audiences at Bricusse's royal levee may have spent some of the time wondering how its six female stars had come to an amicable arrangement about who should have which dressing room. At least *Thomas and the King* had a veneer of historical accuracy about it; there was nothing remotely scholarly about the charade of *Kings and Clowns*.

Lessons about the dangers of the royal musical might have been learned by producers and writers, but they were forgotten by the time **Always** (Victoria Palace, 22 May 1997; 76) reached London. As its announcements explained 'In 1936 Edward VIII chose to abdicate the throne rather than abandon his true love, Wallis Simpson. This extraordinary relationship is brought to life in this remarkable, exquisite and lavish new musical.'[6] The po-faced programme note signs off with the assertion that 'In an age where the young sought desperately for something to believe in, Edward was the ultimate romantic and as such became the role model for the entire escapist generation.' The idea that the weak Edward would work as an 'ultimate romantic' at least gave the audience a hearty laugh before the curtain went up, but *Always* itself (as the title-song told us, 'If always were a place I'd take you there') was intent on taking itself seriously. A lily had been chosen as the show's motif, but not because Edward was probably one of the most lily-livered personalities of his time. No, Wallis had once brought him a bunch of them, and lilies adorned his coffin. As its audience stuffed handkerchiefs into their mouths, the writers William May and Jason Sprague assured themselves a place in theatrical history with three hours of obsequious bilge; it was a surprise that anyone without a forelock was allowed to witness such witless, reverential goings-on.

Ultimately (and *Always* presented itself as 'The Ultimate Love Story'), the writers had written a piece to appeal to those who spent their lives with their heads stuck in the railings of Buckingham Palace. Unfortunately, the Fire Brigade had been unable to free enough of them to fill the Victoria Palace for more than a few weeks. There was simply no *intelligence* about *Always*. To begin, how could the writers have imagined that a romantic musical could be made about two such deeply unattractive people? As Edward VIII (1894–1972), Clive Carter had been tutored to speak in a ridiculously over-elocuted voice, turning him into a sort of high-born Speaking Clock. In fact, he caught the almost wimpish quality of the man, but this achievement cancelled out any belief in England's troubled king as a great lover. Jan Hartley as Wallis Simpson (1895–1986) looked uncannily like the woman, and at least sang well. As her Aunt Bessie, Shani Wallis (no relation) returned to the London stage she had left in the late 1950s, having made clear in interviews how unhappy she was with her role. Her vengeance was to deliver two numbers as if she were doing cabaret at Vegas.

The only genuine cabaret of the evening came when Sheila Ferguson, once of the singing group the Three Degrees, sang 'Love's Carousel'. London's *Evening Standard* described her 'voice that could destroy buildings let alone royal dynasties, accompanied by mincing pierrots and prancing harlequinades with horse's heads', the result being 'sheer, buttock-clenching comic awfulness'. The review continued 'There have been dud musicals this year, but nothing to match this gloriously misguided attempt [...] it is the sheer, cheesy folly of the concept that puts Frank Hauser's hilarious production right up there [...] for connoisseurs of the truly bad musical.'

For those willing to appreciate it, there was much of the Theatre of the Absurd about *Always*. A mature musical leading lady invited to audition for the role of Queen Mary declined when told to turn up in fishnet tights and tap shoes. In fact, Her Majesty did not appear thus attired in the production; *Always* might have been more fun had she done so. Showing anything less than goggling adoration of a royal personage would, presumably, have meant immediate removal from the Victoria Palace to the Tower of London. Things might have been enlivened by dealing with the rumours that Wallis had once worked in a brothel, or the pair's involvement with the Nazis. Come to that, was Wallis really a man in drag? Almost any original or faintly disrespectful idea might have been better than none at all. Instead, there was the spectacle of hat-doffing Welsh miners carolling 'Long May You Reign'; the truth was that the writers simply backed out of the room to show an undying respect. A few weeks after the closure of *Always* – an object lesson in not attempting to turn the tawdry into the beatific – the death of Diana Princess of Wales brought another troubled royal romance sharply into focus. Rumours of various 'Diana' musicals surfaced, floated and were dissipated.

Politics and the British biomusical

Politicians have usually been safe from the British musical. *Always* might have taken some notice of **Mrs Wilson's Diary** (Theatre Royal Stratford East, 21 September 1967; transferred Criterion Theatre, 24 October 1967; 175), a lampoon around the then Prime Minister Harold Wilson (1916–95), originated in the magazine *Private Eye* by Richard Ingrams and John Wells, with music and songs by Jeremy Taylor, produced by Joan Littlewood. 'Bang, my good woman,' said the cartoon beneath the credits, 'goes your hope of an Arts Council grant.'[7] A modest sprinkling of music didn't qualify it as a musical, although the songs provided some of the highlights, including the account of Mary (Mrs) Wilson's (b. 1917) domestic duties in 'Here I Kneel', and her duet with the PM 'Harold and Me'. There was amusement to be had from Mrs Callaghan (her husband Chancellor of the Exchequer soon-to-be Home Secretary James was otherwise engaged) and Wilson's Foreign Secretary George Brown. When the play was made into a TV version, Brown insisted that certain scenes were cut. Not in the least satirical was *The Station Master's Daughter* (Yvonne Arnaud Theatre, Guildford, 11 April 1968; season). The libretto by Frank Harvey, with music by Charles Zwar, had Rose Hill as a Minister for Transport trying to shut down a local railway. Audiences realised that this was meant to be Barbara Castle (1910–2002), but by the time the show opened Castle had moved to another ministerial post, rendering the piece historical.

In 1978 *Evita* became the most successful and famous British musical to deal with politicians, although not British. Ten years later, the desperate state of the British musical unconnected to the Lloyd Webber school was confirmed by *Winnie*, a hotch-potch entertainment about Winston Churchill (1874–1965) seen at the Victoria Palace in 1988. Cyril Ornadel, the show's musical director and part-composer, was to have written its few original songs to slot into the pattern of those that 'Winnie' may have known of if not whistled, with his frequent collaborator Norman Newell. Newell was replaced by the distinguished Arnold Sundgaard, who had collaborated with Kurt Weill and Alec Wilder. Other writers, including Alan Braden and Tony Hatch, submitted songs for consideration. Hubert Gregg obliged by revising his lyrics for the World War II success 'I'm Going to Get Lit Up When the Lights Go on in London'.

There wasn't much integrity about *Winnie*. Orandel was summarily informed that Lionel Bart was to write the show's original songs, but time passed and Bart was unable to produce the material. When the show, already plagued by financial difficulties, opened in Manchester, Orandel was furious to see posters still insisting 'Music by Lionel Bart'; Ornadel was listed in the programme as lyricist. Some of the cast left the production, and the first previews were cancelled. After the show's last night in Manchester, just before opening in London, the show's producer Robin Hardy demanded major changes to the score, provoking a major fall-out with Ornadel and the show's stars, Virginia McKenna and Robert Hardy. A largely negative critical response encouraged Hardy to ask the company to accept a 25 per cent cut in pay. The company decided against accepting. With only twenty-four hours' notice the production was closed, having incurred losses of around £1.5 million.

The British biomusical and social issues

The British musical only infrequently bothered itself with social issues, and when it did things did not always turn out well. Take the 1980 *Barnardo*. Little more than an excuse for a Cockney knees-up and squelching sentimentality, this retelling of the life of Thomas John Barnardo (1845–1905) was pitiful:

one of the lyrics ran 'Fog is always *thick* in / You'll get done real *quick* in / Feel your heart *tick-tick* in London's East End'. *Barnardo* tottered through forty-three performances.

In 1966 Londoners were offered *two* British musicals about the 1888 employees' strike at Bryant & May's matchworks in Bow, East London. The 1,400 employees were all women, complaining at the terrible conditions in which they worked, their inadequate pay and bullying treatment by the management. The factory operated a stringent fining system: latecomers lost half a day's pay, and the pay of those who went to the lavatory without permission was docked. There was also the prospect of developing 'phossy jaw', a form of osteonecrosis caused by the yellow phosphorus used in the production of matches. The condition began with loss of hair, yellowing of the skin, then a greening and a blackening, the secretion of an evil-smelling pus, and death. Fearing a loss of trade, the British government had not followed many other countries in banning the use of the particular type of phosphorus responsible.

The Fabian Annie Besant (1847–1933) was fired by a talk given by Clementina Black to the Fabian Society in June 1888 about the plight of the Bryant & May girls. After visiting the factory to see conditions for herself, Besant wrote an article, 'White Slavery in London' in the *Link*.

> Born in slums, driven to work while still children, undersized because under-fed, oppressed because helpless, flung aside as soon as worked out, who cares if they die or go on to the streets provided only that Bryant & May shareholders get their 23 per cent and Mr Theodore Bryant can erect statues and buy parks? Girls are used to carry boxes on their heads until the hair is rubbed off and the young heads are bald at fifteen years of age. Country clergymen with shares in Bryant & May's draw down on your knee your fifteen year old daughter; pass your hand tenderly over the silky clustering curls, rejoice in the dainty beauty of the thick, shiny tresses.[8]

An awakened public interest prompted the Bryant & May management to force the girls to sign an assurance that they were satisfied with their lot. Those who refused were sacked, and the strike began. While it seems that Besant neither encouraged nor supported the strike, it is clear that her interest helped to polarise reactions. Whatever its causes, the matchgirls' concerted action was an important moment for the organised labour movement, and one that had its effect on the London Dock Strike of 1889.

Without the socialist passion of its librettist, Bill Owen, *The Matchgirls* (Globe Theatre, 1 March 1966; 119) would never have been written. Owen's sympathies with the labour movement (in its least political form) had been nurtured by his early association with London's Unity Theatre, itself developed from the Workers' Theatre movement in the East End. This pioneering organisation took social issues to its working-class audiences, using various forms of presentation to put across its socialist message, perhaps a plea for more social cohesion, or an argument against Fascism. Those forms embraced plays or documentaries or pantomimes, just as *Belle* and *Poppy* used 'light' art forms to convey serious issues.

As early as 1949 Owen had written a play about the matchgirls which had been produced at the Unity. In the event, his libretto for the musical version was possibly its least valuable asset, but its importance should not be overlooked, for here was a British musical dealing with an historical industrial dispute, and linking it to the dockers' strike that would follow by having its heroine in love with one of the men. On the credit side, *The Matchgirls* had a score by a promising newcomer to the genre, the jazz musician Tony Russell; direction and choreography by Gillian Lynne, attempting something almost untried in the British musical – an unusual integration of dance and movement into the very heart of the work; and, not least, a central performance that ranks as one of the finest of our period. In the opinion of the critic Helen Dawson 'Vivienne Martin [as Kate] makes the evening worth weeping through.'[9]

One of the principal difficulties faced by the writers and director was to convey the darkness of the subject while giving the public a lively and enjoyable evening. This was to an extent achieved, even if the problem became evident in the show's opening number 'Phosphorus', a sort of wryly comic hymn to the spectre that haunted the matchgirls' lives, set to a jogging tune. The screw turned when Besant first comes to see for herself, and is given a guided tour by Kate, leader of the girls, in 'Look Around', a chastening and effective dirge on their misery. The pity expressed so deeply in *The Matchgirls* is found again in 'Dear Lady' when Besant receives a letter written by Kate (Charles West sang another 'Dear Lady' in *Strike a Light!*). Here, Owen is quoting an original document.

> Dear Lady they have been trying to get the poor girls to say that it is all lies that has been printed and trying to make us sign papers that it is all lies; dear Lady nobody knows what it is we have put up with and we will not sign them. We thank you very much for the kindness you have shown to us. My dear Lady we hope you will not get into any trouble on our behalf as what you have spoken is quite true.[10]

On the other hand, Owen and Russell dress up their work with liberal doses of Cockney jollity, as in 'Mind You, Bert' and the second act celebration of 'Cockney Sparrers'. These are not the best of *The Matchgirls*, in which Russell's music and orchestration often achieve a deep melancholia. This infuses 'Men' and a gentle duet for Kate and her boyfriend Joe, 'There's Something about You', and the same quality is found in Kate's steely realisation that she has to choose between heart (loving her Joe) and carrying on with the strike in 'Comes a Time'. At its most virile the score leaves no doubt about the aspirations of its heroines, for which Russell writes his strongest pieces: the raffle in the factory ("Atful of 'Ope', also called 'Look at That Hat'); the pulsating Act I closer 'We're Gonna Show 'Em' in which Lynne packed the matchgirls into an aggressive little army driving towards victory; Kate and Joe's defiant claim to live 'This Life of Mine'. The need to musicalise Besant's socialist convictions resulted in her Act II 'I Long to See The Day', a moment of high passion and resolve against the background of so much drabness. It came as a breath of relief to find a scene in a Kentish hop field where 'The Hopping Dance' threw off all the characters' concerns in a joyful routine that is probably the best remembered moment of the score. Whatever criticisms were levelled at it, no one suggested the piece was disingenuous. An original cast recording and amateur performances have helped keep *The Matchgirls* alive.

The second Bryant & May musical to appear in London in 1966, **Strike a Light!** (Piccadilly Theatre, 5 July 1966; 30) began its twelve week long pre-London tour a month after *The Matchgirls* opened at the Globe. Its early closure and lack of a full recording or published script have sent the work to the dustbin of British musicals, making a meaningful comparison with Owen and Russell's version impossible. There is no doubt that everything about *Strike a Light!* was more professional, bigger, and more starry. For its leader of the Bryant & May strike it had Jeannie Carson as Sarah Chapman, making her first return to British musicals since *Love from Judy*, John Fraser in his only London musical as her suitor, and Evelyn Laye as Annie Besant. A more substantial cast, more expensive production values, and a large orchestra proclaimed the new work's superiority over the earlier Bryant & May musical.

Where *The Matchgirls* had gone for the po-faced, *Strike a Light!* went for smiling faces. (There is no photograph I have seen of the production that allows anything but a broad grin from its principals.) There was, after all, no more reason to believe in Miss Laye's genteel interpretation of the formidable Besant than in Marion Grimaldi's impersonation in *The Matchgirls*. *Strike a Light*'s librettist Joyce Adcock explained in a programme note that this was 'not a musical about misery, disease and squalor. It is a musical about courage, vitality and hope'. Wasn't this the very sort of musical the public took to? If this seemed like a gentlewomanly dig at the glum *Matchgirls*, so did the added note that 'the risk of phossy-jaw [...] was very small at the time of the strike'.

So, the previous show had misled us into worrying about those girls! By presenting as a jolly evening of song and dance *Strike a Light!* might have been setting itself up for a critical mauling, but the reviews were warmer than for *The Matchgirls*. The *Stage* found it 'a jolly show, and nothing anywhere near reality, which is certainly entertaining in its way, and romanticises and sentimentalises everything it touches'.[11] By diluting the seriousness of the very premise on which the show was built, *Strike a Light!* won its welcome, but it was not enough to bring in audiences. In an effort to keep the production going, the company worked for two weeks for the basic Equity rate of £15 a week. In a last throw, Carson sang a number from the show on ITV's *Sunday Night at the London Palladium* but she had already vacated her dressing-room at the Piccadilly.

The biomusical and Moral Re-Armament

Less ambitious than any of the above, and less worthy of attention as a serious work was the well-intentioned *Annie* (Westminster Theatre, 27 July 1967; 398). A work of little worth beyond its attempt to steer the hearts and consciences of its audience into a new understanding of what community and good citizenship was, *Annie* was a musical biography of Annie Jaeger (1875–1944), the owner of a hat shop in Stockport in the 1930s. The shop was in the working-class area of Higher Hallgate, standing before a cotton mill, a brewery next door and public houses on every street. Annie was a good neighbour, with a growing concern for the ordinary man and his family. In a programme note Annie's son William recognised that 'So much of the history of our friends in the Labour movement was that of sacrifice, struggle, success and then stagnation when apathy set in and the purpose of doing something for mankind was forgotten.'[12] Annie's concerns came together in a realisation that God was the most important element in her life. Selling her shop, she moved to London's East End to help others create the united home, for this she felt was the secret of personal and spiritual happiness. When the Moral Re-Armament movement was established in 1938, Jaeger became one of its prime movers, exemplifying the role of the ordinary person striving to change the world for the better. Her work extended through Sweden, Holland and the USA. A modest, uneducated remaker of the world who reached out to others. After her death, her son received over 500 letters from families she had helped and inspired.

If goodness was enough reason to make a musical of someone's life, Jaeger was thoroughly deserving. The management of the Moral Re-Armament-owned Westminster Theatre depended on its house writers to provide many of the entertainments (plays, pantomimes and musicals) staged there, and *Annie* was the work of two of them, librettist Alan Thornhill who had written the first Moral Re-Armament play staged at the theatre in 1946, and composer William L. Reed, the sort of name one felt one must have seen on the covers of hymn books. *Annie*'s strong card was its three principals. For the glamorous soprano Margaret Burton (Annie) it was a rare success in a career pockmarked with flops, and she brought an earthiness and natural warmth to her role, some of which she may have accumulated through her time in the TV soap-opera *Coronation Street*.

Playgoers to the Westminster may not have been the most sophisticated of Londoners, but they would have relished Burton's programme photograph, her hair coiled elegantly above her head, the beauty spot, the extravagantly jewelled drop-earrings. The show's young lovers were capably taken by Angela Richards (recently of *On the Level* – the contrast with *Annie* could hardly have been more stark) and Gerard Hely, the refugee leading man of *The Matchgirls*. In all other departments *Annie* was unremarkable, its songs arch and thumpingly unimaginative. Everything was at the mercy of the message, as in the principal number for Annie, 'Open Your Heart' ('Open it wide, then open it wider').

Annie (Margaret Burton) waves goodbye as she leaves Stockport for adventures in London's East End.

"ANNIE"
at the
WESTMINSTER
THEATRE

"Right for you" sings Annie as neighbours and customers try on hats in her shop.

38 Ready for Moral Re-Armament, Margaret Burton leaves Stockport for London in the original London production of *Annie* (1967)

In a world where artistic and moral effort was appreciated, there would already be at least a booklet about the theatrical activities of Moral Re-Armament, with details of its musicals, including *High Diplomacy* and *Space is so Startling*. The aim was often too obviously to proselytise, buying a ticket too much like paying to get into Sunday School. Few of the productions were ever considered serious contenders by the capital's critics, and the musicals tended to negate themselves by never offering major stars or choreography or spectacle or orchestras. A biomusical about Sir Francis Drake (1540–96), not a Moral Re-Armament but a commercial production that originally played the West End, was ***Drake's Dream*** (Shaftesbury Theatre, 7 December 1977; transferred to Westminster Theatre, 1 February 1978; 82). The public was invited to 'come sailing round the world with [the pop-singer leading man] Paul Jones' in a 'funtastic [*sic*] musical adventure for all the family', and Drake's dream, presumably not conflicting with that of Moral Re-Armament and revised for the occasion by the Theatre Royal, Stratford East director Ken Hill, was considered wholesome enough for the Westminster, but not entertaining enough to attract many customers.

The previous year, Moral Re-Armament staged a musical which deserves to be remembered as one of its most ambitious and memorable. ***Ride! Ride!*** (Westminster Theatre, 20 May 1976; 76) was first staged at a Methodist church in Lancashire. Alan Thornhill's libretto had the benefit of Penelope Thwaites' music in this tribute to the religious reformer and founder of Methodism John Wesley (1703–91), using as its driving force the imprisonment in Bedlam of one of his converts, Martha Thompson. A strongly built score revealed at its centre the equivalent of *Annie*'s anthem 'Open Your Heart' in 'The Whole Wide World Is My Parish', reconstructing Wesley's insistence that 'The whole world is my parish'. Directed by Peter Coe (*Oliver!*, *Lock Up Your Daughters*, *Tom Brown's Schooldays*), *Ride! Ride!* (its title referring to the fact that Wesley spent much of his life on horseback, travelling some 250,000 miles across England to take his mission to the people) was a reminder that Moral Re-Armament had made a significant contribution to the British musical, and often found a way of melding a spiritual message with entertainment. Thwaites subsequently prepared a concert version of the score, helping *Ride! Ride!* to an after-life.

A saintly footnote

Ride! Ride! may be a 'religious musical', but there is no doubt to whom the laurel for this genre belongs. In the 1970s Lloyd Webber's *Jesus Christ Superstar* and *Joseph and the Amazing Technicolor Dreamcoat* all but *became* religions; their stupendous success around the world continues almost forty years later. Less fortunate was ***Bernadette*** (Dominion Theatre, 21 June 1990; 28), an account by teacher Maureen Hughes (librettist) and her piano-tuner husband Gwyn (composer) of the miraculous happenings at Lourdes. Maureen Hughes dedicated one of its numbers to her deceased mother. Announcing *Bernadette* as 'The People's

Musical' was in one way accurate, for the production was paid for by 2,500 subscribers who had never before spread their wings as West End 'angels'. In Rome the Pope gave his blessing, and candles were lit at Lourdes at the precise moment the curtain went up on the first night, when Benedict Nightingale of *The Times* saw 'the kind of frolicsome village that exists only in musicals' and wished that, rather than have to criticise the piece, 'I was in a kindlier trade, such as whaling or seal-culling'. Within a week, a *Sunday Correspondent* reporter was in the audience, where 'There was a solitary nun, a group of Irish nurses, a party of convent schoolgirls, a Roman Catholic priest with a coach-load of parishioners and a West End couple with their relatives from New York who couldn't get into *The Phantom of the Opera.*'

10 *Fin de Partie*
John Osborne, Lionel Bart and After

Beginning the end: *The World of Paul Slickey*

When the leading lady of *The World of Paul Slickey* (Palace Theatre, 5 May 1959; 47) gave a two-finger salute to the first night audience as the curtain fell, nobody should have been surprised. She was only doing what its author, John Osborne, had been doing all evening. For so seminal a work, this must be one of the most undiscussed, unremembered, unheard, unmourned British musicals of all time. Its relevance may have been almost completely overlooked, but we should not ignore one blazing fact: it is almost certainly one of the very worst musicals of all time. Or is it? Unfortunately, its 'worseness' has been set in the cement of received opinion. Even Osborne's assiduous biographer John Heilpern gives it short shrift, accepting everything bad that has ever been said about it, and offering little illumination.

Slickey was meant as a major work. It is not a trifle that slid into Osborne's canon when his career edged into the shadows. *Slickey* takes its turn with some Osborne jewels: *Look Back in Anger* (1956), *The Entertainer* (1957), *Epitaph for George Dillon* written with Anthony Creighton (1958), *The World of Paul Slickey* (1959), *Luther* (1961). The list is of works that hold their heads high in critical analysis, except for that 1959 blip. Although the script is still available, only a handful of the songs were ever published, and there is no official original cast, or any other, recording of them.[1] What has been left is a recollection that Osborne once wrote a musical, and for his trouble was chased up Shaftsbury Avenue after its premiere by an angry mob. It really was a case of the Angry Young Man of British theatre inducing mass anger. Anger, it seems, is almost the *raison d'être* of *Slickey* – anyone in doubt need only read the playwrights' dedication to the liars and deceivers, professionals who used their callings as 'instruments of debasement'. 'In this bleak time,' Osborne writes, 'when such men have never had it so good, this entertainment is dedicated to their boredom, their incomprehension, their distaste.'

Three years on from *Look Back in Anger*, Osborne's outrage was alive and kicking, but why in 1959 couldn't he have channelled it into another play? Why did it have to be a musical? Deep down, somewhere amongst all that bile, I suspect Osborne wanted to be the British Lorenz Hart or at least Oscar Hammerstein on an embittered day. A fondness for the sung word can be found elsewhere in his plays. *Look Back in Anger* bursts into song twice, first with Jimmy's 'You Can Quit Hanging Round My Counter Mildred 'Cos You'll Find My Position Is

Closed' (come to think of it, he didn't improve much on this for the *Slickey* lyrics) and then with a Flanagan and Allen routine. *The Entertainer*, of course, really *wants* to be a musical, and might even have been better had it been one. There is a suspicion here that the songs have not been brought into the play for dramatic reasons but that the play has sprung up around the songs. In the context of a broken-backed British music hall, Archie Rice and his dead eyes, through the medium of those on-stage numbers, intermittently hold up a mirror to his own and his audience's unsatisfactory life. 'Thank God I'm Normal' is a fair example of the unthinking absurdity of it all, and when real life creeps in, and when the Income Tax man is waiting with his hook in the wings to haul Archie in, we can sympathise with Archie's 'Why Should I Care?'. In *The Entertainer* Osborne's dialogue is heightened by playing alongside the songs, and Osborne's composer John Addison catches the desperate tawdry tone. *The Entertainer* ultimately makes the most of its musical side in the play's closing scene, when the sentimentality of Archie's reprise of 'Why Should I Care?' is meant to turn the play's emotional screw. In this, Osborne and his composer realised the value of sentiment; it is something that *Slickey* repudiates, to its detriment. In *The Entertainer* we can find refuge from Osborne's spoken dialogue in his songs; in *Slickey* there is no hiding place.

The move from a play with music to full-blown musical was one that Osborne must have thought about. Osborne must have *wanted*, perhaps even *needed*, to write a musical. Having made that decision, he had to make others, and at once difficulties arose. Addison's music for *The Entertainer* is never less than apposite, and he writes tunes. Was he approached for *Slickey*? Was he sent a script? Did he hold up his hands and say 'John, you must be joking!' Anyone approaching this work would have been at once impressed by one thing: Osborne's lyrics seem eminently resistant to setting. It would take an immense leap of imagination to think otherwise, and perhaps Addison was unwilling to take the leap. Osborne chose instead to collaborate with Christopher Whelen, a composer of whom according to Heilpern no one but Osborne's agent had heard. And perhaps to speak of collaboration is inaccurate, for one can hardly expect any composer to have smiled when Osborne handed over such intractable material.

Whelen was not an unknown, and already had one London musical to his credit. In 1958 his music for *School*, based on the play by T. W. Robertson, had been heard in London after its Birmingham premiere; according to Whelen 'The London production was hideous – as were my arrangements, I think.'[2] The *Stage* heard in his melodies 'and even more in his accompaniments, a touch of the modern mode that engages but never startles the ears'.[3] By the time the show reached London, the songs 'please for a time, then lose their impact. They seem to be destined for popular success, and then not to be.'[4] Twenty-five years after *Slickey*, Whelen wrote that 'Musicals are (frankly) a thing of the past, for me. Now and then, as you have done, people express interest. I suppose there must be a flicker of mild historical wonderment that such silly stuff actually *exists*! Never mind: I see you are up to serious intent, and won't knock you.'[5] In 1958, by which time Whelen had composed fourteen scores for Shakespeare plays and was currently commissioned to write four new musicals, including *Ferdinand the Matador*, *Ricky with the Tuft* and *Slickey*, Eric Johns reported that

> Mr Whelen has very definite ideas about English musicals. At their best, he considers they are superior to the American ones because they are written by genuine playwrights and theatre musicians [...] It is a mistake, according to Mr Whelen, for too many cooks to collaborate in the creation of a musical production. The fewer the better – as was in the case of Rodgers and Hammerstein – one for the music, the other for the book and lyrics.
>
> The script and lyrics, written by a genuine playwright, are what Mr Whelen demands before he writes a bar of music. Once he has soaked himself in the words, he tries to get inside the characters and write music which makes them believable. He is content to satisfy his own artistic conscience and hopes the result will meet with the approval of the public.[6]

Selecting Whelen as the composer of *Slickey* may have been Osborne's agent's doing, but we must wonder at how much Osborne knew, or cared, about any of the alternatives. The main advantage of Whelen may have been that he *was* unknown to the British public; Osborne may subconsciously have wanted to be Lorenz Hart but he didn't need a Richard Rodgers, or even a Kurt Weill who might the better have taken his satiric stance on board. While we consider most musicals through their composers, the interest in *Slickey* centres around its librettist; the choice of Whelen is a blank. There was to be no competition between Osborne and his composer. The only reason why Osborne was not his own composer was that he could not compose. There was never a risk that he would approach one of the other current composers of British musical theatre. A true collaboration would have thrown Osborne off course, and we must assume that the quality of *Slickey* was seriously questioned during its creation. For Whelen, this was just another commission in which one suspects he took little interest. For Osborne, Whelen was probably no more than a bystander, and so he seems to us now, until the (unlikely) revival of *Slickey* proves otherwise, and we may test R. B. Marriott's assertion that Whelen was 'destined to become one of our leading light composers'.[7]

We have to ask, did Osborne take any interest in the musical side of the work? If Osborne knew of the conventions of the British musical, he serves only to exploit them to his own largely unsuitable ends. Did Osborne think that *Slickey* would simply not pass muster as a straight play, but that as a musical he could get away with such a vehicle for his venom? The coldness of the work makes it stand almost alone in the canon. Here, after all, is a musical without a shred of romance, sentiment or sentimentality, dream ballets, emotional tugs, orchestral swells, hummable tunes, believable characters, warmth or charm. None of these are needed on voyage. This is the British musical stripped bare, bearing only its garbled message of distrust and dissatisfaction at what Osborne perceives as the *status quo*. Some explanation may be found in the fact that Osborne had conceived the piece as a play years before, in which form it had never found favour. Perhaps making a musical out of it was a method of disguising the product. We can be confident that Osborne was not well versed in recent developments in the British musical. If *Slickey* eventually played its part in that development it was almost entirely accidental. If *Slickey* altered the British musical in one way it was in its insistence not to send out its audience in a happy glow.

So, Osborne had his musical and his composer. Then, although having had no experience of directing a major musical play, he made himself its director. This made way for some serious miscalculations. The casting was odd. There might have been recruits from Theatre Workshop or the Royal Court who would have responded to Osborne's demands, but they were not called in. For the title-role Osborne chose a handsome popular singer of the day, Dennis Lotis, who was agreeable but not a strong stage performer; Lotis wouldn't have recognised satire if it had hit him in the face. Adrienne Corri had no musical experience for her leading lady role, and Jack Watling made a strange bed-fellow as romantic interest. Better parted were Philip Locke as the effete Father Evilgreene, and Marie Löhr as Lady Mortlake, whom Osborne introduces as 'in the long tradition of magnificently gracious ninnies so familiar to English play-goers'.[8] Burdened with an armful of garden blooms, she made her entrance through French windows with the immortal line 'Oh if only one didn't have to work for one's living! It's such a glorious day full of sunshine and flowers.'[9] For a moment, audiences at the Palace must have thought that *Slickey* was to be a satire on the mild drawing-room comedies whose casts Miss Löhr had so often inhabited.

Slickey was for almost its entire length almost certainly not that. Osborne was more intent on lashing out at contemporary British society than the theatrical conventions that decorated it and promulgated a presiding upper-middle-class cosiness. Osborne's mouthpiece is Jack Oakham, alias Paul Slickey, the gossip columnist for the *Daily Racket*. (Note how Jack's alias places him at a distance from his attitudes to the world around him.) A much milder journalist would be the hero of the Slade–Reynolds' *Wildest Dreams*[10] a few months later, and the much milder satires of that show received almost as much derision as did *Slickey*. Besides filling the columns of the *Daily Racket* with titbits about errant politicians, sexual indiscretions, and all the paraphernalia of the unimportant and overdone, Jack, married to Lesley, has a private life in which he is having an affair with his sister-in-law Deirdre Rawley, one of the Mortlake's daughters. 'Our song will be sung when our loins cease to groan' goes the lyric of their love duet 'We'll Be in the Desert and Alone', striking nervousness into any audience even by the end of Scene 2. The song is interrupted by Jack's pronouncement that 'The day is coming when mass diversions of the flesh will be launched like new washing powders by gigantic commercial empires in fierce competition with each other.'

Before ten minutes is past, this puts *Slickey* beyond anything that had ever been attempted in the British musical.

The plot begins. Jack is sent off to Mortlake Hall where Lord Mortlake is mortally ill. If he survives forty-eight hours his family will avoid paying death duties. Thus, Osborne is already on the track of upper-class privilege. If his Lordship dies before the five-year period necessary for exemption, the family will be at the mercy of the Income Tax Man, just like Archie Rice. His wife is a brave soul; she has always been brave. 'I remember,' says Deirdre, 'how she was when they gave away India.' The statuesque Mrs Giltedge-Whyte arrives, hiding the fact that she was once Lord Mortlake's mistress, and hardly sits down before launching into a song about the joys of capital punishment, 'Bring Back the Axe', with its *Daily Racket* (and possibly *Daily Mail*) conviction that Death by Hanging is Too Good For Them.

The shock of seeing Mrs Giltedge-Whyte, and the memories she invokes, are too much for Lord Mortlake, who expires. Osborne's attacks are clumsy but persistent, against drama critics (Jack insists 'I take the theatre too seriously to be a dramatic critic'), or the acting profession (Mrs G-W tells her daughter Gillian 'if I had thought you wanted to be an actress I would never have sent you to the Academy of Dramatic Art'), or anything else that catches his eye. Mrs G-W is, anyway, a hard nut to crack, detecting sentimentality in Gillian. ('I've noticed it before. Ever since we had to eat your bunnies during the war.') Gillian is revealed as the fruit of Lord Mortlake's loins. 'Hardly your fault,' Mrs G-W tells his Lordship. 'Whose fault did you think it was,' asks Lord Mortlake, 'the Lord Chamberlain's?'

En route, Lesley undergoes a sex change, only one of the events that contributed to *Slickey's* infamous reputation. She suggests that so much emotional uncertainty could be dismissed by being a woman all week and a man at the weekend, and Osborne has a song, 'A Woman at the Weekend,' to push the idea home. Sex change in British theatre was something almost unspoken of, even in the increasingly liberal-minded atmosphere of 1959. Setting such stuff to music was an outrage! The playwright William Douglas Home was berated when he built his play *Aunt Edwina* around the same idea. *Aunt Edwina*[11] opened in Eastbourne in September; *Slickey* had first seen light of day in Bournemouth in April. (What sort of grudge did British managements have against the legendarily geriatric populations of these watering holes, that they assaulted them with such offence?) *Aunt Edwina* made sex change its principal theme, but the British critics were outraged by a piece that now sounds like a jolly good jape. The elderly, portly Colonel Edward Ryan, a respected Master of Foxhounds, is visited by his children. His daughter looks out into the garden and sees a woman in a red hat. 'Yes, I know dear,' her mother replies, 'That's what I was going to tell you. That's your father.' The sex change element had only been one strand of *Slickey*. Many elements make up its fabric. One brave day, we may be given a chance to see it staged again.

A sigh of relief: *Oliver!*

Perhaps some of the above suggests why *Slickey* is important in charting the history of the post-war British musical. Osborne broke so many of the rules. Neither the critics nor its audiences were having any of it, although there must have been some who came out of the Palace feeling that something seismic had happened. *Slickey* had few friends. None of the other musicals around in London in 1959 felt like compatriots, either *Candide* or *Lock Up Your Daughters* or *Irma la Douce* or that complete antithesis to *Slickey*, the charm-dripping *Marigold* ('charming, sweet and harmless'[12] according to the *Stage*). *Slickey* could expect no sympathy. The British verismo musical was still seemingly strong, although in another year it would be all but burned out, and the 'little' British musical, the *plein air*, had already been all but bonfired. In its outrage and unique negativity, *Slickey* exacerbated rather than enthralled, and helped clear the way for a work that would take the British musical back into a comfortable place. The place was called *Oliver!* and it would take British musicals back to a world which was acceptable. Those gazing at it were no longer expected to look into a mirror and see themselves.

Lionel Bart, born Begleiter, was of a long line probably the last musical theatre writer to create truly British musicals. His early enforced retirement from the genre began an interregnum of seven years or so when no new writers or composers were able to make any lasting impression. After contributing to various small productions, he began a string of musicals that above all else celebrated Britishness: *Fings Ain't Wot They Used T'Be* (tarts and ponces in contemporary Soho); *Lock Up Your Daughters* (sexual appetites in 1730 London); *Oliver!* (mid-Victorian London courtesy of Dickens); *Blitz!* (East Enders enduring World War II); *Maggie May* (prostitutes and industrial unrest in Liverpool); *Twang* (Robin Hood and his none too Merry Men); *The Londoners* (more Cockney tarts, spivs and ponces) and *Costa Packet* (the same sort of Londoners trying to get away from it all).

Even the most successful of composers of the 1950s would have envied Bart's success rate, the scores coming after an already prolific career as a writer of pop-songs. Unlike Slade or Wilson whose follow-ups to their initial hits had disappointing runs, Bart's were something they could only dream of, as proved by the performances run up by the original productions: *Lock Up Your Daughters* 328 (but a 1962 revival notched up another 664, and there was a film); *Fings* 886; *Oliver!* 2,618 (not counting the Broadway total of 744, and the countless revivals and film); *Blitz!* 568; *Maggie May* 501. There seemed to be only one wrong move, *Twang*, but it was all that was needed for a downfall.

Bart's London musical theatre career was spectacularly successful and brief: six years from his debut as lyricist for *Lock Up Your Daughters* in 1959 to the full stop of *Twang* in 1965. After this débâcle, there were aftershocks. In 1969, *La Strada*, based on Federico Fellini's film and one of many mooted or unfinished or unproduced projects that Bart had long been working on, made it to Broadway for one night only. By the time the show reached New York only three of Bart's songs remained, the rest of the score now by other hands. *La Strada* never had a hope of being seen in Britain, although three years later there were two works that had Bart's name attached. *The Londoners*, a musical from Stephen Lewis's play *Sparrers Can't Sing* (for the film of which Bart had written the popular title-song in 1963) had a season at Stratford East in 1972, as did *Costa Packet*, a 'candy-floss entertainment' about the British passion for package holidays by Bart, Frank Norman and Alan Klein. It was obvious to managements that Bart had gone back to where they felt he belonged: unpretentious roots. He had reason to be grateful for a tribute that was mounted in London in 1977, but on the first night of *Lionel* he took to the stage to tell the audience 'This is the worst show I have ever seen. Don't bother coming to see it.'[13]

Of this at least the public took notice. They knew nothing of his plans for other musicals, an adaptation of Victor Hugo's *The Hunchback of Notre Dame* or a musical about Golda Meir, a musical of *Cyrano de Bergerac* intended for Peter O'Toole, or that no less a distinguished writer than Bertrand Russell wanted to collaborate on a musical of his book *Saturn in the Suburbs*. At one time there had been talk of a highly unlikely writing partnership with Richard Rodgers. With the spectre of *Twang* at Bart's back, there was no chance of any of these reaching fruition. No matter that his previous work *Maggie May* had notched up a long enough run to get through three leading ladies, he found no support.

The central question of Bart's most famous work may not be 'Where Is Love? (more accurately 'Where-ere-ere-ere-ere Is Love?') but 'Whatever Happened to Baby Oliver?'. It was such a modest little thing, almost a starveling of a show, of which its original management had little hope, a puling babe in a world of musical plenty. There is now only one way of getting back to the show as Nature intended: by listening to Decca's original London cast recording. It was almost inevitable that a film version would embellish its landscape; at least Carol Reed's film embellished it carefully. On stage, **Oliver!** (New Theatre, 30 June 1960; 2,618) did without star names. Top-billed Ron Moody as Fagin had been successful in some Myers–Cass revues, and a support actor in the British production of *Candide*.[14] Few of the greater British public knew of him, and even less of the Nancy, Georgia Brown, a graduate from the Royal Court. Her major contribution to the success of the stage production was generally underrated, and often ignored by the critics. When it came to the film, her face didn't fit, and Shani Wallis, fresher-faced, blonde, sweeter-voiced, got the job. Moody kept his place at the heart of the thing, winning plaudits for a performance which was little more than an amalgam of all the characters he had played in all those revues. As usual, the critics were ready to over-praise the competent, and undervalue the good. Paul Whitsun-Jones and Hope Jackman, a perfectly paired Beadle and Widow Corney for the stage, were probably among the latter. No stars, then, but a band of professionals doing their best. At the beginning, they must have felt there was little to make a fuss about. Much more *brouhaha* had been kicked up about many other British musicals. The first production of *Oliver!* didn't even get specially designed costumes. They arrived in trunks from Monty Berman Ltd, and the coiffures were by Wig Creations, although the management splashed out in getting Robert Fielding of Regent Street to see to Nancy's hair. (Did this mean she had to be at his salon for a couple of hours every afternoon? I think not.)

In some ways, the star turned out to be the designer Sean Kenny. Bernard Levin spoke for many when he declared him a genius. Kenny's scenery was enormously effective, a monument of old pieces of wood, but there was nothing spectacular about it; spectacle would come to *Oliver!* later. What Kenny did was to score the scenery; the sets became part of the action, indissolubly. One of the film's problems was that through its medium it was now possible to move beyond the stylised stage evocations of London to actual locations, and once you have a London street that you can pan a camera across it is tempting to fill it with dancing chorus boys and armies of milk-maids and all sorts of pretty adornments. Originally, nobody in *Oliver!* dreamed of cavorting. In the 2008 stage revival the famed British choreographer Matthew Bourne (of the all-male *Swan Lake*) was brought in to do the dances. *Oliver!*'s original production credits no choreographer because there was nothing for a choreographer to do. Peter Coe, its director, hated dancing, and the temptation to plump up the East End revels with fingers-hooked-in-the-waistcoat-costermongering routines was avoided. After all, in Dickens' sorry but ultimately uplifting tale, there really isn't much to dance (or sing) about. Dance does not belong in *Oliver!* Even on the periphery, it does not belong. Adding dance helps turn *Oliver!* into just another musical, which it is not.

Throughout the long run, Coe's production retained a modesty. For the opening performances the programme listed as its chorus ten Boys and thirteen Londoners; towards the end of the run, these numbers had swelled to fourteen Boys and sixteen Londoners. We don't know if Donald Albery, *Oliver!*'s impresario, allowed a couple more instruments into the pit as the run went on, but there was originally no extravagance extended to the theatre's musicians. Such austerity seems appropriate for a play overshadowed by the Poor Law. Aurally, if we are to get back to *Oliver!* in its first form we must acknowledge the original orchestrator Eric Rogers, responsible for the 'Oliver sound'. In the same way that Ronald Binge gave Mantovani the sound with which Mantovani came to be identified, so was Rogers' contribution to *Oliver!* highly distinctive. His responsibilities certainly went beyond sorting out instrumentation. Levin gave Bart the credit for the street cries heard in the introduction to 'Who Will Buy?', comparing these favourably to George Gershwin's street-seller sequence in *Porgy and Bess*, but it was Rogers who would have made Bart's idea work. Bart could do little more than sing his tunes onto a tape recorder; anything approaching orchestration was beyond him.

Rogers' orchestrations provide a basic support to the musical structure without reducing it to a chamber work. He is helped by the fact that Bart never falls back on pastiche; the setting is Victorian, but the music is never Victoriana.

Many other period musicals musically ape their periods. *Pickwick* has a duet, 'Look into Your Heart', which sounds as if it has been rescued from a 1880 piano-stool, and as such it is not convincing. Julian Slade's *Trelawny* here and there apes Victorian music, as in Rose's on-stage at Sadler's Wells' song 'Ever of Thee', and Slade's attempt at 'period' sound in 'Trelawny of The Wells' is another example. In his *Vanity Fair* everything stops for a feeble pastiche parlour song 'Alone the Orphan'.[15] There is even more musical pastiche in *Follow That Girl*, not least in 'Waiting for Our Daughter'. Slade seems unable to write in period without trying to replicate its atmosphere; Bart does not suffer from the need for this. Bart is more cunning, writing songs that perfectly fit into the narrative fabric and time while existing as popular songs. *Pickwick*'s 'If I Ruled the World' sounds like a popular song of the 1960s, and not much like a Victorian one, but 'As Long as He Needs Me' manages somehow to be a popular song and yet sound correctly in place. We have no reason to believe that these songs do not belong to the era within which they are presented. *Oliver!* is perhaps one of the very first post-war British musicals to integrate these possibilities.

This does not mean that the songs seem authentic. Consider Nancy's numbers – 'It's a Fine Life', 'I'd Do Anything', 'As Long as He Needs Me' – there is more Florrie Forde about them than Henry Mayhew. That torch song, with its limited and repetitive use of a few notes, brings echoes of Vincent Youmans. According to some, Bart's songs often brought memories of other songs, songs *they* had already written. Another composer claimed to have written 'Be Back Soon' years before, a fact that Bart privately acknowledged. There were other accusations of plagiarism. There is no doubt that the title-song of *Fings* bore a marked resemblance to the Rodgers and Hart 'Mountain Greenery', but the general public was unworried by such niceties as more and more of Bart's simple little tunes earned more and more radio airplay.

The sing-a-long ease of much of *Oliver!*'s score helped it to success (the 'let's all join in the chorus' quality was proved when Max Bygraves recorded 'Consider Yourself') and, unlike many other songs from other shows, the *Oliver!* songs never lost their reference to their origin. The songs of *Oliver! belonged* to the score of *Oliver!*, as the songs of *My Fair Lady* remained always the songs of *My Fair Lady*. Even out of context, their context is intact in the public mind, in a way that 'If I Ruled the World' is not. An essential part of this has been the sound world of the original *Oliver!*, part Bart, part Rogers, part impresario Donald Albery simply because he was probably tight about the orchestral budget. Those who know the score only through its later manifestations are not to blame for any misunderstanding of what *Oliver!* is: basically, basic. Small, in 1960, was beautiful.

Of course it should be a matter for celebration that as late as 2009 a major London production of *Oliver!* is attracting capacity audiences and destined for another long run. Unfortunately most British musicals (and certainly *Oliver!*) do not lend themselves to reinvention, only to repetition, inflation or constriction. Opera is constantly reinvented. Waiting for the curtain to rise on a new production of *Tristan and Isolde* there is no guarantee that the sets and costumes will be in any way like those of its original production. Wagner might be surprised. Audiences would probably be disappointed if it were otherwise. *Aida* may work well set in its usual Egypt, but it could be made to work in many other settings, and removed to other times. Peter Sellars and the majority of opera directors have turned away from the original conceptions. Bizet survives Jonathan Miller's reinterpretation of *Carmen*. In dance, Matthew Bourne's *Swan Lake* transposes the ballet's heterosexuality to homosexuality, bypassing much criticism by seemingly aligning itself more fully with its composer.

The reinvention of musicals is much more difficult, locked in as so many are to their time and place. *Salad Days* on a building site set? Hardly. A Handel opera on a building site? Why not? With musicals, too, 'period' becomes much more of a problem. It is difficult to imagine doing anything radical with *The Boy Friend* or *The Buccaneer* or *Expresso Bongo*, for they express so forcefully the period to which they are subscribed. It would take a director of great resource, imagination and cheek to try a radical overhaul of *Fings* or *Lock Up Your Daughters* or *Blitz!*, and perhaps this is a matter for regret. The light operas of Offenbach readily respond to change, as demonstrated by the hugely successful revivals done at Sadler's Wells. The director Wendy Toye and others did wonders for those old works. I do not think she would have managed so well with *Salad Days*. Too often, for the British musical there seems no option but aspic.

Anyway, this is the stuff of dreams, for reinventing *Oliver!* is never going to happen. It has been made almost impossible by the way in which its perceived form has been hammered into the public's mind through film and the television series to find a 'new' Nancy (and one, by the way, who will only sing at six of the eight weekly performances; spare a thought for the original actresses who did every performance without demur, and without microphones that remove any need for real singing). Reinvention has never been attempted with the central character of Fagin, although in our day its representation of the Jew is outdated and to some offensive. Moody's original characterisation is implanted in the public mind as the personification of Fagin, perhaps of Jewishness, and certainly as the face of *Oliver!* Meanwhile, as *Oliver!* survives successfully into old age, it has become little more than a commodity, a sure ticket to financial reward, pressing down the enormous archive of British musicals hidden beneath. But, even in its day, the effect of *Oliver!* was something more than it seemed. The mirror held up to modern Britain had been put aside; audiences no longer had to face a musical that reflected their own lives, or the lives of those around them. Away with the purported truths of *Fings Ain't Wot They Used T'Be*, *Expresso Bongo*, *The World of Paul Slickey*, *The Lily White Boys*. The vices that made up the fabric of *Oliver!* turned into a Good Night Out, one that an audience could sit through without recognising any association with its own past.

The first performances, at the Wimbledon tryout, were not a conspicuous triumph; Moody recalled that it did not seem successful, and that nobody was very impressed. Two weeks later, London was on its feet. Critical reaction was good, but not unanimously so. To Alan Brien it was 'little more than a tasty strip-cartoon fillet … served with a thin, sugared gruel of words and music oddly enough ladled from almost the same pot as *Follow That Girl* … What Lionel Bart needs now is a bloody, bawdy, outrageous, unspeakable injustice to start some adrenaline pumping into his words and music.'[16] Richard Findlater criticised the inability of Bart's score 'to reach the peaks even of pastiche melodrama'.[17] Philip Hope-Wallace thought it 'a sad disappointment, a very starveling musical from the workhouse'.[18] All detected what we might describe as a general thinness about the piece; perhaps the continued success of the piece is partly due to the fact that subsequent productions have, in one way or another, fattened it up.

The voice of its detractors was drowned out by public acclaim. A seal of approval came from the royal family, whose members flitted in and out of the New Theatre. On 15 December 1960 the Queen was in the stalls, Row G, accompanied by Prince Philip, her second visit in a fortnight. The Duchess of Gloucester and Prince Richard looked down at her from their box. Two days before the Duke and Duchess of Windsor, no doubt intrigued to see how the lower orders had disported themselves in the days of Victoria, were in the audience. 'An awfully good show,' the Duke remarked on leaving. 'I must get the record.' Less unusually, Princess Margaret and her future husband Tony Armstrong-Jones had seen it that summer, he no doubt eyeing it as a participant in British musicals. (He had designed the sets for John Cranko's *Keep Your Hair On!*)

'An awfully good show' is undoubtedly what *Oliver!* was, and most of the critics endorsed that opinion. Interestingly, it is also the only one of his shows for which Bart was sole author. He certainly got through his collaborators: Laurie Johnson and Bernard Miles for *Lock Up Your Daughters*, Frank Norman (and perhaps Joan Littlewood and most of the cast) for *Fings*, Joan Maitland for *Blitz!*, Alun Owen for *Maggie May*, Harvey Orkin (Littlewood, again) for *Twang*. This suggests that Bart might have done better to ignore them all and plough a lonely furrow. Somehow, his adaptation of Dickens had a brilliance almost unparalleled in British musicals. Dickens' reputation in theatre came with more than a dash of Victorian melodrama, effectively expounded by such barn-storming actors as Sir John Martin-Harvey, whose Sydney Carton in *The Only Way* became one of his most famous portrayals. Turning *Oliver Twist* into a musical presented its own problems, a novel whose very existence rested on grinding poverty, parochial corruption, kidnapping, thievery, the physical and sexual abuse of women, prostitution, domestic violence, child abuse (at the least, physical), and murder. A musical constructed on such themes in a contemporary setting would hardly have made space for the royal limousines outside the New, but this was Dickensian, and therefore palatable. Dickens had not been dusted off from the museum of literature to which he had naturally graduated, but taken out and redressed. Witnessing the vile, cruel world of orphaned Oliver is made entertaining because we distance ourselves from it. This is not about us, or even our past, but a

Victorian Britain which exists only in the pages of picture-books or, when snow falls, on Christmas cards. The sketch is by Boz. The distancing is not apparent in our attitude to Dickens' novel, where the rawness, the actuality, remains; the distancing occurs when it is presented as a musical, that long-sought-for Good Night Out. The songs make all well; this is misfortune made to whistle. This in no way lessens Bart's achievement, for this is a piece which works on its own terms. *Oliver!*'s status as an exemplar of what a musical should be has contributed largely to its continued life.

Oliver! is sometimes held responsible for firing a starting-pistol for the succession of British musicals based on books or plays that littered the 1960s. In fact, there were rather more in the period 1945–60, rather less in 1960–75. Bart showed that there was gold in those hills and that a strong novel (or play) might be the best crutch to support a score in need of a good book. A stage full of piping boys was not a bad idea, either. At least two novels offered that possibility: James Hilton's *Goodbye Mr Chips* and Thomas Hughes' *Tom Brown's Schooldays*, but neither adaptations proved successful. In this matter, as in so much else, *Oliver!* was a signal work which would go unmatched through the next decade and beyond. Those immaculate limousines outside the New give us the hint to the truth about *Oliver!* After all that had come before, the mourning for Novello, the disappointment in Coward, the little musicals of Slade and Wilson and their tiny regiment, the verismo and kitchen-sink, the prostitutes of 1950s London and the daring rarities that chanced their luck in an unsympathetic environment, *Oliver!* – quite apart from being a good work – came as a blessed relief, to which no exception could be taken. That, of course, was then. Now, we might wince at the attitudes it evinces, not least in its depiction of its heroine. Today, too, Fagin's association with his boy gang might well trigger a visit from Social Services.

At the end of a decade, it represented British musical theatre's *fin de siècle*. It came at a pitch of pressure which neither critic nor audience could withstand. In a sense, it obliterated almost everything that had gone before, the romanticism of Novello, the false Broadway accent of such dodos as *Carissima* and *Wedding in Paris*, the whimsy of *Salad Days*, the whispered profanity of *Valmouth*, the slap-happy realism of *The Crooked Mile*, the ugly truths of *The Lily White Boys*, the rude posturing of *The World of Paul Slickey*. Osborne's contempt for everything British (including its audiences) had seemed unpardonable. Lady Mortlake, arriving through those French windows burdened with armfuls of garden blooms signalled Osborne's hatred not only for everything that was meaningless and unthinking about British society, but his contempt for the medium he was exploiting to deliver his message. But Lady Mortlake would surely not have disapproved of *Oliver!* What, after all, was there to disapprove of? And, as time has gone on, and our distance from the Dickens–Bart Victoriana has lengthened, so the efficacy of that arrangement has worked, if not to its advantage, then certainly not to its detriment.

39 Roy Dotrice as Dr Arnold and Judith Bruce as an unlikely school matron
in the original London production of *Tom Brown's Schooldays* (1972)

More Dickens: *Pickwick* ❋ *Two Cities*

Before *Oliver!* no one seems to have seriously considered Dickens as source for a musical. Even so, it was only in 1963 that the next Dickens appeared. *Pickwick* (Saville Theatre, 4 July 1963; 694) needed three writers, Wolf Mankowitz for its book, proving that his once proud claim that he was establishing a definitive 'school' of British musicals had gone awry, Leslie Bricusse for its lyrics and Cyril Ornadel for its score. *Pickwick* was blatant commercialism. Somehow the song titles told you everything before a note had been struck: 'Do as You Would Be Done By', 'That's What I Want for Christmas', 'A Hell of an Election'. The titles tripped out all too easily. Peter Coe, director of *Oliver!*, was brought in to rework the *Oliver!* trick, although the absence of starving children was a disadvantage. The main reason for its London success was the likeable comedian-singer Harry Secombe, who had the right sort of rotundity, in one of those 'born to play it' parts. Pickwick's philosophy expressed in 'If I Ruled the World' ranks as one of the most irritating songs in post-war British musicals. Its enormous popularity was a depressing example of the state the British musical had got itself into by the mid-1960s. *Pickwick* displayed serious gooeyness and a Dickens reduced to Christmas card proportions. At the time of writing, the song has been rediscovered as a jingle to a television advertisement for a telephone company, irritating a whole new generation.

An adaptation of Dickens' *A Tale of Two Cities* could hardly depend on the sort of comical japes that had marked *Pickwick*. *Two Cities* (Palace Theatre, 27 February 1969; 44) had a troubled pre-London tour, a dreadful press and a quick end. It must have seemed a good idea at the time. The show was first announced as starring Keith Michell as Sydney Carton and Margaret Burton as Marie Antoinette. Neither Michell, Burton or Marie Antoinette made the final script, and neither did the original Mme Defarge. Dramatically, the work suffered from comparison with Arthur Benjamin's 1950 opera, celebrated at the following year's Festival of Britain and staged at Sadler's Wells in 1957, and with Rank's skilfully cast film of 1958.

The musical's score looked nowhere but the obvious. *Of course* it began with Dickens' opening sentences ('It was the best of times, it was the worst of times'); *of course* it ended with the hero climbing the scaffold and singing 'It is a far, far better thing I do than I have ever done' as the tinny orchestra hurried to its conclusion before making for the pub; *of course* it had a supposedly comic number in which Carton and his long-suffering clerk told us what an incorrigible cad Carton was. Rather more imaginatively, it had some fun around the scaffold, with a natty 'Knitting Song' and a number called 'The Machine of Doctor Guillotine', but with generally weak stuff at its disposal, it failed to make real the horrors of the Revolution. Perhaps Jeff Wayne's music and Jerry Wayne's lyrics and Constance Cox's adaptation might have benefited from listening to Poulenc's 1957 opera *Dialogues des Carmélites*, in the finale of which a queue of nuns one by one climbs the scaffold. *Two Cities* was hardly in this class, and subsequent adaptations of Dickens failed to make the grade, reaching a nadir in *Hard Times*. Originally staged provincially in 1973, a 2000 London production was completely off the radar of public taste, and it had none of its own. How much more interesting it might have been if writers and composers had turned to his darker works, to *Dombey and Son* or *Our Mutual Friend*, but even in these they might have been misled into over-egging Dickens' uncurbable sentimentality.

Oliver! was almost certainly one of the reasons for so many novels and plays being explored for musical theatre. The predilection for J. M. Barrie was strong, but there was almost as much enthusiasm for the works of H. G. Wells, his books full of that middle-of-the-road philosophy and quirky characters, often the disadvantaged made good, that seemed to sustain the common man's interest in literature in the early twentieth century. *Half a Sixpence* (*Kipps*), showed the way, and others followed, including *Ann Veronica*. It was as if the British musical had a pipe permanently clenched between its teeth, its sources so middle-class, so middle England, so ponderous. The sort of musical that J. B. Priestley might have written, but never did.[19] Before *Oliver!* the works on which musicals were based were just as, if not more, interesting and challenging. Only those of epicurean taste were likely to chance *Zuleika*, based on Max Beerbohm's novel, or *Happy Holiday* based on the old Arnold Ridley repertory theatre staple *The Ghost Train*, a musical that Eric Maschwitz was almost *forced* to write by the impresario to whom he was contracted. More caviare to the general was *The Young Visiters*, an affectionate attempt at musicalising Daisy Ashford's childhood novel.

After *Oliver!*: *Scapa!* ❋ *Blitz!*

To make way for Bart's follow-up to *Oliver!*, another British musical had to be hurried from the scene. *Scapa!* (Adelphi Theatre, 8 March 1962; 44) was an adaptation of Hugh Hastings' play *Seagulls over Sorrento*, which in 1950 had begun 1,551 performances, a record at the time only outrun by a Whitehall farce and *Blithe Spirit*. Now, Hastings wrote book, music and lyrics for his all-male sailor extravaganza, the British musical's equivalent to Benjamin Britten's all-male opera *Billy Budd*. *Seagulls over Sorrento* made Hastings a fortune, and there was money from a film version called *Crest of the Wave*.

None of the reviews seemed to catch even a whiff of the homoeroticism that had filtered down from *Seagulls over Sorrento* and emerged with new vigour in *Scapa!*, complete with scenes where the sailors dressed in women's clothes and cavorted about to a first Act closer called 'Bella'. After the production was cleared out of the Adelphi Hastings escaped England. For several years he was in self-imposed exile following a homosexual imbroglio. Not a note of *Scapa!*'s music was ever commercially recorded, although the author worked with Hastings on assembling a definitive script and score, as all sign of the originals had vanished.

ADELPHI

THEATRE   STRAND, W.C.2

First performance at this theatre Thursday, 8th March, 1962.

PROGRAMME ONE SHILLING

40 All boys together: the all-male nautical shipwreck of *Scapa!*

Hastings had written some attractive numbers, not least the romantic ones sung by the show's leading man David Hughes, who carefully vetted the material given him by the composer, and insisted that his musical director was made MD for the show. 'Some Voice' and 'One Woman' were strong contenders, although it seemed a little strange for Dusty (Hughes' character) to be always singing about 'one woman' when there wasn't the slightest possibility of one. 'Seagull in the Sky', a sort of signature song for the piece, had atmosphere, and the American actor-writer Timothy Gray was brought over to give the show a dash of Broadway zing with 'I Wish I Was an Orchestra'. What had made Hastings want to turn his mega-successful play into a musical in the first place?

> My genes. Mum: vaudeville, ballet mistress, song and dance teacher. Dad: violinist, photographer, farmer. Plus fulfilling an ambition I'd had since the age of sixteen when I was a cow-hand and wrote two ghastly musicals, *Crazy Diana* and *Starlight*. Some of the lyrics weren't bad. *Seagulls over Sorrento* took the labours of Hercules to get on, but the musical went ahead pretty smoothly thanks to the impresario Sandor Gorlinsky. My agent Eric Glass asked me how I perceived such a production. I told him that principally I would like to see a large open deck for dance routines. The internal/external dual set was ingenious. The cocktail bar sub-art-deco front-cloth was quite dreadful. We had an orchestra of twelve, often too loud because there were no mikes on stage. The choreography was first class. However, the morning after the Adelphi opening George Carden flew to Amsterdam and I was appointed to take over direction. I demurred at first but there was nobody else, and the show desperately needed changes. I immediately stopped the use of the follow spot – not nautical and dated. And I had the cocktail front-cloth removed.[20]

The actor-director Henry Kendall was drafted in.

> Henry came up to Liverpool after we had already cut 'Why Should It Happen To Me?' and 'Do Not Trust Him'. He loved the show, finding little to criticise. By the time we got to Dublin I felt it needed a big number early on, and 'Don't Give A Damn' was written and rehearsed almost overnight.

The all-male cast singled out *Scapa!* as something quite distinctive in British musicals.

> In *Seagulls* Lofty (big man, big heart) was played in London by Bernard Lee, David Langton and Brewster Mason – all tall men. For *Scapa!* it was difficult to find an available man who was tall and also had a fine singing voice. David Hughes, somewhat short in stature, was ideal but did not measure up to a naval 'Lofty', hence the change of character name to Dusty. David didn't care for 'Seagulls Sometimes Sing'. During rehearsals I sat in a room at Rediffusion during a TV strike and came up with 'Some Voice' with some guidance from David's musical director, Derek New. David was after some sort of sung soliloquy, hence the verse.

The part of Badger was written for Anthony Newley. He wrote me a sweet letter, blaming his agent for the delay and explaining that he was working on a project for himself – *Stop the World, I Want to Get Off*. Pete Murray was delightful to work with in spite of his self-confessed shortcomings. Edward Woodward was a favourite of Eric and Blanche Glass (and rightly so) and turned up trumps. A fine actor, he also was able to give a hearing to a wonderful singing voice. Timothy Gray, the versatile American who wrote the lyrics to Hugh Martin's music, made a fair fist of Sprog for which he was virtually miscast. He also had a problem with his wig which I then ordered should be returned to its block in wardrobe. His own head of hair was fine.

The opening night had thirteen curtain calls, but the critics were merciless in their condemnation.

It would have run if a play called *The Big Killing*, dying on its feet, had passed its sell-by date at the Princes Theatre, where we had hoped to transfer, having only been allowed a six-week booking at the Adelphi. *The Big Killing* died at the box office and then unexpectedly picked up. Lionel Bart's *Blitz!* had already been given an opening date at the Adelphi by Jack Hylton. So we came off and disbanded. Jack liked *Scapa!* so much that for the last two weeks he generously gave us the theatre rent-free. Despite the critical assassination the box-office was mounting, but every other West End theatre was occupied. Reading the ghastly reviews in the cold light of day I was on the edge of a nervous breakdown. A friend took pity and said 'Try these'. They turned out to be Purple Hearts and, one half of each tablet at a time, they restored the resilience I had developed as an abandoned child from the ages of two to ten.

Hastings' decision to invest heavily in his own musical resulted in his financial collapse, and he ended his days in near penury. *Scapa!* was put away, and *Blitz!* put up. At least in 1962 they shared the by then almost obligatory exclamation mark.

The great noise made by Bart's new musical may have leaked from the Adelphi Theatre to the nearby Vaudeville, where Alan Melville and Charles Zwar's *All Square* was trying to bring back the sophistication and style of an earlier age of revue, with elegant evening dresses and dress suits for the men in the opening number, and an equally smart walk-down. One of *All Square*'s highlights was *Blast!*, a potted pastiche of *Blitz!*, with Beryl Reid in a baggy cardigan and a very silly beret taking off Amelia Bayntun's performance just down the road. One hopes Miss Bayntun was able to see this tribute, for her appearance in **Blitz!** (Adelphi Theatre, 8 May 1962; 568) was the achievement of her career. Before being invited to Bart's flat to hear his music and lyrics (he shared the book with his one-time secretary Joan Maitland) she had played little more than bit parts and sang Marie Lloyd songs at the Players' Theatre for a pittance. Between engagements she was pulling pints at the public house she and her husband ran, the Grapes in Regent Street. *Blitz!* propelled her to stardom, although she was never a star. Her Act II aria, 'So Tell Me', is one of the most dramatically effective in post-war British theatre, but is all but forgotten. When *Blitz!* closed Bayntun, who never missed a performance, went back to obscurity and the old and mild.

It is questionable whether *Blitz!* would be a hit were it written today, but in 1962 there were people walking past the Adelphi who had been through the whole of the real thing. Bart was one of them. Twenty-one-year-olds at the end of the war were still only thirty-eight. The potential for audiences to witness what was by all accounts an eye-boggling recreation of what Hitler had done to London, was enormous. *Blitz!*, largely due to Sean Kenny's dominating sets – the Underground, St Paul's Cathedral, the East End ablaze – turned the show into an attraction, an alternative to visiting the Tower of London or Tussaud's, in a way that perhaps no other British musical had ever quite been. Today, London's part in the war may be experienced in various museums that contrive to bring back the tension and reality of those times. What Kenny and Bart did was to heighten that evocation with a noisy score and mighty scenery and effects. Critics wrote of such sights not having been put on stage since the old days of Drury Lane. Novello would have gaped to behold such sensation drama, and sensation drama that many of the audience had experienced in real life. Here, of course, the sensation was not confined to a scene or two; the blitz was sensation enough, a whole evening of sensation.

The effect this had may have been much more than virtual. This would hardly be enough to make *Blitz!* work as well today as it did half a century ago, although there was much division about how well it worked in 1962. There is also the show's Jewish content. The plot is concerned with one family, the Blitzteins, the mother working her pickled-herring stall and keeping up the family's respectability in the face of the German onslaught. It is inevitable that Bart's knowledge of the Jewish life should have coloured the work. No other composer of the time would have put a Jewish family at its centre of a musical. If Coward had taken up the subject, his central family would have been the same as that at the centre of *This Happy Breed*, dull but good British through and through, with all the usual worries about keeping up appearances and nagging mother-in-laws and taking time out to look at the roses in the backyard and worrying about the kids' tonsils. Putting a family of Jews at the heart of *Blitz!* was for Bart perfectly natural, but may have reduced some people's interest in it; it may have made *Blitz!* harder to respond to. It proved no impediment to *Fiddler on the Roof*. Anyway, when Mrs Blitztein sings 'So Tell Me', discussing her troubled life with her long dead husband, isn't this really a re-run of *Oliver!*'s 'Reviewing The Situation'? For six minutes Mrs Blitztein is Fagin in drag.

The score of *Blitz!* is one of Bart's best, but it is not all good news. There are twenty-one songs, many of which work well. 'Our Hotel' establishes Bart's community singing philosophy, all races and ages and types dossing down in London's Underground, the most complex network of air raid shelters known to man.

'Tell Him – Tell Her' takes the plot forward, introducing the main characters and giving us a good idea of what each is like. The younger generation, Carol Bliztein and Georgie Locke, have none of the prejudices of their elders, while the elders despair of the outlook of the young. There are other effective moments: a great knockabout hymn of defiance for Mrs B in 'Who's This Geezer Hitler?', another defying moment in the four-square 'Another Morning', and a pastiche of a Vera Lynn World War II serenade in 'The Day after Tomorrow'. Lynn recorded the number for the production, played as if over the radio to the listening populace of Britain, dreaming of their sweethearts in the Forces. These targets are well hit, as are the songs for the children: a regret at evacuation in 'We're Going to the Country' and, Bart as his simplest and most touching, 'Mums and Dads', the street urchins aping their misbehaving parents.

Theatre World reported that

> Mrs Blitztein has a strong attraction for young men between the age of twenty and thirty. Miss Bayntun often finds one or two at the stage door when she leaves the theatre. 'I feel they are very lonely,' she said.
>
> 'Young people are often far more lonely, especially in London, than old ones, and they are attracted by Mrs Blitztein because she is a mother, likely to understand. To some extent, they identify Mrs Blitztein with the actress who plays her, and so they come round to have a word with me.'[21]

Amid the turmoil of *Blitz!* a blessedly quiet moment came at the start of Act II, sung by the now blinded Carol. 'Far Away' is Bart at his most straightforward, with another of what one of his leading ladies calls 'Lionel's simple little tunes'.[22] Too many of the numbers don't stand up to the stronger ones. 'Petticoat Lane' is redundant after Toni Palmer has already chirruped about the delights of being 'Down the Lane'. The second act has its share of also-rans in 'Who Wants to Settle Down?' (Georgie clinging to the idea of eternally sowing his oats), 'Is This Gonna Be a Wedding?' and 'Duty Calls', a sort of *Billy Cotton Band Show* comic song about answering the call to arms. Here and there, as with 'As Long as This is England' (or 'Ing Ger Land' as the lyric had it) the score, the *idea*, treads water. Nevertheless, one has to admit the spirit of *Blitz!*, and perhaps submit to it. It solidly established the Britishness of Bart's contribution to the national musical.

Maggie May

Despite a long run, *Blitz!* was never really a hit, but one of those shows whose popularity is self-contained, uncontaminated by being taken to the heart of the public. They belong to a particular time, and are then put away, leaving not a wrack behind. As much may be said of Bart's next work, **Maggie May** (Adelphi Theatre, 22 September 1964; 501). The elements in its making were more disparate than those for *Oliver!* or *Blitz!* Bart had an acknowledged playwright as

41 The front-of-house photograph of Judith Bruce as Maggie
in the original London production of Lionel Bart's *Maggie May*

his collaborator, an establishment designer of costumes in Leslie Hurry, a choreographer (none of his earlier shows had really needed one) in Paddy Stone, a
director unused to musicals in Ted Kotcheff. The elements of Theatre Workshop
that had threaded through his past work were excised. By now it seemed that
Sean Kenny's sets were an indispensable component of any Bart show. Bart had
a ready-made star in Rachel Roberts as the Liverpudlian tart with the obligatory
heart of gold. Years before, he had sent Roberts the script of *Oliver!*, wanting
her as his first Nancy. Barry Humphries as the Balladeer had the opening song,
apt for a work that seemed to start as ballad opera. Had he persisted with this
idea, Bart might have explored facets of his talent that he locked out in the score
he wrote to Alun Owen's book. Owen jumped at the opportunity to write the
play: 'It seemed to me the most natural development of the "love affair" I have
been conducting with Liverpool.'[23] Bart had qualifications for being the Kurt
Weill, or the lightweight Brecht, of British musicals, this at its strongest in *Fings*.
Fings had borne a social conscience (or lack of it), as had *Oliver!* and, strongly,
Blitz!

The sense of community singing that had imbued the naturalness of *Fings* and
Oliver! and *Blitz!* was weakened in *Maggie May*, and Bart was never to recapture
it. A musical about a working-class prostitute seemed an almost ideal starting
point for his skills, and in the Liverpool setting Bart must have felt a confidence
that coincided with the times. Those times and its most popular songs belonged
to The Beatles. By 1964, they were at the pinnacle of success, and Liverpool
flooded British culture. Bart introduced the piece in a manner that no other composer of British musicals could have.

> From an early age when I could first put one-syllable words together, I used to
> take great delight in my prowess at getting an edge of other street urchins around
> me because I was good at thinking-up and singing spontaneous naughty versions
> of the then current pop songs, like 'The Lady In Red', and 'Sally'.
>
> Today, every audience for one of my shows represents, to me, an extension of
> that gang of kids in the East End of London. Every laugh means a free turn on
> someone's roller skates, and every first night is like a kerbside debut perform-
> ance of a brand-new naughty song. You see, I was the first in our gang to know
> all the rude words to 'Our Old Man's A Dustman' (not Lonnie Donegan's version),
> 'Eskimo Nell', 'She Was A Lulu' and 'Maggie May'.
>
> Which brings me to the subject of this piece. When I decided to make a musi-
> cal, loosely based on the characteristics of this time-honoured sailor's heroine,
> Liverpool, her home town, was not a place that quickly sprang to mind as the
> setting for a musical play. I got the idea in late 1961, which was pre-Beatles, when
> most actors and singers who hailed from that manor were doing their best to dis-
> guise their accents. Come to think of it, I took a bit of a liberty even contemplating
> the idea. But I did, and after doing some research, I found that most of Liverpool's
> folk music had Irish-Celtic roots. Now, it is common knowledge, or should be,

that the Irish are, actually, the lost tribe of Israel so it is a good job that I remembered my barmitzvah music.

However, I was lost on the chat. So I told my mate, designer and genius, Sean Kenny, who, without further ado, took me and my rough story-line to Alun Owen, who had already established himself with plays about Liverpool like 'No Trams to Lime Street'. Alun decided to work with us both, but as I was due to spend a stretch in America helping stage 'Oliver' on Broadway, Alun had to go it solo for six months. When I returned he presented me with a giant script and as he handed it over he said, 'I know it's long, boy-chick, but I've written a lot of material for you to make rhyme into songs. In any case, you've got to learn a whole new language.' I said, 'Whaddya mean, a whole new language?' Then he went on about the dialect, saying it was part Irish, part Welsh and part catarrh. Then I asked him if I had to catch catarrh? He told me to drop dead, and that was the beginning of a beautiful relationship.

The piece speaks, I hope. We enjoyed doing it, anyway. Gi's a turn on your roller skates.[24]

Owen and Bart responded with vigour to the bustle of the Liverpool docks, against which Maggie's love for Casey, a working man of principle who leads a wildcat strike and dies for his pains, bloomed and perished. To suggest that the Liverpool setting worked against the show's success is a nonsense; it probably helped it to success. Years later, Liverpool did nothing to harm the runaway success of Willy Russell's *Blood Brothers*. London in 1964, on the brink of swinging, was quite an insular environment, and it may be that another production of *Maggie May* would reveal qualities which it may possess in quantity. This, I suspect, may be one of the great undiscovered British musicals. It is clearly one of the more interesting of those by Bart, and stands above most others of the 1960s. It also offers itself up for reinvention rather more than many others. And then there is Maggie herself, a giant role to be seized by the outstanding musical actress.

Most of the numbers strongly knit with the storyline: there is no extractable duet such as 'Opposites' or simple romantic torch song such as 'Far Away'. *Maggie May* has two love songs, 'It's Yourself' and 'The Land of Promises'. Neither were given maximum assistance by Roberts, whose gravel voice cannot have helped either to favour; those who waited until later in the run to hear her successor Georgia Brown (who had turned down the role originally) or Brown's successor Judith Bruce were more fortunate. The songs were also recorded by Judy Garland, by 1964 nearing the end of her tether, but she finds the true scale of these pieces, and glorifies in them. These two numbers, the closest Bart ever gets to operatic and integral music-drama, represent everything that *Maggie May* is and *Oliver!* and *Blitz!* are not. Once again, Bart is at the foothills of Brecht and Weill, perhaps spurred on by his librettist to scale new heights. And whatever its achievement, *Maggie May* was an event, tipping Bart back into the modern world. It seemed unthinkable that *Pickwick* belonged to the same decade, that only four years before *Maggie May* Slade and Reynolds were celebrating their afternoon-tea dramas in major London musicals. Now, Maggie showed them how to be unashamed about the pleasures of physical love, itself almost an innovation in the British musical. *Theatre World* considered that

> Alun Owen's vivid book is undoubtedly responsible for lifting *Maggie May* above the general run of musicals. The authentic dialogue, blunt and direct, is a tonic after the stilted words of many shows. Lionel Bart's music adequately supports Mr Owen's book, although it lacks the strong originality of the latter's work. Nevertheless the music has vigour [...] In all, *Maggie May* is refreshing adult entertainment, and while hardly classifiable as one of the great shows of our time, deserves the long run it certainly will achieve.[25]

The *Sunday Times* recognised a play for the times, a British musical that put itself in the public fashion: 'The British North, through the novels of John Braine and Alan Sillitoe, the plays of Alun Owen and Shelagh Delaney, with some additional help from The Beatles, has become for Southern audiences a Grimm's folk-tale country where everyone drinks deep, loves hard, fights long and swears loud on an industrial battlefield.' There was something in this. With *Maggie May*, via Owen's play, Bart was playing catch-up with his fellow theatre writers of the late 1950s; *Maggie May* is Bart's Arnold Wesker moment, his Bernard Kops moment, his *A Taste of Honey* moment. In common with all of these, Bart's moment was itself drawing to a close. The *Sunday Times* preferred the new piece to *Blitz!*, although

> both book and music appear intermittent and unintegrated, given to odd pauses and repetitions. And musically Mr Bart is often torn between Brecht and the Beatles. He is at his best when he relies for inspiration on that great composer 'Traditional' with snatches of sea shanties and folk songs woven into simple, direct, flowing melody. I said it was better than *Blitz!* but for those who believe in setting their standards by *Pal Joey*, *Guys and Dolls* and *West Side Story*, better than *Blitz!* is not good enough.[26]

We should note that those works came from an earlier age: *Pal Joey* (1940), *Guys and Dolls* (1950), and more recently *West Side Story* (1957). By the mid-1960s, British musicals, even those as alive and kicking as *Maggie May*, were still being pulled back to comparison with the American shows of an earlier age. The fact that these had pretty good starts as source material (John O'Hara, Damon Runyon and William Shakespeare) and that *Maggie May* was an original work was overlooked. The fact that *Maggie May* effectively eschewed romanticism was not observed. The fact that it married provincialism with prostitution and a theme of industrial discord was forgotten. The forces that had prevented the development, the unforced evolution, of the British musical were still at work in 1965, its composers and writers regularly sent away with the comment that

42 Judith Bruce, with her daughter Nancy, in the star dressing room at the Adelphi, 1965, during the original London production of *Maggie May*

they could do better. But how much better could anyone in the British musical have done with *Maggie May*? How much more allegory could the British musical achieve, the fusion of tart with heart with the city itself?

Of all the great roles in British musicals, Maggie is in the first division. There was probably no greater exponent of the role than Judith Bruce, remembered by more than one of the original cast as the finest of the three who played it. Indeed, Bruce is the only British actress to have played three of the most demanding, dramatic roles in British musicals, Nancy, Irma and Maggie. A natural successor to Georgia Brown, she had already taken over from her in the London *Oliver!* and in 1964 took over from her as Maggie May. At her dress rehearsal with the company in an empty theatre, as Bruce stepped forward to take her bow a woman's voice from the circle called out 'You're no bloody Maggie May.' Bruce was devastated. She went back to her dressing room and looked at herself in the mirror. After a while, she realised the woman had been right. Bruce never discovered who the woman was. 'I knew then that I had to give it everything'. And did.

Twang

Bart was to experience his own *fin de partie* with **Twang** (Shaftesbury Theatre, 20 December 1965; 43), the show of legendary awfulness and – sometimes – two exclamation marks, conceived as a satire on the story of Robin Hood. According to Bart, the Sherwood hero was to be a cross between Errol Flynn and Bugs Bunny. On the day this idea came to him, Bart had a choice between the drawing-board and the wastepaper basket, and made the wrong decision. From the beginning, disaster beckoned, with the composer adrift on a sea of difficulties on which he made unhappy reunions with many from his Theatre Workshop days, and unfortunate new alliances. Almost uniquely in the history of British musical theatre, the sequence of misfortunes that befell *Twang* was chronicled in excruciating detail, too painful, convoluted and trivial to be repeated here.[27]

Joan Littlewood offered her services as director, much to Bart's surprise, as she had hated *Oliver!* and walked out at the intervals of *Blitz!* and *Maggie May*. The viper was at Bart's breast. Littlewood was misguided or mischievous in inflicting her old Theatre Workshop methods of constant tampering with script and concept, and having her actors hide all over the theatre and then pretend to be dying trees. At one point she was seen with Bart's script in a folder on which she had scrawled 'Lionel's Final Fuck-Up'. Leaving everyone exhausted and exasperated, she eventually withdrew, as did the show's impresario Bernard Delfont. On his sea Bart was also missing his skipper Sean Kenny, as for the first time in four shows the designs were by another, Oliver Messel. Many thought his costumes hideous and the sets worse than a third-rate pantomime. The libretto was hopeless, the director out of his depth, the choreographer in despair. At one point Judith Bruce was sent to Manchester as the management wanted her to replace

Toni Eden as Maid Marian; Bruce told them it was so bad she didn't see how her going into it would be of any help.

The show's debut engagement at Birmingham was cancelled, so it opened in Manchester to a decidedly tepid response. Here the critics noted four-letter words, over-exposed bosoms and a near striptease, but couldn't raise enthusiasm for the songs or cast or anything else. Public interest in the ongoing farce was accentuated because Bart's private life was now making as many headlines as his work – a downfall seemed imminent. In an effort to avoid it, Bart was reputed to have almost completely redone the score before opening at the Shaftesbury, but it was too late. The London critics delivered the *coup de grâce*. R. B. Marriott, referring to Bart's sea of difficulties, decided that 'One can hardly say it has emerged from that sea; it is a dank, bedraggled, feeble thing [...] I can think of no good thing to say for the book, which is thin and boring, for the lyrics, which, when one can hear them, are painfully devious or tediously "clever", for the music, which is about as pedestrian as you can imagine ...'[28] Jeremy Rundall in *Plays and Players* diagnosed 'Bart Failure', suggested another title ('Arrers Can't Sing') and thought 'it really has no business on a professional stage before a paying audience'. He suspected 'the fell influence of the committee'. Finally, he thought it

> hopelessly, unprofessionally, self-conscious. Its awareness of being the latest Bart musical never leaves it for a second. If it's Bart, it must be right, and whether or not the audience enjoy themselves the cast is determined to have a ball. It is like gate-crashing a stage party: everyone knows everyone, and you are the outsider. In other words, the piece breaks the first rule of the theatre, observed by every craftsman from Shakespeare to Beckett: a play can only exist in relationship with an audience. To ignore it is death.[29]

Rundall has it right. Lacking either inspiration or any reason for its existence from Bart, *Twang* or, made ridiculous by its louder exclamation, *Twang!!*, was pointless. It remains, indeed, one of the very few true failures of the British musical for which one feels little sympathy. Listening to the original cast recording, the only remnant left of the sad enterprise, it is all too clear that whatever Bart once had was burned out. It reaffirms the belief that the most interesting British musicals had at root a reason for their being; indeed, it seems sometimes as if the least commercially successful of them had more reason than many. In a world riven with disease, poverty, war and needless death, even the least impressive of British musicals remain blameless.

Appendix 1
Original Productions of British Musicals

This list is not intended to be comprehensive. It does, though, provide a general guide, and attempts to give as complete a list of musical numbers as possible. Musicals listed here are discussed within the main body of the book, but there are many others listed here that are not referred to in the text. Most productions listed belong to the period 1945–72, but those from other periods may be arbitrarily included.

Information given for each entry is as follows:

Title of production

Composer

Lyricist

Librettist and, where applicable, details of original work from which the musical's book is adapted

London theatre or, where applicable, provincial theatre where work opened (some transfers are also noted)

Date of first performance in London

Dates of first performances in theatre clubs, provincial productions or outskirt London theatres which may have preceded the London opening are not necessarily included

PC = Principal cast members

MN = Main musical numbers

Where it has been possible to trace this information, all musical numbers are listed. The usual source for these lists is the original theatre programmes of the original production, and / or original scores where available. In a few cases, it has not been possible to trace a list of musical numbers from any source. Some programmes include misprinted titles, and in such cases the author has corrected any obvious errors. Titles of songs may also deviate from those by which they are generally known, but the original programme or score titles have been used in most cases. Changes in the list of musical numbers during the run are noted if known, but it has inevitably not always been possible to trace such changes.

Number of performances. Where there was no London run, this may read [Tour] or [Season].

Ace of Clubs Music, lyrics and book by Noel Coward. Cambridge Theatre, 7 July 1950. PC: Pat Kirkwood, Graham Payn, Sylvia Cecil, Elwyn Brook-Jones, Myles Eason, Jean Carson. MN: Top of the Morning; My Kind of Man; This Could Be True; Nothing Can Last Forever; Something about a Sailor; I'd Never Never Know; Three Juvenile Delinquents; Sail Away; Josephine; Would You Like to Stick a Pin in My Balloon?; In a Boat on a Lake; I Like America; Why Does Love Get in the Way?; Evening in Summer; Time for Baby's Bottle; Chase Me, Charlie. 211 performances.

After the Ball Music, lyrics and book by Noel Coward, based on the play *Lady Windermere's Fan* by Oscar Wilde. Globe Theatre, 10 June 1954. PC: Mary Ellis, Vanessa Lee, Graham Payn, Peter Graves, Shamus Locke. MN: Oh, What a Century It's Been; I Knew That You Would Be My Love; Mr Hopper's Chanty; Sweet Day; Stay on the Side of the Angels; Crème de la Crème; Light Is the Heart; May I Have the Pleasure?; I Offer You My Heart; Why Is It the Woman Who Pays?; Letter Song; Aria; Go, I Beg You, Go; London at Night; Oh, What a Season This Has Been; Farewell Song; Something on a Tray; Faraway Land. [Cut before London: Good Evening, Lady Windermere; What Can It Mean?]. 188 performances.

Aladdin Music, lyrics and book by Sandy Wilson. Lyric Theatre, Hammersmith, 21 December 1979. PC: Richard Freeman, Joe Melia, Aubrey Woods, Elisabeth Welch, Christine McKenna. MN: The Spell; Aladdin; Hang-Chow; The Proclamation; Tuang Kee Po; It Is Written in the Sands; There and Then; Love's a Luxury; Dream about Me; Song of the Genie of the Ring; Song of the Genie of the Lamp; Happy Ever After; Chopsticks; All I Did; Wicked; The Dirge; Life in the Laundry; Give Him the Old Kung Fu. [Season]

Always Music, lyrics and book by William May and Jason Sprague. Victoria Palace, 22 May 1997. PC: Clive Carter, Jan Hartley, Shani Wallis, Sheila Ferguson. MN: Long May You Reign; Someone Special; I Stand before My Destiny; Why?; Love's Carousel; If Always Were a Place; This Time Around; It's the Party of the Year; Hearts Have Their Reasons; The Reason for Life Is to Love; Montage; Invitation Is for Two; Always. 76 performances.

The Amazons Music by John Addison; lyrics by David Heneker; book by Michael Stewart. Nottingham Playhouse, 7 April 1971. PC: Elizabeth Counsell, Sandra Scriven, Fiona Mathieson, Robert Coleman, Joan Turner. MN: There's Nothing Wrong with England; My Boys; The West End's the Worst End; I'm Only Following My Instructions; Knees Up!; Whatever Can Have Happened?; Let's Stick Together; We Shall See What We Shall See; On Parade; A Nice Young Fellow; Don't Follow the Music; She Hates Me; Afternoon Tea; I Thought as Much; The Coast Is Clear; Eurythmics; Gymnastics; Stag Party; Three Pretty Daughters. 21 performances.

Ambassador Music by Don Gohman; lyrics by Hal Hackady; book by Don Ettlinger, based on the novel *The Ambassadors* by Henry James. Her Majesty's Theatre, 19 October 1971. PC: Howard Keel, Danielle Darrieux, Isobel Stuart. MN: A Man You Can Set Your Watch By; It's a Woman; Lambert's Quandary; Lilas; The Right Time the Right Place; Surprise; Charming; All of my Life; What Can You Do with a Nude?; Love Finds the Lonely; Tell Her; La Femme; Young with Him; I Thought I Knew You; What Happened to Paris?; La Nuit d'Amour; Am I Wrong?; Mama; That's What I Need Tonight; You Can Tell a Lady by her Hat; This Utterly Ridiculous Affair; Not Tomorrow; Thank You, No! 86 performances.

And So to Bed Music and lyrics by Vivian Ellis; book by J. B. Fagan, based on his play. New Theatre, 17 October 1951. PC: Leslie Henson, Betty Paul, Jessie Royce Landis, Keith Michell. MN: Ayre and Fa La; A Chine of Beef; If Only Oliver Cromwell Lived Today; Tonight at Eight; Rigaudon; Gaze Not on Swans; Love Me Little, Love Me Long; Taffety Gown; Amo, Amas; Sarabande; Beauty Retire; When a Woman Smiles; And So to Bed; Moppety Mo; Catch; Supper Scene; Bartholomew Fair; The First Oath; The Second Oath. 323 performances.

Ann Veronica Music by Cyril Ornadel; lyrics by David Croft; book by Frank Wells and Ronald Gow, based on the novel by H. G. Wells. Cambridge Theatre, 17 April 1969. PC: Mary Millar, Arthur Lowe, Hy Hazell, Simon Kent, Peter Reeves, Charles West. MN: A Whole Person; I Don't See What Else I Could Have Said; Ann Veronica; Maternity; Opportunity; Sweep Me off My Feet; One Man's Love; Chemical Attraction; I Couldn't Do a Thing Like That; Why Can't I Go to Him?; They Can't Keep Us Down Anymore; Rococo Trot; Stand in Line; Home Sweet Home; Glad to Have You Back; If I Should Lose You; You're a Good Man; Too Much Meat. 44 performances.

Annie Music by William L. Reed; lyrics and book by Alan Thornhill. Westminster Theatre, 27 July 1967. PC: Margaret Burton, Angela Richards, Gerard Hely, Bill Kenwright. MN: Our Town; Annie; Right for You; Remember, Bill; Ribbons and Such; Walking Out; My Cousin in London; I Don't Like Your Hat; It Fair Takes Your Breath Away; Knock, Knock, Knock; Good Morning; I Keeps Myself to Myself; A Cup of You and Me; Who's the Dictator, Jim Parks?; We're Going to Shake the Country; Betwixt and Between; Open Your Heart; Sheep! Sheep! – Come the Day!; The Appeasement Parade; Mending Things; A Basinful of Revolution. 398 performances.

Arc de Triomphe Music and book by Ivor Novello; lyrics by Christopher Hassall. Phoenix Theatre, 9 November 1943. PC: Mary Ellis, Peter Graves, Elisabeth Welch, Raymond Lovell, Olive Gilbert. MN: Prelude; Shepherd Song; Man of My Heart; Easy to Live With; I Wonder Why; Apache Ballet; Josephine; Waking or Sleeping; Royal France; Paris Reminds Me of You; Dark Music; The Phantom Court; Vision Duet; Jeanne D'Arc [operatic sequence with 'France Will Rise Again']. 222 performances.

Balalaika Music by George Posford and Bernard Grun; lyrics and book by Eric Maschwitz. Adelphi Theatre, 22 December 1936. PC: Muriel Angelus, Roger Treville, Betty Warren, Clifford Mollison, Betty Bucknell, George Gerhardt. MN: Where Is the Snow?; The Devil in Red; Red Rose, What Can Your Meaning Be?; Tzigansky Music; If All the World Were Mine; Hail to Thee, Russia; Soldiers' Hymn; Come This Holy Night of Christmas; At the Balalaika; Masha! Masha! Masha!; Ballerina, Sad and Lonely; Be a Casanova!; Ballet (Reflections); Court Mazurka; Nichevo! Nichevo!; Tango and Paso Doble. [Other titles at some time in the run listed in theatre programme: Oh I'm So Tired!; Two Acres and a Cow; Drink to Our Friends!] 570 performances.

Bar Mitzvah Boy Music by Jule Styne; lyrics by Don Black; book by Jack Rosenthal, based on his play. Her Majesty's Theatre, 31 October 1978. PC: Joyce Blair, Harry Towb, Barry Angel, Ray C. Davis, Leonie Cosman, Vivienne Martin. MN: Why?; If Only a Little Bit Sticks; The Bar Mitzvah of Eliot Green; This Time Tomorrow; Thou Shalt Not; The Harolds of This World; We've Done Alright; Simchas; You Wouldn't Be You; The Bar Mitzvah; Rita's Request; Where Is the Music Coming From?; The Sun Shines out of Your Eyes; I've Just Begun. 78 performances.

Barnardo Music, lyrics and book by Ernest Maxin. Royalty Theatre, 22 May 1980. PC: James Smillie, Fiona Fullerton. MN: London's East End; Oy Vey; The Midnight Waltz; Lovely 'Ot Pies; There's a First Time; Snuggle Up; What Children Will Do; You're the Man; Tosh; Welcome to Dreamland; Girls; Cor!; I Feel Sorry for You; I'm a Winner; My Son; Why Don't We Try Again?; Who Needs a Man?; Am I Running out of Time? 43 performances.

Battersea Calypso Music, lyrics and book by James Bernard, Paul Dehn and Ken McGregor. Richmond Hill Hotel, Montego Bay, Jamaica, February 16 1989. PC: Unknown. MN: Battersea Calypso; Brixton Market; What's Bent Never Goes Straight; Shall I Ever Make It?; Love Me for Another Day; Look Up High; Stay with Me; Granny [Water Come to Me Eye]; Jamaican Banana; Lavender Hill; What Became of Love? [Season]

Belinda Fair Music by Jack Strachey; lyrics and book by Eric Maschwitz and Gilbert Lennox. Saville Theatre, 25 March 1949; transferred Strand Theatre, 20 June 1949. PC: John Battles, Adele Dixon, Jerry Verno, Geoffrey Hibbert, Daphne Anderson. MN: Take a Flower; The Golden Days of Good Queen Anne; I Dreamed I Was at Home Again; Love, Love, Love!; I'm off to the Low Countree; Time Now to Say Farewell; No Love. No Heartbreak [*sic*]; Mistress Peregrine; Good Madam Geneva; A Fool There Was; The Gay Little Ladies of Drury Lane; Sweet Nellie Gwynne; Belinda Fair; Awakening of Belinda; Bim, Bim, Bim; Women and Men; Let's Be Merry; Finale and Country Dance. 131 performances.

Belle, or The Ballad of Dr Crippen Music and lyrics by Monty Norman; book by Wolf Mankowitz. Strand Theatre, 4 May 1961. PC: George Benson, Jerry Desmonde, Davy Kaye, Rose Hill, Virginia Vernon, Nicolette Roeg. MN: The Ballad of Dr Crippen [recurring]; Fifty Years Ago; Mister Lasherwood and Mighty Mick; Bird of Paradise; Meet Me at the Strand; You Are Mine; Colonies; The Devil's Bandsman; Hyoscine; Pills, Pills, Pills; Ain't It a Shame; The Surgery Recitative; Song of Our Future; Lovely London; Posthorn Medley; A Pint of Wallop; Mother Song [There's Nobody Like a Fairy Godmother]; The Bravest of Men; Waltzing with You; Belle; I Can't Stop Singing; Policeman's Song; Coldwater, Michigan; Don't Ever Leave Me; The Dit-Dit Song; The Minstrel Show [comprising: I Do Not Wish to Know That; Mister Robinson and Master Jack; Ah Got So Much Trouble]; You Can't Beat a British Crime. 44 performances.

Big Ben Music by Vivian Ellis; lyrics and book by A. P. Herbert. Adelphi Theatre, 17 July 1946. PC: Carole Lynne, Trefor Jones, Gabrielle Brune, Lizbeth Webb. MN: Other Men; My Father Was a Grocer; Come to Britain; The Parade – Sunsuit to Bridaldress; London Town; I Want to See the People Happy; Let Us Go down to the River; I Like to Like; Love Me Not; Do You Remember the Good Old Days?; In Parliament We Offer; The Sun Is on the City; Wheels of the World; Let's Stop Somebody; We Must Be Free; Who's the Lady?; There's a Lot to Be Said for the Lords; The Poodle and the Pug; A Glass of Wine, My Darling; London's Alight Again. 172 performances.

The Biograph Girl Music by David Heneker [with Warner Brown*]; lyrics by David Heneker and Warner Brown; book by Warner Brown. Phoenix Theatre, 19 November 1980. PC: Bruce Barry, Sheila White, Sally Brelsford, Guy Siner. MN: The Moving Picture Show; Working in Flickers; That's What I Get All Day; The Moment I Close

My Eyes; Diggin' Gold Dust; Every Lady Needs a Master*; I Just Wanted to Make Him Laugh*; I Like to Be the Way I Am in My Own Front Parlor [*sic*]; Beyond Babel; A David Griffith Show; More than a Man; The Industry; Gentle Fade; Nineteen Twenty-Five; The Biograph Girl; One of the Pioneers; Put It in the Tissue Paper. 57 performances.

Bitter-Sweet Music, lyrics and book by Noel Coward. His Majesty's Theatre, 12 July 1929. PC: Peggy Wood, George Metaxa, Ivy St Helier. MN: That Wonderful Melody; The Call of Life; If You Could Only Come with Me; I'll See You Again; Tell Me, What Is Love?; The Last Dance; Life in the Morning; Ladies of the Town; If Love Were All; Evermore and a Day; Little Café; Officers' Chorus; Tokay; Bonne Nuit, Merci; Kiss Me; Ta Ra Ra Boom De Ay; Alas, the Time Is Past; Green Carnations; Zigeuner. 697 performances.

Bless the Bride Music by Vivian Ellis; lyrics and book by A. P. Herbert. Adelphi Theatre, 26 April 1947. PC: Lizbeth Webb, Georges Guétary, Betty Paul, Brian Reece, Anona Winn. MN: Croquet! Croquet!; Too Good to Be True; Any Man but Thomas T; En Angleterre, Les Demoiselles; Oh, What Will Mother Say?; I Was Never Kissed Before; Where Is *The Times?*; Come Dance, My Dear; The Silent Heart; Ma Belle Marguerite; God Bless the Family; Ducky; Bless the Bride; Bobbing Bobbing; Bless the Sea; Mon Pauvre Petit Pierre; The Englishman; Un Consommé; A Table for Two; This Is My Lovely Day; The Fish; This Man Could Never Be a Spy; To France; Here's a Kiss for One and Twenty; My Big Moment. 886 performances.

Blitz! Music and lyrics by Lionel Bart; book by Lionel Bart and Joan Maitland. Adelphi Theatre, 8 May 1962. PC: Amelia Bayntun, Bob Grant, Grazina Frame, Graham James, Thomas Kempinski, Toni Palmer, Edward Caddick. MN: Our Hotel; Tell Him – Tell Her!; I Want to Whisper Something; The Day After Tomorrow; Who's This Geezer, Hitler?; We're Going to the Country; Another Morning; Be What You Wanna Be; As Long as This is England; Opposites; Magic Doorway; Bake a Cake; Leave it to the Ladies; Far Away; petticoat Lane; Down the Lane; So Tell Me; Mums and Dads; Who Wants to Settle Down?; Is This Gonna Be a Wedding?; Duty Calls. 568 performances.

Bordello Music by Al Frisch; book by Julian More; lyrics by Julian More and Bernard Spiro. Queen's Theatre, 18 April 1974. PC: Henry Woolf, Stella Moray, Angela Easterling. MN: A Place Like This; Bordello; Yourself; A Country Bride; Apache Dance; Morality; Business Tango; Simple Pleasures; Art Should Be Art / Can-Can; Family Life; If You Should Leave Me; Madame Misia; All the Time in the World; I Love Me; The Girl in Cabin 54; The Way I See It; Belly Dance; Hallucination; What Does It Take? 41 performances.

The Boy Friend Music, lyrics and book by Sandy Wilson. Players' Theatre, 14 April 1953 [Season]; Revised version Wyndham's Theatre, 14 January 1954. PC: Anne Rogers, Anthony Hayes, Joan Sterndale Bennett, Larry Drew, Denise Hirst, Maria Charles, John Rutland, Violetta, Hugh Paddick. MN: Perfect Young Ladies; The Boy Friend; Won't You Charleston with Me?; Fancy Forgetting; I Could Be Happy with You; Sur le Plage; A Room in Bloomsbury; It's Nicer in Nice; The You-Don't-Want-To-Play-With-Me Blues; Safety in Numbers; The Riviera; It's Never Too Late to Fall in Love; Carnival Tango; Poor Little Pierette. 2,084 performances.

The Buccaneer Music, lyrics and book by Sandy Wilson. New Watergate Theatre, 8 September 1953 [Season]; Lyric Theatre, Hammersmith 8 September 1955 for 170 performances. Apollo Theatre, 22 February 1956. PC: Betty Warren, Eliot Makeham, Kenneth Williams, Ronald Radd, Thelma Ruby, Sally Bazely, Pamela Tearle. MN: Good Clean Fun; Captain Fairbrother; It's Commercial; Unromantic Us; The Facts of Life; You'll Find Out; Something's Missing; For Adults Only; Oh, What a Beautiful Brain; Read All about It; Just Another Man; Just Another Girl; In the Good Old U.S.A.; Learn to Do One Thing Well; Why Did It Have to Be Spring?; Behind the Times; Just Pals. 29 performances.

The Burning Boat Music by Geoffrey Wright; lyrics and book by Nicholas Phipps. Royal Court Theatre, 10 March 1955. PC: Bruce Trent, Marion Grimaldi, Diane Todd, Michael Gough, David Rees. MN: Where Do We Go from Here?; Sir Matthew; A Quiet Part of the World; Twelve Tone Tune; The Burning Boat; This Afternoon; Normouth's Having a Festival; Swimming against the Tide; A Girl Ought to Look Like a Girl; Doesn't He Realise?; Marry a Man with a Mind; Now I Know; Running a Festival; A Great Success. 12 performances.

Call it Love? Songs by Sandy Wilson; book by Robert Tanitch. Wyndham's Theatre, 22 June 1960. PC: Lally Bowers, Nicholas Meredith, Norman Warwick, Richard Owens, Karin Clair. MN: Love Play; Love Song in Rag; I Know, Know, Know; Hate Each Other Cha-Cha; Call It Love. 5 performances.

Canterbury Tales Music by Richard Hill and John Hawkins; lyrics by Nevill Coghill; book by Martin Starkie and Nevill Coghill, based on Coghill's translation of Geoffrey Chaucer. Phoenix Theatre, 21 March 1968. PC: Michael Logan, Nicky Henson, Pamela Charles, Jessie Evans, Kenneth J. Warren, Wilfred Brambell. MN: Song of Welcome; Good Night Hymn; Canterbury Day; [*The Miller's Tale:* I Have a Noble Cock; Darling Let Me Teach You How to Kiss; There's Something in My Blood; Pater Noster; There's the Moon]; [*The Priest's Tale:* My Little Feathery Lady; My Husband Is So Clever]; Love Will Conquer All; [*The Steward's Tale:* Fill Your Glass]; Come on and Marry Me Honey; Beer, Beer, Beer; Where Are the Girls of Yesterday?; [*The Merchant's Tale:* Wedding Song; If She Has Never Loved Before; I'll Give My Love a Ring; Sing in Praise of Women's Virtue]; I Am Forever Dated; [*The Wife of Bath's Tale:* What Do Women Most Desire?]; April Song. 2,080 performances.

The Card Music and lyrics by Tony Hatch and Jackie Trent; book by Keith Waterhouse and Willis Hall, based on the novel by Arnold Bennett. Queen's Theatre, 24 July 1973. PC: Jim Dale, Millicent Martin, Marti Webb, Joan Hickson, Dinah Sheridan, John Savident. MN: Hallelujah!; Nine till Five; Lead Me; Universal White Kid Gloves; Nobody Thought of It; Moving On; Come Along and Join Us; That's the Way the Money Grows; The Card; Opposite Your Smile; I Could Be the One; Nothing Succeeds Like Success; The Right Man. 130 performances.

Careless Rapture Music and book by Ivor Novello; lyrics by Christopher Hassall. Theatre Royal, Drury Lane, 11 September 1936. PC: Ivor Novello, Dorothy Dickson, Olive Gilbert, Zena Dare. MN: Thanks to Phyllida Frame; Singing Lesson; Music in May; Why Is There Ever Goodbye?; Studio Duet; Wait for Me; Rose Ballet; Hampstead Scene [comprising: Hi-Ti-Tiddly-Eye; Winnie, Get off the Colonel's Knee; Take a Trip to Hampstead]; We Are the Wives; The Manchuko; Love Made the Song I Sing to You; Chinese Procession; Temple Ballet; The Bridge of Lovers. 295 performances.

Carissima Music by Hans May; lyrics and book by Eric Maschwitz, from the story by Armin Robinson. Palace Theatre, 10 March 1948. PC: Elizabeth Theilmann, Shirl Conway, Robert Shackleton, Guido Lorraine. MN: Morning in the Piazza; Venice in Spring; Santa Rosa; Carnival in Venice; Two in a Gondola; Far in the Blue; Drink Up, Drink Down; The Urchin's Conversion; I'll Be Waiting for Love; Carissima; The Tenement. 466 performances.

Charlie Girl Music and lyrics by David Heneker and John Taylor; book by Hugh and Margaret Williams with Ray Cooney; story conceived by Ross Taylor. Adelphi Theatre, 15 December 1965. PC: Anna Neagle, Joe Brown, Derek Nimmo, Christine Holmes, Hy Hazell, Stuart Damon. MN: The Most Ancestral Home of All; Bells Will Ring; Charlie Girl; I Love Him, I Love Him [subsequently dropped]; The Scooter Scramble [in later programmes renamed 'The Scooter Ballet']; What Would I Get from Being Married?; Let's Do a Deal; The Flippin' 'All [added during run]; My Favourite Occupation ['The Things I Do for You' replaces this in a later programme]; What's the Magic?; I Was Young*; I Hates Money; The Charlie Girl Waltz; The Party of a Lifetime; Like Love [not listed in subsequent programmes]; That's It; Be My Guest; Washington [not in subsequent programmes]; Fish and Chips; Society Twist [not in subsequent programmes]; Society Exposed [not in original programme]; Liverpool [added for Gerry Marsden]; You Never Know What You Can Do. [* For the 1986 London revival this song was replaced by 'When I Hear Music, I Dance']. 2,202 performances.

Chrysanthemum Music by Robb Stewart; lyrics and book by Neville Phillips and Robin Chancellor. Prince of Wales Theatre, 13 November 1958; transferred to Apollo Theatre 18 February 1959. PC: Pat Kirkwood, Hubert Gregg, Roger Gage, Patricia Moore, Raymond Newell. MN: Alexander; Ships at Sea; Sinner Me; Watch Your Step; Mary Ann; The Limehouse Ballet; Sorry You've Been Troubled; Is This Love?; Understanding; Love Is a Game; Double Wedding; At the Wedding; Saturday Night; Thanks to the Weather; No More Love Songs; How Can I Find My Love?; Shanghai Lil; The Fire Brigade; The Fire Mimed Scene. 148 performances.

The Clapham Wonder Music, lyrics and book by Sandy Wilson, based on the novel *The Vet's Daughter* by Barbara Comyns. Marlowe Theatre, Canterbury, 26 April 1978. PC: Jan Todd, Anita Dobson, George Parsons, Liz Bagley. MN: The Clapham Wonder; The Vet's Daughter; Someday; A Lot More to Life than That; The Waterfall; The Strumpet from the Trumpet; Eh, Rosa?; Any Time; You Know What; Everything, London; 'Ow Do You Know If You Like It (Till You've Tried It)?; My Little Tin Trunk and Me; Mrs Gowley's First Round; Don't Change, Lucy; Alice's Ball; Mrs Gowley's Second Round; Come for a Spin; Our Golden Afternoon; A Wine-Coloured Suit (And a Feather Boa). [Season]

The Comedy of Errors Music by Julian Slade; adapted from Shakespeare by Lionel Harris and Robert McNab. Arts Theatre, 28 March 1956. PC: Bernard Cribbins, Frederick Jaeger, Patricia Routledge, Jane Wenham. MN: I Shall No More to Sea; A Cup of Wine; He That Commends Me; Should He Upbraid; Quoth; When Woman Weeps; Come, I Will Fasten; Get Thee from the Door; Teach Me, Dear Creature; The Chain; Who Would Be Jealous?; When You Have Vow'd; Which; Let's Go Hand in Hand. [Season]

Conversation Piece Music, lyrics and book by Noel Coward. His Majesty's Theatre, 16 February 1934. PC: Yvonne Printemps, Noel Coward, Irene Browne, Louis Hayward,

Heather Thatcher, Moya Nugent. MN: The Parade; I'll Follow My Secret Heart; Regency Rakes; Charming, Charming; Dear Little Soldiers; There's Always Something Fishy about the French; English Lesson; There Was Once a Little Village by the Sea; Nevermore. 177 performances.

Crest of the Wave Music and book by Ivor Novello; lyrics by Christopher Hassall. Theatre Royal, Drury Lane, 1 September 1937. PC: Ivor Novello, Dorothy Dickson, Marie Löhr, Peter Graves, Olive Gilbert. MN: Rose of England; Versailles in Tinsel [comprising: Haven of My Heart; Sarabande; Mazurka; Turbillon]; Why Isn't It You?; Nautical; If You Only Knew; Café Scene [comprising: Spring Duet; The Venezuela; Tango]; March of the Ancestors; Oh, Clementine! [aka Lazy Old Mule]; When Hollywood Plays; Christmas Carol; Used to You [unused]. 203 performances.

The Crooked Mile Music by Peter Greenwell; lyrics and book by Peter Wildeblood, based on his novel *West End People*. Cambridge Theatre, 10 September 1959. PC: Elisabeth Welch, Millicent Martin, Jack MacGowran, Elwyn Brook-Jones, John Larsen. MN: Requiem for Joe; Someone Else's Baby; Lollyby; Going Up; If I Ever Fall in Love Again; Buy a Ticket; Horticulture; The Crooked Mile; Cousin Country; Free; Street Scene; Meet the Family; Spare a Penny; The War on Saturday Night; I'll Wait; The Simple Life; Monday Morning March; Other People's Sins; Strike!; Down to Earth; Luigi. 164 performances.

The Crystal Heart Music by Baldwin Bergersen; lyrics and book by William Archibald. Saville Theatre, 19 February 1957. PC: Gladys Cooper, Laurie Payne, Julia Shelley, Dilys Laye. MN: A Year Is a Day; The Anchor's Down; Yes, Aunt; A Girl with a Ribbon; I Wanted to See the World; Hilltop Dance; A Monkey When He Loves; How Strange the Silence; Desperate; Lovely Island; Pretty Little Bluebird; Handsome Husbands; Agnes and Me; Madam, I Beg You; My Heart Won't Learn; When I Dance with My Love; Lovely Bridesmaids; It's So British; It Took Them. 7 performances.

The Dancing Years Music and lyrics by Ivor Novello; lyrics by Christopher Hassall. Theatre Royal, Drury Lane, 23 March 1939. PC: Ivor Novello, Mary Ellis, Roma Beaumont, Olive Gilbert. MN: Dawn Prelude; Uniform; Waltz of My Heart; Masque of Vienna 1911; The Wings of Sleep; Lorelei [including My Life Belongs to You]; I Can Give You the Starlight; My Dearest Dear; Masque of Vienna 1914; Primrose; In Praise of Love; The Leap Year Waltz; Masque of Vienna 1927; Memory Is My Happiness; When It's Spring in Vienna. 187 performances, closing at outbreak of war. Reopened at the Adelphi Theatre 14 March 1942 for 969 performances.

Divorce Me, Darling! Music, lyrics and book by Sandy Wilson. Globe Theatre, 1 February 1965. PC: Joan Heal, Patricia Michael, Philip Gilbert, Anna Sharkey, Cy Young. MN: Here We Are in Nice Again; Someone to Dance With; Challenge Dance; Whatever Happened to Love?; Lights! Music!; Back to Nature; On the Loose; Maisie; The Paradise Hotel; No Harm Done; Together Again; Divorce Me, Darling!; Here Am I (But Where's the Guy?); Out of Step; Fancy Forgetting; You're Absolutely Me; Back Where We Started; Blondes for Danger; Swing-Time Is Here to Stay. 87 performances.

Drake's Dream Music and lyrics by Lynne Riley and Richard Riley; book by Simon Brett. Shaftesbury Theatre, 7 December 1977; revised version by Ken Hill transferred to Westminster Theatre, 1 February 1978. PC: Paul Jones, Donald Scott, Janet Shaw, David Burt, Caro Gurney. MN: Listen All You Seadogs; At the Court of Queen

Elizabeth; I've Always Had a Dream; She Plays a Dangerous Game; Let's Get Going!; Take a Little Time; When the Winds Command Us Away; Weaving Our Webs; Between Today and Tomorrow; Sedition; Gold; Waiting Isn't Easy; Nova Albion; God of the Waters; The Telephone Song; Spice of Life; Fa La La!; Aground; Sailing Around. 82 performances.

Enrico Music by Renato Rascel; lyrics and book by Garinei and Giovannini (English version in collaboration with Peter Myers and Ronald Cass). Piccadilly Theatre, 3 July 1963. PC: Renato Rascel, Roberta D'Esti, Julia Carne, Roger Delgado, Frank Coda, Gloria Paul, Clelia Matania. MN: Buona Sera; Just Round the Corner; Varieta; Bon Giorno; Socialist Anthem; Strike; Com'e Bello; Theresa; The Boater; My Son; The Furlana; Arriverderci Not Addio; The Song of Rome; Ballad; Resistance Song; Boogie Woogie; Made in Italy. 86 performances.

Expresso Bongo Music by David Heneker and Monty Norman; lyrics by Julian More, Monty Norman and David Heneker; book by Wolf Mankowitz and Julian More. Saville Theatre, 23 April 1958. PC: Paul Scofield, Millicent Martin, Hy Hazell, James Kenney, Meier Tzelniker. MN: Don't You Sell Me Down the River; Expresso Party; Nausea; Spoil the Child; Seriously; I Never Had It So Good; The Shrine on the Second Floor; The Dip Is Dipping; He's Got Something for the Public; I Am; Nothing Is for Nothing; There's Nothing Wrong with British Youth Today; We Bought It; Time; Majorca; The Gravy Train. 316 performances.

The Fields of Ambrosia Music by Martin Silvestri; lyrics and book by Joel Higgins, based on an original screenplay by Garrie Bateson. Aldwych Theatre, 31 January 1996. PC: Joel Higgins, Christine Andreas, Marc Joseph, Marc Heenehan. MN: Ball and Chain; Hubbub; The Fields of Ambrosia; How Could This Happen?; Nuthin'; Who Are You?; Reasonable Man; Step Right Up; Too Bad; That Rat Is Dead!; Hungry; Continental Sunday; Alone; The Card Game; The Gallows; Do It for Me; All in This Together; The Getaway; The Breakout. 23 performances.

Fings Ain't Wot They Used T'Be Music and lyrics by Lionel Bart; book by Frank Norman. Theatre Royal, Stratford East 17 February 1959 and revised version 22 December 1959 / Garrick Theatre 11 February 1960. PC: Glynn Edwards, Miriam Karlin, Barbara Windsor, James Booth, Toni Palmer, Wallas Eaton. MN: Prologue; Proceeding in a Westerly Direction; G'Night Dearie; Fings Ain't Wot They Used T'Be; Laying Abaht; Where It's Hot; The Ceiling's Coming Dahn; Contempery; Cochran Will Return; Polka Dots; Meatface; Where Do Little Birds Go?; Big Time; Carve Up!; Cop a Bit of Pride; The Student Ponce. 63 performances [Stratford East]; 897 performances [revised version and Garrick Theatre].

Follow That Girl Music by Julian Slade; lyrics and book by Dorothy Reynolds and Julian Slade. Vaudeville Theatre, 17 March 1960. PC: Susan Hampshire, Peter Gilmore, Marion Grimaldi, Newton Blick, Patricia Routledge, James Cairncross. MN: Tra La La; Where Shall I Find My Love?; I'm Away; Follow That Girl; Solitary Stranger; Life Must Go On; Three Victorian Mermaids; Doh, Ray, Me; Song and Dance; Taken for a Ride; Shopping in Kensington; Waiting for Our Daughter; Lovely Meeting You at Last; Victoria! Victoria!; One, Two, Three, One; Evening in London. 211 performances.

Free as Air Music by Julian Slade; lyrics and book by Dorothy Reynolds and Julian Slade. Savoy Theatre, 6 June 1957. PC: Gillian Lewis, Patricia Bredin, Dorothy

Reynolds, Michael Aldridge, John Trevor, Gerald Harper. MN: I'm Up Early; Let the Grass Grow; Nothing but Sea and Sky; The Boat's In; Free as Air; A Man from the Mainland; Daily Echo; Her Mummy Doesn't Like Me Any More; The Girl from London; I'd Like to Be Like You; Testudo; I've Got My Feet on the Ground; Holiday Island; Geraldine; We're Holding Hands; Terhou. 417 performances.

Gay's the Word Book and music by Ivor Novello; lyrics by Alan Melville. Saville Theatre, 16 February 1951. PC: Cicely Courtneidge; Lizbeth Webb; Thorley Walters. MN: Ruritania; Everything Reminds Me of You; Guards on Parade; It's Bound to Be Right on the Night; Finder Please Return; An Englishman in Love; Teaching Ballet; If Only He'd Looked My Way; Vitality; Teachers' Song; Greek Dance; Sweet Thames; Gaiety Glad; A Matter of Minutes; On Such a Night as This; Bees Are Buzzin'. 504 performances.

A Girl Called Jo Music by John Pritchett, with additional music by Stanley Myers*; lyrics and book by Peter Myers, Alec Grahame and David Climie, based on the novels of Louisa M. Alcott. Piccadilly Theatre, 15 December 1955. PC: Joan Heal, Virginia Vernon, Diane Todd, Marion Grimaldi, Denis Quilley, Edward Woodward. MN: It's a White World*; Jo's Play*; Books; Christmas Eve; Oh, What a Party It Will Be; Going to the Ball; The Galop; When They Play the Polka; Returning from the Ball; Whither You Go, Love; The Wonder of Spring*; The Wedding March; Oh, I'm Such a Fool!; A Girl Called Jo; The Wedding Dance; New York, 1864*; Rely on Me*; Paree!; Jo's Departure from New York; Amy's Letter; Amy in Europe*; Why Do I Feel Like This?; Bread and Cheese and Kisses; My Beth. 141 performances.

Glamorous Night Music and book by Ivor Novello; lyrics by Christopher Hassall. Theatre Royal, Drury Lane, 2 May 1935. PC: Ivor Novello, Mary Ellis, Olive Gilbert, Elisabeth Welch. MN: Suburbia; Her Majesty Militza; Fold Your Wings; Glamorous Night; Shine through My Dreams; When the Gypsy Played; Rumba; Skating Waltz; Shanty Town; The Gypsy Wedding; March of the Gypsies; Krasnian National Anthem; The Girl I Knew; Singing Waltz [aka Waltz of June]; The Royal Wedding. 243 performances.

Golden City Music, lyrics and book by John Toré. Adelphi Theatre, 15 June 1950. PC: Julia Shelley, Judith Whitaker, Norman Lawrence, Eleanor Summerfield, Moyra Fraser. MN: Aunt Janie; The Telephone; It's a Great Occasion; One White Glove; Moonlight on the River; Tivoli Girls; Jacaranda; What More Is There to Say?; The Girl in the Window; When the Candle Burns Low; It's Love, My Darling, It's Love; Coon's Carnival; Let's Go up to Mabel's Saloon; If I Were to Marry You; Braaivleis; Alles Sal Reg Kom (All Will Come Right); Gold-Digging Digger; The Prettiest Girl in the Town. 140 performances.

The Golden Touch Music, lyrics and book by James Gilbert and Julian More. Piccadilly Theatre, 5 May 1960. PC: Cec Linder, Sergio Franchi, Evelyn Ker, Gordon Boyd. MN: Isles of Greece; Way Out; Athens in My Blue Suit; High Life; Hard to Get; It's a Deal; Whisky A' Go' Go; Funny Thing; Art for My Sake; Beatnikology; Lemon on a Tree; Trust; You're So Like Your Father; Battle Hymn of the Colony; Not Enough of Her to Go Round. 12 performances.

Gone with the Wind Music and lyrics by Harold Rome; book by Horton Foote. Theatre Royal, Drury Lane, 3 May 1972. PC: Harve Presnell, June Ritchie, Patricia

Michael, Robert Swann. MN: Today's the Day; Cakewalk; We Belong to You; Tara; Bonnie Blue Flag; Bazaar Hymn; Virginia Reel; Quadrille; Two of a Kind; Blissful Christmas; Tomorrow is Another Day; Ashley's Departure; Where is my Soldier Boy?; Why Did They Die?; Lonely Stranger; A Time for Love; Atlanta Burning; A Soldier's Goodbye; Which Way is Home?; If Only; How Often, How Often; The Wedding; A Southern Lady; Marrying for Fun; Strange and Wonderful; Blueberry Eyes; Little Wonders; Bonnie Gone; It Doesn't Matter Now. 397 performances.

The Good Companions Music by André Previn; lyrics by Johnny Mercer; book by Ronald Harwood, based on the novel by J. B. Priestley. Her Majesty's Theatre, 11 July 1974. PC: John Mills, Judi Dench, Christopher Gable, Marti Webb, Ray C. Davis. MN: Goodbye; Camaraderie; Bruddersford [All Mucked Up; The Pools; Aye, Lad]; Footloose [The Great North Road; Fancy Free; On My Way]; Pleasure of Your Company; Stage Struck; Dance of Life; Good Companions; Slippin' around the Corner; A Little Travelling Music; And Points Beyond; Darkest before the Dawn; Susie for Everybody; Ta, Luv; I'll Tell the World; Stage Door John. 252 performances.

The Good Old Bad Old Days Music, lyrics and book by Leslie Bricusse and Anthony Newley. Prince of Wales Theatre, 20 December 1972. PC: Anthony Newley, Bill Kerr, Julia Sutton, Caroline Villiers. MN: The Good Old Bad Old Days; Mustn't Grumble; The Fool Who Dared to Dream; The Wisdom of the World; Thanksgiving Day; And Women Must Wait; Today; Tomorrow; Yesterday; It's a Musical World; I Do Not Love You; A Cotton Pickin' Moon; The Good Things in Life; What's the Matter, God – Can't You Take a Joke?; They've Got a Cure for Everything on Broadway; The People Tree; Broadway Finale. 309 performances.

Good Time Johnny Music by James Gilbert; lyrics by Julian More and James Gilbert; book by Julian More. Birmingham Repertory Theatre, 16 December 1971. PC: Ronnie Barker, Eric Flynn, Colette Gleeson, Joan Sims. MN: Bed; A Crackerjack; Crackerjack Dance; Above Below; One for a Win, One for a Place; Well, Isn't That Nice; Come a Little Closer, Rosa; Big Lover; Why Should the Devil Have the Best Songs?; Another One for the Poor; Sigmund; Good-Time Johnny [sic]; What Have I Got to Lose?; Don't Come Any Nearer, Vera; Never Have a Clever Idea; That Indefinable Something; Riverside Rag; The Laugh's on Me. [Season]

Goodbye Mr Chips Music and lyrics by Leslie Bricusse; book by Roland Starke, based on the novel by James Hilton. Chichester Festival Theatre, 11 August 1982. PC: John Mills, Colette Gleeson, Nigel Stock. MN: Roll Call; Would I Have Lived My Life Then; Fill the World with Love; Schooldays; That's a Boy; Where Did My Childhood Go?; Boring; Take a Chance; Walk through the World; When I Am Older; The Miracle; A Day Has a Hundred Pockets; You and I; What a Lot of Flowers; When I Was Younger; Goodbye Mr Chips. [Season]

Grab Me a Gondola Music by James Gilbert; lyrics by James Gilbert and Julian More; book by Julian More. Lyric Theatre, 26 December 1956. PC: Joan Heal, Denis Quilley, Jane Wenham, Donald Hewlett, Trefor Jones, Guido Lorraine. MN: Grab Me a Gondola; That's My Biography; Plain in Love; The Motor Car Is Treacherous; Cravin' for the Avon; Bid Him a Fond Goodbye; Lonely in a Crowd; Jimmy's Bar; Man Not a Mouse; Star Quality; Chianti; New to Me; What Are the Facts?; Show Page Ballet; Mink; The Worst Thing That Happened to Me; Rockin' at the Cannon Ball; When I Find That Girl. 673 performances.

Half A Sixpence Music and lyrics by David Heneker; book by Beverley Cross, based on the novel *Kipps* by H. G. Wells. Cambridge Theatre, 21 March 1963. PC: Tommy Steele, Marti Webb, James Grout. MN: All in the Cause of Economy; Half a Sixpence; Money to Burn; The Oak and the Ash; She's Too Far above Me; I'm Not Talking to You; A Proper Gentleman; If the Rain's Got to Fall; The Old Military Canal; Hip, Hip, Hoorah!; The One That's Run Away; Long Ago; Flash! Bang! Wallop!; I Know What I Am; I'll Build a Palace; I Only Want a Little House. 679 performances.

Half in Earnest Music, lyrics and book by Vivian Ellis, based on the play *The Importance of Being Earnest* by Oscar Wilde. Belgrade Theatre, Coventry, 27 March 1958. PC: Marie Löhr, Stephanie Voss, Brian Reece, Bryan Johnson, Phyllida Sewell, Henry Manning. MN: Don't Touch the Cucumber Sandwiches; So Romantic; To Bunbury I Must Go; Teatime Quartet; How Do You Propose to Propose?; The Cloakroom at Victoria; The German Lesson; So Charming; A Sensible Man; Foolish Love; There's No Friend Like a New Friend; Christening Quartette; The Social Scale. [Season]

Half in Earnest was first presented at Bucks County Playhouse, New Hope, Pennsylvania, 29 June 1957. PC: Anna Russell, Jack Cassidy, Sara Seegar. MN: Chopsticks; So Romantic; Bunbury; One Lump or Two?; How Do You Propose to Propose?; The Cloakroom at Victoria; The German Lesson; Where Is My Prince Charming?; A Sensible Man; Foolish Love; There's No Friend Like a New Friend; Where's My Princess Charming?; Christening Quartette; The Social Scale. [Season/Tour]

Happy Holiday Music by George Posford; lyrics and book by Eric Maschwitz, based on the play *The Ghost Train* by Arnold Ridley. Palace Theatre, 22 December 1954. PC: Reg Dixon, Austin Melford, Marie Burke. MN: Carols in the Snow; Happy Holiday; Honeymoon Hotel; The Fellow for Me; Sew a Silver Button on the Moon; The Glenbogle Song; Surprisingly; There Goes Charlie; Laird O'Cockpenny; The Thing That Goes Bump in the Night; A Lovely Day for Dreaming; A Wonderful Wedding in White; Wedding Ballet; The Charm of Growing Old; The Feeling of Falling in Love. 31 performances.

Hard Times Music, lyrics and book by Christopher Tookey and Hugh Thomas. Theatre Royal, Haymarket, 22 May 2000. PC: Roy Hudd, Brian Blessed, Peter Blake, Susan Jane Tanner, Malcolm Rennie, Ann Emery. MN: The Greatest Show on Earth; Fact!; That's What Made Me a Man; Wond'ring Again; Another Town Tomorrow; One of These Days; People Can!; Factory Town; I've Never Heard the Last of It; What Do You Know about Love?; A Modern Marriage Pact; Father of the Bride; Haven't We Met?; A Boy Must Do; Spring; Better Things Shall Be; Mrs Sparsit's Staircase; Ask of Me Anything; When I Was a Boy; My Bounderby Alphabet. 112 performances.

Harmony Close Music by Ronald Cass and Charles Ross; lyrics and book by Charles Ross. Lyric Theatre, Hammersmith, 17 April 1957. PC: Zack Matalon, Jo Ann Bayless, Louie Ramsay, Bernard Cribbins, Rose Hill, Colin Croft, Barry Kent. MN: Opening; Getting Nowhere Fast; Undesirable Elements; Great Big City; London Is a Village; Don't Knock; Goodbye to All That; I Go Round in a Whirl; Nothing to Do in London; Robin's Dream; Goodnight until Today; Lovely Weather for Ducks; Why Should I Care?; Exercising the Dog; I Confess; Life Should Be a Lively Thing. 62 performances.

High Diplomacy Music by William L. Reed and George Fraser; lyrics and book by Alan Thornhill and Hugh Steadman Williams. Westminster Theatre, 5 June 1969. PC: Donald Scott, Patricia Bredin, Muriel Smith. MN: High Diplomacy; What They Say and What They're Meaning; Efficiency; Hail to the Precarious Isles!; Reading People; No Strings Attached; X Marks the Spot; Give 'Em What They Want – Tell 'Em What to Do; Everything That He Does; Is She on Our Side – or Theirs?; For Everyone, Everywhere; Just between You and Me; For Certain; It May All Depend on You; If I Don't Do It, Nobody Else Will; Will There Be a Street in the Future?; It's Crazy! It's Mad!; The Oldest Au Pairs in the Business; The Operator; Children in the Dark. 172 performances.

His Monkey Wife Music, lyrics and book by Sandy Wilson, based on the novel by John Collier. Hampstead Theatre Club, 20 December 1971. PC: June Ritchie, Robert Swann, Bridget Armstrong. MN: Emily's Waltz; Home and Beauty and You; Marriage; In Boboma Tonight; Haverstock Hill; Don't Rush Me; Who Is She?; Dear Human Race; Leave It All to Smithers; Mad about Your Mind; His Monkey Wife; A Girl Like You; Doing the Chimpanzee; Live Like the Blessed Angels. [Season]

Hooray for Daisy! Music by Julian Slade; lyrics and book by Julian Slade and Dorothy Reynolds. Lyric Opera House, Hammersmith, 20 December 1960. PC: Eleanor Drew, Robin Hunter, Angus Mackay, Dorothy Reynolds, Joe Greig, Edward Hardwicke. MN: She's Coming on the 4.48; I Feel as If I'd Never Been Away; No Lullaby; Nice Day; Soft Hoof Shuffle; If Only You Needed Me; How, When and Where; See You on the Moon; Going Up; Wine Is a Thing, Ting-a-Ling; He's Got Absolutely Nothing; Madame, Will You Dine?; It Won't Be the Same; I'm Sorry; Let's Do a Duet; Personally. 51 performances.

House of Cards Music by Peter Greenwell; lyrics and book by Peter Wildeblood, based on David Magarshack's translation of the play *Even a Wise Man Stumbles* by Aleksander Ostrovsky. Players' Theatre, 26 January 1963 [Season]. Phoenix Theatre, 3 October 1963. PC: Patrick Mower, Stella Moray, Geoffrey Hibbert, Barbara Evans, Barbara Couper, Douglas Byng. MN: Give Us the Money; You've Only Got to Ask; If You Were Not So Beautiful; The Mashenka Waltz; I Don't Remember At All; The End of Summer; Thé Dansant; Charity Begins (At Home); The Secret with Women; The Delectable Life; Somewhere There's Someone; Down the Mountainside; A Marriage Has Been Arranged; I Didn't Even Ask Her; Easy to Please; The Political Situation. 27 performances.

I and Albert Music by Charles Strouse; lyrics by Lee Adams; book by Jay Allen. Piccadilly Theatre, 6 November 1972. PC: Polly James, Sven-Bertil Taube; Lewis Fiander; Aubrey Woods. MN: It Has All Begun; Leave It Alone; I've 'Eard the Bloody 'Indoos 'As It Worse; The Victoria and Albert Waltz; This Gentle Land; This Noble Land; I and Albert; His Royal Highness; Enough!; Victoria; This Dear Paradise [replaced by Just You and Me]; All Glass; Draw the Blinds; The Widow at Windsor; No One to Call Me Victoria; When You Speak with a Lady; Go It, Old Girl! 120 performances.

Instant Marriage Music by Laurie Holloway; lyrics and book by Bob Grant. Piccadilly Theatre, 1 August 1964. PC: Bob Grant, Joan Sims, Stephanie Voss, Paul Whitsun-Jones, Tony Holland, Wallas Eaton. MN: Getting Married; Down There; I Not Sleep; Flippin' Strippin'; My Shape; Hands Off, He's Mine; We Get It at Home;

A Good Time Was Had by All; Bad, Bad Day; You've 'Ad Your Lot; I Wish My Love Were Here; Instant Marriage; Up There; Show Him What's What; Shake It About; I'm Gonna Get You. 366 performances.

Irma la Douce Music by Marguerite Monnot; English lyrics and book by Julian More, David Heneker and Monty Norman. Lyric Theatre, 17 July 1958. PC: Elizabeth Seal, Keith Michell, Clive Revill. MN: Valse Milieu; Très Très Snob; The Bridge of Caulaincourt; Our Language of Love; She's Got the Lot; Dis-Donc, Dis-Donc; Le Grisbi Is le Root of le Evil in Man; The Wreck of a Mec; That's a Crime; From a Prison Cell; Irma la Douce; There Is Only One Paris for That; The Freedom of the Seas; Fever Dance; Christmas Child. 1,512 performances.

Jack the Ripper Music by Ron Pember; lyrics and book by Ron Pember and Denis De Marne. Ambassadors Theatre, 17 September 1974. PC: Terese Stevens, Howard Southern, Peter Spraggon, Eleanor McCready, Roy Sone. MN: Saturday Night; Sing Sing; I'm the Girl You All Know; God Bless; Goodbye Day; What a Life; Love; Ripper's Going to Get You; Charlie and Queenie; Half a Dozen Pints; There's a Boat Coming In; There Ain't Any Work Today; Look at Her; Suspects; Policeman's Chorus; Step across the River; Montage. 228 performances.

Joey Joey Music, lyrics and story by Ron Moody; book by Keith Waterhouse and Willis Hall. Saville Theatre, 11 October 1966. PC: Ron Moody, Vivienne Martin, Peter Pratt, Teddy Green, Joe Baker, Gordon Rollings, Ann Hamilton. MN: Typitywitchet; Where You Been Joe?; Friend; Our Place; You My Son; Flowers; Softly and Secretly; Mary; When You Dance with Me; Harlequinade; My Fault; The Life That I Lead; Get Your Coat on Joey; Let's Think about Me for a Change; Hot Codlins; Run across London; You Can't Keep a Good Clown Down; Basket Dance; Darkly Handsome; Winter Harlequinade; Father and Son. 23 performances.

Johnny the Priest Music by Antony Hopkins; lyrics and book by Peter Powell, based on the play *The Telescope* by R. C. Sherriff. Princes Theatre, 19 April 1960. PC: Jeremy Brett, Stephanie Voss, Bunny May, Hope Jackman, Frances Buckeridge, Phyllida Sewell. MN: Doin' the Burp; The Maybury Story; The Little Box; Hellfire; Johnny the Priest; Vicarage Tea; Be Not Afraid; I'm Your Girl; Beyond These Narrow Streets; Rooftops; The Foggy Foggy Blues; He'll Let You Down; Bound Over; Ping Pong; Johnny Earn Peanuts; A Tanner's Worth of Tune; Charge Me; A Boy Called Johnny; Stormy Night; Farewell Johnny. 14 performances.

Joie de Vivre Music by Robert Stolz; lyrics by Paul Dehn; book by Terence Rattigan, based on his play *French Without Tears*. Queen's Theatre, 14 July 1960. PC: Donald Sinden, Joan Heal, Joanna Rigby, Robin Hunter, Jill Martin. MN: Opening Chorus; Why?; There'll Always Be a Navy; Give Me!; Grab It While You Can; Open Your Eyes; Leave the Building; How Can I Tell the Other Man?; Fraternity!; 'Allo, Beeg Boy!; Scottish Can Can; Another Day; The Girl I'm Intending to Marry; The Kiss Was Very, Very Small; Le West End; I'm Sorry but I'm Happy. 4 performances.

Jorrocks Music and lyrics by David Heneker; book by Beverley Cross. New Theatre, 22 September 1966. PC: Joss Ackland, Thelma Ruby, Paul Eddington, Willoughby Goddard, Cheryl Kennedy, Bernard Lloyd. MN: Ask Mr Jorrocks; Belinda; The Happiest Man Alive; Fresh Bloomin' Health; We'd Imagined a Man; Toasts of the Town; The Midsummer Fox; I Don't Want to Say Goodnight; The Opening Meet;

The Hounds of John Jorrocks; Love Your Neighbour; A Little Bit Individual; You Can Depend on Me; I Well Recall the Day; I Don't Want to Behave Like a Lady; Once He's in He'll Never Get Out; The Sport of Kings; Jorrocks. 181 performances.

Keep Your Hair On! Music by John Addison; lyrics and book by John Cranko. Apollo Theatre, 13 February 1958. PC: Rachel Roberts, Betty Marsden, Barbara Windsor, Erik Mörk. MN: True Party Song; Rain; Just a Misfit; Toni's a Phoney; Crowning Glory; Crocodile Tears; One Day; Patent Leather Pumps; A Martyr for the Truth; Help the Lady, Dave; Not What I Call Love; Olaf's Song; Oh I Do, I Do; Never Be a Bore; Bosom Friend; Keep Your Hair On. 20 performances.

King's Rhapsody Devised, written and composed by Ivor Novello; lyrics by Christopher Hassall. Palace Theatre, 15 September 1949. PC: Ivor Novello, Vanessa Lee, Olive Gilbert, Denis Martin, Zena Dare, Phyllis Dare. MN: Dancing Lesson; Birthday Greeting and Dance; Someday My Heart Will Awake; Arrival at Murania; Fly Home Little Heart; Mountain Dove; If This Were Love; Mayor of Perpignan; Gates of Paradise; Take Your Girl; A Violin Began to Play; Muranian Rhapsody; Coronation Scene. 881 performances.

Kings and Clowns Music, lyrics and book by Leslie Bricusse. Phoenix Theatre, 1 March 1978. PC: Frank Finlay, Elizabeth Counsell, Dilys Watling, Maureen Scott, Anna Quayle, Colette Gleeson, Sally Mates, Ray C. Davis. MN: Kings and Clowns; Henry Tudor; Good Times; To Love One Man; Get Rid of Her!; I'm Not!; The Grape and the Vine; A Woman is a Wonderful Thing; In Bed; My Son; Young Together; Tomorrow with Me; Could Anything Be More Beautiful?; Bitch!; The Perfect Woman; Is Sad; Ten Wishes; The End of Love; A Man Is about to Be Born; Sextet. 34 performances.

Kookaburra Music and lyrics by Eric Spear; book by Charles Macarthur Hardy, adapted from the book by Joyce Dennys. Princes Theatre, 26 November 1959. PC: Maggie Fitzgibbon, Gordon Boyd, Julia Shelley. MN: Work to Be Done; Romance; It's a Tough Life; Rain; I Walked with My Love; The Wowsers of the District; A Day Like This; Kookaburra; The Tea Party; God's Own Country; Women; Christmas; The Right Kind of Man; The Mail; England; Grandmother's Piano; Why?; Christmas Party. 42 performances.

The Lily White Boys Music by Tony Kinsey and Bill Le Sage; lyrics by Christopher Logue, in collaboration with Lindsay Anderson, Charles Fox and Oscar Lewenstein; book by Harry Cookson. Royal Court Theatre, 27 January 1960. PC: Albert Finney, Philip Locke, Monty Landis, Georgia Brown, Sally Ann Field, Ann Lynn, Willoughby Goddard, Ronnie Stevens. MN: The Opening Lament; The Song of Reasonable Ambition; The Committee's Point Number; The Young Hero Sings a Song of Self-Understanding; A Youth Leader Advises Neutrality and Respectfulness; The Boys' Spare Chorus; The Solicitor's Song; The Song of Natural Capital; The Girls' Spare Chorus; The Sentimental Number; The Song of The English Salesmen; The Song of Innocent Prosperity; The Song of Practical Values; The Bag of Gold Song; The Quartet; Jeannie on the Price of Ethics; The Song of Good Adjustment by the Company Analyst; The Destiny Duet; The Chorale. 45 performances.

Listen to the Wind Music and lyrics by Vivian Ellis; book by Angela Ainley Jeans. Oxford Playhouse, 15 December 1954; Arts Theatre, 16 December 1955. PC: Gillian

Webb, Miriam Karlin, Richard Palmer, Ronald Barker, Nora Nicholson. MN: Listen to the Wind; Introductions; Timothy's under the Table; When I Grow Up; Who'd Be Governed by a Governess?; The Bread and Butter Song; Twinkle, Twinkle Little Star; Naughty Gale Bird; Miaow! Miaow!; Ten Little Mermaids; Whistle Down the Chimney; When They Grow Up; Thunder Song; Goody Gale Bird. 48 performances.

Liza of Lambeth Music by Cliff Adams; lyrics and book by William Rushton and Berny Stringle, based on the novel by W. Somerset Maugham. Shaftesbury Theatre, 8 June 1976. PC: Angela Richards, Christopher Neil, Patricia Hayes, Bryan Marshall, Michael Robbins. MN: Husbands; Liza; Gawd Bless Her; I Come Down from Wigan; Liza of Lambeth's Mum; Liza Ballet; Prince of Wales; Is This All?; Watch It; Red Jollop; Good Bad Time; Who in his Right Mind?; Dirty Bertie; Tricky Finish; Going down to Chingford on a Chara; Whatever Happens to a Man; Liza Outing; Beautiful Colours; What's the Use of Killing Yourself?; Gilbert and Sullivan; Why Can't We Choose?; I Know I Shouldn't Like It; Between Ourselves; A Little Bit on the Side. 110 performances.

Lock up Your Daughters Music by Laurie Johnson; lyrics by Lionel Bart; book by Bernard Miles, based on the play *Rape upon Rape* by Henry Fielding. Mermaid Theatre, 28 May 1959. PC: Hy Hazell, Richard Wordsworth, Stephanie Voss, Terence Cooper, Frederick Jaeger. MN: All's Well; A Proper Man; It Must Be True; Red Wine and a Wench; 'Tis Plain to See; On the Side; When Does the Ravishing Begin?; Lovely Lover; Lock up Your Daughters; There's a Plot Afoot; Mister Jones; On a Sunny Sunday Morning; If I'd Known You; Kind Fate; I'll Be There. 330 performances.

Lost Empires Music by Denis King; lyrics and book by Keith Waterhouse and Willis Hall, based on the novel *Lost Empires* by J. B. Priestley. Darlington Civic Theatre, 15 May 1985 and tour. PC: Brian Rawlinson, Angela Richards, Peter Adamson, Julia Chambers, Leslie Randall, Peter Ledbury. MN: Till Ready; He's a Shy Boy; You're So Different; The Bill; Quite the Gentleman; Actors; Success; Nice Girls Don't; The Show Must Go On; Twice Nightly; If Autumn Met Spring; Where Is My Love Tonight?; 'Ow's Abaht; A Prediction; Lost Empires; Gag-Time Rag; It Will All Be Over by Christmas. [Tour]

The Love Doctor Music, lyrics and book by Robert Wright and George Forrest suggested by the medical plays of Molière. Piccadilly Theatre, 12 October 1959. PC: Ian Carmichael, Joan Heal, Douglas Byng, Eleanor Drew, Richard Wordsworth, Patricia Routledge, Peter Gilmore. MN: Bleed and Purge; Rich Man, Poor Man; Be-Angelled; Promised; Loose in the Foot; Who Is? You Are!; His Father's Son; She's Appalling, She's Alluring; I Would Love You Still; I Am Your Man; The Parade; Would I Were; Up; Formula, Formulae, Formulorum; The Carefree Heart; Anatomy; The Chase. 16 performances.

Love from Judy Music by Hugh Martin; lyrics by Hugh Martin and Jack Gray; book by Eric Maschwitz and Jean Webster. Saville Theatre, 25 September 1952. PC: Jean Carson, Bill O'Connor, Adelaide Hall, June Whitfield, Audrey Freeman, Johnny Brandon. MN: Mardi Gras; I Never Dream When I'm Asleep; It's Great to Be an Orphan; Goin' Back to School; Dumb, Dumb, Dumb; It's Better Rich; Daddy-Long-Legs; Love from Judy; A Touch of Voodoo; Skipping Rope Hornpipe; Here We Are; Go and Get Your Old Banjo; Kind to Animals; Aint Gonna Marry; My True Love; What Do I See in You? 594 performances.

Maggie May Music and songwords by Lionel Bart; book by Alun Owen. Adelphi Theatre, 22 September 1964. PC: Rachel Roberts, Kenneth Haig, Andrew Keir, Barry Humphries, Diana Quiseekay. MN: The Ballad of the Liver Bird; Lullaby; I Love a Man; Casey; Shine, You Swine; Dey Don't Do Dat T'Day; I Told You So; Right of Way; Stroll On; Away from Home; Maggie, Maggie May; The Land of Promises; Leave Her, Johnny, Leave Her; Carryin' On; There's Only One Union; It's Yourself (It Hurts); The World's a Lovely Place; I'm Me; We Don't All Wear D'Same Size Boots; It's Yourself. 501 performances.

Magyar Melody Revised version of *Paprika* Music by George Posford and Bernard Grun; lyrics by Harold Purcell and Eric Maschwitz; book by Eric Maschwitz, Fred Thompson and Guy Bolton. His Majesty's Theatre, 20 January 1939. PC: Binnie Hale, Roger Treville, Betty Warren, Arthur Margetson. MN: The Lancers; Were Ev'ry Pretty Girl a Song; Czardas; Just Like a Gipsy Band; Magyar Melody; Home Is the Harvest; My Heart Belongs to Budapest; Operetta Scene; Ballet (Moonlight on the Danube); Music for Romance; Mine Alone; We Don't Want to Flirt; A Tandem in the Park; Duel at Dawn. 105 performances.

Make Me an Offer Theatre Royal, Stratford East, 17 October 1959 for 36 performances. New Theatre, 16 December 1959. PC: Daniel Massey, Dilys Laye, Sheila Hancock, Martin Miller, Diana Coupland, Victor Spinetti. MN: The Pram Song; Portobello Road; Dog Eat Dog; First Needle Recitative; I Want a Lock-Up; If I Was a Man; Business Is Business; All Big Fleas; You've Gotta Have Capital; Love Him; Sally's Lullaby; Make Me an Offer; Whatever You Believe; Second Needle Recitative; Break-Up; The Auction; It's Sort of Romantic; Knock-Out; Third Needle Recitative. 267 performances.

Man of Magic Music by Wilfred Wylam; lyrics and book by John Morley and Aubrey Cash. Piccadilly Theatre, 15 November 1966. PC: Stuart Damon, Judith Bruce, Stubby Kaye, Doris Hare, Gaye Brown. MN: Floral Sisters; Man in the Crowd; Fantabulous; The Man Who Captures My Heart; Suddenly; Sling the Gin; Conquer the World; Man of Magic; Don't Bother Me Bub; The Earth Is the Lord's; Like No Other Man; Kester's Crystal Cabbage; You Can't Keep a Good Man Down; This He Knows; Say Your Name. 135 performances.

Mardi Gras Music and lyrics by Alan Blaikley and Ken Howard; book by Melvyn Bragg. Prince of Wales Theatre, 18 March 1975. PC: Lon Satton, Nicky Henson, Pepsi Maycock, Dana Gillespie, Gaye Brown, Aubrey Woods. MN: Mardi Gras (Breeze from the River); Everything about You; From Now On (Immortal, Invisible); Isn't It a Nice Sensation?; I Call the Tune; That's That; The Second Line; That's the Trick*; New Orleans; Love Keeps No Season; I Can See It All; Everybody's Moving; One in a Million*; Make Jazz; Celandine's Blues; When I Feel the Spirit Move Me; The Calinda; Love's Fool; Ash Wednesday* [*listed in theatre programme for part of the run]. 212 performances.

Marigold Music by Charles Zwar; lyrics and book by Alan Melville, based on the play by F. R. Pryor and L. Allen Harker. Savoy Theatre, 27 May 1959; transferred to Saville Theatre 13 July 1959. PC: Sally Smith, Sophie Stewart, Jean Kent, Jeremy Brett, Madeleine Christie, Edith Stevenson, Stephen Hancock. MN: Romance at the Manse; Love Can't Be Learned; Such Will Be Our Life; The New Bohemian Polka; According to Mr Payton; Mr Gloag's Advice; Always Ask Your Heart; Princes Street;

Her Majesty's Health; Wonderful View; Reel; Present Day Youth; Men; Lullaby; Fashionable Pair. 77 performances.

Marilyn! Music by Mort Garson; lyrics and book by Jacques Wilson. Adelphi Theatre, 17 March 1983. PC: Stephanie Lawrence, John Christie, John Bennett, David Firth, Bruce Barry, Judith Bruce. MN: Did You Know Marilyn Monroe?; I Am Camera; Somebody Will Love Me; What Do We Do with the Girl?; Can You Hear Me Mama?; The Most Beautiful Girl of Them All; 8 X 10 Glossies; Where Do You Want Me?; I Never Knew a Girl Like Her Before; Seeing Other Men; Come and Get it Girl; It Happens; The Man Has Got an Eye; I Can See Myself Very Clearly; To Love Somebody; Then the Town Comes Down on Your Head; I'm Going Public; So Happy to See Me; Who's That Girl?; How Do You Like It?; Bigger than Life; A Girl Like You Needs a Little Protection; There's So Much to Do in New York; Dumb Blonde; The Wedding: The Scene Will Play; Beautiful Child; It Was Not Meant to Be; Somewhere a Phone Is Ringing. 156 performances.

The Matchgirls Music by Tony Russell; lyrics and book by Bill Owen. Leatherhead Theatre Club, 23 November 1965 [Season]. Revised version Globe Theatre, 1 March 1966. PC: Vivienne Martin, Marion Grimaldi, Gerard Hely, Cheryl Kennedy, Julia Sutton. MN: Phosphorous; 'Atful of 'Ope; Look Around; Me; Men; Something about You; Mind You Bert; Dear Lady; We're Gonna Show 'Em; Cockney Sparrers; This Life of Mine; Hopping Dance; I Long to See the Day; Comes a Time; An Amendment to a Motion; Waiting. 119 performances.

Mister Venus Music by Trevor H. Stanford (Russ Conway) and Norman Newell; lyrics by Norman Newell; book by Ray Galton and Johnny Speight. Prince of Wales Theatre, 23 October 1958. PC: Frankie Howerd, Anton Diffring, Judy Bruce, June Grant, Alexander Dore, Annette Carell. MN: The Mister Venus Theme (Overture); Time to Celebrate; Love Like Ours; Marble Arch; Love, Love, Love; Stepping out in Society; Song and Dance Man; Every Little Minute; In the Spring; Airport Sequence; It's Been Fun; Tradition; Good Neighbours Ballet; It's in the News. 16 performances.

The Mitford Girls Music by Peter Greenwell; lyrics and book by Caryl Brahms and Ned Sherrin. Globe Theatre, 8 October 1981. PC: Patricia Hodge, Lucy Fenwick, Colette Gleeson, Patricia Michael, Gay Soper, Julia Sutton, Oz Clarke. MN: [excludes existent numbers, listing only original items by Greenwell, Brahms and Sherrin] Imagination; Why Do People Fall in Love?; Why Fall for Love?; The Controversial; I'll Fall in Love; Think of Being Rich; Find Your Partner and Dance; Why Love?; Strange Forces; Travelling Light. 116 performances.

Mr and Mrs Music, lyrics and book by John Taylor, based on the plays *Fumed Oak* and *Still Life* by Noel Coward. Palace Theatre, 11 December 1968. PC: John Neville, Honor Blackman, Hylda Baker, Alan Breeze, Liz Edmiston, Leslie Meadows. MN: *Mr* – Millions of People; Other People's Husbands; Happy Family; I Feel I Want to Dance; And So We Got Married; No More Money; Big Wide World. *Mrs* – If the Right Man Should Ask Me; Father of Two, Mother of Three; Give Us a Kiss; Come Thursday; I Want to Wet My Whistle; Before Today; The Electric Circus; I'll Be Always Loving You; Mr and Mrs. 44 performances.

Mr Burke M.P. Music, lyrics and book by Gerald Frow. Mermaid Theatre, 6 October 1960. PC: Wally Whyton and the Vipers, Sally Miles, Peter Clegg. MN: It's a Rat Race;

Marriage of Convenience; Inanimate; Father Figure; Get a Cause; I'd Move to the Jungle; Underneath the Skin; 95% of Me Loves You; Wear a Smile; It's All Yours; You're Going to Be Caught. 114 performances.

Mrs Wilson's Diary Music by Jeremy Taylor; lyrics by John Wells; book by Richard Ingrams and John Wells. Theatre Royal, Stratford East, 21 September 1967 [Season]; Criterion Theatre, 24 October 1967. PC: Bill Wallis, Myvanwy Jenn, Bob Grant, Peter Reeves, Sandra Caron. MN: Here I Kneel; Who?; Who Are the Bastards Now?; The Terrible Mr Brown; Why Should I Worry?; What Would They Say?; Harold and Me; One Man Band. 175 performances.

Nell! Music and lyrics by John Worth; book by John Worth and Philip Mackie. Richmond Theatre, 8 April 1970. PC: Jackie Trent, Hermione Baddeley, Stuart Damon, Gerard Hely. MN: Tickle 'n Slap; It's a Bargain; China Oranges; I Can Do It; I Must Choose; Bring out Your Dead; Pretty Witty Nell; Around the Corner; No More; Charley the Second; Old Rowley; The King Must Be Fed; I'll Be Near You; 'E 'Ad a Drink with Me; My Little Girl; Funeral Music; It's a Boy; Nell! [Season/Tour]

Oh! My Papa! Music by Paul Burkhard; lyrics and book by Juerg Amstein and Erik Charell. Garrick Theatre 17 July 1957. PC: Peter O'Toole, Rachel Roberts, Laurie Payne, Sonia Rees. MN: Opening Duet; The Cook's Song; Birthday Duet; The Coughing Song; Father's Entrance; Rome Wasn't Built in Just a Day; The Pony Song (My Pony Johnny); The Limit Is the Sky; Oh! My Papa!; Tiri-Lee Tiri-La; Our Love Will Stay This Way; Circus Song; Lion Tamer's Song; Hocus Pocus; Quartet; He Is My Man; Farewell Scene. 45 performances.

Oliver! Music, lyrics and book by Lionel Bart, based on the novel *Oliver Twist* by Charles Dickens. New Theatre, 30 June 1960. PC: Ron Moody, Georgia Brown, Paul Whitsun-Jones, Hope Jackman, Danny Sewell, Keith Hamshere, Martin Horsey. MN: Food, Glorious Food; Oliver!; I Shall Scream; Boy for Sale; That's Your Funeral; Where Is Love?; Consider Yourself; You've Got to Pick a Pocket or Two; It's a Fine Life; I'd Do Anything; Be Back Soon; Oom-Pah-Pah; My Name; As Long as He Needs Me; Who Will Buy?; Reviewing the Situation. 2,618 performances.

On the Level Music by Ron Grainer; lyrics and book by Ronald Millar. Saville Theatre, 19 April 1966. PC: Barrie Ingham, Angela Richards, Gary Bond. MN: G.C.E.; You Can Take It; Strangely Attractive; Thermodynamically Yours; Chaos; A Very Good Friend; Peaceful; Bleep-Bleep; My Girl at the Dance; Let's Make the Most of Now; Where the Action Is; Nostalgia; Love Gets Younger Every Day; On the Level; And Then I'll Go; Chorale. 118 performances.

Once More Darling Music by Cyril Ornadel; lyrics by Norman Newell; book by Ray Cooney and John Chapman, based on their play *Not Now, Darling*. Churchill Theatre, Bromley, 5 June 1978. PC: Norman Vaughan, Jack Douglas, Lynda Baron, Leon Greene, Jan Hunt, Yvonne Marsh. MN: We've Got to Get This Show on the Road; Actually; Claudette; My Wife Doesn't Understand Me; Get 'em Off; Have a Good Time; If You Sit around and Wait; I Was Bored; You; Infidelity; Men; What a Team; Remember Monte Carlo; We Might as Well Be Strangers; Once More Darling. [Tour]

Operette Music, lyrics and book by Noel Coward. His Majesty's Theatre, 16 March 1938. PC: Fritzi Massary, Peggy Wood, Muriel Barron, Max Oldaker. MN: Prologue; Trouville; Countess Mitzi; Dearest Love; Foolish Virgins; The Stately Homes of

England; Where Are the Songs We Sung?; The Island of Bollamazoo; Sing for Joy; Operette. 133 performances.

Our Man Crichton Music by David Lee; lyrics and book by Herbert Kretzmer, based on the play *The Admirable Crichton* by J. M. Barrie. Shaftesbury Theatre, 22 December 1964. PC: Kenneth More, Millicent Martin, George Benson, David Kernan, Patricia Lambert, Dilys Watling, Anna Barry. MN: Tweeny!; Yes, Mr Crichton; Down with the Barriers; Were I as Good; Our Kind of People; Let's Find an Island; London, London – My Home Town; Doesn't Travel Broaden the Mind?; Yesterday's World; I Tries; The Hairpin; Little Darlin'; Oh! For a Husband, Oh! For a Man; I Never Looked for You; Nobody Showed Me How; My Time Will Come. 208 performances.

Pacific 1860 Music, lyrics and book by Noel Coward. Theatre Royal, Drury Lane, 19 December 1946. PC: Mary Martin, Graham Payn, Sylvia Cecil, Daphne Anderson. MN: Family Grace; If I Were a Man; Dear Madam Salvador [Letter Song]; My Horse Has Cast a Shoe; I Wish I Wasn't Quite Such a Big Girl; Ka Tahua; Bright Was the Day; Invitation to the Waltz; His Excellency Regrets; Dear Friends, Forgive Me, Pray; Make Way for Their Excellencies; Funfumbolo; One, Two, Three; This Is a Night for Lovers; I Never Knew; This Is a Changing World; Come Back to the Island; Poor Lady in the Throes of Love; Mother's Lament; Pretty Little Bridesmaids; I Saw No Shadow; Wedding Chorus. 129 performances.

Paprika Music by George Posford and Bernard Grun; lyrics and book by Eric Maschwitz, based on a story by Stephen Nagy. His Majesty's Theatre, 15 September 1938. PC: Betty Warren, Austin Trevor, Barbara Bory, Anthony Eustrel. MN: A Victorian Ball; Home Is the Harvest of Grape and Grain; Ballet (How Life Goes on in Our Village); Child of Hungary; Just Like a Gipsy Band; Magyar Melody; Mine Alone; Theresa of Tokay; Musical Scene from 'Theresa of Tokay'; Grand Palotas; My Heart Belongs to Budapest; Duel at Dawn; A Tandem in the Park; I Lost My Love. 11 performances. Revised and subsequently presented as *Magyar Melody*.

Passion Flower Hotel Music by John Barry; lyrics by Trevor Peacock; book by Wolf Mankowitz, based on the novel by Rosalind Erskine. Prince of Wales Theatre, 24 August 1965. PC: Pauline Collins, Jane Birkin, Karin Fernald, Jean Muir, Francesca Annis, Nicky Henson, Bunny May, David Charkham, Jeremy Clyde, Bill Kenwright. MN: School Song; A Little Hammer; What a Question; What Does This Country Need Today?; The Syndicate; Naughty, Naughty; Tick Which Applies; Bully-Off; Passion Flower Hotel; How Much of the Dream Comes True; A Great Big Nothing; I Love My Love; Beastly, Beastly; Something Different; Don't Stop the Show. 148 performances.

Peg Music and lyrics by David Heneker [original theatre programme lists no librettist, but the book was based on the play *Peg o' My Heart* by J. Hartley Manners]. Phoenix Theatre, 12 April 1984. PC: Siân Phillips, Ann Morrison, Martin Smith, Patricia Michael, John Hewer, Julia Sutton. MN: A Matter of Minutes; That's My Father; Pretty Dresses; Three of a Kind; Peg and Jerry; Come Away with Me / Ethel's Waltz; The Steamers Go By; Peg O' My Heart [by Alfred Bryan and Fred Fisher]; There's a Devil in Me; The Fishing Fleet; How Would You Like Me?; I Want to Dance; Manhattan Hometown; Who Needs Them? / Easy; When a Woman Has to Choose; A Genuine Hall-Marked Alpha-Plus Little Brick. 146 performances.

Perchance to Dream Music, lyrics and book by Ivor Novello. Hippodrome, 21 April 1945. PC: Ivor Novello, Roma Beaumont, Muriel Barron, Olive Gilbert, Robert Andrews, Margaret Rutherford. MN: When the Gentlemen Get Together; Love Is My Reason; The Meeting; The Path My Lady Walks; A Lady Went to Market Fair; When I Curtsied to the King; Highwayman Love; The Triumph of Spring; Autumn Lullaby; A Woman's Heart; We'll Gather Lilacs; The Victorian Wedding; The Glo-Glo; The Elopement; Ghost Finale. 1,022 performances.

The Perils of Scobie Prilt Music, lyrics and book by Julian More and Monty Norman. New Theatre, Oxford, 12 June 1963. PC: Mike Sarne, Nyree Dawn Porter, Nigel Davenport. MN: Night Train to Nipz; Thinks; The Third Mack; You Need Someone; Harris; Russian Roulette; Cahoots; Don't Think about Me; Hullo-Goodbye; The Perils of Scobie Prilt; Fifteen Borders Later; Lights out Little Soldier; The Big But's Base; Under the Influence; Down Your Street; Night Plane to San Cristo; You Can't Make Me. [Tour; closed at end of first week]

Phil the Fluter Music and lyrics by David Heneker and Percy French; book by Beverley Cross and Donal Giltinan. Palace Theatre, 15 November 1969. PC: Evelyn Laye, Stanley Baxter, Mark Wynter, Sarah Atkinson, Caryl Little. MN [all Heneker except where otherwise stated]: If I Had a Chance; Abdul Abulbul Amir [French / Cross]; Mama; A Favour for a Friend; They Don't Make Them Like That Anymore; Good Money; How Would You Like Me?; Phil the Fluter [French / Heneker]; The Mountains of Mourne [French / Heneker]; I Shouldn't Have to Be the One to Tell You; Follow Me; Where Is She? [Moorhouse / Heneker]; You Like It; Are You Right There Michael? [French / Heneker]; That's Why the Poor Man's Dead [Heneker / French]; Wonderful Woman. 123 performances.

Pickwick Music by Cyril Ornadel; lyrics by Leslie Bricusse; book by Wolf Mankowitz, based on the novel *The Pickwick Papers* by Charles Dickens. Saville Theatre, 4 July 1963. PC: Harry Secombe, Jessie Evans, Peter Bull, Anton Rodgers, Teddy Green. MN: Business Is Booming; Debtors' Lament; Talk; That's What I'd Like for Christmas; The Pickwickians; A Bit of a Character; Learn a Little Something; There's Something about You; You Never Met a Feller Like Me; Look into Your Heart; The Winter Waltz; A Hell of an Election; Very; If I Ruled the World; The Trouble with Women; That's the Law; British Justice; Do as You Would Be Done By; Good Old Pickwick. 694 performances.

Pocahontas Music, lyrics and book by Kermit Goell, based on his book *Pocahontas*. Lyric Theatre, 14 November 1963. PC: Anita Gillette, Terence Cooper, Isabelle Lucas, Michael Barrington, Christene Palmer. MN: Prologue: The First Landing; Gold; She Fancied Me; Free as a Bird; You Have to Want to Touch Him; Too Many Miles from London Town; Eagle Dance; London Bridge Is Falling Down; I Love You Johnnie Smith; Things; Virginia; Oranges and Lemons; I Want to Live with You; I Have Lost My Way; Give Me a Sign; Like My True Love Grows; Yes, I Love You; Fit for a Princess; You Can't Keep a Good Man Down; Masque of Christmas. 12 performances.

Popkiss Music by John Addison and David Heneker; lyrics and book by Michael Ashton, based on the play *Rookery Nook* by Ben Travers. Globe Theatre, 22 August 1972. PC: Daniel Massey, Patricia Hodge, John Standing, Isla Blair, Joan Sanderson, Mary Millar. MN: The Trouble with You; The Girl from Up the Road; Tonight Was on the Way; Cheer-O, Mr Popkiss; I'm Not Going Back to Him; You Are Who?; Up the

Stair; Clara; Something Must Have Happened to Me; A Rumour Gets Around; The Life of a Wife; I Know You; Wrong All Along; Doing My Bit. 60 performances.

Poppy Music by Monty Norman; lyrics and book by Peter Nichols. Barbican Theatre, 25 September 1982 [Season]. Revised version Adelphi Theatre, 14 November 1983. PC: Nichola McAuliffe, David Firth, Janet Shaw, Geoffrey Hutchins, Antonia Ellis, Alfred Marks. MN: The Emperor's Greeting; Dunroamin-on-the-Down; Whoa, Boy; The Good Old Days; Why Must I?; In These Chambers; If You Want to Make a Killing; Nostalgie de la Boue; John Companee; Poppy; China Clipper; The Bounty of the Earth; The Emperor's Lament; China Sequence; They All Look the Same to Us; The Blessed Trinity; Sir Richard's Song; Rock-a-Bye Randy; The Dragon Dance; Rat-Tat-Tat-Tat. 97 performances.

The Princess Music and lyrics by Mario Braggiotti; story and choreography by Jo Anna. Strand Theatre, 23 August 1960. PC: Violette Verdy, Pierre Lacotte, Jo Anna, Claudia Cravey, Keith Beckett. MN: No musical numbers listed in programme. 44 performances.

Queenie Music by Ted Manning and Marvin Laird; lyrics and book by Ted Willis. Comedy Theatre, 22 June 1967. PC: Vivienne Martin, Bill Owen, Paul Eddington, Simon Oates, Kevin Colson, Cheryl Kennedy, Neil Fitzwilliam. MN: Ballad; Here Is the Key of the Door, Bill; Birthday Dance; I Can't Help Remembering; Queenie; We're Gonna Be Dead and Gone; Bill's Dance; Special Kind of Man; Starting from Now; Poor Poor Man; This Is the Meaning of Love; That's Beautiful; How Does He Look in the Morning?; Now That the Kissing Has Started; Young People; I Feel Fabulous Tonight; Excuse Me for Speaking My Mind. 20 performances.

Quick, Quick, Slow Music by Monty Norman; lyrics by Julian More; book by David Turner, adapted from his play for television *Way Off Beat*. Birmingham Repertory Theatre, 20 August 1969. PC: John Baddeley, Stella Moray, Jane Freeman, Paul Henry. MN: A Tiny Silver Pot; One Step Ahead; Something to Look Forward To; Nothing to Look Forward To; Going Round in Circles; Ballroom; Gang Bang; Inside Knowledge; In the Middle of the Dance; Mister Antonio Laveline; I Went All the Way; Linda's Place; They Can't Sabotage My Big Night; Arthur's Beautiful Moment; The Wearin' of the Gown; We've Come to the End of the Road, Love. [Season]

Rainbow Square Music by Robert Stolz; lyrics and book by Guy Bolton and Harold Purcell. Stoll Theatre, 21 September 1951. PC: Bruce Trent, Gloria Lane, Matha King, Sonnie Hale, Alfred Marks, Vera Pearce, Doreen [Pip] Hinton. MN: Rhythm of Manhattan; Who Knows?; The Vagabonds' Burletto; Rainbow Square; Wake Up and Whistle; Oh, Marie; Eight Little Music Men; You're So Easy to Know; The Show Must Go On; If I'd Been Wise as I Am Now at 21; Be My Sunday Girl; Fabulous; You'll Still Belong to Me; Follow the Drum; Indian Love Song; Two-Gun Susie; Can-Can; Scena; What a Day! 146 performances.

Ride! Ride! Music by Penelope Thwaites; book and lyrics by Alan Thornhill. Westminster Theatre, 20 May 1976. PC: Gordon Gostelow, Caroline Villiers, Brendan Barry, Richard Owens. MN [Concert Version]: Have You Heard?; He's Just a Little Man; Riding Song 1; Deep in the Blackness; London Street Cries; London Town; Strange City; The Lord Jehovah Reigns [lyric: Isaac Watts]; The Whole Wide World is my Parish; Audrey's Conversion; The Garden of England; Why Me?; He Knows my

Name; Enthusiasm; A Nice Little Change of Air; Say What You Mean; One by One;
Let the Enemies of the Lord; Everyone is Needed; What Thou Hast Done [lyric: John
Wesley]; Riding Song 2; The Travellers' Blessing; Ride Out. 76 performances.

The Roar of the Greasepaint – The Smell of the Crowd   Music, lyrics and book by
Anthony Newley and Leslie Bricusse. Theatre Royal, Nottingham, 3 August 1964.
PC: Norman Wisdom, Willoughby Goddard, Sally Smith, Cy Grant. MN: The Beautiful
Land; A Wonderful Day Like Today; It Isn't Enough; Things to Remember; Put It in
the Book; This Dream; Where Would You Be Without Me?; Look at That Face; My
First Love Song; The Joker; Who Can I Turn To (When Nobody Needs Me)?; A Funny
Funeral; That's What It Is to Be Young; What a Man!; Feeling Good; Nothing Can Stop
Me Now!; My Way; Sweet Beginning. [Tour] The work was subsequently produced in
New York in December 1965, with Newley replacing Norman Wisdom.

Robert and Elizabeth   Music by Ron Grainer; lyrics and book by Ronald Millar,
based on the play *The Barretts of Wimpole Street* by Rudolph Besier. Lyric Theatre,
20 October 1964. PC: June Bronhill, Keith Michell, John Clements, Stella Moray,
Angela Richards, Jeremy Lloyd. MN: The Wimpole Street Song; The Family Moulton-
Barrett; The World Outside; The Moon in My Pocket; I Said Love; Want to Be Well;
You Only to Love Me; The Real Thing; In a Simple Way; I Know Now; Soliloquy; Pass
the Eau De Cologne; What's Natural; I'm the Master Here; Escape Me Never; Hate Me,
Please; Under a Spell; The Girls That Boys Dream About; What the World Calls Love;
Woman and Man; Frustration. 948 performances.

Romance in Candlelight   Music and lyrics by Sam Coslow; book by Eric Maschwitz,
from the original by Siegfried Geyer and Carl Farkas. Piccadilly Theatre, 15 September
1955. PC: Jacques Pils, Roger Dann, Sally Ann Howes, Patricia Burke. MN: Romance
in Candlelight; I Love Them All; Oo-La-La, Boom-Boom-Boom; Live a Little, Love a
Little; Bonjour Finis; I Just Dropped in to Say Goodbye; Toujour L'Amour; The Board
of Directors; Go to Bed; You Have a Way with You; The Lady Was Made to Be Loved;
Fromage; I'm in Your Arms; Formidable; My Heart Says Yes. 53 performances.

Sail Away   Music, lyrics and book by Noel Coward. Savoy Theatre, 21 June 1962.
PC: Elaine Stritch, David Holliday, John Hewer, Edith Day, Grover Dale, Sydney
Arnold, Dorothy Reynolds. MN: Come to Me; Sail Away; Where Shall I Find Him?;
Beatnik Love Affair; Later than Spring; The Passenger's Always Right; Useless Useful
Phrases; The Little Ones ABC; Go Slow Johnny; You're a Long, Long Way from
America; Something Very Strange; Italian Wedding Ballet; Don't Turn Away from
Love; Bronxville Darby and Joan; When You Want Me; Why Do the Wrong People
Travel? 252 performances.

Salad Days   Music by Julian Slade; lyrics and book by Julian Slade and Dorothy
Reynolds. Vaudeville Theatre, 5 August 1954. PC: Eleanor Drew, John Warner, James
Cairncross, Michael Aldridge, Dorothy Reynolds, Christine Finn, Michael Meacham,
Joe Greig, Bob Harris. MN: The Things That Are Done by a Don; We Said We
Wouldn't Look Back; Find Yourself Something to Do; I Sit in the Sun; Oh, Look at
Me!; Hush-Hush; Out of Breath; Cleopatra; Sand in My Eyes; It's Easy to Sing; We're
Looking for a Piano; The Time of My Life; The Saucer Song; We Don't Understand Our
Children. 2,283 performances.

Scapa! Music, lyrics and book by Hugh Hastings, based on his play *Seagulls over Sorrento*. Adelphi Theatre, 8 March 1962. PC: David Hughes, Edward Woodward, Pete Murray, Timothy Gray. MN: Scapa; Don't Give a Damn; I Like It Here; Never Volunteer; Napoli; Seagull in the Sky; Give It All You've Got; Some Voice; Trouble; Nocturne; Bella; Wakey-Wakey; She Had Such a Beautiful Touch; The Sound of Bagpipes; I Wish I Was an Orchestra; A Girl in Every Port; One Woman; A Letter to Mum; Squares Dance. 44 performances.

School Music by Christopher Whelen; lyrics and book by Redmond Phillips, based on the play by Tom Robertson. Princes Theatre, 4 March 1958. PC: Eleanor Drew, James Maxwell, Jean Bayless, Michael Blakemore. MN: A Prince for a Cinderella; What a Lovely Afternoon; We're Men of the World; Beautiful and Rare; Bull or Cow; Teach Them Latin; Mignonette and Marigold; The Examination; Muriel, St Muriel; The Blanc Mange Waltz; School; Far from the City; Can a Shadow Say Goodbye?; I Hang on Your Lips; Places and Faces and People I Love; Every Day's the Day; The Letter Song; Handsome Stranger; Call Me a Cynic. 22 performances.

She Smiled at Me Music and lyrics by Allon Bacon; book based on the play *Caste* by T. W. Robertson. St Martin's Theatre, 2 February 1956. PC: Jean Kent, Peter Byrne, Hugh Paddick, Robin Bailey, Mercy Haystead, Leslie Dwyer, Linda Gray. MN: She Smiled at Me; Pity the Working Man; Shall We Fall in Love?; Stick T'Yer Class; Better Days; Wouldn't It Be Fun?; Nothing to Say; Angelina Smith; Military Man; I Gave My Heart; Music Hall; Life Is an Empty Thing; Marry for Love. 4 performances.

Sing a Rude Song Music by Ron Grainer; lyrics and book by Caryl Brahms and Ned Sherrin, with additional material by Alan Bennett. Garrick Theatre, 26 May 1970. PC: Barbara Windsor, Denis Quilley, Maurice Gibb. MN: That's What They Say; 'Ang Abaht!; Happiness; Whoops Cockie!; I'm in a Mood to Get My Teeth into a Song; Only a Friendly Kiss; Tattenham Corner; I've Been and Gone and Done it; Haven't the Words; You Don't Know What It's Like to Fall in Love at Forty; Waiting on the Off Chance; Waiting for the Royal Train; I'm Nobody in Particular; One of Nature's Ladies; Wave Goodbye!; Sing a Rude Song; Leave Me Here to Linger with the Ladies; [also two original Lloyd songs, My Old Man (Don't Dilly Dally) and The Boy I Love (The Boy in the Gallery)]. Original cast recording includes 'The One and Only', not listed in theatre programme. 71 performances.

So Who Needs Marriage? Music, lyrics and book by Monty Norman. Gardner Centre, Brighton, 8 May 1975. PC: Diana Coupland, Jon Pertwee, Eric Flynn, June Ritchie, Elizabeth Power, John Gower. MN: Do I Want a Divorce?; Welcome to the Club; You've Got Everything to Fight For; Theobald's Ponderings; Picking Holes; How Can I Make You Understand?; Live My Life; Before It's Too Late; Our Yesterday Tune; Nothing Would Please Me More; D.I.V.O.R.C.E.; Fast Approaching the Point of No Return; The Improved Permeosonic Decoder; You Just Can't Win; Don't Shut Me Out; So Who Needs Marriage?; For Want of a Word. [Tour]

Songbook Music, lyrics and book by Monty Norman and Julian More. Globe Theatre, 25 July 1979. PC: David Healey, Gemma Craven, Diane Langton, Anton Rodgers, Andrew C. Wadsworth. MN: Landin' Headfirst on My Feet / Songbook; East River Rhapsody; Your Time Is Diffcrent to Mine; Such Sweet Poison; Mr Destiny; Pretty Face; Je Vous Aime, Milady; Les Halles; Olympics Song; Nazi Party Pooper; I'm Gonna Take Him Home to Momma; Bumpity Bump; Das Mädchen am Fenster; The Girl in the Window; Victory V; April in Winsconsin; Freddie Fox; Happy Hickory; When a Brother Is a Mother to his Sister; Climbin'; Don't Play That Love Song Any More, Marvin; Lovely Sunday Morning; Rusty's Dream Ballet; The Pokenhasset Public Protest Committee; I Accuse; Messages; I Found Love; Don't Play That Love Song Any More; Golden Oldie; Nostalgia. 208 performances.

Stand and Deliver Story, music and lyrics by Monty Norman; book by Wolf Mankowitz. Roundhouse, 24 October 1972. PC: Nicky Henson, Anna Dawson, Elizabeth Mansfield, Derek Godfrey, Pamela Cundell. MN: Jack Sheppard Theme; Our Humble Thanks; Dance on Nothing; What a Strange Life; Jill of All Trades; Look No Further; Do Unto Husbands; The Wheel; Fool to Fall in Love; Jack's Escape; Runaway Jack; When a Woman's in Love; He's Mine; It's Wearing; Tra'lah, Tra'lah; Six Men's Shoulders; By Hook or by Crook; Hanging Day; Stand and Deliver. [Season]

The Station Master's Daughter Music by Charles Zwar; lyrics and book by Frank Harvey. Yvonne Arnaud Theatre, Guildford, 11 April 1968. PC: Rose Hill, Jenny Wren, Hugh Lloyd, Sally Smith, Graham James, Neil Fitzwilliam. MN: No musical numbers listed in programme. [Season]

The Stiffkey Scandals of 1932 Music and lyrics by David Wood; book by David Wright. Queen's Theatre, 12 June 1969. PC: Charles Lewsen, Annie Ross, Terri (Terese) Stevens. MN: Dear Lord and Father of Mankind; 1932; Girls!; Don't Judge by Appearances; I Can't Understand You; The Lament of Inglebert Ralph Thole; Pestering; The Prostitutes' Padre; Playthings; What a Scoop; 3 Maybe [sic]; When My Dreamboat Comes Home; The Church of England; The Fight Goes On; Simple Gifts [traditional, arranged Carl Davis]. 12 performances. Originally staged in 1967 as *A Life in Bedrooms* and restaged as *The Prostitute's Padre* in 1997.

Stop the World – I Want to Get Off Music, lyrics and book by Anthony Newley and Leslie Bricusse. Queen's Theatre, 20 July 1961. PC: Anthony Newley, Anna Quayle. MN: The A B C Song; I Wanna Be Rich; Typically English; A Special Announcement; Lumbered; Welcome to Sludgepool; Gonna Build a Mountain; Glorious Russian; Meilinki Meilchick; Family Fugue; Typische Deutsche; Nag! Nag! Nag!; All American; Once in a Lifetime; Mumbo Jumbo; Welcome to Sunvale; Someone Nice Like You; What Kind of Fool Am I? 478 performances.

Strike a Light! Music by Gordon Caleb, with additional songs by John Taylor*; lyrics and book by Joyce Adcock. Piccadilly Theatre, 5 July 1966. PC: Jean Carson, Evelyn Laye, John Fraser, Charles West, Josephine Blake. MN: Come the Revolution; It's a Fight; Bit of It Now; Everything*; Pawnshop Doorway; Up in the World*; Scandalous; Another Love; When I Read; Let's Make a Night of It; Strike a Light; Summer Evening; Private Enterprise; Dear Lady; Girls Who Go with Sailors; Making Friends*; Vesta Girls; Near Me; Teach Me; I Don't Know the Words. 30 performances.

Summer Song Music by Antonín Dvořák, arranged by Bernard Grun; lyrics by Eric Maschwitz; book by Hy Kraft and Eric Maschwitz. Princes Theatre, 16 February 1956. PC: Sally Ann Howes, David Hughes, Laurence Naismith, Edric Connor, Bonita Primrose, Van Atkins. MN: Flannagan's Trees; Once a Year Is Not Enough; Just around the Corner; Be She Dark, Be She Fair; Cotton Tail; No-One Told Me; Sing Me a Song; Murphy's Pig; Saturday Girl; One Boy Sends You a Rose; Deep Blue Evening; I'm Not So Certain; Centerville Song; Te Deum; The Day You Hit the Highway; Weddin' Gown;

Summer Song; Small Town Sweetheart; New York Ninety-Three; I'll Be Rememb'ring. 148 performances.

Thomas and the King Music by John Williams; lyrics by James Harbert; book by Edward Anhalt. Her Majesty's Theatre, 16 October 1975. PC: Richard Johnson, James Smillie, Dilys Hamlett, Caroline Villiers. MN: Processional; Look around You; Am I Beautiful?; Man of Love; The Question; What Choice Have I?; We Shall Do It!; Improbable as Spring; Power; Consecration; 'Tis Love; Sincerity; The Test; Replay the Game; A New Way to Turn; Will No One Rid Me? 20 performances.

Tom Brown's Schooldays Music by Chris Andrews; lyrics and book by Joan and Jack Maitland, based on the novel by Thomas Hughes. Cambridge Theatre, 9 May 1972. PC: Roy Dotrice, Judith Bruce, Leon Greene, Ray C. Davis, Trudi Van Doorn, Christopher Guard. MN: Petticoat Government; I Like My Children Around; Head Up*; In the Swim; My Way; Three Acres and a Cow; Where Is He?; What is a Man?; Six of the Best*; The Ballad of the Great White Horse; Young Tom; Have a Try; If I Had a Son*; A Boy's Point of View; Vision of Youth; Warwickshire Home; One for Your Nose; Hold Me. [*lyric by Joan Maitland]. 76 performances.

Tough at the Top Music by Vivian Ellis; lyrics and book by A. P. Herbert. Adelphi Theatre, 15 July 1949. PC: George Tozzi, Maria d'Attili, Brian Reece, Carol Raye. MN: Prelude: Her Highness Is Going Away; The Prussian Guard; Pomania, Mother of the Great; Most Gracious Lady; I'm Going Away; I Don't Want to Marry; Blood and Iron; Fortune Makes Some Sad Mistakes; Pomanian National Anthem; Bubbly Ladies; All the Ladies Are Lovely; I Feel a New Fellow; They Talk about Women and Winning; Tough at the Top; I Wish I Could Sing; You Are So Beautiful; I'm on Fire!; The Muffin Man; Really a Rather Nice Man; Hurray for the Hunting and Shooting!; England Is a Lovely Place; This Is Not the End. 154 performances.

Trelawny Music and lyrics by Julian Slade; book by Aubrey Woods, based on the play *Trelawny of The Wells* by Arthur Wing Pinero. Sadler's Wells Theatre, 27 June 1972. PC: Ian Richardson, Max Adrian, Gemma Craven, Elizabeth Power, Teddy Green, David Morton, Joyce Carey, John Gower, John Watts. MN: Pull Yourself Together; Walking On; Ever of Thee; Trelawny of The Wells; On Approval; Rules; Back to The Wells; Old Friends; The One Who Isn't There; We Can't Keep 'Em Waiting; The Turn of Avonia Bunn; Hail to Aladdin; Arthur's Letter; Two Fools; Life; This Time. 177 performances.

Troubador Music by Ray Holder; lyrics and book by Michael Lombardi. Cambridge Theatre, 19 December 1978. PC: John Watts, Kim Braden, Andrew C. Wadsworth. MN: Vendors' Cries; The Wife Beating Song; Troubador; One Only Rose; Woman Is a Cheat; Can Anyone Assist Me?; Panic in the Palace; The Loneliness of Power; Ave Maris Stella; If There Is Love; Aubade; Onward to Jerusalem; We Must Have Jerusalem; Mary's Child; Kalenda Maya. [Original cast recording includes titles not listed in theatre programme: O Admirabile; Melancholy Lover; Islamic Prayer; Mime Dance Interlude; Woman, Whoever You Are.] 76 performances.

Twang* Music and lyrics by Lionel Bart; book by Lionel Bart and Harvey Orkin. Shaftesbury Theatre, 20 December 1965. PC: James Booth, Barbara Windsor, Toni Eden, Long John Baldry, Bernard Bresslaw, Ronnie Corbett, Elric Hooper. MN: May a Man Be Merry; Welcome to Sherwood; Wander; What Makes a Star?; Make an Honest

Woman [of Me]; Roger the Ugly; To the Woods; Dreamchild; With Bells On; Sighs; You Can't Catch Me; Living a Legend; Unseen Hands; Writing on the Wall; Who's [sic] Little Girl Are You?; Follow Your Leader; I'll Be Hanged; Tan-Ta-Ra! [A title-song 'Twang!' is heard on the original cast recording but is not listed in the Shaftesbury Theatre programme.] 43 performances.

*The theatre programme does not give the exclamation marks that often follow the title in other printed sources.

An inserted printed slip in the programme held in the V & A Theatre Collection reads: 'Lionel Bart wishes to announce to this audience that the following TWO SONG ITEMS "Unseen Hands" [...] and "Writing on the Wall" [...] are now in a New show called "SON OF TWANG".'

Twenty Minutes South Music by Peter Greenwell; lyrics and book by Maurice Browning. St Martin's Theatre, 13 July 1955. PC: Daphne Anderson, Louie Ramsay, Donald Scott, Robin Hunter, John Le Mesurier. MN: The 8.27; I Like People; One of the Family; It's a Lovely Evening; This Is Love; Typing, Typing; Never Mind, I'm Delighted; Why Never Ever?; Easy to Say; The Addison Mambo; Sunday Girl; I Shall; Do We?; Having Ourselves a Wonderful Time; Wondering Alone; The 5.27. 101 performances.

Two Cities Music by Jeff Wayne; lyrics by Jerry Wayne; book by Constance Cox, based on *A Tale of Two Cities* by Charles Dickens. Palace Theatre, 27 February 1969. PC: Edward Woodward, Kevin Colson, Nicolette Roeg, Elizabeth Power, Leon Greene. MN: The Best of Times; Street Prologue; Tender Love and Patience; Independent Man / What Would You Do?; Look Alike; And Lucie Is Her Name; Golden-Haired Doll; Suddenly; The Time Is Now; Let 'Em Eat Cake; The Bastille; Two Different People; The Machine of Doctor Guillotine; Only a Fool; Carmagnole; Will We Ever Meet Again?; Knitting Song; Quartet; Long Ago; It's a Far, Far Better Thing. 44 performances.

Valmouth Music, lyrics and book by Sandy Wilson, based on the novel by Ronald Firbank. Lyric Theatre, Hammersmith, 2 October 1958 for 84 performances. Saville Theatre, 27 January 1959. PC: Cleo Laine [replacing Bertice Reading of the Lyric production], Fenella Fielding, Barbara Couper, Betty Hardy, Denise Hirst, Marcia Ashton, Doris Hare, Peter Gilmore, Patsy Rowlands. MN: Valmouth; Magic Fingers; Mustapha; I Loved a Man; All the Girls Were Pretty; What Do I Want with Love; Request Number; Wot Den Can Make Him Come So Slow; Big Best Shoes; Niri-Esther; Cry of the Peacock; Little Girl Baby; The Cathedral of Clemenza; Only a Passing Phase; Where the Trees Are Green with Parrots; My Talking Day; I Will Miss You; Wedding Anthem. 102 performances.

Vanity Fair Music by Julian Slade; lyrics by Robin Miller; book by Robin Miller and Alan Pryce-Jones, based on the novel by William Makepeace Thackeray. Queen's Theatre, 27 November 1962. PC: Frances Cuka, Sybil Thorndike, Eira Heath, Gordon Boyd, Naunton Wayne, Michael Aldridge, George Baker, Joyce Carey, Gabriel Woolf, John Stratton. MN: Vanity Fair; I'm No Angel; Impressed; There He Is; Dear Miss Crawley; Mama; Love, Honour and Obey; Farewell; Advice to Women; Waterloo Waltz; Where Is My Love?; How to Live Well on Nothing a Year; Someone to Believe In; Rebecca; Forgive Me; I Could Be Good; Poor Dear Girl. ['Alone the Orphan' and 'La Vie Bohème' were listed in the programme for the semi-staged London revival in 2001]. 70 performances.

Virtue in Danger Music by James Bernard; lyrics and book by Paul Dehn, based on the play *The Relapse* by John Vanbrugh. Mermaid Theatre, 2 April 1963 / Strand Theatre, 3 June 1963. PC: Patricia Routledge, John Moffatt, Barrie Ingham, Richard Wordsworth, Jane Wenham, Alan Howard, Lewis Fiander, Gwen Nelson, Patsy Byrne. MN: Don't Call Me Sir!; Fortune Thou Art a Bitch!; Stand Back Old Sodom!; I'm in Love with My Husband; Hurry Surgeon!; Let's Fall Together; Hoyden Hath Charms; Nurse, Nurse, Nurse!; Why Do I Feel What I Feel?; Fire a Salute!; Put Him in the Dog House; Wait a Little Longer, Lover; O Take This Ancient Mansion; Say the Word; I Shall Have to Cuckold Someone. 121 performances.

The Water Gipsies Music by Vivian Ellis; lyrics and book by A. P. Herbert, based on his novel. Winter Garden Theatre, 31 August 1955. PC: Dora Bryan, Pamela Charles, Peter Graves, Laurie Payne, Wallas Eaton. MN: Here's Mud in Your Eye; I'm Glad I Was Born; Why Did You Call Me Lily?; Everybody Picks a Winner One Day; Clip-Clop; Who'd Be a Girl?; I Should Worry; When I'm Washing Up; Jane's Prayer; Lily's Tale; He Doesn't Care; I Can't See What He Sees in Her; Castles and Hearts and Roses; Peace and Quiet; Why Should Spring Have All the Flowers?; This Is Our Secret; It Would Cramp My Style; Little Boat; You Never Know with Men. 239 performances.

Wedding in Paris Music by Hans May; lyrics by Sonny Miller; book by Vera Caspary. London Hippodrome, 3 April 1954. PC: Anton Walbrook, Evelyn Laye, Susan Swinford, Jeff Warren. MN: A Wedding in Paris; Angy's Farewell; It's News; The French Lesson; In a Cosy Corner on the Upper Deck; Ship Ballet; The Young in Heart; Fairy Tales; Lovely Lady of the Sands; The Simple Things of Life; It Only Took a Moment; Harbour Ballet; I Have Nothing to Declare but Love; Paris Ballet; The Streets of Gay Paree; A Man Is a Man Is a Man; Tourist Song; How Do I Know It's Love?; I Must Have Been Crazy; Strike Another Match; Pink Ballet; In the Pink. 411 performances.

When in Rome Music by Kramer; lyrics and book by Garinei and Giovannini, adapted by Ted Willis and Ken Ferry; English lyrics by Eric Shaw. Adelphi Theatre, 26 December 1959. PC: Dickie Henderson, June Laverick, Eleanor Summerfield, Frank Leighton, John Hewer, Sheena Marshe. MN: Concertina; Call It Primavera; Simpatica; Street Dance; A Certain Something; It's So Nice to Sleep with No One; When in Rome [lyric: Sonny Miller]; Ballarello; Stop; When You're in Love; Joe's Blues; Wise Guy. 298 performances.

Who's Pinkus? Where's Chelm? Music by Monty Norman; lyrics by Cecil P. Taylor and Monty Norman; book by Cecil P. Taylor. Jeanetta Cochrane Theatre, 3 January 1967. PC: Bernard Bresslaw, Nancy Nevinson. MN: No musical numbers listed in programme. [Season]

Wild Grows the Heather Music by Jack Waller and Joseph Tunbridge; lyrics by Ralph Reader; adapted by Hugh Ross Williamson from the play *The Little Minister* by J. M. Barrie. London Hippodrome, 3 May 1956. PC: Bill O'Connor, Valerie Miller, Madeleine Christie, Peter Sinclair, Eira Heath. MN: Along the Way; Law and Order; A Little Bit of Devil; Wild Grows the Heather; I See Everything I Love in You; Walking to the Kirk; The Quarrel; I Want the Stars to See You; I Once Had a Wonderful Day; A Woman Knows. 28 performances.

Wild Thyme Music by Donald Swann; lyrics and book by Philip Guard. Duke of York's Theatre, 14 July 1955. PC: Denis Quilley, Betty Paul, Jane Wenham, Colin Gordon,

Archie Harradine, Gwen Nelson, Julian Orchard. MN: English Summer; I Hate You; Dreadful Day; Even for a Day; I Can Remember; Hikers' Meeting; The Hikers' Song; Heaven Is Here; Sold for a Song; A Grace; Lullaby; Two Is Company; Lonely Day [reprise of Dreadful Day]; The Beetle and the Butterfly; A Toast; Long Before; Kiss Me Like That Again. 52 performances.

Wildest Dreams Music by Julian Slade; lyrics and book by Dorothy Reynolds and Julian Slade. Vaudeville Theatre, 3 August 1961. PC: Dorothy Reynolds, Angus Mackay, Anna Dawson, John Baddeley. MN: Nelderham; Mrs Birdview's Minuet; Please Aunt Harriet; Till Now; Girl on the Hill [reprised as 'Man on the Hill']; Zoom, Zoom, Zoom; Here Am I; Wildest Dreams; Red or White; You Can't Take Any Luggage; A Man's Room; I'm Holding My Breath; Quite Something; Green and Oxblood Hill; There's a Place We Know; When You're Not There; This Man Loves You. [Cut songs: The Robber's Chorus; On the Tip of My Tongue; Different This Time (melody re-used by Slade in *Vanity Fair*); We Three; Say Something Interesting.] 76 performances.

The World of Paul Slickey Music by Christopher Whelen; lyrics and book by John Osborne. Palace Theatre, 5 May 1959. PC: Dennis Lotis, Marie Löhr, Adrienne Corri, Janet Hamilton-Smith. MN: Don't Think You Can Fool a Guy Like Me; We'll Be in the Desert and Alone; It's a Consideration We'd Do Well to Bear in Mind; Bring Back the Axe; The Mechanics of Success; Tell Me Later; The Income Tax Man; Them; On Ice; I Want to Hear about Beautiful Things; You Can't Get Away with It; A Woman at the Weekend; I'm Hers; If I Could Be. 47 performances.

Wren Music by David Adams and Chuck Mallett; lyrics and book by David Adams. May Fair Theatre, 25 June 1978. PC: Steven Grives, Richard Tate, Donna Donovan. MN: In Praise of Man; Will You Build a Little Church for Me?; Turn Ye to Me; Invention; Saints and Soldiers; Wit; A Country to Love; Monarchy Madness; The Corn Hop Dance; As I Make Love to Thee; Love for All; I Will Arise; Keep a Watch on My Heart; Out of Our Minds; Dreaming Spires. 34 performances.

The Young Visiters Music by Ian Kellam; lyrics and book by Michael Ashton, based on the novel by Daisy Ashford; additional songs* by Richard Kerr and Joan Maitland. Piccadilly Theatre, 23 December 1968. PC: Alfred Marks, Jan Waters, Anna Sharkey, Vivienne Ross, Frank Thornton, Barry Justice. MN: Daisy Ashford's Written a Book; Prettiest in the Face; If I Can Wait; First and Last Love; Rickamere Hall; My Young Visiters and Me; Near You*; That's What a Visiter's For; An English Gentleman; Twice the Man; Crystal Palace; Belted Earl; Quite a Young Earl; Up the Ladder*; The Girl I Was; I'm Not Beautiful; She Is Me; I Will Keep My Righteous Anger Down; Better for Marrying You; In Love with the Girl I See. 63 performances.

Zuleika Music by Peter Tranchell; lyrics and book by James Ferman, based on the novel *Zuleika Dobson* by Max Beerbohm. Saville Theatre, 11 April 1957. PC: Mildred Mayne, David Morton, Patricia Stark, Peter Woodthorpe. MN: Eights Week; City of Repose; Zuleika; Zuleika's Travels; Lovely Time; It's My Doorstep Too!; All Over Again; Nellie O'Mora [lyric by Harry Porter]; Anything Can Happen; The Last Dance of the Evening; What Has She Got?; Always Be Wary of Women; I Want a Man to Say No; Someday; Follow the Fashion; Seventeen Years from Now. 124 performances.

Appendix 2
Adaptations from Other Works, 1946–78

1946	*Evangeline*	James Laver: *Nymph Errant* [novel]
	Sweetheart Mine	Albert Chevalier & Arthur Shirley: *My Old Dutch* [play]
	Good-Night Vienna	Based on the writers' radio play
1948	*Cage Me a Peacock*	Noel Langley: *Cage Me A Peacock* [novel]
	Carissima	Based on a short story by Armin Robinson
1950	*Dear Miss Phoebe*	J. M. Barrie: *Quality Street* [play]
	Blue for a Boy	Franz Arnold & Ernest Bach: *Hurrah, eine Junge!* [play]
	Caprice	Marguerite Steen & Derek Patmore: *French for Love* [play]
1951	*And So to Bed*	J. B. Fagan: *And So to Bed* [play]
	Zip Goes a Million	G. B. McCutcheon & others: *Brewster's Millions* [novel]
1952	*Love from Judy*	Jean Webster: *Daddy-Long-Legs* [novel]
1954	*After the Ball*	Oscar Wilde: *Lady Windermere's Fan* [play]
	Listen to the Wind	Angela Ainley Jeans: *Listen to the Wind* [novel]
	Happy Holiday	Arnold Ridley: *The Ghost Train* [play]
1955	*The Water Gipsies*	A. P. Herbert: *The Water Gipsies* [novel]
	Romance in Candlelight	Siegfried Geyer & Carl Farkas: *By Candlelight* [play]
	Caste (Allon Bacon)	Tom (T. W.) Robertson: *Caste* [play] revived as *She Smiled at Me* (1956)
	Caste (Bill Owen)	Tom (T. W.) Robertson: *Caste* [play]
	A Girl Called Jo	Louisa M. Alcott: *Little Women / Good Wives* [novels]
1956	*She Smiled at Me*	Tom (T. W.) Robertson: *Caste* [play] revised version of *Caste* (1955)
	The Comedy of Errors	Shakespeare: *The Comedy of Errors* [play]
	Wild Grows the Heather	J. M. Barrie: *The Little Minister* [play]
	The Three Caskets	Shakespeare: *The Merchant of Venice* [play]

1957	*School*	Tom (T. W.) Robertson: *School* [play]
	Zuleika	Max Beerbohm: *Zuleika Dobson* [novel]
	Found in a Handbag	Oscar Wilde: *The Importance of Being Earnest* [play]
1958	*Half in Earnest*	Oscar Wilde: *The Importance of Being Earnest* [play]
	Expresso Bongo	Based on story by Wolf Mankowitz
	Wally Pone	Ben Jonson: *Volpone* [play]
	Valmouth	Ronald Firbank: *Valmouth* [novel]
1959	*Ernest*	Oscar Wilde: *The Importance of Being Earnest* [play]
	Marigold	F. R. Pryor & L. Allen Harker: *Marigold* [play]
	Lock Up Your Daughters	Henry Fielding: *Rape upon Rape* [play]
	No Bed for Bacon	Caryl Brahms & S. J. Simon: *No Bed for Bacon* [novel]
	Make Me an Offer	Wolf Mankowitz: *Make Me an Offer* [novel]
	The Crooked Mile	Peter Wildeblood: *West End People* [novel]
	Kookaburra	Joyce Dennys: *Kookaburra* [novel]
1960	*Johnny the Priest*	R. C. Sherriff: *The Telescope* [play]
	Oliver!	Charles Dickens: *Oliver Twist* [novel]
	Joie de Vivre	Terence Rattigan: *French Without Tears* [play]
	Tom Sawyer	Mark Twain: *Tom Sawyer* [novel]
1961	*Belle*	Based on a play by Beverley Cross
	Jane Eyre	Charlotte Brontë: *Jane Eyre* [novel]
1962	*Scapa!*	Hugh Hastings: *Seagulls over Sorrento* [play]
	Walker London	J. M. Barrie: *Walker London* [play]
	Vanity Fair	William Makepeace Thackeray: *Vanity Fair* [novel]
1963	*Half a Sixpence*	H. G. Wells: *Kipps* [novel]
	Virtue in Danger	Sir John Vanbrugh: *The Relapse* [play]
	Pickwick	Charles Dickens: *The Pickwick Papers* [novel]
	House of Cards	Aleksander Ostrovsky: *Even a Wise Man Stumbles* [play]
	Nutmeg and Ginger	Francis Beaumont: *The Knight of the Burning Pestle* [play]

1964	*Robert and Elizabeth*	Rudolph Besier: *The Barretts of Wimpole Street* [play]
	Our Man Crichton	J. M. Barrie: *The Admirable Crichton* [play]
1965	*Four Thousand Brass Halfpennies*	John Dryden: *Amphitryon* [play]
	Passion Flower Hotel	Rosalind Erskine: *Passion Flower Hotel* [novel]
	Sweet Fanny	John Cleland: *Memoirs of a Woman of Pleasure* etc. [novel]
	Something Nasty in the Woodshed	Stella Gibbons: *Cold Comfort Farm* [novel]
1966	*When You're Young*	*Smilin' Through* [film] see *Smilin' Through* (1972)
	Moll Flanders	Daniel Defoe: *Moll Flanders* [novel]
	Jorrocks	Based on the novels of R. S. Surtees
1967	*The Pursuit of Love*	Nancy Mitford: *The Pursuit of Love* [novel]
	The Four Musketeers	Alexandre Dumas: *The Three Musketeers* [novel]
1968	*Canterbury Tales*	Geoffrey Chaucer: *The Canterbury Tales* [poem]
	Viva, Viva	Niccolò Machiavelli: *Clizia* [play]
	She'd Rather Kiss than Spin	Thomas Middleton: *A Mad World, My Masters* [play]
	My Gentleman Pip	Charles Dickens: *Great Expectations* [novel]
	Mr and Mrs	Noel Coward: *Fumed Oak / Still Life* [plays]
	The Young Visiters	Daisy Ashford: *The Young Visiters* [novel]
1969	*Two Cities*	Charles Dickens: *A Tale of Two Cities* [novel]
	'Erb	W. Pett Ridge: *'Erb* [novel]
	Ann Veronica	H. G. Wells: *Ann Veronica* [novel]
	Quick, Quick, Slow	David Turner: *Way Off Beat* [television play]
1970	*Who Was That Lady?*	James Albery: *Pink Dominos* [play]
	Little Women	Louisa M. Alcott: *Little Women* [novel]
	Mandrake	Niccolò Machiavelli: *Mandragola* [play]
	Love on the Dole	Walter Greenwood: *Love on the Dole* [novel]
	No Trams to Lime Street	Alun Owen: *No Trams to Lime Street* [television play]
1971	*The Amazons*	Arthur Wing Pinero: *The Amazons* [play]
	His Monkey Wife	John Collier: *His Monkey Wife* [novel]

1972	*The Mock Doctor*	Molière: *Le Médicin Malgré Lui* [play]
	The Londoners	Stephen Lewis: *Sparrers Can't Sing* [play]
	Tom Brown's Schooldays	Thomas Hughes: *Tom Brown's Schooldays* [novel]
	Trelawny	Arthur Wing Pinero: *Trelawny of the Wells* [play]
	Smilin' Through	*Smilin' Through* /[film] & *When You're Young* (1966)
	Liberty Ranch!	Oliver Goldsmith: *She Stoops to Conquer* [play]
	Popkiss	Ben Travers: *Rookery Nook* [play]
1973	*Dionysus '73*	Euripides: *The Bacchae* [play]
	R Loves J	Peter Ustinov: *Romanoff and Juliet* [play]
	The Card	Arnold Bennett: *The Card* [novel]
	The Water Babies	Charles Kingsley: *The Water-Babies* [novel]
	Hard Times	Charles Dickens: *Hard Times* [novel]
	Treasure Island	R. L. Stevenson: *Treasure Island* [novel]
	Out of Bounds	Arthur Wing Pinero: *The Schoolmistress* [play]
1974	*The Pilgrim's Progress*	John Bunyan: *The Pilgrim's Progress* [allegory]
	Billy	Keith Waterhouse & Willis Hall: *Billy Liar* [novel]
	The Good Companions	J. B. Priestley: *The Good Companions* [novel]
	Shylock	Shakespeare: *The Merchant of Venice* [play] revived as *Fire Angel*
	Dracula	Bram Stoker: *Dracula* [novel]
	Dear Jo	Louisa M. Alcott: *Little Women* [novel]
1975	*Jeeves*	Based on the *Jeeves* books of P. G. Wodehouse
	Pilgrim	John Bunyan: *The Pilgrim's Progress* [allegory]
	Cranford	Based on Elizabeth Gaskell's *Cranford* novels
	Gulliver's Travels	Jonathan Swift: *Gulliver's Travels* [novel]
	Nickleby and Me	Charles Dickens: *Nicholas Nickleby* [novel]
	Great Expectations	Charles Dickens: *Great Expectations* [novel]

1976	*The Lady or the Tiger*	Frank Stockton: *The Lady or the Tiger* [story]
	Liza of Lambeth	Somerset Maugham: *Liza of Lambeth* [novel]
	The Showman	Leopold Lewis: *The Bells* [play]
1977	*Fire Angel*	Shakespeare: *The Merchant of Venice* [play]; *see Shylock* (1974)
	Mr Polly	H. G. Wells: *The History of Mr Polly* [novel]
	Maggie	J. M. Barrie: *What Every Woman Knows* [play]
1978	*The Clapham Wonder*	Barbara Comyns: *The Vet's Daughter* [novel]
	Once More Darling	Ray Cooney & John Chapman: *Not Now, Darling* [play]
	Bar Mitzvah Boy	Jack Rosenthal: *Bar Mitzvah Boy* [television play]
	The Three Musketeers	Alexandre Dumas: *The Three Musketeers* [novel]

Notes

1 Before and After

1 The D'Oyly Carte Opera Company was begun by Richard D'Oyly Carte in August 1879. Its last performance was in London on 27 February 1982.

2 W. S. Gilbert's *Bab Ballads* were published as a collection in 1869.

3 Dion Boucicault (*c.* 1820–1890), Irish dramatist and actor-manager.

4 On his first visit to London in 1913, Irving Berlin met journalists and offered to write words and music of a song for which they suggested a title. 'The Humming Rag' was written in 29 minutes.

5 Neither Myers nor Cass was prolific in musicals. Myers was part-author of *A Girl Called Jo* and Cass part-composer of *Harmony Close*.

6 Television had already celebrated the American musical on 21 May 1937 with a complete version of *On Your Toes* broadcast from the Alexandra Palace (the original British production was playing at the Palace Theatre). The following year there were televised productions of *Magyar Melody* and *Me and My Girl*.

7 The BBC Yearbook for 1960 notes the beginning of 'Musical Playhouse', a series of abbreviated editions of musicals. *The Dancing Years* starred the Hungarian soprano Sari Barabas.

8 J. M. Barrie's play *The Little Minister* (1891) was a work that its author came to dislike.

9 Vivian Ellis, *I'm on a See-Saw*, p. 167.

10 Gervase Hughes, *Composers of Operetta*, p. 234.

11 *Zelma*, *Faint Harmony*, *Day Out* and *Chicanery*.

12 Vivian Ellis, *How to Enjoy your Operation* (London: Frederick Muller, 1963).

13 Ibid p. 45.

14 *You've Never Had It So Good* recorded by Decca in 1960. The four songs banned by the BBC were 'Rip Van Winkle', 'Stock Exchange Art', 'Hengist and Horsa' and 'You've Never Had It So Good'. Presumably the BBC, in earlier days, had banned such Ellis songs as 'Me and My Dog' and 'Pardon My English' (the latter with lyrics by Desmond Carter), both sung by Frances Day and both with a deal of sexual innuendo.

15 *Follow a Star* opened at the Winter Garden in 1930.

16 It should be noted that Tucker's pianist Ted Shapiro also contributed considerable material for Tucker in the production.

17 From Hilaire Belloc's poem 'Jim' (1907).

18 The revue *Streamline*, written by A. P. Herbert and Ronald Jeans, with music by Ellis, was produced at the Palace Theatre in 1934.

19 *Mr Cinders*, starring Bobbie Howes and Binnie Hale, toured extensively in 1928 and opened at the Adelphi Theatre in 1929.

20 Ellis's grandmother, Julia Sophia Woolf, wrote *Carina* to a book by E. L. Blanchard and Cunningham Bridgman. The work was produced at the Opera Comique in 1888. Her other compositions include an Overture for *The Winter's Tale*, performed at the Theatre Royal Drury Lane in 1878, and a Requiem Mass for the death of the Prince Consort.

21 Kenneth Tynan, 'Curtain-Up in Coventry', *Observer*, 29 March 1958.

2 Delusions of Grandeur

1 Gervase Hughes, *Composers of Operetta*, p. 233.

2 *Band Waggon*, December 1949.

3 W. Macqueen-Pope, *Ivor*, p 498.

4 *Musical Standard*, 2 September 1916.

5 In the issue of 27 December 1915.

6 *Huddersfield Daily Chronicle*, 9 September 1915.

7 W. Macqueen-Pope, *Ivor*, p. 96.

8 Sandy Wilson, *Ivor*, p. 105.

9 A brand of theatrical make-up.

10 Peter Noble, *Ivor Novello*, p. 209.

11 Sheridan Morley, *Spread a Little Happiness*, p. 82.

12 Ibid p. 81.

13 Ibid p. 82.

14 Ibid p. 86.

15 Ibid p. 86.

16 *The World* by Augustus Harris and Paul Meritt, Drury Lane Theatre 31 July 1880. The production ran for a successful 120 performances.

17 *Pluck* by Augustus Harris and Henry Pettitt, Drury Lane Theatre 5 August 1882. The production ran for a successful 103 performances.

18 Martin Booth, *English Melodrama*, p. 172.

19 *Crest of the Wave* was not filmed. The 1954 British film *Crest of the Wave* is from Hugh Hastings' play *Seagulls over Sorrento*. This play was eventually turned by its author into the musical *Scapa!*

20 Alan Bott, 'Entertainments à la Carte', *The Tatler*, 22 September 1937.

21 Quoted in Sandy Wilson, *Ivor*, p. 220.

22 *Plays and Players*, August 1968 p. 23.

23 Mary Garden, a Scottish soprano who found fame in Europe and America. She created the role of Mélisande in Debussy's *Pelleas et Mélisande* in 1902, and the title role in Massenet's *Cherubin* (1905).

24 Gustav Charpentier's opera *Louise*, considered as a leading 'verismo' work, was first produced on 2 February 1900, conducted by André Messager at the Paris Opéra-Comique.

25 *The Lisbon Story*'s hit was 'Pedro the Fisherman'.

26 Letter from Harold Hobson to Ivor Novello 17 October 1949.

27 *News Review*, 15 September 1949.

28 Ivor Novello interviewed by Charles Hamblett in *Illustrated*, 17 September 1949.

29 Ibid.

30 From theatre programme for production of *King's Rhapsody*.

31 Novello co-wrote the script for the Hollywood film *Tarzan the Ape Man* (1932), and is said to have created the line 'Me Tarzan, you Jane'.

32 Sheridan Morley, *Spread a Little Happiness*, p. 126.

33 The director Frith Banbury in conversation with the author.

34 Novello had already written a considerable amount of music for *Lily of the Valley*, published for the amateur market as *Valley of Song* in 1963, with additional material by Ronald Hanmer.

35 W. Macqueen-Pope, *Ivor*, p. 522.

36 Ibid.

3 Mastering Operetta

1 Gervase Hughes, *Masters of Operetta*, p. 234.

2 Ivy St Helier's slim reputation as a composer has been eclipsed by her acting career. She contributed songs to *His Girl* (1922), *The Street Singer* (1924) and *The Blue Train* (1927).

3 Quoted in Raymond Mander and Joe Mitchenson, *Theatrical Companion to Coward*, p. 165.

4 James Agate, *Immoment Toys*, pp. 72–5.

5 Jules Massenet's opera *Werther* (1892), based on Goethe's novel *The Sorrows of Young Werther*.

6 ENSA, the Entertainments' National Service Association, begun in 1939 to provide entertainment for troops and workers in Britain and overseas. More popularly, ENSA was known as 'Every Night Something Awful'.

7 Graham Payn, *My Life with Noel Coward*, p. 40.

8 Ibid, p. 44.

9 *The Times*, 20 December 1946.

10 *Theatre World*, February 1947, p. 6.

11 Ibid.

12 Graham Payn, *My Life with Noel Coward*, p. 42.

13 Gordon Duttson in conversation with the author.

14 Butcher's Films specialised in low-budget movies for the Northern market.

15 Gordon Duttson in conversation with the author.

16 Coward Diaries, 1 March 1950.

17 Sheridan Morley, *Spread a Little Happiness*, p. 124.

18 Stephen Citron, *Noel and Cole*.

19 The libretto of *Ace of Clubs* published in *Play Parade*, vol. 6 (London: Heinemann, 1962) includes the lyrics but states that 'Three Juvenile Delinquents' may not be performed in any production of *Ace of Clubs*.

20 Coward Diaries, 7 July 1950.

21 Patricia Kirkwood, *The Time of My Life*, p. 157.

22 *News Chronicle*, 2 July 1950.

23 *Theatre World*, September 1950, p. 6.

24 *Punch*, 16 June 1954.

25 *Plays and Players*, July 1954, pp. 14–15.

26 Coward Diaries, 1 October 1953.

27 Coward Diaries, 17 January 1954.

28 Coward Diaries, 14 March 1955.

29 Richard Beeching's report *The Reshaping of British Railways* was issued in two parts, in 1963 and 1965. It signalled a radical reduction of the railway network in Britain.

4 Pastiche and Esoteric

1 *Plays and Players*, January 1956, p. 5.

2 Fred Kander and John Ebb's *Cabaret* (1966).

3 Diana Souhami, *The Trials of Radclyffe Hall* (London: Weidenfeld & Nicolson, 1998), p. 171.

4 Sandy Wilson in conversation with Mark Shenton, Shaw Theatre 2009.

5 *Plays and Players*, March 1954, p. 3.

6 *Plays and Players*, Christmas 1954, p. 12.

7 Vida Hope, 'The Boy Friend on Broadway', *Plays and Players*, Christmas 1954, p. 12.

8 Peter Byrne in conversation with the author.

9 *Daily Telegraph*, 2 February 1965.

10 *Stage*, 4 February 1965.

11 *Sunday Times*, 7 February 1965.

12 *Little Mary Sunshine*, produced at the Comedy Theatre in 1962, with Patricia Routledge as Little Mary, supported by Bernard Cribbins, Terence Cooper, Joyce Blair, Gita Denise, Erik Chitty and a chorus

that included Anna Dawson, Patricia Michael, Hilary Tindall and Judy Nash.

13 Sandy Wilson quoted in theatre programme for 1997 Chichester Festival Theatre revival of *Divorce Me, Darling!*

14 Barbara Comyns, *The Vet's Daughter*, p. 60.

15 *Stage*, 11 May 1978.

5 Resounding Tinkles

1 Barbara Ehrenreich, *Dancing in the Streets: A History of Collective Joy* (London: Granta, 2008).

2 Julian Slade in conversation with the author.

3 Ibid.

4 Ibid.

5 Jean Marion Taylor in conversation with the author.

6 Peter Myers in conversation with the author.

7 'Peg o' My Heart' (1913). Lyric by Alfred Bryan; music by Fred Fisher.

8 Eugene Ionesco, the Italian playwright of the absurd and surrealist, noted for such works as *The Bald Soprano* (1950) and *Rhinoceros* (1959).

9 Sheridan Morley in *Spread a Little Happiness* wrote '*Follow That Girl* reached its climax with a rousing chorus number solemnly entitled 'Shopping in Kensington' [p. 154]. Not so. 'Shopping in Kensington' is not a finale, is not rousing, and is in fact a duet with no chorus involvement.

10 *Observer*, 20 March 1960.

11 The sketch was by Alec Grahame, with music by Stanley Myers. The item focused much of its satirical attention on *Hooray for Daisy!*

12 Julian Slade in conversation with the author.

13 Ibid.

14 Ibid.

15 Barry Took and Marty Feldman were the authors of the 'Julian and Sandy' sequences in the BBC radio comedy series *Round the Horne* (1965–8). Julian was played by Hugh Paddick, and Sandy by Kenneth Williams.

16 Julian Slade in conversation with the author.

17 *The Time of my Life: A Celebration of the Words and Music of Julian Slade* at Bristol Old Vic, 20 June 2004.

18 *Sunday Express*, 17 July 1955.

19 For another British musical, *Queenie*, Ted Willis wrote dialogue made up of rhyming couplets.

20 Ibid.

21 *News Chronicle*, 15 July 1955.

22 *Evening Standard*, 15 July 1955.

23 *The Tatler*, 27 July 1955.

6 Away from Home

1 Eric Maschwitz (1901–1969), one of the jobbing writers in British musicals, was librettist for *Balalaika* (1936), *Paprika* (1938), *Magyar Melody*, a 1939 reworking of *Paprika*, *Waltz without End* (1942), *Carissima* (1948), *Belinda Fair* (1949), *Zip Goes a Million* (1951), *Happy Holiday* (1954) and *Summer Song* (1956). He was the lyricist for *Evangeline* (1946). He wrote the librettos for *Love from Judy* (1952) and *Romance in Candlelight* (1955).

2 Eric Maschwitz, *No Chip on My Shoulder*, p. 187.

3 Such as the American musicals *Make a Wish* (1951) and *High Spirits* (1964).

4 *Stage*, 21 February 1957.

5 *Theatre World*, August 1957, p. 6.

6 Ian Carmichael, *Will the Real Ian Carmichael*, p. 306.

7 *Plays and Players*, November 1959.

8 *Theatre World*, December 1963, pp. 20–1.

9 *Plays and Players*, December 1965, p. 41.

10 William Topaz McGonagall (1825 or 1830–1902) a Scottish weaver with a not altogether undeserved reputation as the worst poet of all time.

7 Community Singing

1 V. C. Clinton Baddeley, 'Wanted – British Musicals!', *Plays and Players*, November 1953, p. 9.

2 Presumably *Call Me Madam*, music and lyrics by Irving Berlin, book by Howard

Lindsay and Russel Crouse (New York, October 1950; London, March 1952).

3 V. C. Clinton Baddeley, 'Wanted – British Musicals!'

4 *The Grove Family* was an early BBC TV soap opera (1954–7) about the generally unexciting adventures of an ordinary lower-middle-class family.

5 Peter Greenwell in conversation with the author.

6 Liner note for original London cast recording of *Harmony Close*.

7 Angela Thirkell was a popular novelist, obviously a favourite with subscribers to Boots' Libraries; Somerset Maugham would on occasion have shocked their sensibilities.

8 *Calypso* tellingly opened in 1948 only a month prior to the arrival of the first West Indian immigrants in Britain. This 'West Indian' musical comedy had a mostly West Indian cast, its score made up of authentic West Indian music and dances, vibrantly performed. The show was devised by the British dancer, actor and designer Hedley Briggs.

9 *The Jazz Train* was an all-black revue seen at the Piccadilly Theatre in 1955.

10 *Nymphs and Satires*, made up of white and black artists, was an entertainment seen at the Apollo Theatre in 1965.

11 *Cindy-Ella*, or *I Gotta Shoe*, was a retelling of the Cinderella story for a black cast of four by Ned Sherrin and Caryl Brahms. Its score used negro songs, but incorporated some original music by Ron Grainer and Peter Knight. It first played at the Garrick Theatre Christmas 1962.

12 Throughout its long tenure on television and stage, *The Black and White Minstrel Show* never included a black performer.

13 I am indebted to David Huckvale for alerting me to *Battersea Calypso*, further details of which may be found in his book *James Bernard, Composer to Count Dracula*.

14 *International Theatre Annual*, no. 3, p. 31.

15 *Theatre World*, October 1959, p. 10.

16 Bernard Levin, 'Astonishing, This Curtain Up on Real Musical', *Daily Express*, 20 April 1960.

17 W. A. Darlington, 'Songs Blunt Plays Edge', *Daily Telegraph*, 20 April 1960.

8 Specifically British

1 Quoted in sleevenotes for original cast recording of *Passion Flower Hotel*.

2 *Plays and Players*, January 1966, p. 46.

3 *The Glorious Days* was presented at the Palace Theatre in February 1953 for 256 performances.

4 *Plays and Players*, November 1966, p. 13.

5 Ibid.

6 Frank Marcus in *Plays and Players*, September 1966, p. 22.

7 Note in theatre programme for *Peg*.

8 An interesting composer of British musicals whose contributions have been intermittent rather than sustained: *Passion Flower Hotel* (1965), *Billy* (1975) and *Brighton Rock* (2004). *Lolita, My Love* closed *en route* to Broadway in 1971.

9 *Stage*, 13 April 1961.

10 *Stage*, 11 May 1961.

11 Not, alas, a good one. *Dr Crippen* (1962) was a dull affair. The date suggests the producers may have hoped to benefit from the adverse publicity generated by *Belle*.

12 Frances Stephens in *Theatre World Annual*, no. 12, p. 16.

13 *Beyond the Fringe* was written and performed by Alan Bennett, Peter Cook, Jonathan Miller and Dudley Moore. It opened at the Fortune Theatre in May 1961, running for 1,184 performances before transferring to the Mayfair Theatre.

14 *The Lord Chamberlain Regrets*, devised by Peter Myers and Ronald Cass, opened at the Saville Theatre in August 1961, running for 218 performances.

15 *Hang Down Your Head and Die*, devised by David Wright opened at the Comedy Theatre in March 1964, running for 43 performances.

16 Ursula Bloom (1892–1984).

17 Quoted in Tom Cullen, *Crippen: the Mild Murderer*, p. 203.

18 *Sunday Dispatch*, 29 January 1961.

19 Among the few songs known to have been sung by Belle Elmore (1873–1910) in London music halls is the suggestively titled 'She Never Went Further Than That'.

20 Val May in conversation with the author.

21 Quoted in Anthony Dunn, *Wolf Mankowitz (1924–1998): Post-war Playwright and Impresario* (Lecture given at the Art Workers' Guild 13 November 2008).

22 *Stage*, 11 May 1961.

23 At eighty years of age, Stolz was at the end of a career in which his works included the 1930 *White Horse Inn* co-composed with Ralph Benatzky, and *Wild Violets* (1932). Rather closer to the musical style of *Joie de Vivre* was his enchanting score for *The Blue Train* (1927).

24 Patricia Michael in conversation with the author. The same difficulty arose when the actor Roy Dotrice was cast as Dr Arnold in *Tom Brown's Schooldays* (1972). For his songs, delivered from the pulpit of Rugby School's chapel, his leading lady Judith Bruce was placed below, her back to the audience, mouthing the words at him.

25 Ibid.

26 W. A. Darlington, 'Booing at Rattigan Musical', *Daily Telegraph*, 15 July 1960.

27 Milton Shulman, 'I find Rattigan with music is so out-of-touch – but it could be a success', *Evening Standard* 15 July 1960.

28 W. A. Darlington, 'Booing at Rattigan Musical'.

29 Ibid.

30 *Plays and Players*, December 1972, p. 54.

31 Ibid.

32 *Stage*, 29 May 1975.

33 *The Baroness Bazooka*, words and music by Betty Comden and Adolf Green, music by Leonard Bernstein, written in the 1950s for the team's cabaret/revue act 'The Revuers'.

34 Frank Rich, *New York Times*, 4 May 1981.

9 To Whom it May Concern

1 Eric Maschwitz, *No Chip on My Shoulder*, p. 199.

2 Toffee apples.

3 Tom Cullen, *The Prostitutes' Padre: The Story of the Notorious Rector of Stiffkey* (London: Bodley Head, 1975), p. 30.

4 Sheridan Morley's *Spread a Little Happiness*, p. 155: 'Early in 1962, Wolf Mankowitz even tried a musical life of the

mass-murderer Dr Crippen.' Morley also mistakes the year of *Belle*.

5 Theatre programme for *Jack the Ripper*, Ambassadors Theatre.

6 Flyer for *Always* at the Victoria Palace Theatre.

7 Theatre programme for *Mrs Wilson's Diary*, Criterion Theatre.

8 *The Link*, 23 June 1888.

9 Helen Dawson, 'Worth Weeping Through', *Plays and Players*, May 1966, p. 13.

10 Anonymous letter sent to Annie Besant, 4 July 1888.

11 *Stage*, 7 July 1966.

12 William Jaeger, 'Annie Jaeger's Story' in theatre programme for *Annie*.

10 *Fin de Partie*

1 The author considered recording some of them, but they do not readily give themselves up for sympathetic consideration.

2 Letter from Christopher Whelen to the author, 8 February 1986.

3 *Stage*, 21 November 1957.

4 Ibid.

5 Letter from Christopher Whelen to the author, 8 February 1986.

6 Eric Johns, 'Christopher Whelen's Six-Year Plan', *Stage*, 11 September 1958.

7 *Stage*, 8 January 1959.

8 In stage directions for *The World of Paul Slickey*.

9 Script of *The World of Paul* Slickey, p. 204.

10 Mark Raven, the hero of *Wildest Dreams*. I suspect that Julian Slade would have preferred to have been called Mark Raven, a name that would have freed him from the upper-class connotations of his given name.

11 *Aunt Edwina* was soon threatened with closure after opening in London at the Fortune Theatre in late 1959. Several actors declined the offer to play the sex-change role, including Wilfrid Hyde-White, and

Robert Coote who thought it 'disgusting'. William Douglas Home made it his personal mission to keep the play on, but it closed after 110 performances.

12 *Stage*, 4 June 1959.

13 Barry Fantoni, *Independent*, 8 April 1999.

14 *Candide* had music by Leonard Bernstein, a book by Lillian Hellman and lyrics by Richard Wilbur. Opening at the Saville Theatre in 1959, it was off after only sixty performances.

15 'Alone the Orphan' does not appear in the list of songs for the original London production of *Vanity Fair*, but was heard in the brief London revival directed by Stewart Nicholls. Its inclusion suggests that, several decades later, Slade's taste for pastiche had not weakened.

16 Quoted in David Roper, *Bart!*, p. 47.

17 Quoted in Ibid., p. 46.

18 Ibid.

19 At least two British musicals have been made from J. B. Priestley's novels, *The Good Companions* (1929) and *Lost Empires* (1965). Neither musicals were notably successful. *The Good Companions* proved intractable despite a stellar cast; *Lost Empires* was a fairly desperate thing, everything about it weak.

20 Hugh Hastings in conversation with the author.

21 *Theatre World*, July 1962, p. 44.

22 Judith Bruce in conversation with the author.

23 Note in theatre programme for the Adelphi production of *Maggie May*.

24 Ibid.

25 *Theatre World*, November 1964, p. 29.

26 Quoted in David Roper, *Bart!*, p. 75.

27 Jon Bradshaw's two-part feature 'The Truth about *Twang!!*' was published in *Plays and Players* in the issues of April and May 1966.

28 *Stage*, 23 December 1965.

29 Jeremy Rundall 'No Bullseye', *Plays and Players*, February 1966, pp. 16–17.

Select Bibliography

Agate, James, *Immoment Toys: A Survey of Light Entertainment on the London Stage, 1920–1943* (London: Jonathan Cape, 1945)

Arundell, Dennis, *The Story of Sadler's Wells* (London: Hamish Hamilton, 1965)

Baily, Leslie, *The Gilbert and Sullivan Book* (London: Spring Books, 1966)

Bardsley, Garth, *Stop the World: The Biography of Anthony Newley* (London: Oberon Books, 2003)

Birkin, Andrew, *J. M. Barrie and the Lost Boys* (London: Constable, 1979)

Blom, Eric, *Everyman's Dictionary of Music* (London: Dent, 1946)

Booth, Martin, *English Melodrama* (London: Herbert Jenkins, 1965)

Bordman, Gerald, *Days to be Happy, Years to be Sad: The Life and Music of Vincent Youmans* (New York and Oxford: Oxford University Press, 1982)

Bradley, Ian, *Oh Joy! Oh Rapture!: The Enduring Phenomenon of Gilbert and Sullivan* (Oxford: Oxford University Press, 2005)

Bradshaw, Jon, 'Truth about *Twang!!*', *Plays and Players*, April 1966, pp. 51–2; May 1966, pp. 51–4, 72–3

Brown, Ivor, *Theatre, 1954–5* (London: Max Reinhardt, 1955)

—— *Theatre, 1955–6* (London: Max Reinhardt, 1956)

Byng, Douglas, *As You Were* (London: Duckworth, 1970)

Carmichael, Ian, *Will the Real Ian Carmichael ...: A Biography* (London: Macmillan, 1979)

Citron, Stephen, *Noel and Cole: The Sophisticates* (London: Sinclair-Stevenson, 1992)

Collis, Rose, *A Trouser-Wearing Character: The Life and Times of Nancy Spain* (London: Cassell, 1997)

Comyns, Barbara, *The Vet's Daughter* (London: Virago, 1981)

Coward, Noel, *The Lyrics of Noel Coward* (London: Heinemann, 1965)

Croall, Jonathan, *Sybil Thorndike: A Star of Life* (London: Haas, 2008)

Cullen, Tom, *Crippen: The Mild Murderer* (London: The Bodley Head, 1977)

Day, Barry, (editor), *The Letters of Noel Coward* (London: Methuen, 2007)

Diamond, Michael, *Victorian Sensation or, the Spectacular, the Shocking and the Scandalous in Nineteenth-Century Britain* (London: Anthem Press, 2003)

Dunn, Anthony, *Wolf Mankowitz (1924–1998): Post-war Playwright and Impresario* (Lecture given at the Art Workers' Guild 13 November 2008)

Ellis, Vivian, *I'm on a See-Saw* (London: Cedric Chivers, 1953)

Everett, William A., and Paul R. Laird (editors), *The Cambridge Companion to the Musical* (Cambridge: Cambridge University Press, 2nd edn. 2008)

Findlater, Richard, *Grimaldi: King of Clowns* (London: Macgibbon & Kee, 1955)

Fraser, David, *Will: A Portrait of William Douglas Home* (London: Andre Deutsch, 1995)

Gammond, Peter, *A Guide to Popular Music* (London: Phoenix House, 1960)

—— *The Oxford Companion to Popular Music* (Oxford: Oxford University Press, 1991)

Gänzl, Kurt, *The Blackwell Guide to the Musical Theatre on Record* (London: Blackwell Reference, 1990)

—— *The British Musical Theatre*, vol. 1: *1865–1914* (London: Macmillan, 1986)

—— *The British Musical Theatre*, vol.2: *1915–1984* (London: Macmillan, 1986)

Green, Jonathon, *All Dressed Up: The Sixties and the Counter-culture* (London: Jonathan Cape, 1998)

Green, Stanley, *Encyclopaedia of the Musical* (London: Cassell, 1976)

Gregg, Hubert, *Agatha Christie and all that Mousetrap* (London: William Kimber, 1980)

Harding, James, *Cochran: A Biography* (London: Methuen, 1988)

—— *Ivor Novello* (London: W. H. Allen, 1987)

Heilpern, John, *John Osborne: A Patriot for Us* (London: Chatto & Windus, 2006)

Hoare, Philip, *Noel Coward: A Biography* (London: Sinclair-Stevenson, 1995)

Hobson, Harold, (editor), *International Theatre Annual No. 3* (London: John Calder, 1958)

Huckvale, David, *James Bernard, Composer to Count Dracula: A Critical Biography* (Jefferson, NC, and London: McFarland, 2006)

Hughes, Gervase, *Composers of Operetta* (London: Macmillan, 1962)

Hughes, Kathryn, *The Short Life and Long Times of Mrs Beeton* (London: Fourth Estate, 2005)

Jacobs, Arthur, *Arthur Sullivan: A Victorian Musician* (Oxford: Oxford University Press, 1984)

Johns, Eric, *Dames of the Theatre* (London: W. H. Allen, 1974)

—— (editor), *Theatre Review '73* (London: W. H. Allen, 1973)

—— (editor), *British Theatre Review 1974* (Eastbourne: Vance-Offord, 1975)

Kendall, Henry, *I Remember Romano's* (London: Macdonald, 1960)

Kilgarriff, Michael (compiler), *Sing Us One of the Old Songs: A Guide to Popular Song, 1860–1920* (Oxford: Oxford University Press, 1998)

Kirkwood, Pat, *The Time of My Life* (London: Robert Hale, 1999)

Laye, Evelyn, *Boo, to my Friends* (London: Hurst and Blackett, 1958)

Lesley, Cole, *The Life of Noel Coward* (London: Jonathan Cape, 1976)

Littlewood, Joan, *Joan's Book: Joan Littlewood's Peculiar History as She Tells it* (London: Methuen, 1994)

Logue, Christopher, *Prince Charming* (London: Faber & Faber, 1999)

—— *Songs from the Lily-White Boys* (London: Scorpion Press, 1960)

Lowe, Stephen, *Arthur Lowe: A Life* (London: Nick Hern Books, 1996)

Macqueen-Pope, W., *Ivor: The Story of an Achievement: A Biography of Ivor Novello* (London: W. H. Allen, 1951)

Mander, Raymond, and Joe Mitchenson, *Theatrical Companion to Coward: A Pictorial Record of the First Performances of the Theatrical Works of Noel Coward* (London: Rockliff, 1957)

—— *Musical Comedy: A Story in Pictures* (London: Peter Davies, 1969)

Maschwitz, Eric, *No Chip on My Shoulder* (London: Herbert Jenkins, 1957)

Melville, Alan, *Merely Melville: An Autobiography* (London: Hodder & Stoughton, 1970)

More, Kenneth, *More or Less* (London: Hodder & Stoughton, 1978)

Morley, Sheridan, *Spread a Little Happiness: The First Hundred Years of the British Musical* (London: Thames & Hudson, 1987)

Noble, Peter, *Ivor Novello: Man of the Theatre* (London: The Falcon Press, 1951)

Ornadel, Cyril, *Reach for the Moon: A Portrait of my Life* (Sussex: Book Guild, 2007)

Parker, Derek and Julia, *The Story and the Song: A Survey of English Musical Plays, 1916–78* (London: Chappell/Elm Tree Books, 1979)

Payn, Graham, and Barry Day, *My Life with Noel Coward* (New York and London: Applause, 1994)

—— and Sheridan Morley (editors), *The Noel Coward Diaries* (London: Weidenfeld & Nicolson, 1982)

Plays and Players, journals

Rebellato, Dan, *1956 and All That: The Making of Modern British Drama* (London and New York: Routledge, 1999)

Ripley, A. Crooks, *Spectacle: A Book of Things Seen* (London: Brownlee Nineteen Forty-Two, 1945)

Rollins, Cyril, and R. John Witts (compilers), *The D'Oyly Carte Opera Company in Gilbert and Sullivan Operas: A Record of Productions, 1875–1961* (London: Michael Joseph, 1962)

Roper, David, *Bart!: The Unauthorised Life and Times, Ins and Outs, Ups and Downs of Lionel Bart* (London: Pavilion, 1994)

Rose, Richard, *Perchance to Dream: The World of Ivor Novello* (London: Leslie Frewin, 1974)

Seeley, Robert, and Rex Bunnett, *London Musical Shows on Record, 1889–1989: A Hundred Years of London's Musical Theatre* (London: General Gramophone Publications, 1989)

Shellard, Dominic, *British Theatre since the War* (New Haven and London: Yale University Press, 1999)

Sinden, Donald, *A Touch of the Memoirs* (London: Hodder & Stoughton, 1982)

Slattery-Christy, David, *In Search of Ruritania* (Milton Keynes: Author House, 2008)

Stage, yearbooks

Staveacre, Tony, *The Songwriters* (London: BBC, 1980)

Stedman, Jane W., *W. S. Gilbert: A Classic Victorian and his Theatre* (Oxford: Oxford University Press, 1996)

Theatre World, annuals

Theatre World, journals

Traubner, Richard, *Operetta: A Theatrical History* (London: Victor Gollancz, 1984)

Webb, Paul, *Ivor Novello: A Portrait of a Star* (London: Stage Directions, 1999)

Whitehouse, Edmund (compiler), *London Lights: A History of West End Musicals* (Cheltenham: This England Books, 2005)

Who's Who in the Theatre, various editions

Williams, Michael, *Ivor Novello: Screen Idol* (London: BFI Publishing, 2003)

Williamson, Audrey, and Charles Landstone, *The Bristol Old Vic: The First Ten Years* (London: J. Garnett Miller, 1957)

Wilson, A. E., *Post-War Theatre* (London: Home and Van Thal, n.d.)

Wilson, Robin, and Frederic Lloyd, *Gilbert and Sullivan: The D'Oyly Carte Years* (London: Weidenfeld & Nicolson, 1984)

Wilson, Sandy, *I Could Be Happy: An Autobiography* (London: Michael Joseph, 1975)

—— *Ivor* (London: Michael Joseph, 1975)

Windsor, Barbara, *All of Me* (London: Headline, 2000)

Index of Musical Works

Ace of Clubs, 21, **54–9**, 62, 147
Adriana Lecouvreur [opera], 139
After the Ball, 42, **59–62**
Aida [opera], 15, 153, 231
Airs on a Shoestring [revue], 143
Aladdin, 93
All American, 133
All Square [revue], 239
Always, 212–13
Amazons, The, 91, **176–7**
Ambassador, 133
Andrea Chénier [opera], 139
And So to Bed, 12, **196–7**, 211
Ann Veronica, 236
Anna Kraus [opera], 42
Annie [British], 85, **218**
Annie [US], 85
Annie 2, 85
Annie Get Your Gun, 59, 195
Anything Goes, 83
Applause, 133
Arc de Triomphe, 26, **33–4**, 35, 39, 42, 144
Arlette, 17
Art of Living, The [revue], 169
As Dorothy Parker Once Said, 89, 198

Bang Goes the Meringue!, 96
Bar Mitzvah Boy, 91, **134–5**
Barnardo, 214–15
Baroness Bazooka, The [revue item], 192
Battersea Calypso, 145
Bayadère, La [ballet], 15
Beggar's Opera, The, 149, 183, 190
Bella, 116–17
Belle, **179–86**, 194, 205, 207, 208, 210, 216
Bernadette, 220–1
Bet Your Life, 42
Beyond the Rainbow, 131
Big Ben, 11, 139
Billy Budd [opera], 236
Biograph Girl, The, **177**, 206
Bitter-Sweet, 20, **45–7**, 51, 53, 60, 64, 145
Bless the Bride, 8, 10, 11, 12, 98
Blitz!, 45, 150, 158, 227, 231, 232, **239–41**, 243, 244, 245, 247
Blood Brothers, 244

Blue Kitten, The, 46
Bohème, La [opera], 15
Bohemian Girl, The [opera], 18
Bordello, 189–90
Boy Friend, The, 5, 12, 45, 70, 71, **72–6**, 77, 80, 83, 84, 85, 86, 88, 89, 90, 91, 92, 93, 116, 161, 162, 231
Brief Encounter [opera], 69
Brighton Rock, 138
Bring Back Birdie, 85
Buccaneer, The, 12, **76–80**, 91, 93, 231
Burning Boat, The, **115–18**, 119
Bye Bye Birdie, 85, 133

Cabaret, 71
Call it Love?, 83
Calypso [revue], 144
Candide, 115, 227, 228
Caprice, 72, 116
Carefree Heart, The. See Love Doctor, The
Careless Rapture, 21, 22, 23, 26, **28–9**, 35, 42, 70
Carina [opera], 11
Carissima, 5, 233
Carmen [opera], 13, 231
Carousel, 38, 59
Casanova, 26
Cavalcade [play], 47, 53, 54
Charlie Boy, 125
Charlie Girl, 69, 169, **171–4**, 175, 177
Christmas in King Street, 97, 98, 103, 105
Chrysanthemum, 6
Cindy-Ella, 144
Clapham Wonder, The, 6, **91–3**
Clowns in Clover [revue], 10
Cockie! [revue], 206
Coconut Girl, The [sequence in The Girl who Came to Supper], 65
Colette, 198
Come Out to Play. See Ace of Clubs
Comedy of Errors, The, 97
Company, 191
Conversation Piece, 45, 47–9, 64, 73
Coronation Scot [orchestral piece], 11
Costa Packet, 227, 228
Crazy Diana, 238

Crest of the Wave, 21, 22, 26, **30–1**, 34, 35, 39, 42

Crooked Mile, The, 142, 144, 145, 148, 150, **151–7**, 161, 233

Crystal Heart, The, **126–9**, 137, 190

Dancing Years, The, 5, 22, **31–3**, 34, 35, 42

Darling, I Love You, 46

Dean, 206

Dear Love, 46

Dear Miss Phoebe, 39

Desert Song, The, 46

Dialogues des Carmélites [opera], 235–6

Divorce Me, Darling!, **83–9**, 90, 188

Don't Dilly Dally, 205

Drake's Dream, 220

Duenna, The, 97, 112

Enrico, 131

Evita, 91, 214

Expresso Bongo, **146–8**, 151, 153, 154, 169, 171, 176, 179, 231

Extraordinary Women, 72

Family Album, 49

Ferdinand the Matador, 224

Fiddler on the Roof, 134, 240

Fields of Ambrosia, The, 190

Fings Ain't Wot They Used T'Be, 105, 140, 145, **148–51**, 158, 161, 182, 227, 231, 232, 243

Fiorello!, 195

Follow a Star, 10

Follow That Girl, 97, **102–5**, 106, 107, 188, 202, 230, 232

42nd Street, 24, 39

4 to the Bar [revue], 143

Free as Air, 97, 98, **101–2**, 103, 105, 106

Gay Divorce, 83

Gay's the Word, 5, 17, 22, 24–5, 26, **39–41**, 59, 125

Girl Called Jo, A, 102, 188

Girl Friend, The, 73, 84

Girl who Came to Supper, The, 21, 29, 51, **64–6**

Giselle [ballet], 15

Glamorous Night, 15, 17, 20, 21, 22, 23, **25–8**, 35, 42, 47, 144

Gloriana [opera], 13

Glorious Days, The, 172

God Made the Little Red Apple, 208

Golden Boy, 133

Golden City, **123–6**, 144

Golden Moth, The, 18, 39

Golden Touch, The, 187, 188

Gondoliers, The, 1, 97

Gone with the Wind, **134**, 144

Good Time Johnny, 91, 189

Goodbye Mr Chips, 233

Goodbye to Berlin, 71

Grab Me a Gondola, 91, 187, 188

Grand Tour, The, 106

Great Grimaldi, The. See *Joey Joey*

Great Waltz, The, 185, 195, 196

Guys and Dolls, 56, 58, 204, 245

Half a Sixpence, 5, 45, 148, **169–71**, 176, 177, 179, 186, 236

Half in Earnest, 12

Hang Down Your Head and Die [revue], 182–3

Hansel and Gretel [opera], 80

Happy Holiday, 236

Hard Times, 236

Harmony Close, 96, **142–4**, 148, 149, 155

Here Comes the Bride, 46

Hide and Seek, 8

High Diplomacy, 220

High Spirits, **66**, 67

His Monkey Wife, **89–91**, 93, 134

Hoi Polloi. See *Ace of Clubs*

Hooray for Daisy!, 6, 97, **105–7**, 188, 189

House of Cards, 157

House That Jack Built, The [revue], 18

Hunchback of Notre Dame, The, 228

I and Albert, **133–4**, 211

Instant Marriage, 145

Iolanthe, 1, 139

Irma la Douce, 129, 148, 171, 186, 227

It's a Bird, It's a Plane, It's Superman!, 133

Ivanhoe [opera], 3, 11

Jack the Ripper, 93, **208 – 210**

Jazz Train, The [revue], 144

Jeanne d'Arc [opera in *Arc de Triomphe*], 33

Jeeves, 191

Jesus Christ Superstar, 92, 220

Jill Darling, 111

Joey Joey, 13, **198–202**, 204

John, Paul, George, Ringo and Bert, 206

Johnny the Priest, 58, 148, 150, **161–7**, 182, 188

Joie de Vivre, 187–9

Jongleur de Notre Dame, Le [opera], 23

Jorrocks, 174–5

Joseph and the Amazing Technicolor Dreamcoat, 6, 220

Keep Your Hair On!, 232
Kid from Stratford, The, 139
King and I, The, 128
King's Rhapsody, 15, 20, 22, 26, 27, **36–8**, 41, 42, 59, 60, 70, 125
Kings and Clowns, 212
Kismet, 129
Kiss in the Ring. See *Tough at the Top*
Kookaburra, 131

Lady May, 96, 97
Land of Smiles, The, 47
Lautrec, 190
Let Him Have Justice, 210
Life in Bedrooms, A, 208
Lily of the Valley, 42
Lily White Boys, The, 150, **158–61**, 182, 188, 231, 233
Lionel [revue], 228
Lisbon Story, The, 34
Listen to the Wind, 8, 11

Little Mary Sunshine, 85
Living for Pleasure [revue], 144
Lock Up Your Daughters, 220, 227, 231, 232
London Calling! [revue], 45
Londoners, The, 227, 228
Look Who's Here! [revue], 143
Lord Chamberlain Regrets, The [revue], 182
Lorelei [opera in *The Dancing Years*], 32, 33
Louise [opera], 33
Love Doctor, The, **129–30**, 188
Love from Judy, 66, **126**, 144, 217
Love Lies, 46
Lydia Languish, 71, 116

Mack and Mabel, 206
Madama Butterfly [opera], 15
Maggie May, 150, 227, 228, 232, **241–7**
Maid of the Mountains, The, 38
Make a Wish, 66
Make Me an Offer, 147, 151, **158**, 169, 171
Man from Tuscany, The [opera], 42
Man of La Mancha, 42
Man of Magic, 202–4
Mardi Gras, 144
Marie Lloyd Story, The, 205–6
Marigold, 42, 162, 211, 227
Marilyn!, 206
Marquise, The, 137
Matchgirls, The, 92, 208, **215–17**, 218
Me and My Girl, 5, 171
Meet Me by Moonlight, 162
Merrie England [opera], 4

Merry Gentleman, The, 97, 98
Merry Widow, The [opera], 42, 46
Merry-Merry, 46
Mikado, The, 1, 28, 38
Mister Venus, 42
Mitford Girls, The, 157
Model Maid, The [opera in *Operette*], 51
Most Happy Fella, The, 5
Mr and Mrs, 49, **67–9**
Mr Burke M. P., 90
Mr Cinders, 11, 75
Mrs Wilson's Diary, 213–14
My Fair Lady, 65, 133, 230
My Royal Past, 72

Napoleon, 190
Navvy, 138
Nell!, 211
No, No, Nanette, 6, 73, 74, 75
No Strings, 144
Notre-Dame de Paris, 190
Nymphs and Satires [revue], 144

Oh, Henry!, 71
Oh, Kay!, 73
Oh, What a Lovely War!, 16
Oh, My Papa!, 129
Oklahoma!, 5, 11, 23, 38, 53, 59, 123, 125, 131
Oliver!, 5, 38, 45, 140, 174, 178, 188, 200, 202, 220, **227–33**, 235, 241, 243, 244, 247
On the Brighter Side [revue], 106
On the Level, 218
On the Town, 154
On with the Dance [revue], 45
Once More Darling, 91
Once Upon a Mattress, 153
One Touch of Venus, 181
Open Your Eyes, 46
Operette, 3, **51**, 52
Oranges and Lemons [revue], 72
Our Man Crichton, 171
Our Miss Gibbs, 68
Our Nell, 18
Over the Garden Wall. See *Ace of Clubs*

Pacific 1860, 21, 36, **51–4**, 59, 62
Pagliacci [opera], 139
Pal Joey, 57, 147, 245
Passing Fancy. See *The Girl who Came to Supper*
Passion, 190
Passion Flower Hotel, 169, **178–9**, 185, 190, 191
Patience, 140

Peg, 176, **177–8**
Perchance to Dream, 22, **34–6**, 54, 70
Perils of Scobie Prilt, The, **186**, 191
Phil the Fluter, 169, **175–6**
Pickwick, 5, 13, 178, 186, 230, **235**, 245
Pieces of Eight [revue], 149
Pirates of Penzance, The, 38, 100, 184
Please Teacher!, 26, 88
Pocahontas, **132**, 211
Popkiss, 177
Poppy, **193–4**, 211, 216
Porgy and Bess [opera], 229
Princess, The, 131–2
Princess Ida, 3
Prostitute's Padre, The, 208
Puppets [revue], 18

Quick, Quick, Slow, 187

R Loves J, 189
Red Peppers, 49
Ricky with the Tuft, 224
Ride! Ride!, 220
Robert and Elizabeth, **197–8**, 204
Romance!, 91
Rose Marie, 46
Roza, 193
Ruddigore, 26

Sail Away, 21, **62–4**, 111
Salad Days, 5, 12, 45, 72, 76, **95–100**, 101, 118, 119, 145, 150, 165, 187, 197, 231, 233
Sam and Bella, 116
Saturnalia, 91
Scapa!, 5–6, 66, **236–9**
Scarlet Lady. See Pacific 1860
School, 223
See-Saw [revue], 17
Shall we Dance? [film], 31
She Smiled at Me, 80
Show Boat, 126
Side by Side by Sondheim [revue], 192
Sigh No More [revue], 51
Sing a Rude Song, 204–6
Slings and Arrows [revue], 72
So Who Needs Marriage?, 191
Song of Norway, 129, 195
Songbook, 191–3
Sound of Music, The, 42
South Pacific, 37, 42, 128
Southern Maid, A, 17
Space is so Startling, 220
Stand and Deliver, 190–1
Starlight, 238

Station Master's Daughter, The, 214
Stiffkey Scandals of 1932, The, 208
Stop the World – I Want to Get Off, 182, 212, 259
Strada, La, 227–8
Streamline [revue], 10
Strike a Light!, 92, 175, 216, **217**
Student Gypsy, The, 85
Student Prince, The, 33
Summer Song, 144, **195–6**
Swan Lake [ballet], 229, 231
Sweeney Todd, 93

Tabs [revue], 17
Tale of Two Cities [opera], 235
Te Deum [Sullivan], 1
Thaïs [opera], 23
Thanks for Nothing, 205
Theodore and Co., 17
Thespis, 1, 3
This Year of Grace [revue], 45
This'll Make You Whistle, 26
Thomas and the King, 211–12
Threepenny Opera, The, 183
Through the Years, 47
Tom Brown's Schooldays, 220, 233
Tough at the Top, 12
Travelling Music Show, The [revue], 206
Trelawny, 45, 109, **113**, 230
Trial by Jury, 3, 139
Tristan and Isolde [opera], 231
Troilus and Cressida [opera], 42
Troubador, 91, **135–7**, 211
Twang, 176, 227, 232, **247–8**
Twenty Minutes South, 119, **140–2**, 148, 154, 161
Twenty to One, 26
Two Cities, 137, **235–6**

Underneath the Arches, 206
Unsinkable Molly Brown, The, 195

Valmouth, **80–3**, 89, 90, 92, 145, 233
Vanity Fair, 89, **112–13**, 114
Véronique [opera], 4
Vicar of Soho, The, 208
Virtue in Danger, 145, 197

Wally Pone, 150
Waltz Without End, 195
Water Babies, The, 69
Water Gipsies, The, 12
Wedding in Paris, 233
Werther [opera], 49

West Side Story, 58, 131, 162, 165, 166, 245
What a Way to Run a Revolution, 91
When in Rome, 131
White Horse Inn, 26
Who's Hooper?, 17
Who's Pinkus, Where's Chelm?, 187
Wild Grows the Heather, 6
Wild Thyme, 118–22
Wildest Dreams, 97, 98, 102, 105, 106, **107–11**, 112, 113, 182, 188, 225
Wildflower, 46, 75
Winnie, 214

Wonderful Town, 115, 154
Words and Music [revue], 47
World of Paul Slickey, The, 30, 159, 182, 189, **222–6**, 231, 233
Wren, 211

Yeoman of the Guard, The, 1
Young Visiters, The, 236

Zoo, The, 3
Zuleika, 236

General Index

Abbie [book], 114
Ackland, Joss, 174
Ackland, Rodney, 90
Acres, Harry, 46
Adams, Lee, 133–4
Adcock, Joyce, 217
Addinsell, Richard, 15, 144
Addison, John, 177, 223
Adrian, Max, 113
Against the Law [book], 157
Agate, James, 48, 49, 195
Ainsworth, Alyn, 174
Albert, Prince, 133, 211
Albery, Donald, 174, 229, 230
Alcott, Louisa M., 102
Allen, Chesney, 206, 223
Allen, Jay, 133–4
Alwyn, William, 196
Amazons, The [play], 177
Ambassadors, The [novel], 133
Anderson, Daphne, 54, 141
Anderson, Lindsay, 158, 159, 161
Andrews, Bobbie, 42
Andrews, Julie, 71, 75, 116
Andrews Sisters, 192
Anhalt, Edward, 211
Ann Veronica [novel], 236
Anouilh, Jean, 126
April, Elsie, 45
Archibald, William, 126–9, 137
Armstrong-Jones, Anthony, 232
Arnold, Malcolm, 162
Arnold, Tom, 41
Arrighi, Luciana, 134
Ashford, Daisy, 236
Ashton, Barry, 125
Ashwell, Lena, 17
Askey, Arthur, 42
Asquith, Lady Cynthia, 6
Astaire, Fred, 31, 86
Atkins, Van, 196
Attlee, Clement, 51
Auction Sale, The [novel], 114
Aunt Edwina [play], 226
Autumn Crocus [film], 20
Avengers, The [TV series], 67

Bab Ballads [poems], 1
Bach, Johann Sebastian, 15
Bacon, Allon, 80
Baddeley, Hermione, 39, 211
Baddeley, John, 107
Baddeley, V. C. Clinton, 139–40, 143
Baker, Hylda, 67–8
Baker, Joe, 202
Ballad of Reading Gaol, The [poem], 38
Banbury, Frith, 116
Barker, Ronald (Ronnie), 189
Barnardo, Thomas John, 137, 214–15
Barnes, Sydney, 27
Barrett, Elizabeth, 163, 197–8
Barrie, J. M., 6, 11, 39, 236
Barry, Anna, 208
Barry, John, 138, 179
Bart, Lionel, 38, 45, 92, 113, 138, 148–51, 158,
    202, 214, 227–33, 239–48
Bassey, Shirley, 138
Baxter, Stanley, 107, 175, 176
Bayless, Jo Ann, 142
Bayntun, Amelia, 239–41
Beatles, The, 206, 243, 245
Beaton, Cecil, 72
Beaumont, Binkie, 54
Beaumont, Roma, 42
Becaud, Gilbert, 193
Becket, Thomas, 211–12
Beckett, Samuel, 248
Beecham, Sir Thomas, 125
Beeching, Dr Richard, 68
Bee-Gees, The, 205
Beerbohm, Max, 236
Beethoven, Ludwig van, 15
Beeton, Isabella, 116
Belmore, Bertha, 88
Benjamin, Arthur, 235
Bennett, Alan, 204
Benson, George, 183, 208
Benthall, Michael, 123
Bentley, Derek, 210, 211
Bergersen, Baldwin, 126–9, 137
Berkeley, Busby, 85
Berman, Monty, 229
Bernard, James, 145, 197
Bernadette, St., 220–1

Bernstein, Leonard, 67, 115, 154, 192
Besant, Annie, 215–17
Besier, Rudolph, 197
Besoyan, Rick, 85
Beyond the Fringe [revue], 182
Bickerstaffe, Isaac, 140
Big Killing, The [play], 239
Billington, Michael, 33
Billy Budd [opera], 236
Billy Cotton Band Show [radio programme],
    67, 241
Binge, Ronald, 229
Bizet, Georges, 13, 231
Black and White Minstrel Show, The [TV
    and stage], 145
Black, Clementina, 215
Black, David, 71
Black, Don, 134
Blackman, Honor, 67
Blair, Joyce, 135
'Blast!' [revue sketch], 239
Bliss, Arthur, 15
Blithe Spirit [play], 46, 236
Bloom, Ursula, 183
Blyton, Enid, 162
Bohemian Girl, The [film], 18
Bolam, James, 208
Bonnie Prince Charlie [film], 18
Booth, Webster, 197
Bott, Alan, 30
Boucicault, Don, 3
Bourne, Matthew, 229, 231
Bowles, Peter, 208
Boyer, Charles, 109
'Boz', 233
Braden, Alan, 214
Bradley, Buddy, 86
Bragg, Melvyn, 144
Braham, Philip, 18, 75
Brahms, Caryl, 204–5
Brahms, Johannes, 27
Braine, John, 245
Brecht, Bertolt, 243, 244, 245
Breeze, Alan, 67–8
Brent, Romney, 48
Brett, Jeremy, 161, 162
Bricusse, Leslie, 137, 182, 206, 212, 235
Brief Encounter [film], 49, 67
Brien, Alan, 232
Brighton Rock [novel], 138
Bristow, Mary, 201
Britten, Benjamin, 13, 109, 117, 236
Broccoli, Cubby, 186
Bronhill, June, 33, 197 8

Brook, Peter, 148, 186
Brooks, Mel, 192
Brown, George, 214
Brown, Georgia, 161, 228, 244
Brown, Joe, 171, 172
Brown, Molly, 195
Brown, Warner, 177
Browne, Irene, 60
Browning, Maurice, 140–2
Browning, Robert, 28, 163, 197–8
Bruce, Judith, 42, 43, 202–4, 244, 247
Bruce, Judy. *See* Bruce, Judith
Brunskill, Muriel, 123
Bryan, Alfred, 178
Bryan, Dora, 144
Bryant and May Factory, 215–17
Bryant, Theodore, 215
Buchanan, Jack, 18, 26, 88
Buckeridge, Frances, 162, 165
Buckingham, Ray, 123
Bunnage, Avis, 205–6
Burke, Henry, 208
Burton, Margaret, 137, 218, 235
Burton, Richard, 67
Butt, Sir Alfred, 132
Bygraves, Max, 137, 230
Byrd, William, 15
Byrne, Peter, 80

Caddick, Edward, 150
Caesar, Irving, 73
Cairncross, James, 103
Call of the Blood, The [film], 18
Callaghan, Mrs James, 214
Calthrop, Gladys, 52, 53, 56
Calvert, Eddie, 129
Carden, George, 238
Carey, Denis, 102
Carl Rosa Opera Company, 15
Carmichael, Ian, 129
Carnival [film], 18
Carpenter, Humphrey, 114
Carr, Carole, 4
Carson, Jean (Jeannie), 126, 217
Carter, Clive, 212
Carter, Desmond, 10, 11
Casablanca [film], 193
Cash, Aubrey, 202
Cass, Ronald, 4–5, 8, 143, 228
Casson, Lewis, 31
Castle, Barbara, 214
Cavalcade [play], 47
Cecil, Sylvia, 52, 54, 56, 58
Chamberlain, Neville, 31

Chandos, Dale, 114
Chappell, William, 148
Charisse, Cyd, 174
Charles, Maria, 135
Charles II, 211
Charlot, André, 17
Charnin, Martin, 135
Charpentier, Gustave, 33
Chopin, Frederic, 195
Christie, Julie, 85
Churchill, Winston, 34, 51, 85, 214
Cilea, Francesco, 139
Citron, Stephen, 56
Clements, John, 197
Clifford, Max, 207
Clockwork Orange, A [film], 185
Cochran, Charles B., 8, 11, 12, 90, 206
Coe, Peter, 220, 229, 235
Coleman, Terry, 138
Colette, Sidonie-Gabrielle, 198
Collier, Constance, 18
Collier, John, 45, 90
Collins, José, 17, 18
Comden, Betty, 192
Come Dancing [TV series], 187
Comedienne [play], 21
Comyns, Barbara, 45, 83, 91–3
Connolly, Desmond, 93
Connor, Edric, 144, 196
Constanduros, Mabel, 116
Constant Nymph, The [film], 18
Conway, Russ, 42
Cookman, Anthony, 119
Cookson, Harry, 159, 161
Cooney, Ray, 171
Cooper, Gladys, 126–8
Coronation Street [TV series], 218
Corri, Adrienne, 225
Cosh Boy [film], 147
Cosman, Leonie, 134
Cotton, Billy, 241
Courtneidge, Cicely, 5, 8, 10, 18, 39, 41, 66, 88, 192
Coward, Noel, 3, 4, 8, 10, 16–24, 27, 29, 35–6, 45–69, 73, 80, 83, 86, 89, 92, 111, 119, 125, 137, 145, 147, 207, 240
Cox, Constance, 235
Cranko, John, 232
Craven, Gemma, 113
Crawford, Marion, 125
Crazy Gang, The, 206
Creighton, Anthony, 222
Crest of the Wave [film], 236
Cribbins, Bernard, 142

Crippen, Hawley Harvey, 181–6, 194, 207, 210
Crisham, Walter, 31, 39
Croft, Colin, 142
Crosbie, Annette, 105
Cross, Beverley, 169, 174, 175, 179
Cruddas, Audrey, 123
Cuka, Frances, 112

Daddy-Long-Legs [novel], 126
Damon, Stuart, 204, 211
Dankworth, John, 198
Dare, Phyllis, 28
Darlington, W. A., 83, 163, 188, 189, 200
Darrieux, Danielle, 133
Darwin, Charles, 90
Davidson, Harold F., 207–8
Davies, Clara Novello, 17, 18
Davis, Carl, 208
Davis, Ray C., 135
Dawson, Anna, 107, 108
Dawson, Helen, 216
Day, Barry, 53
Day, Frances, 10
Day, Jill, 4
Daydé, Bernard, 129
de Bergerac, Cyrano, 228
de Marne, Dennis, 208–10
Dehn, Paul, 145, 187, 189
Delaney, Shelagh, 245
Delfont, Bernard, 137, 247
Dent, Alan, 31, 59, 119
Desmonde, Jerry, 184
Diana, Princess of Wales, 213
Dibdin, Charles, 1, 140
Dickens, Charles, 137, 168, 186, 200, 227, 232–3, 235–6
Dickson, Dorothy, 28, 29, 31
Dietrich, Marlene, 86, 192
Diffring, Anton, 42
Dillon, Bernard, 205
Disraeli, Benjamin, 133
Donegan, Lonnie, 243
Dors, Diana, 187
Douglass, Stuart, 208
Downhill [film], 18
D'Oyly Carte, Dame Bridget, 97
D'Oyly Carte Opera Company, 1, 3–4, 52, 97
D'Oyly Carte, Richard, 1, 3
Drake, Sir Francis, 220
Drew, Eleanor, 105
Drummond, John, 37
Duke, Edward, 178
Duke, Vernon, 46

Dumas, Alexandre, 211
Dunne, Irene, 52
Duttson, Gordon, 41, 42
Dvořák, Antonin, 195–6

Eaton, Wallas, 145
Ebb, Fred, 70
Eden, Toni, 248
Edward VII, 139
Edward VIII, 212
Edwardes, George, 17
Edwards, Glynn, 150
Edwards, Jimmy, 174
Ehrenreich, Barbara, 95
Elgar, Edward, 123
Elizabeth II, 232
Ellis, Edith, 41
Ellis, Hermione, 11
Ellis, Mary, 15, 27, 32, 33, 34, 39, 42, 59–62
Ellis, Vivian, 8–13, 75, 88, 92, 98, 196–7
Elmore, Belle, 181, 183, 184, 190
Entertainer, The [play], 222, 223
Epitaph for George Dillon [play], 222
Erskine, Rosalind. See Longrigg, Roger
   Erskine
Esslin, Martin, 190–1
Ettlinger, Don, 133
Evans, Edith, 42
Extraordinary Women [novel], 71

Fagan, J. B., 196
Falstaff, Sir John, 91, 189
Faris, Alexander, 189
Farnon, Robert, 33
Farson, Daniel, 205–6
Fazan, Eleanor, 161
Fellini, Federico, 227
Fenn, Jean, 62
Ferguson, Sheila, 213
Ferrer, José, 65, 138
Ffrangcon-Davies, Gwen, 31
Field, Shirley Anne, 161
Field, Sid, 137
Fielding, Fenella, 66, 149
Fielding, Harold, 134, 137, 169, 171, 172, 174,
   175, 202–4
Fielding, Henry, 140
Fielding, Robert, 229
Findlater, Richard, 232
Finney, Albert, 161
Firbank, Ronald, 45, 80–3
Fisher, Fred, 178
Flanagan, Bud, 206, 223
Flynn, Errol, 20, 247

Forbes, Bryan, 137
Ford, Lena Guilbert, 16
Forde, Florrie, 230
Forrest, George, 129, 195
Fortnight in September, The [novel], 163
Forty Years On [play], 111
Foster, Pamela, 33
Fraser, John, 217
Fraser, Moyra, 125
Fraser-Simpson, Harold, 17, 18
French, Percy, 175–6
French for Love [play], 72
French Without Tears [play], 187, 189
Friml, Rudolf, 38, 46
Frow, Gerald, 90
Full House [play], 20
Fumed Oak [play], 67
Furber, Douglas, 18

Galton, Ray, 137
Gamley, Douglas, 112
Gannon, Luke, 207
Garden, Mary, 33
Garinei, Pietro, 131
Garland, Judy, 244
Garland, Patrick, 208
Gatti, Jack, 95
Gay, John, 140, 190
Gay, Noel, 171
Genet, Jean, 126
George V, 64
George VI, 31
German, Edward, 3, 4, 15, 119
Gershwin, George, 4, 229
Gershwin, Ira, 4
Ghost Train, The [play], 236
Gibb, Maurice, 205
Gibbons, Carroll, 46, 75
Gielgud, John, 65
Gilbert, James, 91, 187, 189
Gilbert, Olive, 15, 29, 31, 32, 33, 35, 36, 41, 42
Gilbert, W. S., 1, 26, 27, 28, 38, 69, 75, 97,
   100, 117, 139, 140, 154, 184
Gillette, Anita, 132
Gilmore, Peter, 103
Giltinan, Donal, 175
Gingold, Hermione, 39
Giordano, Umberto, 139
Giovannini, Sandro, 131
Girl who Loved Crippen, The [book], 183
Gish, Lillian, 177
Glass, Blanche, 239
Glass, Eric, 238, 239
Glyn, Elinor, 46

Goell, Kermit, 132
Gohman, Don, 133
Go-Jos, The, 208
Goldfinger [film], 67
Goodbye Mr Chips [novel], 233
Gordon, Colin, 119
Gorlinsky, Sandor, 238
Gounod, Charles, 49
Grainer, Ron, 197–8, 204–5
Grant, Bob, 205
Grass is Greener, The [play], 171
Graves, Peter, 34, 42
Gray, Timothy, 66, 126, 238, 239
Great Waltz, The [film], 185
Green, Adolph, 192
Green, Philip, 123, 125
Green, Teddy, 202
Greene, Graham, 138
Greenwell, Peter, 140–2, 151–7
Gregg, Hubert, 6, 137, 214
Greig, Joe, 105
Greville, Charles Guy Fulke, 30
Grey, Clifford, 11, 17
Grey, Pearl, 17
Grieg, Edvard, 195
Griffith, D. W., 18, 177
Grimaldi, Joseph, 198–202, 211
Grimaldi, Marion, 151, 217
Grimes, Tammy, 66
Grove Family, The [TV series], 141
Grun, Bernard, 195
Guard, Philip, 118–22
Guétary, Georges, 10
Gwyn, Nell, 18, 137, 211

Hackady, Hal, 133
Hackforth, Norman, 59
Hager, Louis Busch, 178
Haggard, Sir Henry Rider, 28
Hale, Binnie, 10, 86
Hall, Adelaide, 144
Hall, Radclyffe, 71
Hall, Willis, 198–202
Hamlet [play], 34, 131
Hammerstein II, Oscar, 4, 23, 37, 53, 106, 125, 222, 224
Hampshire, Susan, 103, 105
Hancock, Tony, 137
Handel, George Frederic, 15
Hanson, John, 33
Happy Hypocrite, The [play], 43
Harbach, Otto, 73
Harbert, James, 211
Harding, James, 16, 26

Hardy, Robert, 214
Hardy, Robin, 214
Hare, Doris, 66
Harris, Bob, 105
Harris, Lionel, 42
Harrison, Rex, 65
Hart, Dunstan, 42
Hart, Lorenz, 28, 56, 150, 222, 224, 230
Hartley, Jan, 213
Harvey, Frank, 214
Harvey, Laurence, 148
Hassall, Christopher, 23, 28, 29, 35, 39, 42, 47, 92
Hastings, Hugh, 5, 236–9
Hatch, Tony, 211, 214
Hauser, Frank, 213
Hay Fever [play], 46, 66
Hayden, Joseph, 15
Hayman, Damaris, 114
Hazell, Hy, 147
Heal, Joan, 88, 129, 187, 188
Hedley, H. B., 46
Heilpern, John, 222, 223
Hellman, Lillian, 115
Helpmann, Robert, 59, 123
Hely, Gerard, 218
Henderson Jnr, Dickie, 131
Henderson, Florence, 65
Heneker, David, 45, 137, 146–8, 158, 169–78, 179
Henry II, 211
Henry V [play], 31
Henry VIII, 71, 137, 212
Henty, G. A., 77
Herbert, Alan P., 8–13, 98, 100, 197
Herman, Jerry, 106, 114, 206
Heyman, Edward, 47
Hill, Ken, 220
Hill, Rose, 142, 214
Hilton, James, 233
Hitchcock, Alfred, 18
Hitler, Adolf, 31–2, 34, 51, 192
Hobson, Harold, 37, 84, 126, 128
Holder, Ray, 135
Holiday Camp [film], 116
Holm, Celeste, 66
Home at Seven [play], 163
Home, William Douglas, 226
Hope, Vida, 75–6, 89, 137
Hope-Wallace, Philip, 232
Hopkins Manuscript, The [novel], 163
Hopkins, Antony, 42, 162–7
Hoskins, Bob, 193
Hossack, Grant, 174

Houdini, Harry, 202–4, 211
How to Enjoy your Operation [book], 8
Howard, Sydney, 46
Howard, Trevor, 67
Howerd, Frankie, 42
Howes, Bobby, 8, 10, 46, 88
Howes, Sally Anne, 196
Hubert, René, 29
Huggins, Mrs, 17
Hughes, David, 196, 238
Hughes, Gervase, 8, 14, 45, 56
Hughes, Gwyn, 220
Hughes, Maria, 201
Hughes, Maureen, 220
Hughes, Spike, 11
Hughes, Thomas, 233
Hugo, Victor, 228
Hulbert, Claude, 46
Hulbert, Jack, 10, 18
Hull, Ethel M., 109
Hume, Kenneth, 138
Humperdinck, Engelbert, 80
Humphries, Barry, 243
Hunchback of Notre Dame, The [novel], 228
Hurley, Alec, 205
Hurry, Leslie, 243
Hutch, Johnny, 202
Hylton, Jack, 239

I Lived With You [film], 20
Importance of Being Earnest, The [play], 12
Ingham, Barrie, 188
Ingrams, Richard, 213
Ionesco, Eugène, 103
Isherwood, Christopher, 70

Jack the Ripper, 208–10
Jackman, Hope, 162, 167–8, 228
Jaeger, Annie, 218
Jaeger, William, 218
James I, 211
James, Henry, 133
James, Jessica, 33
James, Polly, 133
Jeans, Angela Ainley, 8, 11
Jeans, Ronald, 10, 17
Jekyll, Gertrude, 155
Johnson, Amy, 71, 137, 202
Johnson, Celia, 67
Johnson, Laurie, 232
Johnson, Richard, 211
Jones, Paul, 220
Jones, Sidney, 26
Josephine de Beauharnais, 138

Josephs, Wilfred, 204
Journey's End [play], 163
Joyce, Yootha, 150
June, 10

Kalman, Emmerich, 23, 26
Kander, John, 70
Kay, Norman, 205
Kaye, Davy, 184
Kaye, Stubby, 202–4
Keel, Howard, 133
Kelly, Marie, 210
Kendall, Henry, 39, 238
Kennedy, Cheryl, 174
Kenney, James, 146
Kenny, Sean, 161, 229, 240, 243, 244, 247
Keown, Eric, 60
Kent, Jean, 80
Kern, Jerome, 17, 27, 39
Kid for Two Farthings, A [novel], 158
King, Hetty, 184
Kingsley, Charles, 69
Kinsey, Tony, 159
Kipps [novel], 169
Kirby, Kathy, 132
Kirkwood, Patricia, 6, 56, 58, 137
Kitchin, C. H. B., 114
Klein, Alan, 228
Kneeland, Ted, 131
Knight, David, 33
Kops, Bernard, 245
Kostal, Irwin, 134
Kotcheff, Ted, 243
Kraft, Hy, 195
Kretzmer, Herbert, 137
Kurnitz, Harry, 65, 66

La Guardia, Fiorello, 195
Ladies into Action [play], 21
Lady Windermere's Fan [play], 59
Laine, Cleo, 198
Lambert, Gavin, 138
Lambert, J. W., 146
Landis, Monty, 161
Lane, Lupino, 5, 46
Langford, Gordon, 154, 162, 165
Langton, David, 238
Lass o' Laughter [play], 132
Laughton, Charles, 71
Lawrence, Gertrude, 18, 86
Lawrence, Norman, 123
Lawrence, Stephanie, 206
Lawton, Leslie, 89
Laye, Evelyn, 137, 175, 176, 217

Le Neve, Ethel, 181–4
Le Sage, Bill, 159
Lean, David, 67
Lee, Bernard, 238
Lee, Bert, 46
Lee, Vanessa, 37, 42, 60–2
Lehár, Franz, 3, 23, 25, 26, 46, 47
Leigh, Vivien, 64
Léon, Viktor, 46
Leonard, Hugh, 132, 174, 175
Leoncavallo, Ruggiero, 139
Lerner, Alan Jay, 4
Lerner, Goodhart and Hoffman
    [songwriters], 8
Lesley, Cole, 60
Levin, Bernard, 83, 162, 186, 229
Lewis, Rosa, 137
Lewis, Stephen, 228
Lewsen, Charles, 208
Liberace, 143
Lillie, Beatrice, 66
Linley, Thomas, 1
Liszt, Franz, 27
Little Minister, The [play], 6
Littler, Emile, 126
Littler, Prince, 54
Littlewood, Joan, 105, 149, 150, 151, 158, 161,
    205, 213, 232, 247
Lloyd, Marie, 204, 206, 239
Locke, Philip, 161, 225
Lockwood, Margaret, 35
Lodger, The [film], 18
Loesser, Frank, 5, 56, 58
Loewe, Frederick, 4
Logan, Joshua, 37
Logue, Christopher, 158–61
Löhr, Marie, 225
Lombardi, Michael, 135–7
Longrigg, Roger Erskine, 178
Look Back in Anger [play], 222
Losey, Joseph, 138
Lotis, Dennis, 142, 225
Lupino, Stanley, 88
Luther [play], 222
Lynn, Ann, 161
Lynn, Vera, 241
Lynne, Gillian, 133, 138, 216, 217

Macbeth [play], 131
MacDonald, Jeanette, 46, 72
MacGowran, Jack, 151, 154, 155
Mackay, Angus, 107, 108
Mackay, Barry, 20
Mackenzie, Compton, 71

Mackintosh, Cameron, 6, 76, 113, 115
Macqueen-Pope, W., 17, 43–4
Macrae, Arthur, 144
Madden, Cecil, 205
Main Chance, The [novel], 157
Maitland, Joan, 232, 239
Mander, Raymond, 52, 60, 66
Mankowitz, Wolf, 146–8, 158, 169, 175,
    178–86, 190–1, 235
Manners, J. Hartley, 177
Mantovani, 56, 229
Marconi, Guglielmo, 184
Marcus, Frank, 175
Margaret Rose, Princess, 114, 232
Marowitz, Charles, 187
Marquise, The [play], 137
Marriott, R. B., 83, 89, 111, 129, 159, 179, 202,
    224, 248
Marsden, Betty, 107
Marshall, Norman, 162
Martin, Hugh, 66, 126, 239
Martin, Margaret, 134
Martin, Mary, 42, 52–4, 56
Martin, Millicent, 147, 151, 155
Martin, Vivienne, 135, 201, 216
Martin-Harvey, Sir John, 232
Mary, Queen (Mary of Teck), 213
Maschwitz, Eric, 5, 126, 195–6, 236
Mason, Brewster, 238
Mason, Derrick, 138
Massary, Fritzi, 51
Massenet, Jules, 23, 49
Masteroff, Joe, 71
Matalon, Zack, 142
Matcham, Frank, 204
Matthews, Jessie, 86, 88, 137
Maugham, W. Somerset, 142
May, Bunny, 161, 162, 165
May, Hans, 5
May, Val, 174, 185
May, William, 212
Mayer III, David, 198
Mayerl, Billy, 26, 46, 75, 193
Mayhew, Henry, 230
McAlister, David, 38
McDaniel, Hattie, 144
McGlinn, John, 61
McGonagall, William Topaz, 135
McGregor, Ken, 145
McKenna, Virginia, 214
Meir, Golda, 228
Melbourne, William Lamb, 133
Melville, Alan, 23, 39–42, 66, 211, 239
Mendelssohn, Felix, 15

Merman, Ethel, 86, 88
Messager, André, 4
Messell, Oliver, 247
Meyer, Jean, 154
Michael, Patricia, 187–8, 189
Michell, Keith, 65, 66, 137, 197–8, 235
Michener, James, 37
Miles, Bernard, 232
Millar, Ronald, 197–8
Miller, Anthony, 182
Miller, Jonathan, 230
Miller, Robin, 112
Miller, Valerie, 6
Mills & Boon [publishers], 33
Mills, Hayley, 113
Mitchell, Margaret, 134
Mitchenson, Joe, 52, 60, 66
Molière, 129
Mollison, William, 72
Monckton, Lionel, 26, 75, 98
Monnot, Marguérite, 148, 192
Monroe, Marilyn, 206
Monsey, Derek, 118, 119
Moody, Ron, 91, 198–202, 228, 231
Moore, Harry, 205
Moral Re-Armament, 218–20
More, Julian, 91, 146–8, 159, 169, 179, 186–7, 189, 191–3
Morgan, Arthur, 41
Morgan, Diana, 137
Moritt, Fred G., 197
Morley, John, 71, 137, 202
Morley, Sheridan, 22–5, 39, 53, 56–7, 88, 210
Morris, Libby, 89
Moule, Ruby. See Lee, Vanessa
Mozart, Wolfgang Amadeus, 15
Mr Norris Changes Trains [novel], 71
Munnings, Hilda. See Sokolova, Lydia
My Royal Past [book], 72
Myers, Peter, 4–5, 102, 182, 228

Naismith, Laurence, 196
Napoleon, 138, 190
Nash, Ogden, 181
Navarro, Ramon, 18
Neagle, Anna, 20, 46, 133, 171, 172, 174, 175
Nearest and Dearest [TV series], 67
Nelder, Mr and Mrs, 107
Neville, John, 67
New, Derek, 238
Newell, Norman, 214
Newley, Anthony, 137, 182, 206, 212, 239
Nichols, Peter, 193–4
Nightingale, Benedict, 221

Nimmo, Derek, 171
No Trams to Lime Street [play], 244
Noble, Peter, 22
Norman, Frank, 148–51, 161, 228, 232
Norman, Monty, 146–8, 158, 169, 178, 179–87, 190–4
Novello, Ivor, 5, 10, 14–44, 49, 53, 54, 59, 62, 70, 72, 75, 80, 88, 92, 97, 105, 119, 125, 139, 144, 233, 240
Nunn, Trevor, 134

O'Brien, Timothy, 201
O'Hara, John, 245
O'Shea, Tessie, 65
O'Toole, Peter, 228
Oakley, Annie, 195
Offenbach, Jacques, 47, 105, 231
Oliver Twist [novel], 168
Olivier, Laurence, 64
Only Way, The [play], 232
Orchard, Julian, 119
Origin of Species, The [book], 90
Orkin, Harvey, 232
Ornadel, Cyril, 91, 214, 235
Osborne, John, 159, 222–6, 233
Other Theatre, The [book], 162
Owen, Alun, 232, 243, 244, 245
Owen, Bill, 215–17

Paddick, Hugh, 113
Palmer, Toni, 150, 241
Pankotia, Zsiga, 182
Parker, Dorothy, 198
Parnell, Val, 56
Parnes, Larry, 135, 210
Parr-Davies, Harry, 38
Parsons, Donovan, 18
Patmore, Derek, 72
Paul, Betty, 119
Payn, Graham, 52–4, 56, 58, 66
Pearce, Vera, 46, 88
Pears, Peter, 117
Peg o' My Heart [play], 177
Pember, Ron, 208–10
Pennies from Heaven [TV], 193
Pepys, Samuel, 12, 196–7
Person Unknown [play], 172
Pertwee, Jon, 191
Pertwee, Michael, 38
Phillips, Siân, 178
Phipps, Nicholas, 117–18
Piaf, Edith, 192
Piccadilly Ten, The, 208
Pickford, Mary, 177

Pickwick Papers, The [novel], 186
Pinero, Arthur Wing, 17, 91, 113, 137, 177
Pirandello, Luigi, 126
Pluck [play], 25–6
Plummer, Christopher, 65
Pocahontas, Princess, 211
Porter, Cole, 88
Potter, Dennis, 193
Poulenc, Francis, 235
Powell, Peter, 162, 163, 165
Prancing Nigger [novel], 80
Presley, Elvis, 143
Presnell, Harve, 134
Previn, André, 69
Price, Dennis, 20
Priestley, J. B., 236
Prime of Miss Jean Brodie, The [play], 111
Primrose, Bonita, 196
Prince and the Showgirl, The [play], 64
Prince, Hal, 71, 116
Printemps, Yvonne, 48, 51, 52
Private Eye [journal], 182
Privates on Parade [play], 193
Pryce-Jones, Alan, 112
Puccini, Giacomo, 15, 27, 92, 183
Purcell, Henry, 15

Quality Street [play], 39
Quayle, Anna, 138
Quilley, Denis, 66, 107, 118, 205

Ramsay, Louise, 142
Randolph, Elsie, 26, 88
Rascel, Renato, 131
Rat, The [film], 18
Rattigan, Terence, 64, 65, 187–9
Ravensbrück Concentration Camp, 32
Raye, Martha, 88
Reed, Carol, 228
Reed, William L., 218
Reid, Beryl, 239
Reizenstein, Franz, 42
Return of the Rat, The [film], 18
Reynolds, Dorothy, 5, 6, 95–113, 114, 116, 150,
    159, 182, 225, 245
Rice, Peter, 133
Rice, Tim, 91
Rich, Frank, 193
Richard, Cliff, 143
Richards, Angela, 198, 218
Richardson, Ian, 113
Ridley, Arnold, 236
Ritchie, June, 134
Rix, Brian, 146

Roberts, Rachel, 243, 244
Robertson, Patrick, 208
Robertson, T. W., 80, 223
Robinson, Harry, 185
Rodgers, Richard, 4, 37, 53, 56, 73, 125, 150,
    224, 228, 230
Roeg, Nicolette, 184
Rogers, Eric, 229, 230
Rogers, Ginger, 5, 86
Rolling Stones, The, 85
Rollings, Gordon, 201–2
Romanoff and Juliet [play], 189
Rome, Harold, 134
Rookery Nook [play], 177
Rosenthal, Jack, 134
Ross, Annie, 208
Ross, Charles, 142–4
Round the Horne [radio series], 113
Routledge, Patricia, 103
Rubens, Paul, 26
Rundall, Jeremy, 248
Runyon, Damon, 56, 245
Russell, Bertrand, 228
Russell, Ken, 76
Russell, Tony, 208, 216–17
Russell, Willy, 206, 244

Sagan, Leontine, 41
Sailor Beware [play], 12
Sainthill, Loudon, 185
Sala, G. A., 26
Sansom, William, 116
Sargent, Sir Malcolm, 125
Sarne, Mike, 186
Saturn in the Suburbs [book], 228
Schlesinger, John, 133–4
Schoenberg, Arnold, 118
Schwartz, Arthur, 46
Scofield, Paul, 146, 148
Scott, Hutchinson, 103
Seagulls over Sorrento [play], 5, 236–8
Searle, Ronald, 119–22
Secombe, Harry, 235
Sellars, Peter, 231
Sennett, Mack, 177
Shakespeare, William, 4, 11, 31, 34, 245, 248
Shall we Dance? [film], 31
Shaw, Roland, 64
She [novel], 28
Shelley, Julia, 123
Sheppard, Jack, 190, 208
Sheridan, Richard Brinsley, 71
Sherriff, R. C., 162, 163
Sherrin, Ned, 204–5

Shulman, Milton, 103, 119, 188–9
Shute, Nevil, 131
Sickert, Walter, 204
Simpson, Alan, 137
Simpson, N. F., 126
Simpson, Wallis, 212–13
Sims, Joan, 189
Sinclair, Barry, 33
Sinden, Donald, 187–8
Sisters Cora, The, 17
Slade, Julian, 5, 6, 45, 89, 92, 95–115, 150, 182, 225, 227, 230, 245
Smillie, James, 211
Sokolova, Lydia, 31
Sondheim, Stephen, 24, 190, 191, 192
Spain, Nancy, 116
Sparrrers Can't Sing [play], 228
Spence, Johnnie, 67, 68
Sprague, Jason, 212
St Helier, Ivy, 47
Staiger, Libi, 5
Steele, Tommy, 137, 169
Steen, Marguerite, 72
Stein, Gertrude, 13
Stein, Leo, 46
Stephens, Frances, 59, 181
Stephenson, B. C., 3
Stevens, Marti, 66
Stevens, Terri, 208–10
Stewart, Michael, 129, 177
Stewart, Robb, 45, 46
Still Life [play], 49, 62, 67
Stolz, Robert, 187, 189
Stone, Paddy, 243
Stott, Wally, 64
Strachey, Jack, 75
Strada, La [film], 227
Stritch, Elaine, 62
Strouse, Charles, 133–4
Stuart, Isobel, 133
Styne, Jule, 134
Sullivan, Arthur Seymour, 1, 38, 69, 75, 97, 139
Summerfield, Eleanor, 123
Sunday Night at the London Palladium [TV], 5, 217
Sundgaard, Arnold, 214
Surtees, Robert Smith, 174
Swann, Donald, 118–22
Swann, Robert, 33
Symphony in Two Flats [film], 18

Talbot, Howard, 17
Tale of Two Cities, A [novel], 137

Tanitch, Robert, 83
Tarzan of the Apes [film], 39
Taste of Honey, A [play], 112, 245
Tatler, Arthur, 185
Taube, Sven-Bertil, 133
Taylor, C. F. (Metal Tanks) Ltd., 202
Taylor, Cecil P., 187
Taylor, Jean Marion, 98
Taylor, Jeremy, 213
Taylor, John Russell, 172
Taylor, John, 67–9, 137, 171–4
Taylor, Ross, 67, 171
Telescope, The [play], 162
Tempest, Marie, 128
Tennent, Harry, 27
Thackeray, William Makepeace, 112
Thirkell, Angela, 142
This Happy Breed [play], 65, 240
This is Sylvia [book], 73
Thompson, Jimmy, 208
Thompson, Kay, 66
Thompson, Martha, 220
Thorndike, Dame Sybil, 112
Thorne, Ken, 64, 135
Thornhill, Alan, 218, 220
Three Degrees, The, 213
Three Musketeers, The [novel], 211
Thwaites, Penelope, 220
Tilley, Vesta, 184
Tom Brown's Schooldays [novel], 233
To-night at 8.30 [plays], 67
Toré, John, 123–4
Toulouse-Lautrec, Henri de, 189–90
Toye, Wendy, 118, 190, 231
Travers, Ben, 177
Treble, Sepha, 86
Trelawny of the Wells [play], 113, 137
Trent, Jackie, 211
Triumph of the Rat [film], 18
Trollope, Joanna, 114
Troubridge, Una, 71
Troy, Louise, 66
Tucker, Sophie, 10
Tunbridge, Joseph, 6, 26, 46, 72, 75, 88
Tynan, Kenneth, 12

Unterfucker, Hans, 46
Ustinov, Peter, 189

Valentino, Rudolph, 18
Vane, Sybil, 16
Vanity Fair [novel], 112
Veidt, Conrad, 30
Vercoe, Rosemary, 208

Verdon, Gwen, 66
Vernon, Virginia, 183
Vet's Daughter, The [novel], 83, 91–4
Vickers, John, 182
Victoria, Queen, 48, 133, 211, 232
Vinaver, Steven, 88
Voltaire, 115
Vortex, The [film], 18
Voss, Stephanie, 161, 162

Wagner, Richard, 15
Waller, Jack, 6, 26, 46, 72, 88
Wallis, Shani, 213, 228
Walton, William, 11, 15, 42
War and Peace [novel], 131
Ward, Dorothy, 17
Wardle, Irving, 103–5
Water-Babies, The [novel], 69
Waterhouse, Keith, 198–202
Waters, Jan, 66
Waterstone, Tim, 114
Watling, Jack, 225
Way of Life, A [book], 157
Wayne, Jeff, 235
Wayne, Jerry, 235
We Proudly Present [play], 21
Webber, Andrew Lloyd, 6, 13, 22, 91, 97, 111,
     191, 220
Webster, Jean, 126
Weill, Kurt, 71, 147, 181, 214, 224, 243, 244
Welch, Elisabeth, 28, 34, 144, 154, 155
Well of Loneliness, The [novel], 71
Wells, H. G., 169, 236
Wells, John, 213
Wesker, Arnold, 245
Wesley, Charles, 220
West End People [novel], 153, 157
West, Charles, 216
Weston, R. P., 46
Whelen, Christopher, 223–4
Whistler, Rex, 48
Whitaker, Judith, 123
White Rose, The [film], 18
Whitsun-Jones, Paul, 228
Wicked Lady, The [film], 35
Widney, Stone, 133

Wilcox, Herbert, 20
Wilde, Oscar, 12, 38, 46, 59, 60, 61
Wildeblood, Peter, 145, 151–7
Wilder, Alec, 214
Williams, Hugh, 171
Williams, John, 211
Williams, Lloyd, 41
Williams, Margaret, 171
Williams, Tennessee, 128
Wilson, Harold, 213–14
Wilson, Mary, 213–14
Wilson, Sandy, 6, 16, 20, 45, 70–94, 116, 134,
     135, 137, 141, 149, 202, 212, 227
Wilton, Robb, 179
Windsor, Barbara, 150, 205
Winspear, Violet, 109
Wisdom, Norman, 200
Wodehouse, P. G., 18, 39, 178, 191
Wolfenden, John, 144, 157
Wood, David, 208
Wood, Haydn, 46
Wood, Peggy, 51
Wood, Sir Henry, 125
Woodforde-Finden, Amy, 143
Woodward, Edward, 66, 137
Woolley, Reginald, 88, 154, 167, 210
World, The [play], 25
Worth, John, 211
Wren, Sir Christopher, 211
Wright, Bill, 41
Wright, David, 208
Wright, Geoffrey, 70, 71, 72, 116–18
Wright, Robert, 129, 195
Wylam, Wilfred. *See* Josephs, Wilfred
Wynter, Mark, 175, 176

Youmans, Vincent, 46, 47, 73, 75, 230
Young Visiters, The [novel], 236

Ziegler, Anne, 197
Zinkeisen, Doris, 48
Zuleika Dobson [novel], 236
Zwar, Charles, 211, 214, 239